When in Boston

When in Boston

A Time Line & Almanac

∾ JIM VRABEL

in association with The Bostonian Society

Northeastern University Press · BOSTON

Northeastern University Press

Library of Congress Cataloging-in-Publication Data
Vrabel, Jim.
    When in Boston : a time line & almanac / Jim Vrabel.
        p.   cm.
    Includes bibliographical references and index.
    ISBN 1-55553-620-4 (pbk. : alk. paper)—ISBN 1-55553-621-2 (cloth : alk. paper)
    1. Boston (Mass.)—History—Chronology.   2. Boston (Mass.)—History—
Miscellanea.   I. Title.
F73.3V73   2004
974.4'61'00202—dc22   2004005749

Designed by Gary Gore

Composed in Minion by Coghill Composition, Richmond, Virginia. Printed and bound by Thomson-Shore, Inc., Dexter, Michigan. The paper is Joy Offset, an acid-free stock.

MANUFACTURED IN THE UNITED STATES OF AMERICA
08   07   06   05   04   5   4   3   2   1

To Nancy Richard and all the other archivists and librarians in the city for the work they do to preserve and make accessible Boston's history

Contents

Illustrations

Legend

The events described in *When in Boston* are arranged chronologically by year. Within each year, events are arranged by category. The categories—in the order they appear—are:

	Population/Immigration
	Planning/Development
	Buildings: Public/Commercial/Residential
	Transportation/Water/Municipal Services
	Parks/Public Art/Cemeteries
	Settlement/War/Boston History
	Politics & Government
	Social Change
	Society/Hotels/Restaurants/Visitors
	Crime/Public Safety/Law
	Disasters & Tragedies
	Nature
	Religion
	Education
	Health/Science/Technology
	Business & Labor
	Media
	The Arts: Visual Art/Letters & Literature/Music/Theater/Popular Culture
	Sports/Recreation

Foreword

As any enthusiast captivated with the history of Boston soon learns, there is good news and there is bad news. The good news is that Boston's age is so great (nearly four hundred years), and its history so colorful, that it never ceases to provide topics for historians to explore and narratives for readers to enjoy. Politics and religion, war and peace, education and medicine, science and economics, fine arts and architecture, philosophy and literature, immigration and transportation, sports and recreation—these and many other topics can be found in the extraordinary number of books and articles about Boston.

The bad news is that the amount of material relating to Boston history is so enormous, and the number of publications so extensive, that it is almost impossible for readers and researchers to recall the location of certain references, remember the date of particular events, or come up with the correct titles of specific prominent figures. Where did I see that reference? What year was that election held? When did they launch that ship? When was so-and-so mayor? When did that battle take place? What book contained that particular quotation? Where can I find what the city's population was just before the Civil War? These are the kinds of questions that haunt writers when they are trying to go back and verify a fact, locate a date, or find the original source of a statement. It was all very frustrating until Jim Vrabel came along.

I first met Jim Vrabel over a cup of coffee when we were talking about his recent experiences as co-author of a biographical study of Pope John Paul II. From there we wandered off into a broader discussion of Boston history and local politics, and I was greatly impressed with the range of Jim's knowledge about the city of Boston. Some of his information, I learned, came from his own long-standing fascination with the city's history; some of it came from his firsthand experiences working in city government as assistant director of the Mayor's Office of Neighborhood Services, executive assistant to the Boston School Committee, and, finally, in his current position as senior research analyst and editor at the Boston Redevelopment Authority.

Toward the end of our conversation, I asked Jim if he was involved in any other projects now that the book about Pope John Paul II had been published. Almost as an afterthought, he reached into his briefcase and pulled out a sizable manuscript that was obviously still in progress and handed it to me. As soon as I looked at it, lights flashed and whistles blew. It was great! I wanted a copy for myself. Jim had developed an impressive compendium of facts, figures, and events in Boston, arranged as a continuous time line. Starting with the early voyages of discovery, the native people who occupied these shores, and the arrival of John Winthrop and the Puritans, the subjects move chronologically through the colonial period to the struggle for independence and the formation of the Constitution that made Boston part of the new nation. From the social and industrial changes of the early nineteenth century to the fight for women's rights and the crusade against slavery, *When in Boston* offers the reader events and personalities of the Civil War period and the postwar years, when immigration changed the face of the city. In addition to ethnic diversity, Vrabel describes the libraries, museums, theaters, and music halls that went up in the city at a time when professional sports teams were just making their appearance. Modern Boston politics, the creation of a New Boston, the rise of racial conflict, the busing crisis, and the new waves of immigrants are among the innumerable topics that will either refresh readers' memories or provide them with all sorts of new information.

Jim Vrabel not only compiles this impressive list of subjects, topics, people, buildings, places, activities, and events associated with Boston history, all arranged in chronological order, but also further divides the material into categories that include Population/Immigration, Planning/Development, Politics, Social Change, Religion, Education, the Arts, and even Sports/Recreation, making it possible for readers to go back and extract the specific information they are interested in. There is no doubt that *When in Boston* will prove to be an invaluable research tool for academics, scholars, researchers, graduate students, librarians, archivists, museum directors, newspaper editors, and all those whose professional lives and careers are centered on the study of Boston. But this handy, single-volume reference work will also be a very welcome addition to the bookshelves and libraries of all those general readers who love the city and its history. Vrabel has succeeded in his task, not only because of his extensive personal knowledge about Boston history, but also because of his innate love of order and his keen sense of what's important to remember about the city's past.

THOMAS H. O'CONNOR
Boston College

Acknowledgments

First and foremost, I want to thank Thomas H. O'Connor, Professor of History, Emeritus, and University Historian at Boston College, for the kindness he extended to a stranger. His immediate enthusiasm, generosity, and encouragement helped to make this book a reality.

Similarly, I want to thank William Fowler, executive director of the Massachusetts Historical Society, for his instant enthusiasm and support for this project. I want to thank Peter Drummey, librarian at the Massachusetts Historical Society, for so thoroughly reviewing this text and sharing his encyclopedic knowledge of Boston history. My thanks likewise go to Robert J. Allison, Associate Professor of History and director of University Archives at Suffolk University, for wading through each entry and professing to enjoy every step.

I want to thank Nancy Richard, director of Library and Special Collections at the Bostonian Society, for taking in a hungry researcher off the street and serving up all of the Boston history he could consume. I want to thank the rest of the Bostonian Society library staff for their help, suggestions, and encouragement: Sylvia Weedman, library assistant; Anne Vosikas, project archivist; Natalie Greenberg and Liz Doucett, volunteers; and Sue Goganian, director of Education and Public Programs.

For making available the resources of the Boston Public Library, I want to thank Mary Frances O'Brien, assistant to the director of Public Service, and all the other members of the BPL staff who were so generous with their time and knowledge: Marta Pardee-King, curator of social sciences; Mary Devine and Linda MacIver, reference librarians; Henry Scannell, curator of newspapers and microtext; Metro Voloshin, reference librarian; Diane Ota, curator of music; Evelyn Lannon, reference librarian and assistant to the curator of fine arts; Gayle Fithian, government documents librarian; Aaron Schmidt, of the Print Department.

I want to thank John Cronin, chief librarian at the *Boston Herald,* for his support of this project, and for opening that newspaper's text and photo files to me on all those Wednesday nights. I want to thank Tom Sheehan, copy editor at the *Boston Globe,* for making that newspaper's electronic files available in the wee hours, and reporter Mitch Zukoff for sharing facts from his upcoming book on Charles Ponzi.

I want to express my gratitude to all of the other archivists and librarians in Boston who provided me with information and direction: Dave Nathan, John McColgan, and Kristen Swett at the Boston City Archives; Stephen Nonack and Mary Warnement at the Boston Athenaeum; Robert Fleming at Emerson College; Bridget Carr at the Boston Symphony Orchestra; Donna Wells at the Boston Police Department; Garry Haggerty and Ralph Rosen at Berklee College of Music; George Sanborn at the State Transportation Library: Siobahn Wheeler at the Vose Galleries; Emily Beatty at the Boston University Medical Center; Libby Bouvier at the Massachusetts Supreme Judicial Court; Martha Clark at the State Archives; Betty Siegel at the State House Library; Michael Steinitz at the Massachusetts Historical Commission.

I want to thank the following historians and students of Boston history for their help: James Green, Professor of History at the University of Massachusetts; Dick Johnson, director of the New England Sports Museum; Jack Grinold, Sports Information Director at Northeastern University; Gil Santos of WBZ-Radio; Albert Rex of the Boston Preservation Alliance; Nancy Hannan of the Hyde Park Historical Society; Dr. William Reid of the South Boston Historical Society; Dr. William Marchione and Jeff Buschel of the Allston-Brighton Historical Society; and Bill Walczak of Codman Square in Dorchester. At City Hall, I want to thank for their help John Donovan, Jr., at the Boston Election Department; Margaret Dyson at the Boston Parks Department; John Sheehan at the Public Works Department; Jim Creamer at the Department of Neighborhood Development; and Ophelia Pedraza at the Boston School Committee.

For their encouragement, I want to thank former Massachusetts governor Michael Dukakis, now Professor of Political Science at Northeastern University; Paul Guzzi, president and chief executive officer of the Greater Boston Chamber of Commerce; Hubie Jones, former dean of the School of Social Work at Boston University; and Clare Cotton, former president of the Association of Independent Colleges and Universities in Massachusetts. I want to thank my neighbors Larry Johnson, for creating the Web site WhenInBoston.com, Steve Rochinski, for introducing me to Nicolas Slonimsky, and Allan MacDougall, for belying the adage that if you remember the sixties you did not participate in them.

For their friendship, information (baseball and otherwise), photographs, graphic design help, and other advice, I want to thank Richard Tourangeau, Marilyn Miller, Larry Rothstein, and Scott Kaiser. For their friendship and for sharing their love and knowledge of Boston, I want to thank Bob Consalvo, Greg Perkins, John Avault, Rolf Goetze, and Cathy Frye at the Boston Redevelopment Authority. For helping to make this history and this city better, I want to thank Lew Finfer.

At Northeastern University Press, which has done so much to preserve and promote Boston history, my thanks and gratitude go to Bob Gormley, executive editor, for his faith in this project and wise counsel; to Jill Bahcall, associate director for guiding it to its completion; to Ann Twombly, art and production director, for her commitment to completing this book under difficult circumstances, and for making it as accurate, visually appealing, and reader-friendly as it is; and to copy editor Deborah Kops, for smoothing out the rough spots in my fact-laden prose.

Finally, I want to thank my wife, Eiric, and my daughter, Zoe, for allowing me to shirk family responsibilities during the last three years in order to work on this project, and my sister, Susan, for worrying that it would never be done.

Preface

Historians have a difficult job. They have to try to reconstruct a whole past from the pieces available in the present, and they must try to tell history as a story. To advance the narrative, they are forced to choose only some of those pieces and ignore the rest. "Ignorance is the first requirement of the historian," Lytton Strachey wrote in *Eminent Victorians*, "ignorance, which simplifies and clarifies, which selects and omits."

I am not a historian. In *When in Boston*, I have tried to collect as many of the significant pieces of Boston history as possible. But since I have not tried to tell a story, I have not been forced to simplify or clarify. I have had to select and omit—but only to pare down into a single volume all that I had collected. I have also rearranged ("fast-forwarded" to finish a sequence of related events) and enhanced (primarily through quotation), but only, as Edward Weeks once wrote, "to break away from the ploddings of chronology and to group the material in a series of galaxies."

This book is not a history of Boston; it is a time-line history. Time lines are always simplified and often arbitrary, but a time line can open up and clarify history by spreading it out in a straight line. Time lines are lists, and people like lists. They make information accessible, remember-able. Lists are a start. They can provide a platform of information that can spur and support greater—and deeper—understanding.

Although a time line can present only one event at a time, it can also illustrate what else was being said, done, and thought in that historical vicinity. *When in Boston*, for example, reveals:

- *that not only did the Indians beat William Blackstone and John Winthrop to the Boston area, but so did quite a few other European settlers*
- *that before the struggle for independence, Boston's founding fathers and mothers struggled against nature, disease, fire, superstition—and each other*
- *that Adams, Hancock, and Revere didn't do all the heavy lifting during the Revolution, and there was still a lot of work left to do afterwards to establish a town and then a city on many hills*
- *that not only did Quakers, Catholics, and abolitionists have to fight for acceptance in Boston, but so did immigrants, women, workers, and minorities—and not just at first, but for many years after*
- *that the city's important institutions and organizations—from the Boston Public Library, Museum of Fine Arts, and Boston Symphony Orchestra to the Catholic Youth Organization, Women's Educational and Industrial Union, and Ten Point Coalition—didn't just happen by accident, but were the result of wealthy men giving something back to the city, and less well off men and women working to make Boston a better place to live*
- *that Boston's colorful brand of politics didn't begin—or end—with James Michael Curley, and that the city's passion for sports isn't confined to the fortunes—or misfortunes—of the Boston Red Sox*
- *that conflict is nothing new in Boston; it has ranged from the conflicts over religion,*

revolution, abolition, immigration, and industrialization in earlier times to conflicts over war, urban renewal, integration, and gentrification today—and none have been simple matters of right and wrong, good guys and bad guys, white and black.

The entries that make up *When in Boston* are arranged chronologically by year. The events of each year are divided into categories ranging from Population/Immigration and Planning/Development, to Politics and Social Change, Education, the Arts, and Sports. I had attempted, initially, to attribute the source of each piece of information, but abandoned the effort when the footnotes overran the text. I later found solace in Samuel Eliot Morison's preface to *The Oxford History of the American People*: "Since this is not a textbook, but a history written especially for my fellow citizens to read and enjoy, footnote references, . . . and other 'scholarly apparatus' have been suppressed."

I hope this book is read and enjoyed by my fellow citizens—from scholars trying to pin down a date to neighbors trying to remember when a church was built, from voters wanting to be better informed to visitors wanting to know what the heck they are looking at, from hard-core history buffs seeking answers to hard-bitten bartenders called on to settle bets. I hope the book does even more, though. *When in Boston* is meant to tell the *who*, *what*, and *where* as well as the *when* of Boston history. But it is also meant to promote other books by the real historians who tell the *how* and *why* of Boston history (such as Justin Winsor, Samuel Eliot Morison, Herbert Gans, and Walter Muir Whitehill in years past, Robert Allison, Robert Hayden, William Marchione, Thomas O'Connor, Douglass Shand-Tucci, and Susan Wilson today).

This book is the result of three years of research. All of the information in it comes from published, secondary sources. Except for official Web sites, I avoided the Internet. In addition to the sources listed in the bibliography, I pored over thousands of newspaper articles—online, in microfiche, and, in the case of the old *Record American*, in yellowed clippings folded into small envelopes and stuffed into file cabinets. I also mined the files of the Bostonian Society and Boston Public Library and used material provided by various neighborhood historical societies. Early on, I learned that compiling the events that make up Boston history was difficult enough, but tying dates to those events was more difficult still. I learned how often dates are missing, which is why historians so often employ phrases beginning with "by" or "as of" prior to a given date. Sometimes I was forced to choose among conflicting dates provided by different sources. Although I sought the day and month for each event, I often had to settle for just the year.

One of the benefits of my research was finding out how much of Boston's history is available and has been saved, especially by the great institutions we are so lucky to have in this city: the Bostonian Society, the Massachusetts Historical Society, the Boston Public Library, the Boston Athenaeum, and others. One of the disappointments, though, was finding out how much of that history is hard to get at, not yet written, or lost. We take more pride in preserving our history in Boston than we should. We have invested too little in saving and gathering it, making it accessible, and getting it down on paper. As much as I enjoyed the digging, I came away convinced that the ground should not have been that hard.

I am pleased at how much I have been able to collect in *When in Boston*, but I know there is much more out there to be gathered. There are more sources I might have consulted, more people I might have talked to. But I was just one man—without a grant, an advance, or the promise of publication, and with a day job, and a family who wanted to see me occasionally. I consider this a good start. I am responsible for perpetuating any errors repeated in this text. Readers with corrections and suggested additions can send them to WhenInBoston.com (with source citations when possible). Perhaps a revised (multivolume) edition will follow.

I want to acknowledge another shortcoming of this and most books of history—the failure to sufficiently acknowledge the lives and contributions of ordinary people. History is not only written by the winners; too often it is saved by and written about only them. Most people have all they can do to earn a living; they don't have the time or confidence to reflect on their lives. As Thomas O'Connor wrote in *The Boston Irish*: "They harbored the conviction that they were not good enough, important enough, deserving enough, influential enough to be considered part of real history." I think most of us feel that way, and that it is a feeling that should be resisted.

I once ran a youth leadership program for a group of high school juniors brought together from all over the city for a crash course on Boston—past, present, and future. One session involved a bus tour of the neighborhoods. Bill Fowler, then a history professor at Northeastern University, and I were the tour guides. Through most of the trip, the kids were their usual ebullient selves, interrupting our attempts to "teach history" by pointing out the windows to where they lived, went to school, or hung out. That changed, though, when we drove through Roxbury, Dorchester, and Mattapan. As Bill and I began to explain BBURG (see 1961 and 1968), the thirty-two young people on the bus grew silent. They stopped looking out the windows and looked at us, listening intently as we described how decisions made twenty-five years before by bankers and politicians continued to affect the lives of these teenagers, their families, and their neighbors today. The kids seemed, suddenly, to get it—to make the connection between areas mistakenly divided into "history" and "real life." It was a moment in my own personal history in Boston that I will never forget.

Most books on Boston history include a quotation from the Boston-educated philosopher George Santayana. But instead of merely repeating his familiar warning ("Those who cannot remember the past are condemned to repeat it"), I would like to close with something more upbeat. "The more you know," the author of *The Last Puritan* once wrote, "the more beautiful everything is." My hope is that the city and its history will be more beautiful and more meaningful the more people know what happened—and when—in Boston.

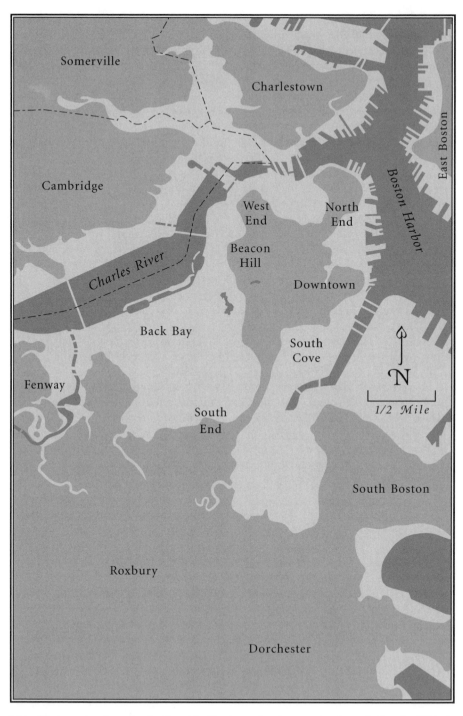

Map of Boston and environs showing the original land areas (medium gray) and areas built on landfill (pale gray). (Map by Charles Bahne)

To 1650

1000

 (ca.) According to Norse legend, Leif, son of Eric the Red, arrives in America. Although no physical evidence has been found to show that he ventures this far south, his description of a place where a river (possibly today's Charles) runs through a lake (possibly the Back Bay) into the sea (possibly Boston Harbor) prompts some historians to speculate that he reaches today's Boston. Anne Whitney's statue of Leif Ericson is dedicated on the Commonwealth Avenue mall near Kenmore Square on October 29, 1887. Its creation was championed by Eben Norton Horsford, a former Harvard professor of nutrition who made a fortune developing a formula for baking powder.

1586

 Sir Francis Drake is thought to visit Cape Cod. Earlier Drake had coined the name "New England," applying it to California on his voyage around the world in 1577.
George Weymouth explores New England, returning to England with three kidnapped Indians. The three live at the home of Sir Ferdinando Gorges and are taught English, so that Gorges can learn more about their homeland.

1600

 By this time, eastern Algonquin Indians have come to inhabit the area in which today's Boston lies. The local tribes include the *Massachusetts* (from *massa* for "great" and *wachusetts* for "mountain place"—a reference to the Great Blue Hill), *Nipmucks*, *Pocumtucks*, and *Pokanokets* (or *Wampanoags*).

1602

 Bartholomew Gosnold explores Massachusetts Bay, Cape Cod, and the islands off southeastern Massachusetts.

1604

Samuel de Champlain charts the Massachusetts coast and is thought to enter Boston Harbor (which the Indians call *Quonehassit*).

NOTE: "Old-style" dates (those used prior to England's adoption of the Gregorian calendar in 1752) have been retained. However, events taking place between January 1 and March 24 in years prior to 1752 (when March 25 marked the beginning of the calendar year) have been moved into the following ("New-style," or modern) year.

An asterisk after the last date in an entry indicates that a related entry can be found in that later year.

Trimount in 1630, decoration from Engine 15, by Samuel Lancaster Gerry and James Burt, oil on panel, 1836. (Courtesy of the Bostonian Society)

1614

Capt. John Smith explores Boston Harbor. A year later, he writes *A Description of New England*, which includes a mention of "Massachusetts Bay" and the river that the Indians called the *Quineboquin* (which means "twisting" or "winding"). Later, he reportedly tells the young Prince (later King) Charles to change the names on his map to some "good English ones," and the prince proceeds to name the river after himself.

1615–1619

A series of epidemics from diseases brought by the European explorers and settlers (such as chicken pox, measles, scarlet fever, and smallpox) kills 80 to 90 percent of the estimated seventy-five thousand Indians who had been living in New England. The population along the Massachusetts coast is reduced from approximately three thousand to five hundred.

1617

So many Indians die of disease in the area that is today South Boston that they lie unburied. For many years, surviving members of the tribe return to hold memorial services there; they name the place *Mattapannock* (meaning "a place where evil is spread about"). English settlers later shorten the name to Mattapan and apply it to an area of what they call Dorchester.

1619

David Thompson, an agent for Sir Ferdinando Gorges, explores Boston Harbor. He returns in 1626, establishes a trading post on what is today Thompson

Island, and dies in 1628, leaving a widow and infant son, John, who continue to live on the island. According to some accounts, the widow Thompson soon marries Samuel Maverick and moves with him to New York; according to Sweetser in *King's Handbook of Boston Harbor*, soon after the arrival of the Puritans, "the good Episcopalian lady abandoned her snug Atlantis, and sailed away to where she could hear once more the familiar 'Let your light so shine' in some distant prelatical realms." John Thompson returns and exercises his claim to the island in 1648.

1620

November 3. James I creates the Council for New England, which grants a patent to a group of merchants in Plymouth, England, for the northern part of the area called Virginia. Much of the land later goes to one of the members of the group, Sir Ferdinando Gorges.

November 11. The Mayflower Compact is signed by the Pilgrims on board ship off Provincetown. The document calls for formation of a "body politick." The Pilgrims land at Plymouth on December 11.

1621

September 29. Myles Standish of the Plymouth Colony leads a party that explores Boston Harbor, landing at today's Squantum, Savin Hill, and Charlestown. A member of the group, William Trevore, claims today's Thompson Island for David Thompson. Afterward, Standish reports: "Better harbors for shipping cannot be, than there are. At the entrance of the bay are many rocks and islands, and in all likelihood, very good fishing ground. Many, yea, most of the islands have been inhabited, some being cleared from end to end, but the people are all dead or removed."

1622

May. An advance party of ten lands at *Wessagussett* (later Weymouth) in an attempt to establish a trading post. Others follow in August. "Insufficiently clad and starving," according to the historian Justin Winsor, "the would-be settlers mixed freely with the neighboring Indians, first begging and then stealing from them, and thus incurring anger while they ceased to inspire fear." The settlers disperse to Plymouth, Maine, and back to England in the spring of 1623.

1623

The Dorchester Company establishes a settlement on Cape Ann (today's Gloucester). Some of the members soon after establish a smaller settlement at Nantasket.

September. Robert Gorges leads a second attempt—this time successful—to settle at Wessagussett. Gorges returns to England a year later. Settlers remaining include Samuel Maverick, Thomas Walford, and William Blackstone (or Blaxton).

1625

Summer. Captain Wollaston leads a party that settles at *Passangesset* (later Mount Wollaston, then Merry Mount, and finally Quincy). He later sails for Virginia with most of the company. Thomas Morton emerges as the leader of the remaining settlers, and he is later arrested by Standish for trading guns, ammunition, and spirits with the Indians for skins.

(ca.) Samuel Maverick establishes a trading post at *Winnisimmett*, today's Chelsea.

(ca.) Thomas Walford leads a party that settles in *Mishawum*, today's Charlestown.

(ca.) William Blackstone becomes the first European settler of today's Boston. A twenty-seven-year-old Anglican clergyman described by the historian Walter Muir Whitehill as "a bachelor with a taste for his own company," he settles on the 783-acre peninsula that the Indians call *Mushauwomuk* (variously described as meaning "living (or flowing) waters," "where there is going by boat," or "crossing place"). Blackstone builds a cabin near today's Beacon and Spruce Streets, complete with library, prompting the literary critic Van Wyck Brooks to later write, "There had been books on the slope of Beacon Hill when the wolves still howled on the summit." Blackstone cultivates a garden and an apple orchard and also reportedly indulges in strong drink, associates with Indians, and rides his tame white bull along the beach.

1626

There are by now five settlements in the area containing approximately fifty people: Wessagussett, Passangesset, Mishawum, Winnisimmet, and Nantasket.

(ca.) The English settlers in the area shorten the name of today's Boston to *Shawmut*, then variously call the peninsula Trimount, Tramount, or Trimountaine for its three hills: Windmill to the north (today's Copp's Hill); Corn or Fort to the south (today leveled); and Trimount in the center (today's Beacon Hill). The Trimount itself has three peaks: Cotton or Pemberton in the east; Centry or Sentry in the center; and West or Mount Vernon on the west.

1628

March 19. The Council for New England, meeting in Plymouth, England, conveys to the "Governor and Company of the Massachusetts Bay in New England" the land that lies between the Merrimack and Charles Rivers.

June 20. John Endicott, appointed governor of the Massachusetts Bay Colony in England, leads a group that settles at *Naumkeag*, which they rename Salem in 1629.

1629

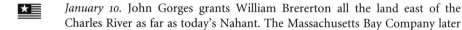

A fort is built on Town Hill in Charlestown as protection against Indian attacks.

January 10. John Gorges grants William Brererton all the land east of the Charles River as far as today's Nahant. The Massachusetts Bay Company later

refuses to recognize the grant, and instead gives Brererton two islands in Boston Harbor (later called Noddles and Hog or Breed's Islands). Brererton remains in England, however. William Noddle, formerly of Salem, settles on one of the islands. He later drowns while carrying wood over in his canoe in the summer of 1632.

March 4. Charles I grants a charter to the Massachusetts Bay Company for land that extends from three miles north of the Merrimack River to three miles south of the Charles River. The company is by now made up of a group of Puritans who have bought up controlling shares, including John Winthrop and Matthew Craddock, who is named governor on April 30.

July 4. Brothers Ralph, Richard, and William Sprague lead a party from Naumkeag that settles at Mishawum. After being granted status as an independent town by Charles I, the settlers rename it Charlestown.

August 26. Members of the Massachusetts Bay Company sign the Agreement at Cambridge, which states that "the whole government, together with the patent of the said plantation . . . remain with us and others who shall inhabit upon the said plantation."

October 20. A "General Court" of the Massachusetts Bay Colony elects John Winthrop governor, John Humphrey deputy, and eighteen others "assistants."

March. In a letter to Endicott at Naumkeag, Matthew Craddock writes, "be not unmindful of the main end of our plantation, by endeavoring to bring the Indians to the knowledge of the Gospel."

Thomas Walford and his family are asked to leave Charlestown because they are members of the Church of England. They eventually move to today's Portsmouth, New Hampshire.

1630

The Great House is built at today's City Square in Charlestown. It later serves as the home of Winthrop and others, a meeting place, a school, and the Three Cranes Tavern. The building is burned down by the British, with much of Charlestown, in June 1775.

King's Chapel Burying Ground is established. The first in Boston, it is located on the site of Isaac Johnson's garden, and he is said to be the first to be buried here. Other graves include those of Mary Chilton (the only Pilgrim to move to Boston), Rev. John Cotton, William Dawes, Govs. John Endicott and John Winthrop and Winthrop's son and grandson (both governors of Connecticut), Gov. William Shirley, and Elizabeth Pain (the reputed model for Hester Prynne, the heroine in Nathaniel Hawthorne's *The Scarlet Letter*).

The Phips Street Burying Ground is established in Charlestown. Graves include that of Nathaniel Gorham, president of the Continental Congress.

The Roxbury (later Eliot) Burying Ground is established at the corner of Eustis and Washington Streets in Roxbury. Graves include those of Govs. Thomas and Joseph Dudley, John Eliot, members of the Willard family, and veterans of the French and Indian War.

Portrait of John Winthrop, second governor of Massachusetts. Engraving by O'Pelton. (Courtesy of the Bostonian Society)

March 20. The *Mary and John*, with 140 passengers aboard, sets sail from England. It is one of eleven ships carrying approximately seven hundred members of the Massachusetts Bay Company that depart between February and May.

March 22. The *Arbella* sets sail from Southampton, England, carrying the Massachusetts Bay Company's charter. En route, John Winthrop writes and probably delivers an address entitled "A Modell of Christian Charity." In it he declares: "For wee must Consider that wee shall be as a Citty upon a Hill. The eies of all people are uppon Us." (The words are adapted from Matthew 5:14, "Ye are the light of the world. A city that is set on a hill cannot be hid.")

Early June. Dorchester is settled by passengers from the *Mary and John*. Landing at a place they call Rocky Hill (today's Savin Hill), the new inhabitants establish homes near today's Edward Everett Square. "Had not the waters of Dorchester Bay been more shallow than those of the other side of Dorchester Heights," Justin Winsor writes 250 years later, "we should probably have had to record the annexation of Boston to Dorchester instead of the reverse."

June 12. The *Arbella* and four other ships land at Salem. Members of the Massachusetts Bay Company find many of the settlers sick and without food, and they are turned away from Salem's church for not being "covented members." The result, according to Thomas Dudley, is that "Salem where we landed pleased us not."

June 17. Governor Winthrop leads a party that explores Boston Harbor in hopes of finding a better site for a settlement. After staying the night with Samuel Maverick in Winnisimmett, he decides that the members of the Massachusetts Bay Company should join the existing settlement at Charlestown.

Late June/early July. The remainder of the Massachusetts Bay Company moves from Salem to Charlestown. Other ships arrive from England, bringing more settlers. By the end of the summer, the population reaches an estimated fifteen hundred. Most live in tents, but Winthrop and the other "gentlemen" live in the Great House, renamed the Governor's House, which they purchase from its owner, who has returned to Salem.

Late July. Wracked by illness, the Charlestown settlers decide to disperse to the eight "primary towns" already established in the area. Dudley writes: "this dispersion troubled some of us; but help it we could not." Sir Richard Saltonstall leads one group to Watertown; William Pynchon, another to Roxbury; other groups go to Dorchester, *Mistick* (later Medford), and Saugus.

August. William Blackstone informs the Charlestown settlers of the presence of freshwater springs on the Shawmut Peninsula. He also invites Isaac Johnson, whom he had known in England, to share his cabin on the Shawmut Peninsula. Approximately 150 additional members of the group follow, moving across the harbor and living in huts and wigwams. After Johnson dies at the end of September, Blackstone invites Winthrop, Dudley, Rev. John Wilson, and other leaders of the group into his home. Three hundred years later, John Paramino's Founders Monument is dedicated on Boston Common on September 16, 1930.

August 23. The first meeting of the Court of Assistants is held aboard the *Arbella* at Charlestown.

September 7. Boston is named. At the second meeting of the Court of Assistants, held at the Governor's House in Charlestown, it is voted "that Trimountaine shalbe called Boston," after the town in Lincolnshire from which many of the Puritans had come, that Mattapan shall be called Dorchester, "and the towne upon Charles River," Watertown.

October 8. The Court of Assistants votes to establish the town of Roxbury (originally Rocksborough or Rocksbury, after the pudding stone found there). It includes today's West Roxbury, Jamaica Plain, and Roslindale.

October 19. The General Court is established, and the government is officially transferred from Charlestown to Boston. According to Winthrop, the settlers "had all things to doe, as in the beginning of the world."

November 8. The sky over Boston is darkened by the flight of thousands of pigeons.

December 26. Boston Harbor is reportedly frozen "far down" the bay.

June 6. The First Church in Dorchester holds its first service in temporary quarters. The first church building opens at the corner of today's East Cottage and Pleasant Streets a year later. John Maverick and John Warham are the first ministers. After the original building is destroyed by fire, a new one is built in 1645, then is moved by oxen to Meeting House Hill in 1670. The sixth and current building on the site, designed by Cabot, Everett, and Mead, opens in 1897.

July 30. The First Church in Boston is established, initially in Charlestown. It is the third church in the English settlements (after those in Salem and Dorchester); John Wilson is the first teacher. The congregation initially worships under a large tree, "the Charlestown Oak," then moves to Boston in September. A mud-walled, thatched-roof church opens on King Street (at today's 27 State Street) in 1632. It is replaced by a new church in Cornhill Square (at today's 209 Washington Street) in 1639. That building is destroyed by fire in October 1711, and replaced by "The Old Brick," dedicated on May 3, 1713. The congregation becomes Unitarian in the 1780s, and moves to a new church, designed by Asher Benjamin, on Chauncy Street in 1808. The current church, designed by Ware and Van Brunt, at 66 Marlborough Street in the Back Bay, is dedicated on December 10, 1868. Almost destroyed by a fire in 1968, the church is rebuilt, designed by Paul Rudolph, and reopens and merges with the Second Church in 1970.

 Two doctors are among the members of Winthrop's fleet: William Gager, who dies soon after his arrival, and Richard Palgrave, who lives for another twenty years.

1631

 Boston's population is approximately 175.

 May 14. Thomas Williams receives a charter from the Court of Assistants to operate the first ferry service, connecting Boston to Chelsea. His original passenger boats are later replaced by scows capable of carrying freight and livestock.
June 14. The Charlestown ferry to Boston opens. Established by Edward Converse, it continues to operate until the first bridge is constructed in 1786.*

 Spring. Deputy Gov. Thomas Dudley moves to the newly established settlement of Newtowne (later Cambridge). Governor Winthrop begins to build a house there, but is persuaded to remain in Boston and instead has the unfinished house dismantled and reassembled near Town Cove.
May 18. In the first election held in Boston, Winthrop is reelected governor "by the general consent of the Whole Court, manifested by the erection of hands. . . ."

 February 22. A day of thanksgiving in Boston is declared one day after the *Lyon* returns from England, carrying a much-needed shipment of food.
March. Massachusetts sachem *Chickataubut* ("house-a-fire") visits Boston "with his sannops and squaws." A dinner is held in the chief's honor, where, according to Winthrop, he "behaved himself as soberly as an Englishman." Chickataubut returns in April, seeking to trade for a new suit. Winthrop, however, orders his tailor to put the chief "into a very good new suit from head to foot," at the governor's own expense.

 March 22. The General Court bans gambling, passing a law that requires "all persons whatsoever that have cards, dice or tables in their houses shall make away with them before the next court convenes under pain of punishment."
April 12. The General Court creates the Boston Night Watch. The first police patrol in the Colonies, it is described as "a court of Guard upon the Neck,

between Roxburie and Boston, whereupon shall always be resident an officer and six men."

September 27. Josiah Plaistowe is convicted of stealing four baskets of corn from an Indian. He is forced to return eight baskets and pay a fine of five pounds, and he is deprived of his title of "gentleman."

March 16. A fire in Thomas Sharp's wooden chimney burns down his thatched-roof house. The first fire recorded in Boston history, it prompts Deputy Governor Dudley to issue an order that "No man shall build his chimney with wood, nor cover his house with thatch."

November 2. The First Church in Charlestown is established. Thomas James is the first pastor. The congregation meets initially under the Charlestown Oak, then in the Great House. The first church building is constructed in 1636. A new church is later dedicated next door on August 5, 1716, and is destroyed by the British in 1775. A new building opens in 1783. The current brick meeting-house is dedicated on March 5, 1803, and remodeled in 1852.

March 4. Nicholas Knopp is fined five pounds for the manufacture of quack medicines.

The first place of safe deposit in the Colonies is established in Dorchester. There, according to town records, "A sentinel was kept at the gate every night; and thither the people carried their plate and most valuable articles every evening. . . ."

1632

Boston's population is estimated at slightly more than 200.

The Boston Neck, an isthmus forty yards wide that flooded at high tide, is fortified to protect the town from Indian attacks. A gate is erected across it in 1640. Another fortification is built there in 1714, and some type of barrier or guard post is maintained until 1832.

October 3. The General Court is permanently established in Boston, which is declared "the fittest place for publique meetings of any place in the Bay."

August 2. Richard Hopkins is "whipt & branded with a hott iron on one of his cheekes, for selling peeces & powdr Y shott to the Indeans."
Smoking is banned in public. A law is passed that prohibits the use of "tobacco in any inne, or common victual house, except in a private room there, so as the master of said house nor any guest there shall take offence." The fine for breaking the law is two shillings and sixpence for every offense.

December 25. Boston Harbor is once again reported frozen "far down" the bay, and the winter of 1632–1633 is particularly harsh.

Summer. The First Church in Roxbury opens at today's John Eliot Square. Thomas Weld is the first pastor and John Eliot the first "teacher." He preaches there for more than sixty years. New churches are built on the site in 1674, 1741, and 1746. The current church, designed by William Blaney, contains a bell cast by Paul Revere and a clock built by Simon Willard. It is dedicated on June 7, 1804.

A smallpox epidemic kills a number of Indians, including the Massachusetts sachem Chickataubut.

August. A windmill is set up on Copp's Hill to grind corn. Moved from Watertown "because it would not grind there except in a westerly wind," it is the first windmill to operate in the Colonies and continues in service for many years.

1633

Boston's population is estimated at approximately 290.

The General Court rules "that the Indians had a just right to such lands as they possessed and improved by subduing the same."
Samuel Maverick settles on Noddles Island. He subsequently moves to New York and returns to Boston and then to England.

The Dorchester North Burying Ground is established. Among the graves eventually included are those of Rev. Richard Mather and William Stoughton, chief justice of the witch trial courts. The cemetery also includes the Capen stone, which marks the grave of Bernard Capen and is thought to be the oldest gravestone in New England. It is inscribed November 8, 1638.

May 29. John Winthrop is reelected governor and Thomas Dudley, deputy governor.
October 8. The first town meeting in the Colonies is held in the Dorchester meetinghouse "to sette down such orders as may tend to the generall good."

March 4. Robert Coles of Roxbury is found guilty of drunkenness and ordered to "weare about his neck & soe hange upon his outward garment a D made of redd clothe & sett upon white; to contynue for a yeare and not to leave it off at any tyme when he comes amongst company under penalty of XLs."

March 4. Thursday public lectures are established in Boston churches. The practice continues until approximately 1833.

A smallpox epidemic occurs, chiefly among the Indians, reducing their population even further.

1634

Boston's population is estimated at 400.
William Wood's tract, *New England Prospect: A True, Lively, and Experimentall Description of That Part of America, Commonly Called New England*, is pub-

A view of Boston Common. (Courtesy of the Bostonian Society)

lished in London. It encourages emigration to Boston, which it describes as being free from "three great annoyances, of Woolves, Rattle-snakes, and Mus-ketos."

April 1. The General Court orders every town to record the ownership and transfer of property.
Boston enacts the first local property tax in the Colonies.
Long Island is annexed to Boston.

July. The first fort is built on Castle Island. A mud-walled structure, it is re-placed by Fort William and Mary in 1689. After being badly damaged by a fire on March 21, 1673, it is replaced by Castle William in 1705, which is rebuilt in 1788. It is replaced by Fort Independence in 1803, which is in turn replaced by a second Fort Independence in 1851.*

August. Boston Common is established. The first public open space property in the Colonies, it is acquired when the town purchases forty-four of the fifty acres it had allowed William Blackstone to retain. The thirty-pound purchase price is raised by asking citizens who can afford it to contribute six shillings each. Later records describe how "The Town laid out a place for a trayning field; which is used for that purpose & for the feeding of Cattell." When some advocate selling the land for development in 1640, the town orders: "Hence-forth there shalbe noe land granted for hous-plott or garden out of Comon Field."

October. The reclusive Blackstone leaves Boston, complaining: "I left England on account of the Bishops. I fear that I may have to leave here on account of the Brethren." He eventually settles at a place he calls Study Hill near today's Cumberland, Rhode Island.

May 14. Citizens, upset at learning that, under the charter, elections were supposed to have been held annually—but were not—turn Winthrop out of office and elect Thomas Dudley governor.
September 1. Boston's first town elections are held and the town's "occasions" (selectmen) are chosen.

May 6. The town passes a law that absence from church shall be punishable by a fine of ten shillings or imprisonment for an unspecified amount of time.

The first marketplace in Boston is established on the site of today's Old State House. The General Court directs that the market be "kept on Thursdays, on which days the Public Lecture was held." The historian Esther Forbes later describes how "long before sunrise, country people streamed towards the narrow neck. The town was awakened by the rattle of wooden wheels, the hooves of horses, the cries of drovers . . . [bringing in] prodigious sacks of grain, slaughtered hens, hams, firkins of butter."
March 4. Samuel Cole opens an "ordinary" on Merchant's Row near Dock Square (at today's 239 Washington Street). The first tavern in Boston, its prices for both food and drink are set by the General Court. It later becomes the Ship Tavern.
John Cogan opens the first store in Boston. Located on the north side of King Street (today's 2 State Street), it is actually more of a trading post. Cogan is appointed by the General Court as the sole agent in town with the authority to buy and resell goods. The system soon fails, however, and other merchants are allowed to open shops.
Israel Stoughton builds the first waterwheel in the Colonies in Dorchester. He uses it to power a gristmill, which he builds at Lower Mills on the *Neponset* (an Indian word for "at the spread-out place") River in 1634.

1635

January 1. Boston's population is estimated at approximately 575.

The town enacts its first zoning ordinance. The order reads: "there shall noe house at all be built in this towne neere unto any of the streets and laynes therein but with the advise and consent of the overseers of the towne's occasions for the avoyding of disorderly building to the inconvenience of streets and laynes and for the more comely and Commodius ordering of them."

January. A beacon is erected on Centry Hill (thereafter Beacon Hill) "to give notice to the country of any danger." It is rebuilt in 1768, torn down by British troops in 1775, and replaced in 1776. Blown down in a storm in November 1789, it is replaced by a monument in 1791, which is torn down in 1811 and replaced by a replica nearby in 1898.

May 6. John Haynes is elected governor.

The first town jail ("gaol") opens on Prison Lane (now Court Street and the site of City Hall Annex). Built of wood with barred windows, it is later described by Hawthorne in *The Scarlet Letter*. Replaced by the Bridewell on Centry Lane (today's Park Street) in 1720, the jail moves to Leverett Street in 1822, to Charles Street in 1851, and to its current location on Nashua Street in 1991.

August 16. The Great Colonial Hurricane strikes Boston. According to John Winthrop, the storm "blew down many hundreds of trees . . . overthrew some houses, and drove the ships from their anchors," including the four-hundred-ton *Great Hope*.

April 3. Latin School is established when the town meeting votes to entreat "Our Brother Philomen Pormort to become schole master for the teaching and nourtering of children with us." The oldest public school in America, its graduates would include Cotton Mather, Sam Adams, John Hancock, Charles Bulfinch, Ralph Waldo Emerson, Edward Everett Hale, George Santayana, and Leonard Bernstein (Benjamin Franklin attended the school, but never finished). Classes are held in Pormort's home until 1643.*

1636

March 9. Noddles Island (part of today's East Boston) is annexed to Boston. The town sells the island to Samuel Shrimpton in 1670. Shrimpton's family owns the island for the next 160 years.

The Pequot War is fought. It begins after members of that tribe kill John Oldham, of Watertown, on Block Island. The General Court dispatches a force that includes men from Boston, who join other European settlers, as well as Mohegan and Narragansett Indians. They all but wipe out the Pequot tribe in fighting that takes place primarily in Connecticut.

May 25. Henry Vane is elected governor. Called the "Boy Governor" because he is only twenty-five years old, he takes office during a time of religious and civil unrest.
Capt. Robert Keayne's disposition of a stray pig prompts a lengthy court suit, which according to some accounts contributes to the separation of the General Court into two houses, the Magistrates and the Deputies, on March 7, 1644.

June 18. William Witherell opens the first school in Charlestown in the Great House. A new school building is subsequently constructed on Windmill Hill.
October 28. Harvard College is established. The General Court awards four hundred pounds for construction of "a schoale or colledge . . . the next Court to appoint where and what building." A year later, the General Court directs that the school be located in Newtowne, and changes the community's name to Cambridge, after the university town in England. The college opens in 1638.*

1637

The five islands that later make up East Boston (Noddles, Hog or Breed's, Governor's, Apple, and Bird) are annexed to Boston.

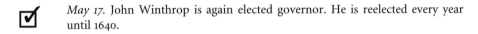 *May 17.* John Winthrop is again elected governor. He is reelected every year until 1640.

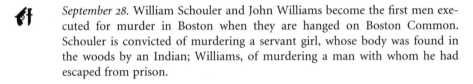 *September 28.* William Schouler and John Williams become the first men executed for murder in Boston when they are hanged on Boston Common. Schouler is convicted of murdering a servant girl, whose body was found in the woods by an Indian; Williams, of murdering a man with whom he had escaped from prison.

Winter 1637–1638. The town is almost abandoned because of a shortage of firewood. John Winthrop later writes to his son, "We in Boston were almost ready to brake up for want of wood."

November 8. Anne Hutchinson is banished for heresy. A midwife and lay healer, she is also an Antinominan and believes that grace alone is necessary for salvation, rather than in combination with good works. Although she had many supporters in the town (including Governor Vane), her critics include Winthrop, who confides in his journal, "if she had attended to her household affairs and such things as belong to women, and not gone out of her way and calling to meddle in such things as are proper for men, whose minds are stronger." Hutchinson, her husband, and their fourteen children move to Rhode Island. After her husband's death, Hutchinson moves to New York. She and five of the children are killed by Indians at Pelham in 1643.

1638

Commenting on Boston's increasing population, John Winthrop writes, "there came over this summer, twenty ships and at least three thousand persons."

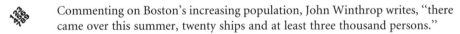 *March 13.* The Ancient and Honorable Artillery Company is chartered. Originally called the Military Company of Massachusetts, the organization assumes its current name in 1738. Robert Keayne is the first commander. The company's headquarters are later located in the Town House, then, beginning in 1746 and continuing to the present, in Faneuil Hall.

The first slaves arrive in Boston from the West Indies aboard the *Desire.*

June 27. Thomas Lechford arrives in Boston from England. The town's first lawyer, he is soon accused of trying to influence a jury and banned from appearing in court; he later returns to England in 1641.
December 10. Dorothy Talbye is hanged in Boston for murdering her child. She is later described by Winthrop as "a member of the church of Salem, and of good esteem for godliness &c; but, falling at difference with her husband, through melancholy or spiritual delusions, she sometimes attempted to kill him, and her children, and herself."

Harvard College opens. It is named for Rev. John Harvard, a twenty-seven-year-old minister who dies of consumption after only one year in Charlestown and leaves his 320-volume library and half his estate (779 pounds, 17 shillings, and twopence sterling) to the new college. Nathaniel Eaton is the first master. He is subsequently accused of beating students—and faculty—with a walnut cudgel, and his wife of mixing goat dung in the hasty pudding. The couple flees to Virginia at the end of the school year, and the college closes temporarily, reopening in 1640.*

A printing press is established in Cambridge. The first in the Colonies, it is brought from England by Rev. John Glover, who dies en route. Glover's widow and Stephen Daye, the printer who accompanied the press, establish a shop. The first printed material is "The Freeman's Oath," on a half-sheet of paper; the second, an "Almanack" prepared by Capt. William Peirce. The General Court soon passes a law prohibiting presses from being established anywhere but in Cambridge.

1639

A "Wharf and Crayne" is completed at which ships can be loaded and unloaded. The town has fifteen private wharves by 1645.

Mother Brook is created. The first major canal in the Colonies, it is built by the town of Dedham to divert water from the Charles River in order to power waterwheels on the Neponset River.

November 5. A post office, the first in the Colonies, is established in a tavern located near the corner of today's Washington and Devonshire Streets. The tavern proprietor Richard Fairbanks is Boston's first postmaster. Designated as the place for "all letters from beyond the sea, or [that] are to be sent thither," the post office handles only overseas mail. Those wishing to send or receive mail within the Colonies must make their own arrangements with private travelers.

Edward Palmer becomes the first man placed in the stocks in Boston. The builder of the device, he is punished for submitting a bill that is judged to be exorbitant. A few months later, a convicted bigamist is sentenced to be "set in the stocks for one hour on Lecture Day for two weeks so that all maids and widows might see him and not become number three."

May 20. Dorchester residents vote to establish the Mather School. The first free, public elementary school in America supported by taxes, it opens soon after on Settlers Street (today's Pleasant Street) with six boys in the first class. The school is supported by the fees paid by farmers who graze their cattle on Thompson Island. Girls are first admitted in 1748. The current school building, designed by Cram, Goodhue, and Ferguson, opens on Meeting House Hill in 1905.

A shopkeeper, Robert Keayne, is fined two hundred pounds by the court for overcharging customers. Although the fine is later reduced to eighty pounds, Keayne is also criticized by the church for "selling his wares at excessive Rates, to the Dishonor of Gods name . . . and the Publique scandal of the Cuntry."

1640

Boston's population is estimated at 1,200.

Centry Lane (today's Park Street) is constructed to allow access to the town beacon.
April 20. A ferry begins operating between Charlestown and Chelsea.

March 30. An ordinance is passed that prohibits use of any more of the Common lands "without consent of the major part of the inhabitants of the town," and forbids use "for house plotts or garden to any person."

May 13. Thomas Dudley is elected governor.

May 27. An explosion aboard the *Mary Rose* sinks the British man-of-war in Boston Harbor, killing fourteen people. Shortly before the ammunition explosion, the captain had declined Gov. John Winthrop's invitation to bring his crew ashore for church services, declaring they would hold their own services on board the ship.

Fall. Harvard College reopens. Henry Dunster is named the school's first president. He is succeeded by Charles Chauncy (1654), Leonard Hoar (1672), Uriah Oakes (1675), John Rogers (1682), and Increase Mather (1685–1701*).

Stephen Daye prints *The Whole Booke of Psalmes* (later known as the *Bay Psalm Book*) in Cambridge. The first book published in the Colonies, the 128-page quarto is sold in the shop of Hezekiah Usher, the first bookseller in Boston. The ninth edition of the book, published in 1698, contains the first musical notation in any book printed in the Colonies.

1641

November 29. Valentine Hill and Associates are granted the rights to fill and build wharves and warehouses in Bendall's Cove (today's Dock Square).

Francis Willoughby opens the first shipyard in Charlestown.
The 160-ton *Trial* is launched. The first full-size ship built in Boston, it is later credited with initiating Boston's foreign trade. The *Trial* sails for Bilbao, Spain, with a cargo of fish in 1643 and returns, via the West Indies, laden with "wine, fruit, oil, iron and wood," on March 23, 1644.

June 2. Richard Bellingham is elected governor. His subsequent marriage, at age fifty, to Penelope Pelham, aged twenty, reportedly shocks the town.

The winter of 1641–1642 is particularly severe, with deep snow and a frozen harbor.
The General Court passes the first law against cruelty to animals. The law states "that no man shall exercise any tyranny or cruelty towards any brute creatures which are usually kept for the use of man."

An African-American maidservant is welcomed into a Dorchester church, according to John Winthrop, because of her "sound knowledge and true godliness."

John Harrison establishes the first rope-making operation in Boston at the corner of today's Summer and Purchase Streets.

1642

March 27. It is voted that beer should be provided at town meetings.
May 18. John Winthrop is again elected governor. He is reelected in 1643.

The General Court passes an ordinance requiring each town to provide for the education of its children. A similar and more specific law is passed in 1789.*

July 23. Edward Bendall fashions the first diving bell in America. He uses it to salvage the wreck of the *Mary Rose* in Boston Harbor.

1643

July 31. A group of businessmen is given the right to develop the marshy area of North Cove, provided they build one or more gristmills and "maynteyne the same for ever." Mill Creek (in the area of today's Blackstone Street) is dug to power the mill, and a dam constructed in 1644 to create Mill Pond. A drawbridge is built over the creek and replaced by a fixed bridge in 1712. The filling of the creek begins in 1828 and is completed in 1833.

May 10. The General Court divides the Massachusetts Bay Colony into four shires: Suffolk (including Boston and seven neighboring towns), Norfolk, Essex, and Middlesex.
The town's elected leaders are first called "selectmen." Previously, they had been referred to as "the ten men," "the nine men," or "the town's men." They are elected annually beginning in 1645.

Anne Clarke is granted the first divorce in America—from her husband, Denis, who had fathered four children, two by her and two by another woman.

January 18. On this day, according to Ebenezer Clapp's *History of Dorchester*, "there were strange sights seen about Castle Island, and the Governor's Island . . . in form like a man, that would sometimes cast flames and sparkles of fire. This was seen about eight of the clock in the evening by many. About the same time a voice was heard between Boston and Dorchester upon the water in a dreadful manner, crying out, 'Boy, boy, come away, come away. . . .' About fourteen days after, the same voice was heard in the like dreadful manner; divers sober persons were witnesses thereof, at both times, on the other side of the town, toward Noddles Island."

The first Latin School building is constructed on today's School Street, at the rear of the site now occupied by King's Chapel. It is replaced by another building, near today's Old City Hall, in 1704; then by another, on the site of today's Parker House, in 1748. While this building is being repaired in 1785, classes are held in Faneuil Hall. A new school is built on the same site in 1812. Latin School moves to a shared building with the English High School on Bedford Street in 1844, then to another such building in the South End in 1880, which is dedicated in 1881.*

1644

May 29. John Endicott is again elected governor.

A group of Boston businessmen sends a ship to Africa for "gold dust Negroes." It is the first mention of slaves being imported directly from Africa to Boston.

August 26. A large meteor lights the sky and "causes consternation." Honeybees are first imported to Boston.

Rev. John Cotton's *The Keys of the Kingdom of Heaven* is published.

1645

Eleven ships arrive from England carrying "linen, woolens, shoes and stockings and other useful goods."

May 24. Thomas Dudley is again elected governor.
The town of Dorchester adopts the "Directory," which contains regulations for conducting town meetings.

The ship *Rainbowe* reportedly attempts to deliver a load of slaves from Guinea, West Africa, to Boston, only to have the ship's officers seized and the Africans returned home at public expense.

August 31. Roxbury Latin School is founded by Rev. John Eliot. Originally called the Roxburie Free Schoole (although free only to the sons of its donors), it is later described as "the oldest school in continuous existence in North America" (because, unlike Boston Latin, its classes are not interrupted during the Revolution). Rev. Eliot's brother, Philip, is the first headmaster. Graduates would include Gen. Joseph Warren, Dr. Paul Dudley White, and Walter Muir Whitehill. Classes are held in rented rooms until 1652.*

A tidal-powered gristmill is constructed in Charlestown.

1646

The North Battery is built at Merry's Point (today's Battery Wharf) in the North End.

May 6. John Winthrop is again elected governor. He is reelected in 1647 and 1648, and dies on March 26, 1649.

 October 28. Rev. John Eliot preaches to the Nonantum chief Waban and others of the tribe in today's Brighton. Later known as the "Apostle to the Indians," Eliot reportedly speaks for more than an hour in the Indian language, and is afterwards asked if God will understand prayers offered in the Indian tongue.

1647

 John Cotton's *Singing of Psalme A Gospel-Ordinance* is published in London. It is the most comprehensive study of American church music to be published prior to the Revolution.

 The General Court orders "that every township, after the Lord hath increased them to the number of fifty households, shall appoint one to teach all children to write and read; and when any town shall increase to the number of one hundred families, they shall set up a grammar school, the master thereof to be able to instruct youth so far as they may be fitted for the University." Later called "the old deluder Satan Act," its purpose is to promote "knowledge of the Scriptures." The law calls for supervision of the schools by "no existing body of officials but charged the Town as a whole with this important duty." In complying, the Boston Public School system is established, the first in America. Despite the wording of the law, the town's selectmen act as supervisors of the schools.

1648

 (ca.) The Blake House is built on Cottage Street in Dorchester. The oldest house in today's Boston, it is purchased by the city, turned over to the Dorchester Historical Society, and moved to its current location at 735 Columbia Road in 1895 in one of the first instances of moving a historic building to preserve it.

 June 5. Margaret Jones of Charlestown is hanged on Boston Common for engaging in witchcraft. A midwife or lay healer, she had been convicted of putting a fatal spell on a neighbor's cow. She is the first of four women who would be executed for witchcraft in what today is Boston. A total of thirty-seven people would be put to death for witchcraft in all of New England. In comparison, during the sixteenth and seventeenth centuries, an estimated thirty thousand would be executed for witchcraft in England and Scotland, seventy-five thousand in France, and one hundred thousand in Germany.

 The General Court establishes a quarantine on all ships coming into Boston from the West Indies. A year later, the court repeals the order, "seeing it hath pleased God to stay the sicknes there."

 October 18. The General Court allows "the shoomakers of Boston" to "assemble and meet together in Boston at such . . . times as they shall appoynt." The

resulting association is considered to be the first labor organization in America. A coopers' association is also formed this year. Both draw up list of rates and work rules for their respective trades.

1649

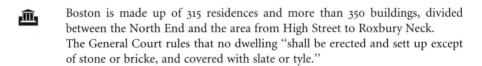

April. Solomon Franco becomes the first Jew to visit Boston. Accompanying a cargo shipped to Maj. Gen. Edward Gibbons, Franco becomes embroiled in a dispute over his promised commission, which Gibbons claims should have been paid by the shipper of the goods. Franco is ordered to leave town, and does soon after.

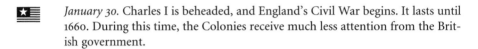

Boston is made up of 315 residences and more than 350 buildings, divided between the North End and the area from High Street to Roxbury Neck.
The General Court rules that no dwelling "shall be erected and sett up except of stone or bricke, and covered with slate or tyle."

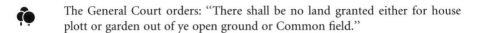

The General Court orders: "There shall be no land granted either for house plott or garden out of ye open ground or Common field."

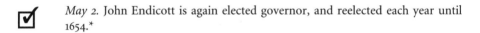

January 30. Charles I is beheaded, and England's Civil War begins. It lasts until 1660. During this time, the Colonies receive much less attention from the British government.

May 2. John Endicott is again elected governor, and reelected each year until 1654.*

Cooking fires in houses are ordered to be extinguished or covered from 9:00 P.M. to 4:30 A.M. to guard against night fires.
December. Eight persons drown when they fall through the ice in Boston Harbor.

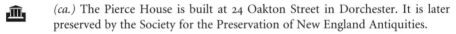

Rev. John Cotton's *The Way of Congregational Churches* is published.

1650

Boston's population is estimated at 2,000.

(*ca.*) The Pierce House is built at 24 Oakton Street in Dorchester. It is later preserved by the Society for the Preservation of New England Antiquities.

June 5. The Second Church (Old North Meeting House) opens in North Square. The congregation formed the previous year. Samuel Mather and John Mayo are the first pastors. Their successors include Increase and Cotton Mather. The church burns down on November 26, 1676. It is rebuilt, but then torn down for firewood by British soldiers in the winter of 1775–1776. The congregation merges with that of the New Brick Church and moves to Hanover Street in 1779.*

December. Father Druillettes, a Jesuit missionary, is allowed to enter Boston, but only because he is on a diplomatic mission to forge an alliance between the English and French settlers against the Iroquois. During his visit, he reportedly celebrates the first Catholic Mass in Boston, in a private room supplied by his host, Major Gibbons.

1651 to 1700

1651

October 3. To curtail ostentation, the General Court declares: "If a man was not worth 200 pounds, he should not wear gold or silver lace or buttons, nor great boots. Women worth less than 200 pounds are forbidden to wear silk or tiffany hoods or scarfs."

(ca.) Alice Lake of Dorchester is executed for being a witch.
September 24. John Eliot establishes a community of what are called "praying Indians" in *Natick* (which means "the place of the hills"). During King Philip's War, members of the community are taken to Deer Island on October 30, 1675. Some are allowed to return in May 1678, by which time the town has been incorporated as the town of Natick.

1652

(ca.) The flat conduit, a twelve-foot-square wooden "reservoir," is built near today's Dock Square, becoming the first municipal water supply in the Colonies. The water is carried through wooden pipes from nearby springs and used by subscribers, as well as by the town for fighting fires.

Arson of a dwelling house is made a capital crime.
May 31. The General Court orders that no "garbage, dead beast or stinkering things" be deposited on Boston streets.

Roxbury Latin opens its first school building off Guild Row in today's Dudley Square. The building is replaced in 1742, again in 1789, and then enlarged in 1819. The school moves to a new building on Kearsage Avenue in Roxbury in 1860, then to its current campus, designed by Perry, Shaw, and Hepburn, on the former Codman estate at 101 St. Theresa Avenue in West Roxbury in 1927.

1653

April 14. The first of Boston's "Great Fires" kills three children and destroys eight houses in the area of today's State and Washington Streets.
The town enacts its first fire code. It requires every household to provide a ladder and "a pole of about 12 feet long, with a good large sob at the end of it, to rech to the rofe." The town also appoints a ladder inspector and buys several ladders and "fower strong Iron Crooks" to pull down houses.

A distillery is set up in Boston. The liquor it produces is called "rum," which at this time means any potent drink.

1654

In his book *Wonder-Working Providence*, Edward Johnson describes Boston as "crowded on the Sea-bankes and wharfed out with great industry and cost."

May 3. Richard Bellingham is again elected governor.

Boston residents are forbidden to keep Quaker writings.

May 3. The General Court votes "that the youth thereof be educated, not only in good literature but sound doctrine," but not by teachers "that have manifested themselves unsound in the faith, or scandalous in their lives."

1655

May 23. John Endicott is again elected governor and is forced by the newly passed residency requirement to move into Boston from Salem. He is reelected every year until 1665.*

Ann Austin and Mary Fisher become the first Quakers to arrive in Boston. Eight more Quaker women join them a few months later. All are arrested, jailed, and deported. Soon after, the General Court orders that all Quakers are to have their ears cut off or tongues pierced with a hot iron. A year later, the penalty for being a Quaker is increased to death.

1656

Bostian Ken is described as the owner of a house and "four acres planted in wheat" in Dorchester. He is believed to be the first African-American property owner in today's Boston.

August 25. An ordinance is passed prohibiting the galloping of horses in the town.
Another ordinance names "the bridge to the North End" as the only place where butchers might "throw their beasts' entrails and garbid, without penalty of a fine."

June 19. Anne Hibbens is hanged for witchcraft. The sister of Governor Bellingham, she had earlier been excommunicated from the church for usurping her husband's authority by berating a carpenter for overcharging for his work.

1657

At the urging of Rev. John Eliot, the town of Dorchester sets aside six thousand acres at Ponkapoag as a reservation for the Neponset Indians. It is believed to be the first Indian reservation in the Colonies.

The Town House is built at the corner of today's Washington and State Streets. Construction of the wooden building is supported by a bequest from the merchant Robert Keayne for a place "for Merchants, Mr of Shipps and Strangers as well as the Towne . . . to meet in." The building is destroyed in the Great Fire of 1711 and replaced in 1713.*

The Scots Charitable Society is established. Incorporated in 1786, it is the oldest charitable organization in Boston and, perhaps, in the Colonies.

The Green Dragon Tavern is established on Union Street; Richard Pullen is the proprietor. One of the earliest taverns in Boston, it becomes a popular meeting place, first for Masonic groups, then for Colonists resisting British rule, as well as the British themselves. The building is later used by the Massachusetts Charitable Association and torn down in 1828. Today, a tavern of the same name is located at 11 Marshall Street.

The first House of Correction opens on today's Court Street. Built to confine those who might be "debauched and live idly," it is replaced on the same site by the Bridewell in 1704. The prison moves to South Boston in 1823, Deer Island in 1882, and its current site in the South Bay in 1991.
The General Court prohibits the sale of all liquors to the Indians, "whither knoune by the name of rumme, strong water, wine, strong beere, brandy, cidar, perry, or any other strong liquors, going vnder any other name what-souer."
Arthur Howland is convicted of possessing "seditious" materials.

June 14. A General Council of the Churches meets in Boston. It declares that all those baptized in infancy are to be regarded as members of the church and entitled to all privileges—with the exception of "the Lord's Supper." The decision is reaffirmed at another synod in 1662.

1658

At his death, Stephen Winthrop leaves a bequest of "fifteene pounds" to be used for the poor. The first such recorded bequest to the poor in Boston, it is joined by one given by William Paddy on November 29.

1659

Copp's Hill Burying Ground is established. The second-oldest in Boston, it is named for the shoemaker William Copp. Its graves would include those of Prince Hall, Cotton, Increase, and Samuel Mather, and John Webster (the murderer of George Parkman; his body lies in an unmarked grave).

William Blackstone returns to Boston. After selling the last six acres of his property and marrying the widow Stevenson, he returns with her and her sixteen-year-old daughter to Study Hill. Blackstone dies on May 26, 1675, and is buried in what is today Cumberland, Rhode Island. His house and library are destroyed by fire during King Philip's War a year later. The city of Boston names Blackstone Street (formerly Mill Creek) after him in 1834.

October 27. Two Quakers, Marmaduke Stevenson and William Robinson, are hanged on Boston Common. A third, Mary Dyer, is about to be hanged, but her son persuades authorities to spare her. She is escorted out of Massachusetts and warned not to return, but Dyer does return, a year later, "persuaded that her death was necessary." She is hanged on Boston Common on June 1, 1660.

1660

 Boston's population is estimated at 3,000.

 The Granary Burying Ground is established on the site of the former town granary (on today's Tremont Street). Originally called the South Burying Ground, it is the third-oldest in Boston. Its graves would include those of Samuel Adams, four of the five the victims of the Boston Massacre, Peter Faneuil, John Hancock, James Otis, Paul Revere, and Elizabeth Foster Vergoose (thought to have been the writer of the Mother Goose nursery rhymes).

 Charles II is "restored" to the throne and England is once again is ruled by a king.
The British Parliament enacts the Navigation Acts, which require the Colonies to trade exclusively with England.

 (ca.) The King's Head Tavern is built on North Street. It is torn down in July 1870.

 Winter. Rev. Samuel Danforth of Roxbury notes in his church records: "The Lord was pleased to visite vs, with epidemical colds, coughs, agues, and fevers."

1661

 August 7. News of the "restoration" and accession to the English throne by Charles II reaches Boston.

 The Anchor Tavern opens on King Street.

 May 28. Judah Brown and Peter Pierson receive twenty strokes from a whip in Boston for being Quakers. They are then tied to a cart, taken to Roxbury, and given ten more strokes there.

1662

 An estimated 40,000 English colonists inhabit New England. They outnumber Indians by approximately two to one.

 The Great Bridge opens, connecting today's Allston with Cambridge near today's Harvard Square. Swept away by a high tide in 1685, it is rebuilt in 1690, and replaced first by the North Harvard Bridge, then by the current Nicholas Longworth Anderson Bridge in 1915.

 The town's Almshouse (later called the House of Industry) is built at the corner of today's Park and Beacon Streets. Eventually, provision is made "for the separation of the vicious from the worthy poor." The building is destroyed by fire in 1682 and rebuilt in 1686. A new Almshouse, designed by Charles Bulfinch, opens on Leverett Street on May 18, 1802. It moves to South Boston in 1825, Deer Island in 1852, Rainsford Island in 1866, West Roxbury in 1877, and Long Island in 1891.

October 18. The Wampanoag chief Metacom (King Philip) visits Boston, having succeeded his father, Massasoit, who died earlier in the year. Under Metacom's leadership, the relationship between the Indians and the European settlers deteriorates.

 General Atherton is killed on Boston Common when his horse collides with a cow. Atherton was on his way home from reviewing his troops. According to an account of the incident, "the cow also suffered."

 The Half-Way Covenant is adopted. It allows membership in the Puritan church for those who have not made a public declaration of their faith, but who appear to lead moral lives.

Charles II sends what would be called "the king's missive" to Governor Endicott, declaring that Quakers should not be put to death, but instead sent back to England for trial.

 The first town censor is named. Although not an official position in modern times, the role is filled until 1975.

1663

 The first Custom House opens on Richmond Street near North Square. Succeeding locations would include Scollay Square, Tremont and Court Streets, and State Street. It moves to a new building on Custom House Street in 1810. That building is torn down in 1846 and replaced in 1847.*

 The Englishman John Josselyn visits Boston. Returning to London, he later writes: "The houses are for the most part raised on the sea banks, and wharfed out with great industry and cost; many of them standing upon piles, close together on each side of the street, as in London, and furnished with many fair shops. . . . The town is rich and populous. On the south there is a small, but pleasant, Common, where the Gallants, a little before sunset, walk with their Marmalet-madams, as we do in Morefields, till the nine o'clock bell rings them home to their respective habitations. When presently, the Constables walk their rounds to see good order kept, and to take up the people."

 December. John Eliot's complete "Indian Bible," *Up-biblum God*, is printed by Samuel Greene and Marmaduke Johnson in Cambridge. The only remaining copy of the book is owned by the Roxbury Latin School. His translation of the New Testament was published on September 5, 1661.

1664

 Royal commissioners from England visit Boston. They order that the town stop minting its own money, and that citizens say "God save the king" after royal proclamations are read aloud.

Fifteen Quakers (twelve men and three women) are "whipped through three towns"—that is, whipped in Boston and then in two other neighboring communities.

The British State Papers declare that "Boston . . . had a great trade with Barbadoes in fish and other provisions; 300 vessels traded to the West Indies, Virginia, Madeira, etc., and 1,300 boats fished in the waters about Cape Sable, and there was a great mackerel fishery in Cape Cod Bay."

1665

The South Battery is built at the site of today's Rowes Wharf.
The Royal Commissioners compile a report on Boston. It reads, in part, "Their houses are generally wooden, their streets crooked, with little decency and no uniformity."

MAMUSSE
WUNNEETUPANATAMWE
UP-BIBLUM GOD
NANEESWE
NUKKONE TESTAMENT
KAH WONK
WUSKU TESTAMENT.

Ne quoshkinnumok nashpe Wuttinneumoh *CHRIST* noh asoowesit

JOHN .ELIOT·

CAMBRIDGE,
Printeuoop nashpe *Samuel Green* kah *Marmaduke Johnson.*
1663.

John Eliot's Indian Bible. (Reproduced by permission of the Houghton Library, Harvard University)

May 3. Richard Bellingham is again elected governor. He is reelected every year until 1672.*

July. Capt. Richard Davenport, commander of Fort William and Mary on Castle Island, is struck and killed by lightning while lying on his cot in the barracks.

Rev. Samuel Danforth's *Astronomical Description of the Comet of 1664, with Brief Theological Applications Thereof* is published.

1666

March 28. The First Baptist Church is established. After meeting in private homes, the congregation dedicates a new church at the corner of Salem and Stillman Streets in the North End on February 15, 1679. Closed by order of the General Court in 1680, it is later rebuilt and reopens on the same site, moves to the North End in 1829, Beacon Hill in 1854, and its current location, in the former Brattle Square Church in the Back Bay, in 1882.

Smallpox kills forty residents of the town.

John Eliot's *Indian Grammar* is printed by Marmaduke Johnson in Cambridge.

1668

Robert Stanton builds the first house in today's Hyde Park.

1669

The first stagecoaches are used in Boston.

A town ordinance is passed prohibiting rogues, idlers, jugglers, and fiddlers.

May 12. The Third Church (also known as the Cedar Meeting House) opens on the former site of John Winthrop's garden on today's Washington Street. Formed by dissidents from the First Church, it remains Congregationalist throughout the years. The building is destroyed by the Great Fire of 1711 and is rebuilt. People begin calling it the "Old South" Church in 1719, when another church is built nearby. The current church building opens in 1730.*

1670

Boston is the third-busiest port in the British Empire and the leading port in the American colonies.

August 13. The Wampanoag chief Metacom again visits Boston.

An Indian is convicted of the murder of Zachary Smith in a Dedham forest and is hanged on Boston Common.

(ca.) According to Winsor, "the town, or possibly the colony, established in Boston a collection of books for public use sometime before the Indian outbreak of 1675." He speculates that this library was probably the repository of the "ancient books" described as being destroyed when the Town House burns in 1747.

1671

September 1. Englishman John Josselyn again visits Boston. He later describes "the Inhabitants exceedingly afflicted with griping of the guts, and Feaver, and Ague, and bloody Flux."

1672

December 12. John Leverett is appointed acting governor.

The tavernkeeper and widow Alice Thomas is whipped and then banished for giving patrons "the opportunity to commit carnall wickedness" and for being "a common Baud." She is allowed to return a year later, however, after contributing money for construction of a seawall to protect the harbor.

John Josselyn's *New England Rarities Discovered: In Birds, Beasts, Fishes, Serpents, and Plants of That Country* is published in London. Professor Joseph Lovering later calls the book, the result of two trips to Boston and the area, "a curious medley of science and nonsense."

1673

February 5. The first mail arrives in Boston from New York via the Boston Post Road. The beginning of a regular postal service, the 250-mile trip takes two weeks. Sarah Knight of Charlestown later becomes the first female postal rider (although she is accompanied by a man). Service is interrupted a year later, first by the Dutch siege of New York, then by King Philip's War. Service resumes in 1685, becomes weekly in 1711, and is increased to three times a week in 1814. Daily service begins in 1880.

May 7. John Leverett is elected governor. He is reelected every year until his death in 1678.

A law is passed prohibiting the operation of dancing schools in Boston, but a fencing school is allowed to open.

1674

Samuel Sewall begins the diary he would keep until 1729 (except for the years between 1677 and 1685). It is published in 1878–82.

The Charlestown Poor Fund is established.

The first Sunday school in the Colonies is reportedly established at the First Church in Roxbury—although credit for establishing the first Sunday school is later also given to Christ Church in 1815 and Park Street Church in 1818.

September 9. John Foster establishes a print shop near the corner of today's Boylston and Tremont Streets. The first in Boston, it is allowed after repeal of the 1638 law confining printing presses to Cambridge. His first publication is the text of a sixty-three-page sermon preached at the inauguration of Gov. John Leverett.

1675

June 8. King Philip's War begins. During the war, two-thirds of the settlements in New England are attacked and an estimated eight hundred European settlers are killed. An estimated three thousand Indians are also killed. The Nonantum Indians, who had been converted to Christianity by John Eliot, are rounded up and interned on Deer Island. Some are later freed, some sold into slavery, some executed. "This usage of them is worse than death," Eliot later writes. "The designe of Christ in these last days, is not to extirpate nations, but to gospelize them." The war ends when the Wampanoag leader Metacom (King Philip) is killed in Bridgewater on August 12, 1676. His decapitated and quartered body is brought to Boston for exhibition three days later.

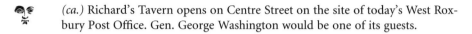 *(ca.)* Richard's Tavern opens on Centre Street on the site of today's West Roxbury Post Office. Gen. George Washington would be one of its guests.

Maurice Brett is found guilty of "filthy carriage." He is sentenced to stand at the gallows with a rope around his neck, where he is given thirty-nine lashes and then banished. When he complains at the severity of the punishment, he is also fined twenty shillings and sentenced to have his ears first nailed to the pillory and then cut off.

June 27. An eclipse of the moon frightens Boston residents. Several ministers deliver sermons regarding its ominous portent.
September 8. A hurricane hits Boston, damaging ships docked at the wharves and anchored in the harbor.

Increase Mather's *The Wicked Man's Portion* becomes the first book to be published in Boston.

Thirty merchants in Boston are estimated to be worth between ten thousand and twenty thousand pounds, and the Boston fleet is estimated to contain 430 large vessels. William Harris writes: "Boston's merchants seem to be rich men, and their houses are handsomely furnished as most in London."
John Langworthy is ridden "upon a pole and by violence" from the North End to the town dock by ship carpenters for being "an interloper" who "had never served his time to the trade."

1676

May 3. Mrs. Mary Rowlandson of Lancaster arrives in Boston after being freed from captivity by Indians. In a book about her experiences, she later credits "some Boston gentlewomen and Mr. Usher" for raising the twenty-pound ransom she calls "the price of my redemption."
August. "About 30 Indian prisoners-of-war" are hanged on Boston Common.

October. John Sparry opens the first coffeehouse in America.

November 27. The Great Fire of 1676 breaks out. The blaze destroys the Second Church and forty-five houses in the North Square area, but a sudden rainstorm prevents further damage and saves the Rev. Increase Mather's one-thousand-book library.

Edward Randolph writes of Boston: "It is the great care of the merchants to keep their ships in constant employ, which makes them trye all ports to force a trade, whereby they abound with all sorts of commodities, and Boston may be esteemed the mart town of the West Indies."

1677

John Speed's map of New England is published in William Hubbard's *A Narrative of the Troubles with the Indians in New England*. It is the first map produced and published in America.

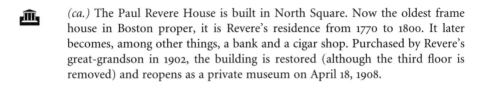

(ca.) The Paul Revere House is built in North Square. Now the oldest frame house in Boston proper, it is Revere's residence from 1770 to 1800. It later becomes, among other things, a bank and a cigar shop. Purchased by Revere's great-grandson in 1902, the building is restored (although the third floor is removed) and reopens as a private museum on April 18, 1908.

The first Quaker meetinghouse in Boston opens. The congregation moves to Brattle Street in 1694, and in 1710 to Congress Street, where a cemetery is established nearby. The congregation dissolves in 1808. The cemetery land is sold and the graves moved to Lynn in 1827.
May 22. The General Court orders cages to be erected for the confinement and exhibition of Sabbath-breakers.

January 21. Rev. Thomas Thatcher's "A Brief Rule to Guide the Common People of New England How to Order Themselves and Theirs in the Small Pocks, or Measles" is published. The first medical pamphlet published in the Colonies, it is reprinted in 1702.

Henry Phillips opens a bookshop under the stairs of the Town House.

1678

James Russell builds the first dry dock in North America in Charlestown. Its purpose is described as "for taking in of shipps & vessells for repayring vnder water."

Reacting to the growth of intemperate drinking, the town of Roxbury restricts the sale of wine and liquor to only one "ordinary." "This prohibitory enactment," according to Winsor, "did not long remain in force."

Thomas Atkins is appointed Boston's first fire chief.

Smallpox kills eight hundred in Boston. Similar numbers die of the disease in 1702 and 1710.

1679

The Province House is completed at what is today 327 Washington Street. Built by Peter Sargeant, it is the most elaborate home of the day and later serves as the setting for some of Hawthorne's *Twice-Told Tales*. Purchased by the town in 1716, it serves as the royal governor's mansion. It is sold in 1779, and becomes a tavern in 1834. Despite efforts to preserve it, the building is demolished in 1922. Only the garden steps, between Province and Bosworth Streets, remain today.

May 28. Simon Bradstreet is elected governor. He is reelected every year until he is replaced by a royal governor in 1686.*

August 8. The Great Fire of 1679 destroys eighty homes and seventy ware-houses.
August 29. A fire commission is established. Eight fire companies are organized and the town acquires a fire "engine" from England.

 As a result of overcrowding at Latin School, two free "primitive" (elementary) schools are established "for the teaching of children to write and cipher."

1680

 Boston's population is estimated at 4,500.

 The Old Feather Store is built in Dock Square. A Boston landmark for many years, it is known for its gabled roof and rough plaster walls. The building is torn down in 1860.

 Two travelers, Danker and Sluyter, describe Boston: "All the houses are made of small, thin, cedar shingles, nailed against frames, and then filled in with brick and other stuff; and so are their churches. For this reason these towns are so liable to fires, as have already happened several times; and the wonder to me is that the whole city has not been burnt down, so light and dry are the materials."

 March 16. Boston is authorized to send three representatives to the General Court. All other towns are limited to two.

 Church representatives from the five New England colonies meet in Boston and draft "A Confession of Faith." It is agreed that congregations may choose which parts of the text to incorporate into their own covenants.

1681

 The Barricado is completed along the route of today's Atlantic Avenue. A 2,200-foot-long breakwater, it is built as a defense against possible attack by the Dutch or French, but it proves unnecessary and soon falls into disrepair.

 July 22. A child is killed when the Roxbury homes of Joshua Lamb and a neighbor burn down. It is subsequently discovered that the fire was set by a slave called Black Maria. She is executed on Boston Common on October 2. "The severity of the sentence," the historian Robert Twombly later writes, "can be attributed to the death and to public hysteria over a rash of conflagrations set by servants of several races in and around Boston."

1682

 Increase Mather's *Heaven's Alarm to the World* is published. In it he contends that the appearance of Halley's comet this year is a sign of God's displeasure with the world. Two years earlier, Mather had written *Cometographia* in response to Newton's comet of 1680.

1683

November 7. The General Court passes an ordinance declaring, "henceforth no Dwelling-house, Warehouse, Shop, Barn, Stable, or any other Housing (in Boston), shall be Erected and set up in Boston, except of Stone or Brick." The law is generally ignored.

The town charter is amended to prohibit the town from ever selling Boston Common.
The Westerly Burying Ground is established at today's Centre and LaGrange Streets in West Roxbury.

The Great Fire of 1683 occurs.

(ca.) The *New England Primer* is first published by Benjamin Harris. Reportedly the first schoolbook printed in America, it includes the prayer "Now I Lay Me Down to Sleep" and is later estimated to have sold more than five million copies.

1684

October 23. The British Parliament revokes the Massachusetts Bay Colony charter, on the grounds that the colony has not upheld English laws or shown sufficient deference to Charles II.

Joseph Gatchell is found guilty of blasphemy and sentenced "to stand in pillory, have his head and hand put in & have his toung drawne forth out of his mouth, & peirct through with a hott iron."

A district writing school opens in today's Scollay Square. The town's first, it is established to teach boys unable to attend the Latin School. Expanded in 1715 and 1753, it closes in 1790. The writing schools are first open to girls—from April 20 to October 20 only—in 1789.

The town of Dorchester grants John Trescott the right to build a lumber mill on the Neponset River. He acquires the land and builds the mill a year later.

1685

(ca.) A chart of Boston Harbor is produced by Thomas Pound, a pirate as well as a cartographer. His chart is used for the next sixty years.
March 19. Town meeting appoints a committee to purchase any claim by Indians, "legal or pretended" to "Deare Island, the Necke of Boston, or any parte thereof." Wampatuck, grandson of the Massachusetts sachem Chickataubut, soon after signs a deed testifying that his grandfather "did grant, sell, alienate, and confirm unto them and their assigns forever" said land, in return for what is reported to be a large sum of money. Historians later speculate that the purchase was made to protect property owners in light of the revocation of the Massachusetts Bay charter by the British Parliament.

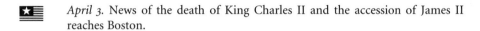 *April 3.* News of the death of King Charles II and the accession of James II reaches Boston.

November 5. The first annual "Pope's Night" is celebrated in Boston on the anniversary of Guy Fawkes Day. Festivities include a parade and the burning of effigies of Satan as well as the pope and other prominent Catholics. The "holiday" often features battles between groups from the North and South Ends as well as attacks on Catholic residents. Pope's Night is particularly violent in 1755, 1762, and 1764, and it is celebrated officially for the last time in 1774.

1686

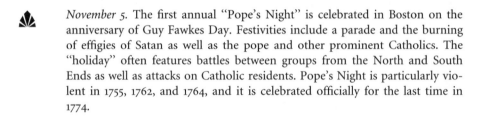 *December 20.* Sir Edmund Andros arrives in Boston. Appointed the first royal governor of the newly created Dominion of New England, he imposes taxes, forces landowners to pay a fee to retain their land, limits the residents' freedom to travel, and reduces the number of town meetings to one each year. He also declares that he considers Indian signatures on land titles to be "of no more worth than the scratch of a bear paw."

March 11. James Morgan is convicted of murder and hanged on Boston Common in the first execution in seven years. People come from as far as fifty miles away to witness it. The prison where Morgan had been kept is described as a "house of meagre looks and ill smells . . . the suburbs of hell, and the persons much the same as these."

A group of French Huguenots establishes a short-lived Presbyterian Church on School Street.
June 15. The first Episcopal service in Boston is held in the Deputies Room of the Town House.

March. John Dunton arrives in Boston with a consignment of books. He later declares the Mather library "the glory of New England, if not all of America," and describes how the wealthy Boston merchant John Usher "got his estate by book selling."

1687

In the annual town election, only "freemen"—those with a taxable estate of at least eighty pounds—are eligible to vote. There are only twenty-four such freemen in the town.

March 25. The first Episcopal service is held at South Church after Governor Andros demands use of one of the existing Congregational churches by the "Established Church."

1688

June 9. Sampson Sheafe is "attacked, knocked down and robbed by two ruffians" on Boston Common.

April 3. Fourteen houses burn "near the draw-bridge."

November 16. Mary "Goody" Glover is hanged on Boston Common. The fourth and last person to be executed for witchcraft in Boston, Glover had been accused by her mistress's thirteen-year-old daughter, Martha Goodwin, after Glover had scolded the girl. Glover was convicted partly because of her inability to recite the Lord's Prayer in English, rather than in Latin, as she knew it. Her last words are reportedly "I die a Catholic."

1689

April 4. News reaches Boston that James II has been deposed and William and Mary of Orange have succeeded him to the throne in "the Bloodless Revolution."
April 18. Gov. Edmund Andros is deposed. Forced to flee to the fort on Fort Hill, he surrenders two days later, is imprisoned at Castle Island, and is then sent back to England.
King William's War begins. It lasts until 1697.

January 27. Capt. James Hawkins and seven pirates are hanged on Boston Common.

June 8. King's Chapel is dedicated. The first Episcopal church in Boston, it is renamed Queen's Chapel during the reign of Queen Anne, from 1702 to 1714. The small, wooden chapel is enlarged in 1710. It houses the first pipe organ in America in 1714, and is replaced by the current granite building in 1754.*
Cotton Mather's *Memorable Providences, Relating to Witchcrafts and Possessions* is published.

July 10. The Eliot School is established in Jamaica Plain. Founded by Rev. John Eliot "for the teaching and instructing of the children of that end of the town," the school is moved to its current location in 1831 and dedicated on January 17, 1832. It later becomes a school for arts and crafts.

1690

Boston's population is estimated at 7,000.

"Freemanship" and the right to vote are extended to all those paying taxes of at least four shillings or holding property valued at six pounds or more.

The Great Fire of 1690 occurs.

May 21. John Eliot dies at the age of eighty-six. Winsor later describes him as a "venerable and Christ-like man. . . . Had he been a Roman Catholic he would assuredly have been canonized."

February 12. A smallpox epidemic breaks out in Boston, forcing the General Court to move to Charlestown temporarily.

$ Paper money is printed in Boston. The first paper money issued in America, it is printed from plates engraved by John Cony and used to pay the soldiers who took part in an unsuccessful attack on Quebec.

●⚬ *September 25.* The first issue of *Publick Occurrences: Both Foreign and Domestic* appears. The first newspaper in the Colonies, it is published by Benjamin Harris. The next day it is banned for an article entitled "Reflections of a very high Nature and sundry doubtful and uncertain Reports." All remaining copies are destroyed.

1691

★▤ *October 7.* A new charter is issued by William III joining the Massachusetts Bay and Plymouth colonies into the royal Province of Massachusetts Bay. Under its terms, the king appoints the governor, and the people elect twenty-eight councilors (eighteen from Massachusetts, four of these from Boston). The new charter also removes religious requirements for officeholders and guarantees religious tolerance for all—except Catholics. It goes into effect on May 16, 1692.

🔥 *June 30.* Another Great Fire occurs in Boston.

✳ A smallpox epidemic strikes Dorchester, killing fifty-seven people.

1692

♯ The General Court passes another zoning law for Boston. This one limits commercial activity to certain parts of the town.

★▤ *May.* Sir William Phips arrives in Boston as the first royal governor of the Province of Massachusetts Bay. He brings with him a copy of the new royal charter.

☑ The town passes the Township Act, requiring that to be considered a "freeman" and eligible to vote, a man must have an estate valued at twenty pounds or more and pay a poll tax. An estimated 350 men qualify—of a male population of 3,000.

🖐 The office of Sheriff of Suffolk County is established. The sheriff's duties have more to do with executing warrants and preventing disturbances of the peace than detecting or preventing crime.

⚖ *May.* Lt. Gov. William Stoughton of Dorchester and Samuel Sewall of Boston are appointed to the special Court of Oyer and Terminer to preside over the witchcraft trials in Salem, which begin in June. Although Cotton Mather would later be blamed for stirring up the witchcraft hysteria, he declares in one sermon: "It were better that ten suspected witches should escape, than that one innocent person be condemned." Twenty people are subsequently convicted and executed—nineteen by hanging and one by being pressed to death with stones.

1693

Governor Phips issues a proclamation freeing the approximately 150 persons still imprisoned for witchcraft.
Cotton Mather's *Wonders of the Invisible World* is published. The book reportedly adds to the witchcraft hysteria. The poet Robert Lowell later describes Mather as "a power-crazed mind, bent on destroying darkness with darkness."

1694

December 4. William Stoughton is appointed acting royal governor of the Province of Massachusetts Bay.

Hannah Newell is convicted of "Adultery by her owne confession." She is sentenced to receive "Fifteen stripes Severally to be laid on upon her naked back at the Common Whipping post." Her lover, Lambert Despar, is given twenty-five lashes and sentenced to "stand upon the Pillory for the space of the full hower with Adultery in Capitall letters written upon his brest."

1695

The list of Boston residents includes one described only as "Samuel the Jew."

1696

A fort is erected on Governor's Island.

1697

Town meeting debates whether to build a town market. The suggestion is defeated, as it is when taken up again in 1701, 1714, and 1717.

A law is passed prohibiting families from owning more than one dog.

The winter of 1697–1698 is described as "the terriblest winter of the century."

January 14. Reflecting on the role he played as one of the judges in the Salem witchcraft trials, Samuel Sewall writes in his diary: "I take the blame and shame."

1698

The first road map to be printed for public use in America appears in Tulley's *Almanack*. The map includes a list of towns, roads, and distances from Boston, as well as a list of tavernkeepers in the area.

The Charter House is built by William Clough on today's Charter Street in the North End. It received its name from the mistaken belief that the original Massachusetts charter had at one time been hidden inside. After being declared unsafe for occupancy, the building is torn down in 1931.

Kissing is declared "a fineable offense (if caught)."

1699

Edward Ward, a visitor from England, describes Bostonians this way: "The Inhabitants seem very Religious, showing many outward and visible Signs of an inward and Spiritual Grace: But tho' they wear in their Faces the Innocence of Doves, you will find them in their Dealings, as Subtile as Serpents, Interest is their Faith, Money their God, and Large Possessions the only Heaven they covet."

May 26. Richard Coote, earl of Bellomont, is appointed royal governor of the Province of Massachusetts Bay.

When Mrs. Eunice Wait's slave Sebastian expresses the wish to marry Mrs. Thair's slave Jane, Mrs. Thair insists that "Sebastian should have one day in six for the support of Jane, his intended wife, and her children, if it should please God to give her any." Complaining that the demand is excessive, Mrs. Wait appeals to Judge Samuel Sewall. He adjusts the demand to five pounds per year. The marriage, presumably, takes place.

July 6. Captain Kidd is arrested for piracy at a house near what is now the corner of Washington and Milk Streets on a warrant issued by New England Governor Lord Bellomont. Kidd had been hired by a group of investors (which included Bellomont) to hunt pirates in Africa, but either turned pirate himself or was falsely accused of doing so. He is imprisoned, shipped to England, tried, found guilty, and hanged. His body is placed on a gibbet and left to rot.

December 12. The Brattle Square Church opens. Benjamin Coleman is the first pastor. A new church is built in 1720. It is replaced by a church designed by Thomas Dawes on today's City Hall Plaza, dedicated on July 25, 1773. A new church, designed by H. H. Richardson, opens at 110 Commonwealth Avenue in 1872. The frieze on the tower, designed by Frédéric-Auguste Bartholdi, is completed in 1877. Some of the figures on it are said to be modeled after Emerson, Hawthorne, Longfellow, Sumner, and other Boston-area personages. Called the "Church of the Holy Bean Blowers" because of the trumpet-carrying angels on the turret, the church later becomes the First Baptist Church.

1700

Boston's population is estimated at 6,700.

July 17. William Stoughton is again appointed acting royal governor.

June 12. Samuel Sewall's *The Selling of Joseph: A Memorial* is published. The first antislavery tract to appear in the Colonies, it contains the passage "[Liberty is] the real value unto life; none ought to part with it themselves or deprive others of it but upon mature Consideration." There are an estimated four hundred slaves in Boston at this time, almost double the number there had been in 1676.

Local pirate Joseph Bradish escapes from the town jail, reportedly assisted by a relative—the jail keeper Caleb Rey.

1701 to 1750

1701

Selectmen order that each of the town's 110 streets, lanes, and alleys be given official names. The task is reported to be completed on May 3, 1708.

In lieu of a royal governor, the Council is appointed to govern the province.

Selectmen vote to request their representatives at the General Court to "put a period to negroes being slaves."

May 10. Members of the Boston Night Watch are authorized to carry a "Hook with a Bill," a wooden staff with a spike at the end of it. The next day, the watchmen are ordered to see that all house lights are extinguished at a fixed hour.
May. An ordinance is passed requiring a license for establishments selling alcoholic drinks.

Increase Mather moves from Boston to Cambridge to comply with the residency requirement for presidents of Harvard, but he soon resigns and moves back, explaining: "Should I leave off preaching to 1500 souls . . . only to expound to forty or fifty Children, a few of them capable of edification by such Exercises." Samuel Willard acts as president of Harvard until 1707. John Leverett becomes the first layman appointed president in 1708. He is succeeded by Benjamin Wadsworth (1725), Edward Holyoke (1737), Samuel Locke (1770), Samuel Langdon (1774), and Joseph Willard (1781). Eliphalet Pearson leads Harvard in 1804, when Joseph Willard dies in office. Samuel Webber becomes president in 1806, and is succeeded by John Thornton Kirkland (1810–1828*).

1702

May 28. News of the death of King William III and the accession of Queen Anne is marked by a twenty-one-gun salute in Boston.
Cotton Mather's *Magnalia Christi Americana: The First Book of the New-English History, Reporting the Design whereon, the Manner wherein, and the People whereby, the Several Colonies of New England were Planted* is published in London. In it he declares: "Boston, 'tis a marvellous thing a plague has not laid thee desolate!"

June 11. Joseph Dudley is appointed royal governor of the Province of Massachusetts Bay.

March. Another Great Fire strikes Boston.

 September 13. "Simon the Jew" is baptized by Rev. Bradstreet in Charlestown. He is reported to be the first Jewish convert to Christianity in Boston.
Cotton Mather's *Meat Out of the Eater, or Funeral Discourses Occasioned by the Death of Several Relatives* is published.

1704

 April 19. Selectmen authorize the expenditure of one hundred pounds to pave those streets in Boston judged "most needful, having particular regard to the hiway right to old Mrs. Stoddard's house."

 Troops from Boston join Col. Benjamin Church's expedition launched against the French to retaliate for an Indian raid on the town of Deerfield.

 June 30. Seven pirates are hanged on the banks of the Charles River.

 April 24. The first issue of the *Boston News-Letter* appears. Boston's second newspaper and the first to publish regularly in the Colonies, the one-sheet weekly is produced by postmaster John Campbell. Made up of news, rumors, gossip, and items clipped from month-old English newspapers, it continues under its various names and ceases publication on February 29, 1776.

1705

 November 13. The settlement known as Muddy River is set off from Boston and becomes the town of Brookline.

 Cromwell's Head Tavern opens at 19 School Street. Visitors would include George Washington, John Paul Jones, and the Marquis de Lafayette. It closes in 1800.

1706

 The Powder House is built on Boston Common. It is guarded at all times by two men, and a watch house is built on the adjacent hill. Town meeting votes to remove the Powder House after concluding that "the town will do nothing concerning it" in 1750.

 Cotton Mather's *The Negro Christianized* is published. In it he calls for the humane treatment of slaves, whom he describes as "Men, and not Beasts, that you have bought."

1707

 May 13. A force of fifteen hundred troops sails from Boston to attack Port Royal in Canada. The expedition would be a complete failure.

1708

A group of businessmen led by Elisha Cooke is granted land on Boston Neck (from today's Herald Street to East Berkeley Street), on the condition that they erect barriers to "secure and keep off the sea."
Seventy-eight wharves extend out into the harbor from Boston and Charlestown.

March 14. A committee is formed to "draft a charter of incorporation" for "the better government of the town." But the town votes against applying for a charter as a city a year later. Similar proposals are defeated in 1784, 1792, 1794, and 1815. Josiah Quincy later writes that one problem with the town meetings at Faneuil Hall was that "those only who obtained places near the moderator could even hear the discussion. A few busy or interested individuals easily obtained the management of the most important affairs in an assembly in which the greater number could have neither voice nor hearing."

A woodcut depicting the new flag of the United Kingdom appears in the *Boston News-Letter*. It is the first newspaper illustration produced in the Colonies.

1709

The Crafts House is built by Ebenezer Crafts on today's Huntington Avenue across from Parker Hill. It is demolished in 1900.
A small earthworks fort is built at the foot of Boston Common and militiamen train nearby.

February. An event called the Great Tide floods wharves, cellars, and the lower floors of houses and warehouses around the docks.

A committee is established to supervise the Latin School. Its members, "Gentlemen, of Liberal Education, Together with Some of ye Revd Ministers of the town," are to visit the school annually.

1710

Boston's population is estimated at 9,000.

(ca.) The Lemuel Clapp House is built on Willow Court in Dorchester. Enlarged in 1765, it is moved to its current present location at 199 Boston Street in 1957 and restored thereafter.

Because of a food shortage, a mob attacks a grain ship about to leave Boston Harbor. Their complaint, according to the historian Gary Nash, is that the ship's owner, Andrew Belcher, "chose to export grain to the Caribbean, at a handsome profit, rather than sell it for a smaller profit to hungry townspeople." Similar food riots take place in 1711 and 1713.

1711

The Moses Pierce–Hichborn House is built at 19 North Square in the North End. In 1948 it is one of the city's oldest brick houses, and a police raid on an illegal gambling operation there sparks public attention and a successful effort to preserve the building.

October 2. Another "Great Fire" burns more than one-third of the town. After breaking out in the rear of the Ship Tavern, the blaze destroys a hundred buildings in the Cornhill area, including the Town House, the First Church, and the Third Church. The fire prompts the establishment of fire wards, each with a warden responsible for putting out fires. The wardens direct volunteer fire companies, which compete to be first on the scene since their only pay comes in the form of goods salvaged from fires.

January 8. Boston Harbor freezes as far out as Long Island.

1712

Jonathan Wardell receives the first taxi license (hackney coach) in Boston. The proprietor of the Orange Tree Tavern, he operates the taxi outside his business on Hanover Street.

The Walter Street Burying Ground is established on Peter's Hill in today's Roslindale. The land later passes into the ownership of the Weld and Bussey families, and is today part of Arnold Arboretum.

The Bunch of Grapes Tavern opens at the corner of today's State and Kilby Streets. The building is torn down in 1798 to make way for construction of the New England Bank.

March 19. A law is passed that prohibits "fiddling, piping, or any musical form, singing, dancing, and reveling in taverns or public houses" on Sunday.

November 2. The Second Church in Roxbury opens on today's Walter Street in West Roxbury. It is originally called the Walter Street Meeting House, and Ebenezer Thayer is the first pastor. Theodore Parker serves as pastor from 1837 to 1846. A new church is built at the corner of today's Centre and Corey streets in 1773. It is replaced in 1821. The current church, designed by A. W. Longfellow, opens in 1900. Stained glass windows by Louis Comfort Tiffany are added between 1894 and 1927.

March. A committee is established to "inspect the Free writing Schools which are Supported at the Townes Charge."

June 1–8. The town prints an advertisement directing "all persons who have any of the town's library or can give notice of any books or other things belonging to ye Town House before ye late fire, to inform ye town's treasurer thereof in order to ye being returned."

The State House, ca. 1794. Watercolor by unknown artist. (Courtesy of the Bostonian Society)

1713

May 5. The second Town House is dedicated at today's 206 Washington Street. Called the State House beginning in 1780 and the Old State House after 1798, it is the oldest public building in Boston and second-oldest in the United States (after the Governor's Palace in Santa Fe). The architect is thought to be Robert Twelves. The building contains a merchants' hall on the first floor, and court and council chambers on the second floor. A visitors' gallery, the first in any legislative assembly in the world, is added in 1767, but later removed. The building is damaged by fires on December 9, 1747; March 20, 1760; and November 21, 1832. The building is renovated by Isaiah Rogers in 1830, and preserved in 1879.*

An epidemic of measles strikes the town.

1714

(ca.) The Capen House is built by Hopestill Capen at 41 Union Street. The building serves as headquarters of Ebenezer Hancock, paymaster of the Continental Army, during the Revolutionary War. The duke of Chartres lives on the second floor during the French Revolution, earning his living by giving French lessons, before returning to France to become King Louis Philippe in 1830. Isaiah Thomas publishes the *Massachusetts Spy* on the third floor from 1771 to 1775. The building becomes a restaurant in 1826.*

A town granary is constructed next to Boston Common to store grain in times of plenty and sell it to the poor at below-market prices during times of shortage. It is replaced by a new building in 1729, but according to town records, it is not well maintained: "the weevils have taken the wheat, and mice annoy the corn much, being very numerous." A replacement is built on the site of today's Park Street Church in 1737, and removed in 1809.

May 31. The town post office announces regular hours for delivery and receipt of mail.

May 5. The Middle Street Meeting House (also called the New North Church) is dedicated on Hanover Street. John Webb is the first pastor. The wooden church is rebuilt in 1730, then replaced by a Bulfinch-designed brick building in 1804. Originally Episcopal, it becomes Unitarian in 1813, with Rev. Francis Parkman, father of the historian, serving as a minister. The church is purchased by the Catholic Archdiocese of Boston in 1846, renamed St. Stephen's, and restored in 1965.

1715

Long Wharf is completed. The longest pier in the Colonies, it is built by a group led by Capt. Oliver Noyes. The wharf is over 1,500 feet long, is 54 feet wide, and has a 30-foot roadway down its center. Eventually it is lined with warehouses and shops. The Boston Fish Pier locates here initially, then moves first to Commercial Wharf, to T Wharf in 1884, and to its current location in 1912.*

The Ebenezer Clough House is built on Unity Street in the North End. Today it is one of the oldest existing brick houses in Boston.

February 4. The Council is again appointed to govern the Province of Massachusetts Bay, until Joseph Dudley is appointed governor on March 21. Elizeus Burgess is appointed to replace him on November 9, but never comes to Massachusetts; William Tailer serves as acting governor in his stead.

The town is divided into eight wards.

June 4. Margaret Callahan is hanged on Boston Common for murder.

1716

September 14. Boston Light goes into service on Little Brewster Island and eventually becomes the oldest continuously operated and occupied lighthouse in America. A cannon is placed there as the first fog signal in the Colonies in 1719, and then replaced by a bell in 1852. Boston Light is damaged by the "Great Storm" of 1723, by a fire in 1751, and by Colonists seeking to deprive the British of its use in 1775. Destroyed by the retreating British forces on June 13, 1776, it is rebuilt in 1783 and taken over by the federal government in 1790.

October 5. Samuel Shute is appointed royal governor.

A French Huguenot chapel opens at today's 20 School Street. It becomes a Congregationalist church in 1748, is abandoned in 1784, and becomes a Catholic church in 1788.*

Cotton Mather begins a series of complaints about the quality of the singing in church, declaring that "the Psalmody in our Assembly must be better provided for."

1717

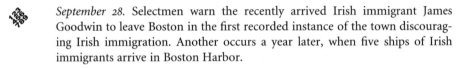

September 28. Selectmen warn the recently arrived Irish immigrant James Goodwin to leave Boston in the first recorded instance of the town discouraging Irish immigration. Another occurs a year later, when five ships of Irish immigrants arrive in Boston Harbor.

A clock is installed on the roof of the Old Brick Church on Cornhill (today's Washington) Street. It is the first clock erected on the exterior of a building in Boston.

November. Lighthouse keeper George Worthylake, his wife, daughter, and two others drown while returning from Boston. Twelve-year-old Benjamin Franklin later immortalizes the incident in a poem, "The Light-house Tragedy."

February 27–March 7. "The Great Snow" begins. The storm reportedly adds six feet to the total snowfall for the winter, which reaches as much as ten or twenty feet in some parts of New England. Cotton Mather writes, "As mighty a snow, as perhaps has been known in the memory of Man, is at this Time lying on the Ground."

A quarantine hospital opens on Spectacle Island. It moves to Rainsford Island in 1737, to Deer Island in 1849, and to Gallops Island in 1867.

1718

(ca.) T Wharf is completed, built by the Minot family. The first granite wharf warehouse in Boston is built upon it in 1834, and the Boston Fish Pier relocates here in 1884, remaining until 1912.*

October 11. The Fire Society is established. The first private fire aid organization in America, it is made up of twenty members who agree to fight any fires that strike one another's property.

A residence and apothecary shop is built for Dr. Thomas Crease at the corner of today's Washington and School Streets. It is located on property originally owned by Isaac Johnson and later the site of Anne Hutchinson's home. The building becomes a bookstore in 1829.*

1719

December 17. The appearance of the aurora borealis is first recorded in Boston. The flashing lights in the night sky alarm many residents; some of them assume the lights portend the end of the world.

December 12. The first issue of the *Boston Gazette* appears. Boston's second successful newspaper, it is published by the town's new postmaster, William Brooker, when his predecessor, John Campbell, refuses to relinquish control of the first. That paper, the *Boston News-Letter*, claims its rival's "sheets smell more strongly of beer than of midnight oil." The *Gazette* ceases publication on September 17, 1798.

 Thomas Fleet publishes *Tales of Mother Goose.*

1720

 Boston's population is estimated at 12,000, the largest of any town in the Colonies. An estimated 2,000 residents are African Americans.
Irish immigrants are required to register within five days of arriving in Boston.

 The Royal Exchange Tavern opens at what is today 28 State Street.

 Isaac Lopez is elected town constable. The first Jewish resident to hold the job, he is a merchant who later establishes a timber yard near the town windmill.

 When Rev. Peter Thatcher is installed as the minister of the New North Church, members of the congregation who opposed his appointment, according to Whitehill, "stormed into the gallery and expressed their contempt for the proceedings by pissing over the railing onto the heads of those below." They subsequently secede, form their own congregation, and open the "New Brick" Church between Hanover and Richmond Streets in 1721. The congregation welcomes and merges with the Second Church in 1779.*

1721

 March. The committee supervising the writing schools is reorganized. The town votes "that the Select men and Such as they Shal desire to Assist them be Inspectors of the Gramer and Wrighting Schools for the year ensuing."

 June 26. Dr. Zabdiel Boylston first uses inoculation to combat smallpox in Boston. Rev. Cotton Mather is the leading proponent of the experiment. According to some accounts, Rev. Mather was told about the practice being used in Africa by one of his slaves, Onesimus; according to others, he had read about it in a publication by the Royal Society in London. Only Boylston, among the town's doctors, agrees to try it. First he administers it to his six-year-old son, his "negro man Jack," and a "negro boy, of 2½," then to townspeople. Opponents nearly lynch Boylston and they set fire to Rev. Mather's house, but the experiment is a success. While over 800 people die of the disease, only 6 of the 247 people Boylston inoculates succumb to it.

 August 7. The first issue of the *New England Courant* appears. The town's third successful newspaper, it is published by James Franklin from his shop at the corner of today's Franklin and Court Streets. The weekly newspaper continues publication until 1727.

 John Tufts's *A Very Plain and Easy Introduction to the Singing of Psalm Tunes* and Thomas Walter's *Grounds and Rules of Musick* are published. Both contain "free-hand music engraving" and are printed for the Boston bookseller Samuel Gerrish.

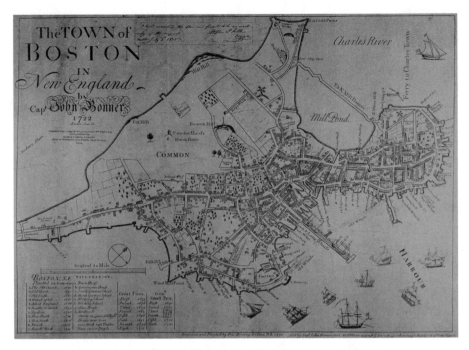

"The Town of Boston in New England" by Capt. John Bonner, 1722. (Courtesy of the Bostonian Society)

1722

John Bonner's map "The Town of Boston in New England" is published. The first detailed map of the town, it is described by the *Boston News-Letter* as "A Curious Ingraven Map of the Town of Boston, with all of the streets, lanes, Alleys, Wharffs & Houses, the Like never done before." The map is revised and reprinted in 1729, 1732, 1733, 1739, 1743, and 1769.

November 27. An eclipse of the sun occurs, which is later described in an article by Thomas Robie.

April 30. Judah Monis, a Jew, is appointed to the Harvard faculty to teach Hebrew and the Old Testament—but only after he agrees to convert to Christianity. He later becomes the first student with a Jewish background to graduate from Harvard, or any college in the Colonies, when he receives a master's degree from the school.

April 2. Benjamin Franklin's first article appears in the *New England Courant* under the name Silence Dogood. Franklin is named publisher of the newspaper on February 11, 1723, after his brother James is barred by authorities from continuing in the position because of what are considered to be offensive articles. A few months later, seventeen-year-old Benjamin breaks his indenture agreement with his brother and runs away, sailing to New York and then walking to Philadelphia. James Franklin then runs an advertisement for a "likely lad for an apprentice" on September 30, 1723.

The first billiard parlor in the Colonies opens in Charlestown.

1723

Boston's Record Commissioners warn that Irish immigrants "may become a Town Charge," and town meeting passes an ordinance requiring them to register their presence in the town.

January 1. William Dummer is appointed acting royal governor.

August 25. Aquitamong, reputed to be a 112-year-old Indian, visits Boston.

February. A "Great Tide" surprises the residents of the town.

December 29. Christ Church (later known as Old North Church) is dedicated at 193 Salem Street. Designed by William Price, it is the oldest church building in today's Boston. Timothy Cutler is the first pastor. The steeple

Old North Church (Christ Church, Salem Street). Engraving by Dearborn for The History of Boston. *(Courtesy of the Bostonian Society)*

and the weather vane by Deacon Shem Drowne are added in 1740. The church bells, cast in England by Abel Rudhall in 1744 and hung by Paul Revere in 1754, are the oldest in the Colonies. The steeple is toppled by the Great Gale of October 9, 1804, and a new one, designed by Charles Bulfinch, is erected in 1807. The church is restored in 1912 by R. Clipston Sturgis and Henry Ross. Hurricane Carol blows the new steeple down on August 31, 1954, and it is replaced by a replica of the original.

1724

March 9. Selectmen's meetings are opened with a prayer for the first time, with Rev. Cotton Mather performing the duty.

Daniel Neal's *History of New England* is published in London. In it he writes, "a Gentleman from London would almost think himself at home at Boston, when he observes the numbers of people, their Houses, their Furniture, their Tables, their Dress and Conversation, which, perhaps, is as splendid and showy, as that of the most considerable Tradesmen in London."
August 1. The accession to the throne of George I is celebrated on Boston Common.
August 22. Capt. Johnson Harmon attends the town meeting and displays the scalps of twenty-seven Norridgewock Indians, as well as that of Sebastian Ralle

(or Rale), a Jesuit missionary killed in the raid he had recently led against what is described as "the enemy."

May 3. The pirates John Rose Archer and William White are gibbeted and hanged in chains on Bird Island. Five days later, Capt. Andrew Harriden arrives in Boston Harbor with a pirate ship captured from the notorious Capt. Phillips—along with Phillips's head in a pickle barrel.

"A Pacificatory Letter about Psalmody, or Singing of Psalms" is published as an anonymous letter. In it the author attempts to mediate the dispute raging in pulpits throughout the town regarding the continued use of the "old way of singing," unaccompanied and led by a deacon, versus the adoption of the more modern way, with music, under the direction of a singing master.

Joseph Marion opens the Sun Fire Office of Boston at what is today 22 State Street. The first insurance company in America, it offers only marine coverage. An attempt by Marion to offer other kinds of policies in 1728 fails, and they are not offered again in Boston for seventy years.

1725

William Burgis's map "A South East View of ye Great Town of Boston in New England in America" is published. He produces a second map in 1728.

(ca.) The Chamberlain House is built at 266 Poplar Street. It is now the oldest house in Roslindale.
(ca.) The Ebenezer Smith House is built at 15–17 Peaceable Street. It is now the oldest house in the Brighton Center area.

December 15. A peace treaty with the Indians is signed at the Town House. In his diary, Jeremiah Bumsted writes, "Ye Indian hostages signed ye artikles for peace att ye Council chamber."

Contrary to William Wood's 1634 advertisement, wolves and rattlesnakes—and bears—*do* trouble Boston residents this year.

Arriving from England, Peter Pelham becomes the first portrait painter in Boston and also establishes the first art school, located near the Town Dock.

1726

Hoop petticoats are banned in Boston.

June 12. Pirates Samuel Cole, Henry Grenville, and William Fly are hanged on Boston Common. The first two are buried at Nix's Mate, while Fly's body is hung in chains there as a warning to sailors passing by.

1727

The Vassall Mansion is built at the corner of today's Washington and Summer Streets. It is torn down to make way for the six-story granite C. F. Hovey dry goods store in 1854, which is, in turn, torn down to make way for the Jordan Marsh building in 1951.

October 29. Residents of Boston are awakened by an earthquake. The sound is described as "horrid rumbling, like the noise of many coaches together driving on the paved stones," and is said to have been felt through "the whole country north of the Delaware River."

March 20. The first issue of the *New England Weekly Journal* appears. Boston's fourth newspaper, it merges with the *Gazette* in 1741.

1728

July 19. William Burnett is appointed royal governor.

July 3. After an argument in the Royal Exchange Tavern, Henry Phillips kills his friend Benjamin Woodbridge in a duel on Boston Common. Phillips subsequently flees to France and dies there, reportedly from loneliness and a broken heart. Woodbridge is buried in the Granary Burying Ground. To discourage future duels, a town ordinance is passed requiring the victor in a duel "to be imprisoned 12 months without bail" and the vanquished to be buried "near the usual place of public execution with a stake driven through the body."

The first paper mill in New England is established at Lower Mills in Dorchester.

1729

July. Demonstrators protest a ship carrying diseased Irish immigrants, which anchors in Boston Harbor

September 7. William Dummer is again appointed acting royal governor.

A Scotch-Irish Presbyterian congregation begins meeting in a converted barn on Long Lane, near the waterfront. Rev. John Moorhead is the first pastor. In 1744 the building is replaced by the Federal Street Church, designed by Charles Bulfinch in the Gothic style, then by a brick building in 1809. The congregation becomes Congregational in 1780, then Unitarian in 1786. William Ellery Channing serves as pastor from 1803 to 1842, and the congregation moves to the new Arlington Street Church in the Back Bay in 1861.*

Arithmetick, Vulgar and Decimal is published. It is considered to be the first mathematics textbook printed in America.

1730

 Boston's population is estimated at 13,000.

 September. Boston celebrates the town's one hundredth anniversary with its first jubilee. It consists of orations delivered at various churches, including one by Rev. Foxcroft at the Old South Meeting House. A jubilee celebration is held every fifty years from this time forward.

 June 11. William Tailer is again appointed acting royal governor. He is succeeded by Jonathan Belcher on August 10.

 April 26. The Third Church (later known as Old South Meeting House) opens at today's 310 Washington Street. Thomas Thatcher is the first pastor. For many years the church offers the largest meeting space in the town. The building is damaged by British soldiers during the Siege of Boston. Repaired and reoccupied on March 2, 1783, it is barely spared by the Great Fire of 1872. Brick additions are made to either side in 1873. The congregation moves to the "new" Old South Church in the Back Bay in 1875.*

 An exhibit of works of the Scottish-born artist John Smibart is held, the first art exhibit in Boston. Smibart, the foremost portrait painter in town at the time, is later described by the art historian Arthur Dexter as working in "a Puritan society [that] was not favorable to art."

1731

 The first known public musical concerts in Boston—and the Colonies—are held. Subscription concerts begin in 1761, and rival musicians and organizations begin to compete for attention after 1770.

1732

 Town officials are alarmed at a rumor that a Catholic priest is in the area and that he is planning to say a Mass on March 17, described as "what they call St. Patrick's Day."

1733

 The British Parliament passes the Molasses Act, taxing its import from the West Indies. The law is later rescinded but reenacted in 1764, sparking protests in Boston for disrupting the "molasses, rum, and slaves" triangle so important to Boston's trading economy.

July 30. The First Lodge of Freemasons in America is organized at the Bunch of Grapes Tavern at today's 53 State Street. Founded by Henry Price and later named the St. John's Lodge, it is the first Masonic lodge in America and the first fraternal society in Boston. Early members include Sam Adams, John Hancock, Paul Revere, and Joseph Warren.

1734

February 28. A polar bear is exhibited in Boston and pronounced "a great curiosity."

June 4. After the town finally approves their construction, public markets are opened at North Square, Dock Square, and the South End. The Dock Square market is destroyed by a mob dressed as clergymen protesting the high regulated prices being charged there on March 24, 1737.

October 10. The first issue of the *Boston Post-Boy* appears. The weekly newspaper continues until 1775.

1735

The first wharf is built in what is today South Boston, and a ferry begins service to Boston.

March 9. The number of wards in the town is increased from eight to twelve, a system that remains in place until 1822.
June 27. The General Court, in issuing an abatement of the province tax, grants Boston 69,120 acres of land in the western part of the state (today's towns of Charlemont, Colrain, and Pittsfield). The town of Boston later sells the land for 3,660 pounds.

May 28. George Brownwell opens Boston's first dancing school.

August 15. Trinity Church opens at the corner of today's Summer and Washington Streets. It was founded in April 1728 "by reason that the [King's] Chapel is full and no pews are to be bought by newcomers." Addington Davenport is the first pastor. The building is replaced by a larger church, designed by George Brimmer, at the corner of Washington and Summer Streets in 1829. That building is destroyed by the Great Fire of 1872. After renting Huntington Hall for four years, the congregation moves to its current church in the Back Bay in 1877.*

1736

Robert Boyd, captain of the brigantine *Bootle* out of Cork, which is anchored in Boston Harbor, is summoned before town authorities. He is made to promise not to allow any of his passengers to "come on Shaor."

The first volume of Thomas Prince's *Chronological History of New England* is published. According to Winsor, the book "extends only over the earliest years of Boston's history, not going beyond 1633, as the author, seeking a start, began with the Flood." A second volume is begun in 1755, but only three chapters are completed before the author's death.

Dr. William Douglass's *The Practical History of a New Epidemical Eruptive Miliary Fever, with an Angina Ulcusculosa Which Prevailed in Boston, New England, in the Years 1735 and 1736* is published. It is an account of an epidemic of what is today thought to be diphtheria striking the town. Douglass also organizes the town's first medical society this year.

1737

Thomas Hancock's granite mansion is built on Beacon Street overlooking Boston Common. The first stone building in Boston and home of the town's wealthiest merchant, it is later occupied by his nephew John Hancock. Despite one of the first efforts at preservation in Boston history, the house is torn down in June 1863.

April 13. The "Boston Stone" is inserted into the wall of the building at 9 Marshall Street. A piece of granite originally brought from England by Thomas Child for grinding paint, it is used to protect the facade from passing vehicles. A neighbor then proposes that it be used like the London Stone—as a point from which distances to Boston are measured. The stone is later transferred to the base of the building that currently occupies the site.

January 3. The Old West Church is organized. A meeting house opens on Lynde Street later in the year. William Hooper is the first pastor. He is succeeded by Jonathan Mayhew in 1747, regarded by some as the first Universalist preacher in America. The church is burned down by the British in 1775 because they suspect signals are being sent from its steeple to the Continental Army in Cambridge. It is replaced by a building designed by Asher Benjamin in 1806. The congregation dissolves in 1882, and the building becomes a branch of the Boston Public Library in 1896, and a Methodist church in 1962.

Andrew Faneuil dies. A bachelor and one of Boston's wealthiest merchants, he leaves his fortune to his nephew, Peter—but only after Peter's older brother, Benjamin, refuses the condition that goes with it, that whoever accepts the inheritance must never marry.

1738

A town workhouse "for the idle and dissolute poor" opens on Centry Lane. A house of industry "for the unfortunate poor" is later opened in South Boston in 1822.
March 17. The Irish Charitable Society is established to assist Irish immigrants. Its founding on this date "in observance of the Feast Day of Ireland's National Apostle" also marks the first celebration of St. Patrick's Day in the Colonies. The organization is still in existence today.

1739

January 8. The settlement of Rumney Marsh is set apart from Boston as the town of Chelsea.

$ John Colman establishes the first private bank in Boston. It is closed a year later when Parliament prohibits the issuance of paper money in the Colonies.

1740

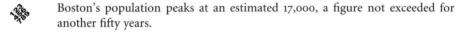 Boston's population peaks at an estimated 17,000, a figure not exceeded for another fifty years.

The town passes an ordinance authorizing payment to the first volunteer fire company to reach the scene of a fire.

June 7. "A good fat bear" is killed at Meeting House Hill in Roxbury.
The winter of 1740–1741 is one of the longest and harshest in years.

October 12. The revivalist Methodist minister George Whitefield preaches to a crowd on Boston Common that is estimated at thirty thousand people—nearly twice the population of the town. It is described later as the high point of "the Great Awakening" in Boston. Some who attend the four-week crusade are afterward diagnosed by physicians as "Rendered insane by listening to Rev. Whitefield."

$ *July 14.* Peter Faneuil's offer to build a market building for the town is approved at town meeting by a slim margin of 367 to 360, but only after he agrees to add a one-thousand-seat public meeting hall above the market, and on condition that strolling vendors are guaranteed the right to continue to do business in the area.

1741

August 14. William Shirley is appointed royal governor.
The First Corps of Cadets is chartered as the bodyguard for Massachusetts' royal governors.

The town granary is looted by a mob.

1742

September 13. Faneuil Hall, designed by John Smibart, opens. The first floor serves as a market, the second floor as the town hall and the home of the state legislature and the Supreme Judicial Court. Francis Hatch later describes the combination: "Here orators/In ages past/Have mounted their attack/Undaunted by proximity/Of sausage on the rack." Closed periodically between 1747 and 1753, the wooden building is damaged by fire on January 13, 1761. It is rebuilt and reopens on March 14, 1763, and is rebuilt and enlarged in 1806.*
November 1. The grasshopper weather vane is installed on Faneuil Hall. Designed by Shem Drowne, the figure is, according to some reports, the symbol from the Faneuil family crest; according to others, it is an imitation of a practice by British banks. Knocked down by an earthquake on November 18, 1755, and damaged by fire on January 13, 1761, the weather vane is moved from the

Faneuil Hall, 1775. Engraving by C. B. Hall in Massachusetts Magazine. *(Courtesy of the Bostonian Society)*

center of the building to the east end in 1852, damaged in a ceremony in 1899, and stolen and then recovered in 1974.

Boston Common is declared "out of bounds" for African Americans and Native Americans. The restriction is not officially lifted until July 4, 1836.

The British Coffee House opens on King Street.

Only three ships are ordered from the Boston shipyard this year; much of the shipbuilding industry moves to Newbury.

A bowling green is built at the base of Fort Hill.

1743

A census records Boston's population as 16,382, the largest of any town in the Colonies, exceeding estimates for Philadelphia (13,000) and New York (11,000).

William Price's *A New Plan of ye Great Town of Boston in New England in America with the Many Additionall Buildings and New Streets to the Year 1743* is published. Price, a cabinetmaker and merchant, has updated John Bonner's map of 1722, adding new streets, graphics, and information in the margins—and leaving Bonner's name off the revised edition.

American Horticultural Magazine begins publication in Boston.

The first issue of *Christian History* appears. Edited by Thomas Prince, Jr., it claims to be "the first religious newspaper in the world."

March 14. Peter Faneuil's funeral is one of the first public gatherings held in the hall named for him. He is described by the *Boston Weekly Newsletter* as "the most publick spirited man, in all regards, that ever yet appeared on the Northern continent of America."

Boston bakers engage in the first strike in the town's history. They refuse to bake bread until they are allowed to increase their prices, which, unlike those of other trades of the time, are regulated by the government.

A Discourse Uttr'd in Part at Ammauskeeg-Falls in the Fishing Season, 1739 is published in Boston. It is considered the first book on fishing—or any sport—to be published in the Colonies.

1744

The "Parting Stone" is erected in Roxbury's Eliot Square. Placed there by Chief Justice Paul Dudley, it marks the spot where the Post Road branches north to Cambridge and Watertown and south to Dedham and Rhode Island.

King George's War against France begins. Notice of its declaration reaches Boston on June 2, and twenty cannon arrive at Fort William on Castle Island on December 27. The war lasts until 1748.

Rev. George Whitefield returns to Boston for another round of preaching. He is reportedly met at Long Wharf by a Dr. Clancy, who declares, "Mr. Whitefield, I am sorry to see you come back again!" "So is the devil," Rev. Whitefield replies.

The First Church in Brighton is established at the corner of Washington and Market Streets. Initially it is a chapel of the First Church in Cambridge; a new building is dedicated on the same site on June 22, 1809. The current church is built in Chestnut Hill in 1895.

June 19. An advertisement in the *Boston Gazette* describes "All Sorts of Drugs and Medicines, both Chymical and Galenical." It is an allusion to the two prevailing schools of medical practice at the time: those advocating "chemical" medicines, which include minerals and a few herbal compounds, and those advocating herbal medicines alone.

1745

June 16. A combined force of Colonial and British troops captures the French fortress of Louisburg in Nova Scotia. Commanded by Sir William Pepperell, the expedition had left Boston on March 24. News of the victory reaches Boston on July 3, prompting rejoicing in the street and bonfires and celebrations on Boston Common. The victory enables the New England colonies to continue to dominate trade with the West Indies and fishing on George's Bank. Louisburg Square on Beacon Hill is later named for the successful expedition.

A visiting Englishman, Joseph Bennett, describes how Boston ladies "visit, drink tea and indulge every piece of gentility to the height of the mode, and neglect the affairs of their families with as good a grace as the first ladies in London."

The Lamb Tavern is established at what is later 555 Washington Street. It is torn down to make way for construction of the Adams House Hotel in 1846.

1746

The Edward Everett Hale House is built in Dorchester. The site is now occupied by a Dunkin' Donuts.

Anticipating trouble with England, Colonial troops organize and drill on Boston Common.

A town petition refers to shipbuilding as "the ancient and almost only manufacture the town of Boston ever had."

1747

(ca.) The Shirley-Eustis House is completed at 31 Shirley Street in Roxbury. Designed by Peter Harrison, it is built for the royal governor, William Shirley. Used by the Colonists as a barracks and hospital during the Revolution, it later becomes the home of Dr. William Eustis, a surgeon and governor of the Commonwealth of Massachusetts. Today it is a museum.

November 17. The Impressment Riot breaks out. A mob attacks British sailors from the warship *Preston* who are attempting to force merchant seamen to serve in the English Navy. Several British officers are seized, three days of rioting follow, and Governor Shirley is forced to take refuge at Castle William. The officers are eventually released, and the British fleet leaves Boston.

1748

The Port of Boston is extremely busy, with 540 vessels leaving and 430 entering, not counting coasting or fishing vessels.

March 14. An advertisement in the *Boston Post-Boy* announces publication of "A Treatis, Proving *(a Posteriori)* That Most of the Disorders Incident to the Fair Sex, Are Owing to Flatulencies not Seasonally Vented." The ad is a reprint of a spoof published three years earlier in London, although with a less scatological title.

1749

September 11. Spencer Phips is appointed acting royal governor.

1750

(ca.) The Dillaway-Thomas House is built at today's 183 Roxbury Street. The parsonage for the First Church, it is built for Charles Dillaway, headmaster of

Roxbury Latin School. Purchased by the city in 1927, it is later preserved by the Roxbury Historical Association and the Massachusetts Department of Environmental Management.

 March. Thomas Otway's *The Orphan—or Unhappy Marriage* is performed in the British Coffee House. Reportedly the first play presented in Boston, it prompts the General Court to pass a law prohibiting plays "tending to increase immorality, impiety and contempt of religion." The law is not repealed until 1797.

1751 to 1800

1751

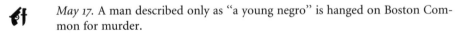 *May 17.* A man described only as "a young negro" is hanged on Boston Common for murder.

1752

The St. Andrew's Lodge of Freemasons is organized. Made up of members who have separated from the St. John's Lodge, it meets at the Green Dragon Tavern and receives a charter from Scotland in 1760.

January–August. The town's longest smallpox epidemic occurs. Selectmen later report that 514 of the 5,544 stricken die, while only 31 of the 2,109 who were inoculated succumb to the disease.

The Concert Hall opens on Hanover Street. Built by the musician Stephen Deblois, it is demolished in May 1869 to allow for the widening of Hanover Street.

1753

August 7. William Shirley is again appointed royal governor.

(ca.) Thomas Johnston builds the first organs to be manufactured in Boston. They are modeled after English chamber and church organs.

1754

The Manufactory House opens on today's Tremont Street. Built as a factory employing women to spin linen cloth, it operates for a few years. It is rented out as a residence to families in 1768, becomes home to the Massachusetts Bank in 1784, and is today the site of Suffolk Law School.

The Boston Marine Society is incorporated under its first name, the Fellowship Club. Founded by a group of sea captains in 1742, it is the oldest marine society in America.

August 11. The second King's Chapel opens, designed by Peter Harrison. The exterior is made from the first granite taken from quarries in Quincy. The church's pulpit is reportedly the oldest in continuous use in the country. The front portico is added in 1789, but the steeple is never completed, owing to lack of funds. British officers worship here during the Siege of Boston, then members of the congregation of the Old South Church attend services here until their church is repaired. It reopens as the First Episcopal Church, with James Freeman as pastor, in 1783, and becomes the first Unitarian Church in Boston in 1785. Because of continuing anti-British sentiments, it is called Stone Chapel from 1776 to the 1830s.

 Mr. Fowle, a printer, is imprisoned for refusing to disclose the names of the authors of *Monster of Monsters*, a satire of the General Court. Those authors are later described as "a club of the most celebrated wits of this country who were very well known, but escaped legal censure."

1755

 May 2. The *Success, Mermaid,* and *Siren* sail from Boston to Acadia, Maine, carrying settlers who refuse to swear allegiance to England. Longfellow later immortalizes their expulsion in his poem "Evangeline."

November 18. An earthquake shakes Boston for more than four minutes. Occurring seventeen days after the Lisbon, Portugal, earthquake, it topples ten chimneys and the weather vane on Faneuil Hall, and causes old springs to dry up and new springs to flow.

1756

 September 1. The Central Burying Ground is established on Boston Common. As in many cemeteries of the time, the markers are not necessarily set above those buried below. One unmarked grave belongs to the artist Gilbert Stuart.

 The Seven Years' War (also known as the French and Indian War) begins. It lasts until 1763.
George Washington makes his first visit to Boston. The purpose of his trip is to have Governor Shirley, the commander-in-chief in America, confirm that Washington, a colonel in the Virginia forces, outranks a captain in the Maryland forces in terms of military seniority.

September 25. Spencer Phips is again appointed acting royal governor.

October 8. The General Court passes a law prohibiting "all riotous, tumultuous and disorderly assemblies." The legislation comes after what is described as "many and great Disorders . . . committed by tumultuous Companies of men, children and negroes, carrying about with them Pageants, or other Shows through the streets and Lanes of the Town of Boston."

1757

 April 4. The Council is again appointed to govern the Province of Massachusetts Bay. Thomas Pownall is appointed royal governor on August 3.

 A daredevil, John Childs, wearing leather wings, slides down a rope stretching from the steeple of the North Church. He repeats the feat a second time, this time firing two pistols during his descent. The stunt attracts such a large crowd that the town's selectmen order him to stop.

1758

September 18. Some forty-five hundred British troops, under the command of Gen. Jeffrey Amherst, camp on Boston Common. They leave soon after on a march to Quebec.

1759

A Poor Widows' Fund is established by Joanna Brooker and others in Boston.

November 14. A serious fire breaks out at the lower end of Milk Street.

April 3. Halley's comet is observed—as predicted—by Harvard mathematics professor John Winthrop. A descendant of Governor Winthrop, he is sometimes described as the first astronomer in America.

The wearing of nightgowns by students is forbidden at Harvard College.

1760

A census records Boston's population as 15,631, making it the third-largest town in the Colonies after Philadelphia (23,750) and New York (18,000).

The Loring-Greenough House is completed at 12 South Street, in Jamaica Plain. Built for the Loyalist British navy commander Joshua Loring, it serves as headquarters for Gen. Nathaniel Greene during the Siege of Boston, and then becomes the first military hospital in Boston. Owned later by the Greenough family, it is purchased in 1924 by the Tuesday Club, a women's literary society, which saves it from demolition. Preserved as a museum, it remains open to the public today.

July 17. Charlestown holds a lottery to raise money to pay for paving Main Street. Twelve thousand dollars worth of chances are sold, $10,800 in prize money is distributed, and the remainder is used to pay for the paving.

December 25. News of the death of King George II and accession of George III is announced from the balcony of the Town House. The news prompts many in Boston to hope for better relations with England, but these hopes prove to be short-lived.

Only 1,500 of the 3,750 white adult male residents of Boston are estimated to qualify for the right to vote.
June 3. Thomas Hutchinson is appointed acting royal governor. He is succeeded by Francis Bernard on August 2. Initially popular with the Colonists, Bernard flees to England amid rising anti-British sentiments in 1769.

(ca.) The Whiting Tavern is built on Centre Street between Elgin and Temple Streets in what is today West Roxbury. It is demolished in 1892.

 March 20. A Great Fire burns over three hundred houses, warehouses, and shops in the Dock Square and waterfront area. The town's new tax collector, Samuel Adams, refrains temporarily from collecting taxes from the fire victims.

 High taxes (67 percent on real and personal property), imposed to pay for services and the care of the poor, reportedly cause many of Boston's merchants to move out of the town.

1761

 February 24. James Otis denounces the Writs of Assistance in a fiery, four-hour speech at the Town House (today's Old State House). The recently passed laws enable customs officials to search houses and warehouses for smuggled goods. In his speech Otis uses the phrase "taxation without representation." John Adams later writes, "Otis was a flame of fire . . . then and there the child independence was born."

 There are five public schools in Boston: Latin School, a grammar school on Bennet Street, and three "writing" (elementary) schools.

 May 9. Harvard professor John Winthrop sails for Newfoundland to chart the transit of Venus, which, according to a letter to the General Court, "has been observed but once before since the Creation of the World." The trip is considered the first publicly supported scientific expedition in the Colonies.

1762

 A rumor that an Anglican bishop has been appointed to sit in Boston upsets the overwhelmingly Congregational town.

1763

 February 10. The Treaty of Paris ends the Seven Years' (French and Indian) War.
The British Parliament passes the first two of the Grenville Acts, named for the British prime minister Sir George Grenville. The Proclamation Act prohibits Colonists from crossing the Appalachian Mountains and settling in the Ohio Valley, while the Currency Act prohibits Colonists from coining money or issuing currency. The Sugar Act, imposing duties on goods imported into America, including molasses and sugar, and exported from America to any country but England, is passed the following year.

1764

 The Market Street Burying Ground is established in Brighton.

 May 24. A Committee of Correspondence is organized in Boston to communicate with similar committees in other colonies.

August. Boston merchants declare an embargo on importing lace and ruffles from England.

September. Boston mechanics agree to wear only leather made in America.

James Otis's *The Rights of the British Colonies Asserted and Proved* is published. The first volume of Gov. Thomas Hutchinson's *History of Massachusetts Bay* is published. As the second volume is being finished, Hutchinson's house is sacked by a mob on August 26, 1765. He flees with his daughter, leaving the manuscript behind. It is saved, however, by Rev. Andrew Eliot and published in 1767. The third volume is published after Hutchinson's death by his grandson in 1828.

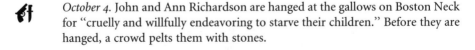 *October 4.* John and Ann Richardson are hanged at the gallows on Boston Neck for "cruelly and willfully endeavoring to starve their children." Before they are hanged, a crowd pelts them with stones.

November 5. During the annual Pope's Night celebration, a five-year-old boy is run over and killed by a wagon carrying a float with an effigy of the pope. Samuel Smith, a ship carpenter and leader of the North End crowd, and Ebenezer MacIntosh, a leather worker and leader of the South End crowd, are tried for causing the fatal accident, but are acquitted.

January–April. Another smallpox epidemic forces businesses to close and many people to flee the town. Inoculating hospitals are opened at Point Shirley and Castle William. Because of the epidemic, the General Court is moved temporarily, first to Cambridge and then to Concord.

John Mein, a Scotsman, establishes the first circulating library in Boston. He sells subscriptions for the use of his personal library of more than twelve hundred volumes. Mein advertises that he was persuaded to start the library "by the repeated requests of a number of gentlemen, the friends of literature."

Lt. Richard Byron's *Three Views of Boston* are completed. Painted by an officer in the Royal Navy, they are later donated by the earl of Carlisle to the City of Boston, and are now the property of the Bostonian Society.

1765

The Adams Street Bridge is completed over the Neponset River in Dorchester Lower Mills, connecting Dorchester and Milton. Because much of the original structure remains, it is considered to be the oldest existing bridge in Boston.

February 27. The Stamp Act is passed by the British Parliament. The law requires the purchase of government stamps for all legal documents and newspapers in the Colonies. It goes into effect on November 1, prompting demonstrations and a boycott of British goods, which leads to food shortages during the winter.

August 14. The Liberty Tree is said to be "consecrated" at the corner of today's Washington and Essex Streets. For the first time, members of the group calling themselves the Sons of Liberty meet to protest the Stamp Act. They hang effigies of the Boston stamp distributor, Andrew Oliver, and other British officials from the tree, march into town, and attack Oliver's house, which prompts his resignation. The site of many meetings and demonstrations prior to the Revolutionary War, the tree is said to have been planted in 1646. It is chopped down for firewood by British troops in 1775, and a British soldier is reportedly killed by its fall.

November 5. Rather than engage in their traditional Pope's Night hostilities, leaders of the North End and South End pledge "no mischiefs would arise by their means." Instead, they add effigies of "tyranny, oppression and slavery" to that of the Pope, parade to one another's strongholds, then to the Liberty Tree, "under the shadows of which they refreshed themselves for a while," according to the *Boston Gazette.*

Jeremiah Gridley establishes a "law club or sodality" for the study of law and training of lawyers. John Adams is a member. Sometimes called the "father of the Boston Bar," Gridley later advises: "Pursue the study of law, rather than the gain of it. Pursue the gain of it enough to keep out of the briers; but give your main attention to the study of it."

The Baker Chocolate Company opens in Dorchester Lower Mills. Originally the John Hannan Mill, it is joined with one owned by Dr. James Baker in 1772. The current complex, designed by Winslow and Wetherell, is completed in 1892. The company is bought by General Foods in 1927. The mills are closed in 1968 and converted into condominiums in 1983.

John Singleton Copley's painting *Henry Pelham* (also known as *Boy with a Squirrel*) is completed. After it is shown later in London, Benjamin West declares its coloring the equal of a Titian painting.

Jonathan Blackburn, Boston's second successful portrait painter, leaves town. The art historian A. T. Perkins later speculates he left because of the increasing popularity of Copley.

Horse races are first held on Boston Neck.

1766

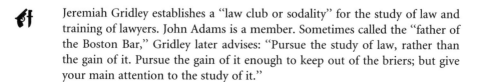

The Declaratory Act is passed by the British Parliament, establishing taxes, albeit small, on various imports. Its passage prompts Boston's town meeting to declare: "We will form an immediate and universal combination to eat nothing, drink nothing, wear nothing from Great Britain. . . . our strength consists in union."

March 17. The *Boston Gazette* declares that blood should be spilled before the Stamp Act is accepted by the Colonies. On the same day, in England, the king receives the repeal of the law, voted the day before in the House of Lords.

May 16. News of the repeal of the Stamp Act reaches Boston. Three days later, the official notice is proclaimed from the balcony of the Town House (today's Old State House). Church bells are rung, guns are fired, and fireworks are set off in celebration.

The selectmen vote to request of their representatives at the General Court "That for the total abolishing of slavery among us, That you move for a law to prohibit the importation and purchasing of slaves for the future."

The Brattle Tavern opens at the corner of Franklin Avenue and Brattle Street. Later it is reportedly the oldest continuously operated tavern in the country, and it is one of the last buildings torn down in Scollay Square in 1963.

John Baker, an Englishman, becomes the first dentist in Boston.
John Hales, "Surveyor and Typographer," publishes his calculations on the speed at which people walk along the mall on Boston Common.

1767

The Ebenezer Hancock House is built at 10 Marshall Street. Inherited by John Hancock from his uncle Thomas, it is occupied by John's brother, Ebenezer, during the Revolution. It becomes the site of the country's oldest continually operating shoe store, from 1798 to 1963.

June 29. The Townsend Acts are passed by the British Parliament, imposing duties on various goods and prompting another boycott of English goods. The British government reportedly collects 21,000 pounds in tax levies—and loses an estimated 1.7 million pounds in trade.
October 28. Town meeting votes "to encourage the use and consumption of all articles manufactured in any of the British Colonies, and more especially in this province, and not to purchase any articles imported from abroad." Soon after, a list of luxury items that residents agree not to buy and merchants agree not to import is published.

Another rumor spreads that an Anglican priest in Boston has written a letter asking for the appointment of an Anglican bishop.

December 21. The first issue of the *Boston Chronicle* appears.

Phillis Wheatley publishes her first poem, "On Messrs. Hussey and Coffin," in the *Newport Mercury*; it is also the first poem published by an African American in the Colonies. Wheatley is a fifteen-year-old slave who arrived in Boston seven years before from Senegal and lives in the home of Mrs. Susanna Wheatley of King Street.

1768

Elisha Brown denies use of the Manufactory House to British troops. One of the last tenants in the building, he barricades himself inside for seventeen days, refusing to leave so that the British troops can be garrisoned there. The maneuver proves successful, and the troops are ultimately quartered in Faneuil Hall instead. Brown's tombstone in the Granary Burying Ground reads, "bravely and successfully opposed a whole British regt. in their violent attempt to FORCE him from his *legal Habitation*."

June 10. John Hancock's sloop, *Liberty*, is seized on its return from Madeira, carrying a cargo of wine. Charged with smuggling because Hancock did not pay the duties imposed by the Townsend Acts, he is arrested, which prompts the extension of the boycott in Boston to all goods from England on which a duty is charged.

August 1. The Boston Society for the Encouragement of Trade, an organization of merchants, meets at Faneuil Hall. The members vote for a boycott of all English goods—except for essentials—beginning January 1, 1769. Later, town meeting votes to encourage residents not to patronize merchants who do not follow the boycott.

September 30. Twelve ships arrive in Boston Harbor carrying two British regiments. Part of what is later described as a threat "to overawe the inhabitants," the troops come ashore the next day at Long Wharf "with drums beating and fifes playing."

October 15. Gen. Thomas Gage arrives in Boston, and the military occupation by British troops begins.

December 19. Paul Revere places an advertisement in the *Boston Gazette* to those "unfortunate as to lose their Fore-Teeth by Accident, and other ways," offering "artificial Ones that look as well as the Natural."

John Singleton Copley's painting *Paul Revere* is completed.

1769

August 2. Thomas Hutchinson is again appointed acting royal governor.

January 30. A fire breaks out in the town jail. Prisoners are rescued and British soldiers aid town residents in the emergency.

September 5. James Otis is struck on the head in a fight with John Robinson, a British customs official, in front of the British Coffee House, and left mentally unbalanced by the blow. He leaves Boston to live in the country in 1770.

July 17. The *Boston Gazette* advertises that a small red cow "strayed away from the Common. . . . Whosoever hath or shall stop said Cow, are desired to inform the Printers hereof, and they shall be Rewarded for their Trouble."

The painter John Singleton Copley marries Susan Clarke, the daughter of Richard Clarke, a wealthy Boston merchant and a Tory. Soon after, Copley acquires a house and eighteen acres of land on Beacon Hill next to the Hancock mansion.

"The Liberty Song" is published in the *Boston Gazette*. The first patriotic song to be published in America, it is reprinted from a broadside by John Mein and John Fleming that was printed on July 18, 1768.

The opera *Love in a Village* is performed. The prohibition by the town against plays is avoided by billing it as a "reading."

1770

February 23. Eleven-year-old Christopher Seider (sometimes written as Snider) is shot by the Loyalist merchant Ebenezer Richardson. He was a member of a crowd protesting another merchant suspected of defying the boycott of British goods. Seider's subsequent funeral on February 28 is, according to Thomas Hutchinson, "the largest perhaps ever known in America."

March 5. The Boston Massacre takes place. After a crowd pelts the British sentry Hugh White with snowballs—and possibly other missiles—outside today's 60 State Street, Capt. William Preston and seven British soldiers intervene. The crowd taunts the soldiers, more missiles are thrown, and the soldiers open fire, although Preston later denies giving the order to do so. Five colonists are killed: Crispus Attucks, a runaway slave from Framingham; Samuel Gray, a ropemaker; James Caldwell, a seaman; seventeen-year-old Samuel Maverick; and Patrick Carr, an Irish tailor. The next day, thousands of armed and angry Colonists pour into town, and the British troops are removed to forts in Boston Harbor to avoid further incidents. A public funeral is held for four of the victims (all but Carr, the only Catholic) at Faneuil Hall on March 8. All are buried—as is Christopher Seider—at the Granary Burying Ground.

April. The British Parliament repeals all the taxes levied under the Townsend Acts—except for the one on tea, which is retained as a symbol of the "supremacy of Parliament" and a declaration of its right "to govern the colonies." News of the action reaches Boston soon after.

October 24. Captain Preston and his soldiers stand trial at the Town House before Judge Benjamin Lynde for their part in the Boston Massacre. The judge's charge to the jury includes the first known use of the phrase "reasonable doubt." They are defended by Josiah Quincy and John Adams. Adams tells the jury: "Facts are stubborn things, and whatever our wishes, our inclinations, or the dictums of our passions, they cannot alter the state of facts and evidence." Captain Preston and four of the soldiers are acquitted on October 30. Hugh White and another soldier are convicted of manslaughter, but escape death sentences through a legal technicality and are punished instead by being branded with the letter "M" on their left thumbs. All of the soldiers are soon sent back to England.

March 26. Paul Revere is accused of plagiarism for printing a reproduction of the Boston Massacre picture by Henry Pelham.

October 20. A gale kills more than one hundred people and destroys a hundred vessels in Massachusetts Bay.

December 11. The First Church in Jamaica Plain opens on Centre Street, originally the Third Parish of the First Church in Roxbury. Rev. William Gordon is the first pastor. He later returns to England and writes the *History of the American Revolution*, the first published account of the conflict. The church becomes independent in 1773. The First Church Burying Ground is established in 1785. The current church, designed by Nathaniel J. Bradlee, opens at 6 Eliot Street in 1854.

The Bloody Massacre. *Engraving by Paul Revere, 1770. (Courtesy of the Bostonian Society)*

July 17. The first issue of the *Massachusetts Spy* appears. Published by Zechariah Fowle and Isaiah Thomas, the newspaper ceases publication in Boston on April 6, 1775, then moves to Worcester and resumes publication soon after.

The first volume of William Billings's *New-England Psalm Singer* is published. It is the first compilation of works by a single American composer to be published.

1771

March 5. James Lovell delivers the first annual Boston Massacre Oration. The custom continues until 1783,* when it is decided to mark July Fourth with an oration instead.

March 20. Because of the anti-British sentiment in Boston, the General Court is moved to Cambridge by order of Royal Governor Hutchinson.

February 8. A benefit concert is held at Concert Hall. The first major orchestra concert in Boston on record, it is organized by Josiah Flagg and features the violinist W. S. Morgan and the Sixty-Fourth Regiment Military Band. They play selections from compositions by Bach, Handel, and others.

The first open-air concerts are held on Boston Common this summer. John Hancock pays for the performances, as well as for construction of a bandstand and the planting of a long row of lime trees opposite his mansion.

1772

Town meeting declares that "ambition and lust of power above the law are . . . predominant passions in the breasts of most men."

Town leaders vote to allow "liberty of conscience" to most Christian sects. "Catholics or Papists" are excluded, however, because they are considered "subservice of society."

Phillis Wheatley convinces a panel of prominent Bostonians, including seven ministers, John Hancock, and Governor Hutchinson, that she is, indeed, the author of her poems.

1773

September 7. The first stagecoach route to New York is established. Leaving from the Royal Exchange Tavern on State Street, the vehicles take six days to make the trip.

December 16. The Boston Tea Party is held. The citizens of Boston are upset by the Tea Act, even though, as Governor Hutchinson points out, "the poor people in America drank the same tea in quality at three shillings a pound which people in England drank at six shillings." A group meets at Faneuil Hall and votes to ask Governor Hutchinson to send three recently arrived ships laden with tea (the *Dartmouth*, *Eleanor*, and *Beaver*) back to England. The meeting moves to the larger Old South Meeting House, where the crowd is informed that Hutchinson has refused the request. A group of approximately fifty men, crudely disguised as Mohawk Indians and led by Sam Adams, then proceeds to Griffin's Wharf. The mob boards the three ships and dumps 342 chests of tea (worth more than one million of today's dollars) into Boston Harbor. Paul Revere rides for New York and Philadelphia to spread news of the protest the next day.
Polly Sumner, a doll belonging to the Sumner family, arrives in Boston on board one of the Tea Party ships. The *New England Magazine* publishes a story in 1893 describing Boston's history through the doll's eyes. Acquired by the Bostonian Society in 1919, the doll has received numerous letters from children ever since.

Caesar Hendricks takes his master to court for "detaining him in slavery." An all-white jury frees him and awards him damages.

September 27. The town of Dorchester sells fourteen acres of land to George Clark for construction of a paper mill at today's 864 River Street in Hyde Park.

The longest continuously operating paper manufacturing site in the United States, it is taken over by William Sumner in 1786, and by Tileston and Hollingsworth on September 19, 1836. The James River Company operates the mill from 1983 to 1987, the Hyde Park Paper Company beginning in 1989, and the Bay State Paper Company in 1995.

Phillis Wheatley's *Poems on Various Subjects, Religious and Moral* is published in England, after being rejected by Boston publishers. After visiting London and returning to Boston, Wheatley is given her freedom, but she continues to live with the Wheatley family for a number of years. She marries John Peters, a free African-American man, in 1778, and dies in poverty in 1784.

Engraving of Phillis Wheatley from the frontispiece of Poems on Various Subjects, Religious and Moral, *by Phillis Wheatley, Negro Servant to Mr. John Wheatley, of Boston, in New England. (Courtesy of the Bostonian Society)*

1774

March 31. The first oil lamps are used for street lighting.

March 25. The British Parliament passes the Coercive Acts. They include the Boston Port Bill, which closes the port of Boston until the East India Company and the British customs office are reimbursed for their losses as a result of the Boston Tea Party; the Massachusetts Government Act, which places virtually all power in the hands of the royal governor and moves the capital of the Province of Massachusetts Bay to Salem; and the Quartering Act, which allows troops to be housed in private homes.
May. Parliament annuls the Massachusetts royal charter.
May 17. Gen. Thomas Gage is appointed royal governor and the civilian government of the Massachusetts Bay Colony is replaced with a military one. Gage moves the official port of entry to Marblehead on June 1. He orders the fortifications on Boston Neck strengthened and all outbound travelers searched. Four British regiments are camped on Boston Common by September and are joined by eleven more regiments by the end of the year. In England, the philosopher and member of Parliament Edmund Burke later declares: "the cause of Boston is become the cause of all America. By these acts of oppression, you have made Boston the Lord Mayor of America."
September 1. Valentine Ducat, a British soldier, is shot dead on Boston Common for desertion, which prompts a protest from residents. William Ferguson is executed for the same offense on December 24.
September 9. The Suffolk Resolves are approved by delegates from Boston and neighboring towns at a meeting in the Milton home of Daniel Vose. A protest against the Coercive Acts (which they describe as the "Intolerable Acts") and a

call for resistance to the British, they are carried by Paul Revere to Philadelphia, where they are endorsed by the First Continental Congress on September 17.

 The American Coffee House opens on King Street.

 Four feet of snow reportedly falls in Boston in twenty-four hours.

 June. John Singleton Copley, America's most accomplished portrait painter, leaves Boston for England. His departure is prompted both by the praise his work is receiving in London and by his in-laws' Loyalist sympathies.

1775

 Boston's population is estimated at 16,000—before the Siege of Boston. The population does not reach its former level of 17,000 until 1785.

 J. W. F. Des Barres's chart of Boston is published; it is used by the British during the siege.

 March 5. Dr. Joseph Warren delivers the annual Boston Massacre Oration at the Old South Church. Dressed in a toga to symbolize the seriousness of the occasion, Warren is forced to climb through a window to enter the building because the hall is so crowded.

April 18. Paul Revere makes his famous ride. Sexton Robert Newman hangs two lamps in the tower of the Old North Church to signal that approximately eight hundred British troops are being ferried across Boston Harbor en route to seize military supplies stored in Concord. Revere, who is rowed across to Charlestown at the same time, is only one of approximately forty riders sent out to alert Colonists north and west of Boston. He and William Dawes are detained by British soldiers in Lexington, and never reach Concord.

April 19. The Battles of Lexington and Concord are fought, and the Revolutionary War begins.

April 20. The Siege of Boston begins. Colonial troops surround the town, making the British virtual captives. Setting up their headquarters at the British Coffee House (on the site of today's 66 State Street), the British order residents to turn in their weapons and prohibit them from leaving the town. Patriots flee the town, however, while Tories from surrounding communities stream in.

June 17. The Battle of Bunker Hill is fought in Charlestown, although misnamed since it is actually fought on neighboring Breed's Hill. Led by Gen. William Howe, the British are ultimately victorious, but their losses (over a thousand killed or wounded) greatly exceed those of the Colonists (approximately four hundred), who are led by Gen. Israel Putnam and Col. William Prescott. Prescott may or may not have issued the order "Don't fire until you see the whites of their eyes" (a well-known military command that originated in the Prussian Army), but he reportedly did say: "Show the bastards. You show them." During and after the battle, the British burn down most of Charlestown—more than five hundred buildings.

July. According to the historian Richard Frothingham, the population of Boston was "stated at 6,753; the number of troops with their dependents, women and children, at 13,600." He notes, "the town became sickly both among the people and the troops." During the harsh winter, the British troops cut down trees and tear down over one hundred buildings—including Governor Winthrop's house—for firewood. They also produce skits at Faneuil Hall ridiculing the Colonists and convert the Old South Church into a riding school and stable.

 March 6. Prince Hall and fourteen other African Americans are inducted into British Military Masonic Lodge No. 441 after being refused membership in the Grand Lodge of Massachusetts. Originally called African Lodge No. 1, it is the only lodge in the United States with a British charter. Later renamed the Prince Hall Lodge, it is located today at 18 Washington Street in Dorchester.

 May 17. The Great Fire of 1775 destroys twenty-five warehouses in Boston. The fire reportedly starts as a result of the careless handling of cartridges by a British soldier.

 November 5. General Washington prohibits members of the Continental Army from engaging in any of the traditional Pope's Night activities to avoid friction between Catholics and Protestants.

 April 19. Latin School suspends classes. Headmaster John Lovell reportedly delivers the news to students by announcing, "War's begun and school's done; *deponite libros*." Classes resume on June 5, 1776, under the direction of a new headmaster because Lovell, a Loyalist, had sailed for Halifax as a guest of the British, along with his son, a Patriot who was taken along as a prisoner.

 Benjamin Church, Jr., a Boston surgeon and director-general of the Continental Army's Hospital Department, is found to be a traitor.

 December 29. Busy Body is performed by British officers and their wives at Faneuil Hall. Gen. John Burgoyne's play *The Blockade of Boston* is performed for the Loyalist residents who remain in the town.

1776

 Boston's population drops to 2,719.

 June. The Roxbury High Fort is completed on today's Fort Hill in Roxbury. It is demolished when the Cochituate Standpipe is erected there for water storage in 1869. Frederick Law Olmsted designs a park on the site in 1895, and the water tower is converted into an observation tower in 1906.

 March 4. After being persuaded to abandon his own plan to attack Boston in the winter by crossing the ice-covered Charles River, General Washington implements one advanced by his generals. At night, under cover of a diversionary bombardment from Charlestown, Colonial forces seize Dorchester Heights, then train cannons brought by Henry Knox from Fort Ticonderoga on the town and harbor of Boston.
March 17. The British evacuate Boston. After a surrender is negotiated, approximately nine thousand British troops and one thousand Loyalists board 125

ships in Boston Harbor and leave town. The Colonial army then enters Boston to find it in ruins.

June 13. Boston Light is destroyed by British forces that had remained in the area. During the attack, Mary Burton, a Loyalist aboard one of the British ships, is killed. Her husband, William, is allowed to bury her at Long Island. According to legend, her ghost later appears on the island, dressed in a red cloak, and is called "the Woman in Scarlet."

July 18. At 1:00 P.M., the Declaration of Independence is first read in Boston at the Town House. Col. Thomas Crafts reads it in the Council Chambers, while Suffolk County Sheriff William Greenleaf reads it simultaneously from the balcony to the crowd gathered below. In the celebration that follows, the carved figures of the lion and unicorn, symbols of English rule, are torn down from the building and burnt in a bonfire, along with the signs from the Royal Coffee House and street signs from King and Queen Streets. Replicas of the lion and unicorn ornaments are once more affixed to the Old State House in 1992.

The Brighton Cattle Market is established by Jonathan Winship and his son to feed the Colonial troops during the Siege of Boston. Afterward, it continues as both a stockyard and slaughterhouse.

The London Harness Company is established. Described as the oldest continuously operated business in Boston, the company traces its beginning to this year, when Zachariah Hick opens a saddlery and harness shop in Boston. He is later joined by a trunkmaker, W. W. Winship, for whom the company is subsequently named. The W. W. Winship Company is acquired by the London Harness Company (established in Concord, N.H., in 1847), which moves to Boston in 1890 and assumes its current name in 1897. Located initially on Devonshire Street, the company moved to its current location at 60 Franklin Street in 1919.

Merchants from the North Shore, including the Cabots, Lowells, Higginsons, and Pickerings, begin moving to Boston, replacing the Loyalist merchants who left town during the British evacuation.

1777

Thomas Page's *A Plan of the Town of Boston* and Henry Pelham's *A Plan of Boston in New England and Its Environs* are published.

May 26. Town meeting declines to vote to form a new government, declaring, "a suitable time will properly come before the people at large to delegate a select number for that purpose, and that alone."

October 5. Elijah Woodward is shot on Boston Common for desertion.

1778

John Hancock hosts a dinner for the French count Charles Hector d'Estaing and his officers to thank the French for the loan they have made the Colonial government. When the milk runs out during the meal, Hancock's wife, Dorothy, dispatches servants to milk all of the cows on Boston Common—and send anyone who complains to her.

June 21. The Wednesday Evening Club, one of Boston's first dining clubs, is organized. Its membership is made up of four clergymen, four doctors, four lawyers, and four "merchants, manufacturers and gentlemen of literature and leisure." The club continues, with an expanded membership, today.

September 19. A circus opens on Boston Common.

John Singleton Copley's painting *Watson and the Shark* is completed.

1779

Lotteries are held to finance the repair of Long Wharf and of streets in Charlestown.

The Declaration of Independence is hailed in Boston (copyright 1943 by the New England Mutual Life Insurance Company, now MetLife). (Courtesy of the Bostonian Society)

May 1. The General Court orders the estates of Loyalists to be confiscated for the benefit of the government.

September 1. The first Massachusetts Constitutional Convention opens in Cambridge. Subsequent meetings are held at the Town House (today's Old State House) in Boston.

The winter of 1779–1780 is particularly severe.

The Second Church merges with and moves to the New Brick Church between Hanover and Richmond Streets in the North End. The congregation becomes Unitarian in 1802. Ralph Waldo Emerson serves as minister from 1829 to 1832. The church is rebuilt in 1845 and torn down in 1871. The congregation moves to the Freeman Place chapel in 1850, then merges with and moves to the Church of the Savior on Bedford Street in 1854. That building is taken down, reassembled on Boylston Street, and dedicated on September 17, 1874. A new church, designed by Ralph Adams Cram, at 874 Beacon Street is dedicated on November 8, 1914. The congregation merges with and moves to the First Church at 66 Marlborough Street in 1970.

1780

The Jonathan Winship House is completed in Brighton Center. Converted to the Brighton Hotel by Samuel Dudley in 1820, it is today the site of the Brighton Police Station, designed by Edmund March Wheelwright and built in 1914. *(ca.)* The Spooner-Lambert House is built in Roxbury.

June 7. The Massachusetts Constitution is adopted at the Town House. Written by John Adams, it is the oldest written constitution in continued use in the world and contains the phrase: "to the end it may be a government of laws and not of men."

October 25. The Commonwealth of Massachusetts is established. John Hancock, elected on September 4, serves as governor from 1780 to 1785 and from 1787 to 1793. The new government operates from the Town House, which is now called the State House.

The Warren Tavern opens at today's 2 Pleasant Street in Charlestown. It becomes the oldest continuously operated tavern in the United States. The building is enlarged in 1786 and renovated in 1972, and remains in operation today. A French visitor named Blanchard writes: "The women are tall, well formed, of regular features; their complexion is generally only pale, without any color. They have fewer attractions and less ease of manner than our French women, but more dignity."

September 10. Counterfeiters are hanged on Boston Common.

May 19. The "Dark Day" occurs. The sun is mysteriously obscured, which causes great alarm in the town. It later turns out that the darkness was caused by smoke from a forest fire in Maine.

February 11. African-American residents are granted use of Faneuil Hall for religious services.

Simon Willard moves to Boston. He and his brothers Aaron, Benjamin, and Ephraim soon begin producing clocks, including the first "banjo" clock built in the United States.

May 4. The American Academy of Arts and Sciences is established. The second-oldest scientific society in the United States, it is later described in *The Memorial History of Boston* as "essentially a Boston institution." Its headquarters are later located at the Boston Athenaeum on State Street, and at the former Faulkner Farm in Jamaica Plain, and in Cambridge after 1981.

1781

The Norfolk House is built in Roxbury. Originally the home of Joseph Ruggles, it later becomes known as Highland Hall, then Norfolk Hall. Enlarged in 1850, the current building served as the home of the Roxbury Neighborhood House and as a branch library for many years.

October 26. An extra edition of the *Boston Gazette* announces Washington's victory over Cornwallis at Yorktown on October 17. The victory is celebrated with a huge bonfire on Boston Common on November 2.

October 25. Slavery is abolished in Massachusetts. In *Commonwealth v. Jennison*, a Massachusetts court frees the slave Quock Walker from his master, Nathaniel Jennison. The court finds that in declaring "All men are born free and equal," the state's 1780 constitution effectively abolished slavery in the state. The Massachusetts Supreme Judicial Court upholds the decision in 1783.

Laws against Sunday activities are first called Blue Laws because they are printed on blue paper.

 November 1. The Massachusetts Medical Society is incorporated in Boston. The first major medical society in America, it is later described as being notable for being "formed of both Loyalists and Patriots . . . before the surrender of Yorktown."

1782

 The French, seventy-four-gun man-of-war *Le Magnifique* runs aground and sinks off Lovell's Island. Since the Boston Harbor pilot David Darling was at the helm, the Revolutionary government gives the French a new seventy-four-gun warship, *America*, prompting John Paul Jones, who would have commanded the new ship, to resign. Darling loses his job, but obtains another as sexton at the Old North Church. There, he is taunted by graffiti written on the church door, which reads: "Don't you run this ship ashore/As you did the seventy four."

 December 25. A fire destroys all the North Mills on the Mill Pond.

 September 19. Harvard Medical School is founded. The third medical school in the United States (after the University of Pennsylvania and King's College, later renamed Columbia University), its creation is spurred by Dr. John Warren, who later leaves his body to the school for dissection. Classes begin the following year in Cambridge. The school moves to Boston in 1815, initially to rented quarters in the Washington Street area, to Mason Street in 1816, then to a new building on North Grove Street, across from Massachusetts General Hospital, in 1847. It moves to a new building at the corner of Boylston and Exeter Streets in the Back Bay in 1883, then to its current location in the Fenway in 1906.*

 Gilbert Stuart's *Portrait of a Gentleman Skating* is completed.

1783

 The filling of the Town Dock begins. It is completed in 1784.

 October 20. The first stagecoach runs between Boston and Hartford along the Post Road.

 April 1. News of a preliminary peace agreement, ending the war with England, reaches Boston. The peace proclamation is read from the balcony of today's Old State House on April 23, and the Treaty of Paris is signed on September 3.

July 4. Boston is the first town to designate—and celebrate—Independence Day as an official holiday. John Warren, brother of Joseph, the "martyr of Bunker Hill," delivers the first annual Fourth of July oration at Faneuil Hall.

April 17. The General Court establishes the position of inspector of police. It is the first use of the word "police" in Boston history.

May 23. James Otis is killed by a bolt of lightning while standing in the doorway of his home in Andover. A few years earlier, Otis had written to his sister, "I hope when God Almighty, in his righteous Providence, shall take me out of time into eternity, that it will be by a flash of lightning." He is buried at the Granary Burying Ground.

After the British Parliament passes the Orders in Council, limiting imports from the United States, Massachusetts retaliates by placing duties on English goods. Because the other states do not do the same, however, Boston loses much of its trade to other American ports.

1784

The Sacred Cod is donated to the state by John Rowe. "A memorial to the importance of cod fishing to the welfare of the Commonwealth," the four-by-eleven-foot pine sculpture is initially displayed in the Old State House, then moved to the chambers of the House of Representatives in the new State House on March 7, 1895. The cod is kidnapped by students on the staff of the *Harvard Lampoon* on April 26, 1933, and returned four days later. It is stolen again in 1968, but found soon after hidden within the State House.

An article entitled "Sentiments on Libertinism" appears in the *Boston Magazine.* In it the author (using the pen name Daphne) declares it unfair that a single act of infidelity "forever deprive women of all that renders life valuable" while "the base betrayer [the man] is suffered to triumph in the success of his unmanly arts, and to pass unpunished even by a frown."

Hannah Adams's *An Alphabetic Compendium of the Various Sects* (*Dictionary of All Religions*) is published.

Dorchester residents vote "that such girls as can read in the Psalter be allowed to go to the Grammar School from the first day of June to the first day of October."

July 5. The Manufactory House, later renamed the Massachusetts Bank, opens on Tremont Street. The second commercial bank in the United States (after the Bank of North America in Philadelphia), it is chartered on March 18th. The bank acquires and merges with the First National Bank of Boston in 1903, is later renamed BankBoston, and is acquired by the Fleet Financial Group in 1999 and Bank of America in 2004.

Ebenezer Battelle opens a bookstore on Marlborough Street. It evolves into the Little, Brown and Company in 1837.*

1785

 July 4. A great celebration—including what are described as "ludicrous scenes"—marks Independence Day.

 March 14. A state prison is established on Castle Island. Previously, the town jail was also used as the state prison. A new state prison is built in Charlestown in 1805.*

 The First Universalist Church opens in the wooden church at the corner of Hanover and North Bennet Streets that was built by those who had seceded from the Old North Church. Rev. George Richards is the first pastor. He is succeeded by John Murray, later called the "Father of Universalism," in 1795. The church is replaced by a brick structure in 1838. The society is dissolved in 1864.

 January 7. French balloonist François Blanchard makes the first successful balloon flight across the English Channel, accompanied by Dr. John Jeffries of Boston. Jeffries is allowed to go along after agreeing to pay for the cost of the trip—and to jump overboard if necessary to lighten the load.

 July. After American ships are prohibited from bringing anything but American goods into British ports, the export of any goods from the United States in British ships is prohibited until England's restriction is lifted. There is not a single British ship in Boston Harbor at this time.

1786

 June 17. The Charles River Bridge opens, connecting the North End to Charlestown. The event attracts twenty thousand spectators—more than the entire population of the town. Some chant, "You Charlestown Pigs,/Put on your wigs,/And come over to Boston town." A Madam Healy pays five hundred dollars to be the first person to cross the bridge, and she is driven over in a carriage drawn by four white horses. The drawbridge is left open from 1836 to 1841. Originally a toll bridge, it is made a free bridge on April 30, 1858, and replaced by the current Charlestown (also called Prison Point) Bridge on November 27, 1899. It is renamed for Judge John Gilmore, a former state representative from Charlestown, in 1974.

 January 6. An earthquake shakes the town and damages property. Another occurs on November 9.
December. A "Great Tide" produces a high tide that is ten inches higher than normal.

 Joseph Pope constructs the first orrery—a three-dimensional, moving display of the solar system—in Boston in his home on Washington Street. It is later sold to Harvard College and moved there on February 27, 1789.

John Trumbull's painting *The Death of General Warren at the Battle of Bunker's Hill, 17 June 1775* is completed.

The Musical Society, directed by William Selby, performs at King's Chapel. One of the most ambitious concerts in Boston to date, it includes the first selections from Handel's *Messiah* to be performed in America.

1787

Charles Bulfinch returns to Boston from a yearlong "Grand Tour of Europe" and, in his words, goes about "pursuing no business but giving gratuitous advice in architecture." "Much as one might like to say something new about Bulfinch here," the architectural historian Douglass Shand-Tucci later writes, "the old and venerable idea that he virtually created Boston architecturally is more or less true."

Prince Hall leads two unsuccessful petition drives on behalf of fellow African-American residents: One requests that they be allowed to return to Africa to form a new Christian nation. The other asks that schools for African-American children be established, arguing that "our children . . . now receive no benefit from the free schools in the town of Boston, which we think is a great grievance."

November 22. John Sheehan, a native of Cork, Ireland, and a Catholic, is hanged on Boston Common for burglary. The *Centinel* later reports, "except for the burglary for which he suffered, [he] does not appear, by his life, to have been guilty of many atrocious offences."

April 20. A fire breaks out in the Hollis Street Church, which eventually destroys more than one hundred buildings and sixty homes.

A correspondent for Philadelphia's *Columbian Magazine* writes of Boston: "Arts and sciences seem to have made greater progress here, than in any part of America."

1788

The Frog Pond begins as a "small mud hole" on Boston Common. It is curbed in 1826, and paved in 1848.

February 6. Massachusetts ratifies the Constitution of the United States at a convention held in the Lane Street Meeting House (later the Federal Street Church) on the site of today's FleetBoston plaza.

The General Court passes a law making the slave trade illegal in Massachusetts.

Brissot de Warville writes of Boston women: "They unite simplicity of morals with that French politeness and delicacy of manners which render virtue more amiable. The young women here enjoy the liberty they do in England,—that they did in Geneva when morals were there, and the Republic existed; and they do not abuse it."

Frog Pond, Boston Common, as it appears today. (Photograph by Richard Tourangeau)

May 8. Archibald and Joseph Taylor are hanged on Boston Neck for robbing a Mr. Cunningham. According to reports, "the robbery was committed near the spot of execution."

November 2. The first public Catholic Mass in Boston takes place in the Church of the Holy Cross at today's 20 School Street. It is celebrated by l'Abbé de la Poterie, a former chaplain for the French navy. The building had been a French Huguenot chapel until it was acquired by the small French and Irish Catholic congregation. Father John Thayer, a Boston native and former Congregational minister who had converted to Catholicism, becomes the pastor in 1790. The church is replaced in 1803.*

January 8. The *Boston Gazette* editorializes: "Until we manufacture more it is absurd to celebrate the Fourth of July as the birth-day of our independence. We are still a dependent people; and what is worse, after the blood and treasure we have expended, we are actually taxed by Great Britain. Our imports help to fill her revenue and to pay the interest of a debt contracted in an attempt to enslave us."

The first glassworks in Boston is established. It begins to produce window glass in 1793.

1789

October 24. George Washington makes the first presidential visit to Boston. He is greeted with a procession to the State House through an arch designed by Bulfinch and a colonnade by Thomas Dawes—but not greeted by Gov. John

Hancock. Hancock soon relents, however. Carried on a litter and pleading an attack of gout, he visits Washington at the Ingersoll Inn at the corner of today's Tremont and Court Streets. The meeting comes to be seen as a symbol of Americans' acceptance of federal authority over that of individual states. In Washington's honor, part of Orange Street is named for him, but the rest of the street is not renamed until 1824.*

 A rash of burglaries plagues the town and prompts criticism of the Boston Night Watch.
October 8. Two men and a woman are hanged at Boston Neck for robbery.
The federal court convenes for the first time in Boston.

 Selectmen vote to allow "the Blacks to have the use of Mr. Vinal's school for public worship on the afternoon of the Lord's Day."
December 25. Boston becomes the first town in New England to officially observe Christmas.

 October 16. After the Massachusetts legislature again passes a law requiring the provision of schooling for girls, Boston town meeting votes to establish a school system in which "children of both sexes were to be admitted, boys for the year round, and girls from April to October." The town also votes to establish one writing and one reading school in the southern, central, and northern parts of the town.
October 20. The Boston School Committee is established. Authorized by the General Court earlier in the year, the committee is made up of twenty-one members (the nine selectmen and a representative from each of the twelve wards). Its responsibility is "to exercise all the Powers relating to the Schools and School Masters."

 November 21. Dr. John Jeffries, a surgeon and former Loyalist, holds the first public lecture on anatomy in Boston. A mob, disturbed by Jeffries's promotion of dissection and by his political views, disrupts the meeting.

Sarah Wentworth Morton (under the pen name of Philenia) publishes *The Power of Sympathy*. It is considered to be the first novel published in America; it is later found to have been written by her neighbor William Hill Brown.
December 10. An "Orang Outang" is exhibited in the town.

1790

 According to the first United States Census Bureau decennial census, Boston's population is 18,320, the third-largest of any city in the United States (behind New York and Philadelphia). Of that number, 18,254 are described as "free white persons" and 66 as "All other free persons except for Indians not taxed." The separate towns of Roxbury, Dorchester, and Charlestown have an additional combined population of 5,531, with 95 classified as nonwhite.

(ca.) The Deacon John Larkin House is built at 55 Main Street in Charlestown. The owner became famous for loaning his horse, Brown Beauty, to Paul Revere

on April 18, 1775. (The horse was taken by the British when Revere was captured and never returned.)

The William Sumner House is built on River Street in today's Hyde Park.

April 17. Upon his death in Philadelphia, Benjamin Franklin leaves a bequest (later called the Franklin Fund) to the "Inhabitants of the Town of Boston . . . for whatever that may make living in the town more convenient to its people and render it more agreeable to strangers resorting thither for health or a temporary residence." The Franklin Fund continues today and supports primarily educational initiatives.

John Winthrop's *History of New England* is published. Only the first two of the planned three volumes appear.

A town committee reports: "The almshouse in Boston is, perhaps, the only instance known where persons of every description and disease are lodged under the same roof and in some instances in the same contagious apartments, by which means the sick are disturbed by the noise of the healthy, and the infirm rendered liable to the vices and diseases of the diseased and profligate."

November 1. A balloonist ascends in front of the Green Dragon Tavern.

"When the first census of the United States was taken in 1790," the investment bankers Henry Kidder and Francis Peabody later write, "the whole population of the country was a little short of four millions, of whom nearly or quite one fourth were directly dependent upon Boston as their financial and commercial capital."

August 9. The *Columbia* returns to Boston. The first American ship to circumnavigate the globe, it left Boston on September 30, 1787. Owned by customers of the Massachusetts Bank and commanded by Capt. Robert Gray, the *Columbia* is credited with opening up a new triangular trade route for Boston merchants. Goods manufactured in New England are exchanged in the Pacific Northwest for furs, which are in turn exchanged in China for tea, textiles, and porcelain. The Boston merchant Thomas Handasyd Perkins was in China when the *Columbia* arrived there. After returning to Boston, he follows the same business formula, beginning in 1803.*

(ca.) Benjamin Crehore builds the first pianos in the Boston area. He lives and works in Milton and, for a time, maintains a shop in Dorchester.

1791

June 18. Bulfinch's sixty-foot Doric column with eagle and tablets is erected on the site of the former town beacon. The first monument in the United States to commemorate the Revolution, it is torn down in 1811 when the top of Beacon Hill is removed. The eagle and tablets are installed in Doric Hall in the State House in 1861, then included as part of the replica of Bulfinch's monument, which is erected behind the State House in 1898.

February 19. The Massachusetts Historical Society is incorporated. The oldest organization of its kind in the country, it is founded by Rev. Jeremy Belknap and others. At first it is located in the attic of Faneuil Hall. Then it relocates to the Manufactory House, then to the arch of the Tontine Crescent, and then to 30 Tremont Street in 1833. It moves to its current quarters at 1154 Boylston Street, designed by Edmund March Wheelwright, on April 14, 1899.

March 30. Charles Bulfinch is elected to his first term on the Board of Selectmen. He is reelected annually for the next four years, resigns to concentrate on his business, then is elected again in 1799. He serves as chairman of the board until 1817.

April 6. John Stewart is hanged on Boston Common for several robberies committed at the Pearl Street home of Captain Rust. It is reported that the "plunder" is found in a tomb on Copp's Hill and the burglar was "traced and caught one stormy night."

June 11. The Columbian Museum opens at the American Coffee House. An exhibit of wax figures presented by Daniel Bowen, it is considered Boston's first museum. The exhibit moves to the top floor of a schoolhouse on Hollis Street, then to a new building—Boston's first specially built museum—at the corner of Bromfield and Tremont Streets in 1795. The museum moves to new quarters on Tremont Street next to King's Chapel Burying Ground in 1806. Destroyed by fire on May 17, 1807, it is rebuilt on the same site.
Hans Gram's *Death Song of an Indian Chief* is published. It is thought to be the first orchestral score published in the United States.

1792

August. Father François Antoine Matignon arrives in Boston, fleeing the revolution in France. He proceeds to heal the rift that has developed between French and Irish Catholics in Boston.

Smallpox again strikes Boston. Thousands volunteer for inoculation, and a hospital to isolate patients is constructed in South Boston.

August 1. The State Street Bank and Trust Company is established. Originally called the Union Bank, it is the second oldest in Boston. Located for many years at 33 State Street, it moves to 71 Federal Street in 1930, then to its current location in 1966.

The Old Farmer's Almanac/Yankee Publishing Company is established. It is the oldest publishing company in Boston.

August 10. The New Exhibition Room (also called the Board Alley Theatre), the first theater in Boston, opens in a converted stable on today's Hawley Street. The opening night performance is more a variety show than a play. When Sheridan's *A School for Scandal* opens on December 3, the performance is stopped and the sheriff arrests the cast and manager for violating the laws against theatrical exhibitions. As a result of public protests, the arrests are waived and the performances continue.

1793

January. The town meeting approves a proposal whereby the Commonwealth of Massachusetts donates the Old State House and the Province House to Boston and, in return, the town provides a new State House for the Commonwealth.

November 23. The West Boston Bridge opens at Cambridge Street, connecting Boston to Cambridge. Originally a toll bridge, it is made a free bridge on February 1, 1858. It is replaced by another bridge, designed by Edmund March Wheelwright, in 1907, renamed the Longfellow Bridge in 1927. (It is popularly known as the "Salt and Pepper Bridge" for its distinctive towers.)

January 23. The town celebrates the success of the French Revolution at what is renamed Liberty Square. The festivities include roasting a thousand-pound ox and placing its horns at the top of a sixty-foot "liberty pole."

March 13. All of the town's fire "machines are damaged by incendiaries."

January 21. The first Franklin medals are distributed to the top scholars in Boston's schools.

The first Boston Chamber of Commerce is established. At first it is only a grain exchange. A second chamber is established in 1836 and continues until 1843. A third, produced by a merger of the Boston Commercial Exchange and the Boston Produce Exchange, is formed in 1885. The chamber and the Boston Merchants Association merge to form a new Boston Chamber of Commerce in 1909. The organization opens it own building at 80 Federal Street on October 6, 1924. The membership is broadened and the name changed to the Greater Boston Chamber of Commerce in 1952.

Bostonian Royall Tyler's *The Contrast* is performed at the New Exhibition Room. The play makes fun of Americans who imitate the English. The theater is torn down soon after, despite the fact that theatrical exhibitions are legalized on April 4, 1793.

1794

The Mount Vernon Proprietors (Harrison Gray Otis, Charles Bulfinch, Jonathan Mason, William Scollay, and Joseph Woodward; Hepsibah Swan joined later) are incorporated to develop Beacon Hill as a residential area. The expatriate artist John Singleton Copley sells his eighteen acres on Beacon Hill to the group in June 1795. After learning the price that his agent agreed to was much less than the land is worth, Copley goes to court, unsuccessfully, to nullify the sale.

The French chef Jean Baptiste Gilbert Playpat opens Julien's Restorator at the corner of Milk and Congress Streets. Until now restaurants are called "cookhouses," but Julien names his establishment after the French word *restaurant*. It becomes famous for its consommé and cheese fondue. The building is torn down in 1824.

July 30. The Great Fire of 1794 destroys nearly one hundred homes and other buildings as well as seven ropewalks in the Pearl Street area. The town votes to donate the marshy land at the foot of Boston Common so the owners of the ropewalks can relocate there, providing they build a seawall. To create the resulting development, the first filling of the Back Bay takes place. The new ropewalks burn down again, however, in 1806 and 1819, and the city buys back some of the land for the proposed Public Garden in February 1824.*

A windmill is set up on Boston Neck.

Susanna Haswell Rowson's *Charlotte Temple* is first published in America. It is the best-selling novel in the United States up to that time.
June 17. The Boston Library Society is incorporated. Located initially in the lower rooms in the arch in the Tontine Crescent, the organization incorporates as the Boston Public Library in 1848.*
William Billings's *The Continental Harmony* is published.
February 3. The Boston Theatre, designed by Charles Bulfinch, opens on Federal Street with a concert of classical, military, and popular music, and performances of *Gustavus Vasa* and *Modern Antiques* by an English theater company. The first true theater in Boston, it is nevertheless advertised as "a school of virtue." Performers would include James Fennel (the first to perform Shakespearean readings in Boston), Edwin Forrest, Edmund Kean, and William Macready. The building burns down on February 2, 1798, is rebuilt, and reopens in October. For the next thirty years, it is Boston's premier—and only—theater. Converted to a concert and lecture hall and renamed the Odeon in 1835, it is turned back into a playhouse in 1846. It closes in 1852 and is torn down shortly thereafter to make way for the second Boston Theatre, which opens in 1854.*

1795

Patrick Jeffrey erects a brick building at the intersection of today's Court and Tremont Streets. Purchased a few years later by William Scollay, an apothecary, it comes to be called Scollay's Building. The area is named Scollay Square in 1838, and the building torn down in 1871. The area is rededicated as Scollay Square on April 29, 1987.
The north side of Bulfinch's Tontine Crescent, a row of town houses, opens on Franklin Street. Although it is eventually completed, subscriptions come in so slowly that Bulfinch is forced to declare bankruptcy a year later. The buildings are torn down to make way for commercial buildings in 1858.

February 27. The Jamaica–Pond Aqueduct Company is incorporated. Boston's first public water service, it receives a charter from the General Court and purchases the water rights to Jamaica Pond in 1796. Then it builds a forty-five-

mile system of wooden pipes to bring water into Boston and Roxbury. The city buys the rights and the plant on May 5, 1851.

A canal is built from Boston Harbor to today's Eustis Street in Roxbury and is later called the Fort Point Channel. Much of the canal is filled in by 1878.

Gov. Samuel Adams signs legislation to create the state capital in Boston after Worcester, Plymouth, and other towns have competed unsuccessfully for the designation. Dorothy Hancock sells a portion of the family's land on Beacon Hill for construction of the state capitol building on April 27. The town votes to move the workhouse and almshouse from Park Street.

March 15. The Massachusetts Charitable Mechanics Association is organized. The labor union is open to several trades; Paul Revere is the first president. After initially using Faneuil Hall for its triennial exhibitions, the organization builds the first Mechanics Hall, designed by Hammatt Billings, at the corner of Bedford and Chauncy Streets in 1860. It moves to a second Mechanics Hall, designed by William Gibbons, at 97–135 Huntington Avenue in 1882. That building is torn down to make way for the Prudential Center in 1959.

The Bell-in-Hand Tavern opens under the Exchange Coffee House in Congress Square at today's Exchange and State Streets. The oldest continuously operated tavern in Boston, it is named for the previous occupation of its first proprietor, James Wilson, the former Boston town crier. The tavern moves to Pi Alley in 1853, a location the lawyer Rufus Choate later describes as "ignominious but convenient." Lucius Beebe later describes the atmosphere: "If a patron fell down among the cuspidors he was likely to go undiscovered for days and, as the chances were that he was a reporter from one of the adjacent offices of Newspaper Row, his acquaintances would pool their intellectual resources in the front room and send to his office reasonably convincing dispatches fabricated over his byline." The tavern later moves to Devonshire Street, then to its current location at 45–55 Union Street in Dock Square.

February 22. Iceboat racing between South Boston and Squantum is inaugurated.

1796

The Ashkenazi immigrant Israel Baer Kursheedt arrives in Boston. Finding only one Jewish family in the town and no synagogue, he soon returns to Europe.

The first Harrison Gray Otis House, designed by Charles Bulfinch, is completed at 141 Cambridge Street. It is converted into a ladies' Turkish bath in the 1830s, then into a patent medicine shop and a ladies' boardinghouse. The building is now owned by and serves as headquarters for Historic New England (formerly the Society for the Preservation of New England Antiquities).

The African Society is organized. Founded by a group of African-American residents, its goals are to aid the poor and promote an end to slavery.

May 1. Members of the Boston Night Watch are provided with rattles to announce fires or to call on other watchmen for help. They carry them until May 1868.

October 3. Father Jean-Louis Lefebvre de Cheverus arrives in Boston. A former student of Father Matingon's, he assists him by ministering to distant parishes and to the Indians in Maine.

The Boston Dispensary is established in Bartlett's apothecary shop on Corn Hill. The first permanent medical institution in New England and third in the United States, it moves to the South Cove in 1856, first to Ash Street, then to Bennett Street in 1883. It merges with the Floating Hospital and Pratt Diagnostic Clinic to form the New England Medical Center in 1965.

The Boston Lock and Safe Company and the Victor Coffee Company are established. They remain in business today.
Shreve, Crump and Low is established. The oldest continually operated jewelry store in the United States, it is founded by the silversmith and watchmaker John McFarlane on Marlborough Street (today's Washington Street). The company is later taken over by, in succession, John Low, Benjamin Shreve, and Charles Crump. Incorporated in 1869, the store moves to 225 Washington Street in 1850, to 147 Tremont/47–55 West Street in 1891, and to 330 Boylston and Arlington Streets in 1929. It is scheduled to move to 440 Boylston Street in 2005.

Gilbert Stuart paints unfinished portraits of George and Martha Washington. Acquired by the Boston Athenaeum in 1831, they are lent to the Museum of Fine Arts in 1876. In order to raise funds, the Athenaeum makes the controversial decision to sell the two paintings in 1979. In response to protests by Boston's citizens, who objected to the works' leaving the city, a compromise is devised: the paintings are sold jointly to the MFA and the Smithsonian Institution's National Portrait Gallery in Washington, to be displayed together in alternating three-year cycles at each location, beginning in 1980.

1797

The architect Asher Benjamin's *The Country Builder's Assistant* is published.

October 21. The USS *Constitution* is launched from Edmund Hart's shipyard on the site of today's U.S. Coast Guard base in the North End. Designed by Joshua Humphrey, it becomes the oldest commissioned ship in the U.S. Navy and winner of all forty-two of her battles, including a victory over the HMS *Guerrière* off Nova Scotia on August 19, 1812, later called one of the greatest sea battles of all time. It is there the ship received its nickname, "Old Ironsides," after a sailor reportedly exclaims: "Huzza! Her sides are made of iron!" The U.S. Navy decommissions the ship and considers scrapping the frigate in 1830. Thanks, in part, to the poem "Old Ironsides" by twenty-one-year-old Oliver Wendell Holmes in the September 16, 1830, edition of the *Boston Daily Advertiser*, the ship is saved. It is rebuilt and recommissioned, and Capt. "Mad Jack"

The State House and Beacon Hill between Hancock and Temple Streets. Lithograph after a drawing by J. R. Smith, 1811–1812. (Courtesy of the Bostonian Society)

Percival sails it around the world from 1844 to 1851. The ship is brought to Boston in 1897, and the U.S. Navy considers using the *Constitution* for target practice in 1904, but is deterred by a campaign by the Massachusetts Society of the Daughters of 1812. The *Constitution* is again rebuilt and sails under its own power for the first time in 116 years on July 21, 1997.

 Hannah Webster Foster's novel *The Coquette, or the History of Eliza Wharton* is published.

The Bostonian John Burk's play *The Battle of Bunker Hill—and the Death of General Warren* is performed at the Haymarket Theatre.

1798

 January 11. The Massachusetts State House, designed by Bulfinch, opens with a procession from what now becomes the Old State House. The pine cone (which looks like a pineapple) atop the dome is meant to symbolize the importance of lumbering to the economy of the state, which still includes present-day Maine. The building's red bricks are painted white in 1825, then yellow, then are restored to their natural color in 1928. The dome, originally white-washed wooden shingles, is sheathed in copper by Paul Revere and Son in 1802, painted gold in 1861, then covered in twenty-three-karat gold leaf in 1874. The dome is first illuminated on September 27, 1898. It is painted gray in 1942 to camouflage it for the duration of World War II. An addition to the front of the building by Isaiah Rogers is completed in 1831, and another, to the rear, by Gridley J. F. Bryant, is finished in 1856. The long, yellow-brick rear addition by Charles Brigham is completed in 1895, and the white marble wings by Chapman, Sturgis, and Andrews in 1917.

 A school for African-American children is established. After Prince Hall unsuccessfully petitions the legislature to allow African-American children to attend public schools, African-American residents establish their own school in the home of Hall's son Primus at the corner of today's Hancock and Revere Streets on Beacon Hill. Elijah Sylvester, a white man, is the first teacher. The school moves to the African Meeting House in 1808, then to the Smith School on Belknap Street (today's Joy Street) in 1835.*

A yellow fever epidemic strikes the town.
A U.S. Marine hospital opens as part of the new Fort Independence on Castle Island. Considered the first public health facility in the United States, it provides treatment for seamen. It moves to Charlestown in 1803, then to Chelsea, and becomes the Chelsea Naval Hospital in 1826.

The Massachusetts Mutual Fire Insurance Company is incorporated. Founded by Moses Michael Hayes, Paul Revere, and others, it is the first successful property insurance company in the United States.

The musician Gottlieb Graupner arrives in Boston from Germany via Canada and South Carolina. As a performer, teacher, author, and promoter, he becomes the leading figure in bringing "modern," secular music to Boston.

1799

The Mount Vernon Proprietors reject Bulfinch's plan for a residential area on Beacon Hill and adopt one by Mather Withington instead.

Nathaniel Bowditch's revision of the English book *The Practical Navigator* is published. He is said to have corrected eight thousand errors that appeared in the original edition.
William Tewksbury moves to Deer Island. By 1825 he and his family would be credited with saving thirty-one lives from shipwrecks.

A group of citizens successfully protests a plan to construct a gun house on Boston Common. The action is later called one of the first environmental protection efforts in the United States.

Hannah Adams's *A Summary History of New England* is published.

April 1. The first election is held in which votes are counted by wards.
July 31. President John Adams visits Boston, and a reception is held in his honor.
December 24. News of the death of George Washington reaches Boston. Church bells toll all day.

May 10. Charles Bulfinch is appointed the first superintendent of police. His salary in the job allows him to continue as the unpaid chairman of the Board of Selectmen. At the time, the police force consists of twelve constables and twenty watchmen.

February 13. The Boston Board of Health is established, the first such board in America. Its duties are "to examine into all Nuisances & other causes injurious to the Health of the Inhabitants . . . and order such Nuisances to be removed." Paul Revere is the first president. Authority for health matters is transferred from the Board of Health to the mayor and aldermen in 1822. They appoint the city's first health commissioner on May 1, 1824.

$

October 6. The Boston Committee of Safety publishes the names of sixteen hatters fined for charging more than the fixed price of thirty-five shillings for a hat.

The merchant Elias Haskett Derby dies, leaving what is reportedly the largest private fortune in the United States up to that time.

1800

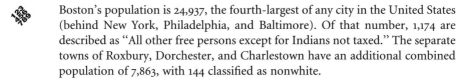

Boston's population is 24,937, the fourth-largest of any city in the United States (behind New York, Philadelphia, and Baltimore). Of that number, 1,174 are described as "All other free persons except for Indians not taxed." The separate towns of Roxbury, Dorchester, and Charlestown have an additional combined population of 7,863, with 144 classified as nonwhite.

Grove Hall is built as a country house for Thomas Kilby Jones at the corner of Blue Hill Avenue and Washington Street in Roxbury. It later becomes a summer hotel, then a hospital and a sanitarium, and is destroyed by a fire in July 1898.

(ca.) No. 44 Hull Street is built in the North End. Only ten feet wide, it is the narrowest building in the town and is said to have been constructed solely to block the view of a neighbor. It remains in use today.

June 17. The Charlestown Navy Yard opens at Moulton's Point. The yard is used not only to build new ships, but also to repair and convert existing ships belonging to the U.S. Navy. The first ship launched there is the USS *Frolic* in 1813. The first wharf is completed that same year, and various wharves, buildings, and barracks are added thereafter. The federal government closes Charlestown Navy Yard in 1974. Part of it is later included in the Boston National Historic Park.

April 23. A satirical article in the *Centinel* describes the various types of beaux in Boston: "the Frenchified American beau, the dapper beau, the college beau," and even "the shopkeeper beau."

June 2. The Boston Municipal Court is established with William Minot presiding as the first judge. Its name is changed to Boston Superior Court on July 2, 1866.

November. The Boston Musical Academy is established. The first music school in Boston, it is founded by Gottlieb Graupner, Francis Mallet, and Filipo Trajetta. The partners quarrel, however, and the school closes in 1802.

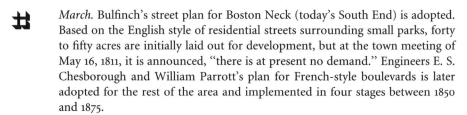

1801 to 1825

1801

March. Bulfinch's street plan for Boston Neck (today's South End) is adopted. Based on the English style of residential streets surrounding small parks, forty to fifty acres are initially laid out for development, but at the town meeting of May 16, 1811, it is announced, "there is at present no demand." Engineers E. S. Chesborough and William Parrott's plan for French-style boulevards is later adopted for the rest of the area and implemented in four stages between 1850 and 1875.

The General Court orders Boston to maintain a continuous night watch. An ordinance is passed naming the first selectman (and later the mayor) superintendent of police.

(ca.) James Marston's painting *The Old State House and State Street* is completed.

1802

The second Harrison Gray Otis House, designed by Bulfinch, is completed at 85 Mount Vernon Street. One of the only freestanding mansions on Beacon Hill, it serves as the fictional residence for the eponymous hero of the 1968 movie *The Thomas Crown Affair.*
A Federal-style mansion called Pinebank is built as a summer house for the China trade merchant James Perkins at Jamaica Pond. It burns down in 1848 and is replaced by a second Pinebank, designed by Jean Lemoulnier in the mansard style, for James's son Edward Newton Perkins. After another fire in 1868, the third Pinebank, designed by Sturgis and Brigham, is completed in 1870. Acquired by the city in 1892, it serves as headquarters of the Parks Department, becomes the home of the Children's Museum from 1913 to 1936, and then is used again by the Parks Department and the Pinebank Center for the Arts in 1975. It is closed after another fire in 1978.

Nathaniel Bowditch's *The New American Practical Navigator* is published. Although it is over five hundred pages long and its formulas take as many as four hours to compute, the book is welcomed because it enables navigators to establish longitude and ascertain positions to within twelve miles.

The Board of Health orders vaccination against smallpox, imposes quarantines, and takes steps to improve sanitation and hygiene in the town.

$ Amos Upham opens a store in a Federal-style house at the corner of Dudley, Stoughton, and Boston Streets in Dorchester, later called Uphams Corner. It is replaced by a commercial building in 1884.

February 8. Thousands of people pay twenty-five cents each to see a leopard at the Columbian Museum.

1803

The leveling of Mount Vernon begins. The destruction of the former "red light district" had prompted one of the Mount Vernon Proprietors, Jonathan Mason, to write to another, Harrison Gray Otis: "We are contracting to pull down Copley Hill, or to speak with mere chasteness, Mt. Whoredom. If you should not in the future resort to it with the same pleasure, you may possibly with more profit." Much of the work is done using a gravity railroad, the first railroad in the United States, developed, according to some accounts, by Silas Whitney, and according to others by a Mr. Sargent or a Mr. Hunt. The material deposited at the bottom of the hill creates the first half of Charles Street. The leveling is completed in 1805.

A group of businessmen (including Gardiner Green, Jonathan Mason, Harrison Gray Otis, and William Tudor) begin development of the South Boston peninsula, and petition for annexation by Boston on condition that a bridge be built. Their attempt is criticized by the *Boston Chronicle* in January 1804. It warns, "a few chattering lawyers in combination with men who are able to monopolize every dollar in the banks, will henceforth generate project after project . . . and under a pretended act of generosity will eventually bear down every opposition to their plans."

The Middlesex Canal opens. Engineered by Loammi Baldwin, the twenty-seven-mile, sixteen-lock canal runs between Boston and Billerica, enabling boats to bring goods such as textiles and Chelmsford granite from the Merrimack Valley directly into Boston Harbor. The canal is later extended to Concord, New Hampshire, but its importance decreases after the development of railroads. The last boat passes through the canal in April 1852.

March 22. Robert Pierpoint and Abiel Story are ordered to stand in the pillory at State Street for destroying a vessel to defraud an insurance company.

September 29. The Church of the Holy Cross, the first Catholic Church built in Boston, is dedicated at today's 214 Devonshire Street. Bulfinch donated the plans and a number of distinguished Protestants, including John Quincy Adams, contributed toward its construction. The church becomes a cathedral in 1808, closes in 1860, is torn down in 1868, and is replaced in 1875.*

$ John Perkins Cushing, the sixteen-year-old nephew of Thomas Handasyd Perkins, sails from Boston for China. Perkins arrives at Whampoa on January 1, 1804, and quickly establishes a close relationship with the Chinese merchant Houqua, later described as the richest man in the world. The Perkins Company trades furs, ginseng, cash, cotton, and, beginning in 1816 through the Sturgis

India and Central Wharves, with the Norris and Baxter dining saloon in the foreground, 1857. (Courtesy of the Bostonian Society)

Company, opium, for Chinese tea, silks, and porcelain. Boston men dominate the China trade until it declines in the 1830s.

Peter Brooks retires from the marine insurance business at the age of thirty-six. Said to be Boston's first millionaire, he declares that he has made enough money "to turn any man's head."

 November. The first issue of the *Monthly Anthology, or Magazine of Polite Literature* appears. It is published by the Anthology Society, founded by Rev. William Emerson and others, which is incorporated on October 17, 1805.

1804

 March 6. Dorchester Neck is annexed to Boston. Renamed South Boston, the addition increases the size of the town by 795 acres. The area is slow to attract residents, however. The architectural historian Walter Kilham later writes that the failure of fashionable Bostonians to flock to "the breezy hills of South Boston with their splendid marine views is one of the unsolved questions in Boston's history."

May. The filling of Front Street, today's Harrison Avenue, begins. Carried out by the Front Street Corporation, it is completed in 1805.

India Wharf, built by Francis Cabot Lowell, is completed. The wharf buildings are completed in 1807. Part of the wharf is torn down in 1962, and it is today the site of Harbor Towers.

 The Thomas Amory House is completed at 9 Park Street. Designed by Charles Bulfinch for a wealthy merchant, it is the largest house in Boston at the time.

After Amory goes bankrupt, the house becomes a boardinghouse for politicians. It is divided in half in 1806. The Harvard historian George Ticknor occupies the southern half and compiles there the largest private library in the United States at the time.

Bulfinch's Nichols House is completed at 55 Mount Vernon Street. Eventually the home of the landscape architect Rose Standish Nichols, it becomes, upon her death there in 1960, the only private residential museum on Beacon Hill.

October 9. The "Great Gale," described as a "snow hurricane," strikes the town and blows down the steeple of the Old North Church.

Hannah Adams's *The Truth and Excellence of the Christian Religion Exhibited* is published.

Miss Beach's Academy opens on Meetinghouse Hill in Dorchester. A private school for girls founded by Clementina Beach and Judith Saunders, it continues until 1846.

1805

The Broad Street Associates begin to fill Broad and India Streets, under the direction of Uriah Cotting. As a result of the development, the waterfront area has wide streets and large warehouses, which are completed in 1807.

The John Phillips House, designed by Charles Bulfinch, is built at 1 Walnut Street on Beacon Hill. The home of Boston's first mayor, it is also the birthplace of his son, the abolitionist Wendell Phillips, who later writes: "Boston boys had reason to be thankful for their birth right. . . . the noble deeds and sacred places of the old town are the poetry of history and the keenest ripeners of character."

(ca.) The John Hawes House is built at today's 568 E. Fifth Street in South Boston. It is today the oldest house in the area.

October 1. The South Bridge (also called the Dover Street Bridge) opens, connecting Dover Street to South Boston. It becomes such a popular place for lovers to stroll that Josiah Quincy, Jr., later dubs it "the Bridge of Sighs." Originally a toll bridge, it is sold to the city and opens for free travel in 1833. The bridge is rebuilt in 1857, 1877, 1894, and 2002.

The Milton Turnpike (later called Dorchester Avenue) opens, connecting Boston to Lower Mills. Initially a toll road, it becomes a public way in 1852.

April 15. John Nichols becomes the last man to stand in the town's pillory on King Street (today's State Street). Convicted of counterfeiting, he is confined for one hour.

December. Charlestown State Prison opens. Designed by Bulfinch and modeled after the Paris Bastille, it is enlarged by Alexander Parris, Gridley J. F. Bryant, and Louis Dwight in 1809, 1826, and 1850, respectively. Insane inmates are transferred to Worcester in 1844, and aged and infirm inmates to Bridgewater in 1901. The facility is condemned in 1878, but reopens in 1884. It finally closes in 1956 and is torn down in 1957.

The Boston Medical Library is founded. Located initially in rented rooms at 19 Boylston Place, it moves to its own building at 8 The Fenway in 1901. For many years the only independent medical library in the United States, it merges with the Countway Library of Harvard Medical School in 1936.

Gilbert Stuart returns from Europe to Boston, where he lives until his death twenty years later. Born in Rhode Island, he is the premiere portrait painter of the time. "He seemed," the painter Washington Allston later writes, "to dive into the thoughts of men; for they were made to rise and speak on the surface." Stuart did not feel appreciated in Boston, however. He called it a cage, and complained that "a grocer will make more by buying a cargo of molasses in a day than my labor can make in a year."
The Roxbury Public Library is established. Reorganized as the Social Library in 1831 and the Roxbury Athenaeum in 1848, it merges with the Fellowes Athenaeum (established in 1866) in 1873, and later becomes part of the Boston Public Library system.

1806

March 10. Faneuil Hall reopens. Designed by Charles Bulfinch and built of brick, it is is twice the size of its wooden predecessor and includes an added third floor. It serves as one of Boston's most important meeting places ever since and is restored in 1992.
The William Clapp House is built in Dorchester. Enlarged in 1839, it is acquired by the Dorchester Historical Society in 1945.

March 1. The town adopts a system of fines for fast driving.
August 4. The "Bloody Monday" killing occurs. The attorney Benjamin Austin, Jr., is shot and killed by another attorney, Thomas Selfridge, in the middle of State Street. Their dispute had to do with payment of a bill, as well as tensions between Federalists and Republicans. Charged with manslaughter, Selfridge is acquitted on the grounds of justifiable homicide.

April 16. A total eclipse of the sun is witnessed by the residents of Boston.

March 1. Jenny Bancroft reportedly causes "a revival of witchcraft excitement" and is ordered to leave the town.
December 6. The First African Baptist Church, later renamed the African Meeting House, is dedicated on today's Smith Court on Beacon Hill. It is built almost exclusively by African-American labor. Cato Gardner led the fundraising efforts, which produced contributions from both the black and white communities. The congregation had been formed the year before and met in Faneuil Hall. Thomas Paul is the first pastor. The building is renovated in 1855, then sold to the Anshei Libovitz congregation of Hasidic Jews in 1898. Purchased by the Museum of Afro-American History in 1972, it is restored and reopened as a museum on January 31, 1988.

The African Meeting House, at Smith Court at Joy Street. Photograph by Josiah J. Hawes, ca. 1860. (Courtesy of the Bostonian Society)

There are 1,760 students in the Boston public schools—1,030 boys and 730 girls.

February 13. The Favorite, packed with 130 tons of ice, sails from Boston for the West Indies. The Boston businessman Frederic Tudor's venture is derided in Boston newspapers as a "slippery one" in which "his assets will perceptibly melt away." By the 1830s, however, Tudor is dubbed the "Ice King," and fifty thousand tons of ice are being shipped annually from Tudor Wharf in Charleston to destinations as far away as Calcutta and Rio de Janeiro. The industry eventually does "melt away," however, after the invention of ice-making machinery in the 1860s.

July 4. The Independence Day celebration on Boston Common includes a fight between a man and a bear.

1807

February 24. Brighton incorporates as a town separate from Cambridge.
Independence Wharf, begun in 1803, is completed.
The filling of Mill Pond begins, eventually creating the area known today as the Bulfinch Triangle. The filling is completed in 1828.

The Peter Trott House is built at 37 Bennett Street. It is today the oldest building in today's Chinatown.

October 9. The Worcester Turnpike, later renamed Route 9, is completed.

The Third Baptist Church, designed by Asher Benjamin, later called the Charles Street Meeting House, opens on Charles Street. Speakers from its pulpit would include Frederick Douglass, William Lloyd Garrison, Wendell Phillips, Harriet Tubman, and Sojourner Truth. The building is sold to the Charles Street A.M.E. Church in 1876, to the Charles Street Meeting House Society in 1939, and to the Universalist Church of America in 1948. The architect John Sharratt purchases and renovates the building for commercial and residential use in 1982.

South Boston residents establish and support their own school. The Boston School Committee does not provide support until 1811.

December. President Thomas Jefferson's Embargo Act goes into effect. Since more than one-third of British imports pass through the Port of Boston, the law hurts the town financially. Some Boston merchants petition the president to end the embargo; others ignore the law.

February 13. The Boston Athenaeum, founded by members of the Anthology Society, is incorporated. The first reading room opens in Joy's Building on Congress Street on January 1, 1807. The private library moves to Scollay's Buildings on Congress Street, to the Rufus Amory House on Tremont Street in 1809, to the James Perkins House on Pearl Street in 1822, then to its current location on Beacon Street in 1849.*

1808

Violence breaks out between African-American residents celebrating the end of slavery in Massachusetts and white residents. The first serious racial incident in Boston, it reportedly had as much to do with turf issues as racial issues.

The Exchange Coffee House opens at the corner of today's State and Congress Streets. The first and most luxurious hotel in the United States, it is destroyed by a fire on November 3, 1818. Rebuilt on a smaller scale, it reopens on January 8, 1822. The first floor is converted to a tavern, which closes on April 1, 1854, and the building is torn down shortly thereafter.

January 1. The Second Church in Dorchester is dedicated and eventually becomes the oldest Congregational meetinghouse still in use in Boston. John Codman is the first pastor.
April 18. Jean-Louis Lefebvre de Cheverus is appointed the first Catholic bishop of Boston. Accepting the post after Father Matignon refuses the honor, Cheverus is installed on November 1, 1810.

The Massachusetts Medical Society publishes *Pharmacopeia*. It is the forerunner of the *Pharmacopeia of the United States*, which is published in 1820.

1809

August 30. The Canal (later the Craigie) Bridge opens, connecting Barton's Point in Boston to Lechmere Point in Cambridge. Originally a toll bridge, it is made a free bridge on February 1, 1858.

December 30. Masquerade balls are forbidden by the selectmen.

 February 5. Responding to complaints from citizens, the selectmen forbid fishmongers to blow their horns in the street to attract customers.

 January 23. Boston Harbor is blockaded as part of the British retaliatory embargo. The United States' embargo is repealed in March, but is replaced by the Non-Intercourse Act, which also curbs trade. As a result, the city's merchants develop trade relationships with Southern planters, which the historian Samuel Eliot Morison later describes as "the marriage of wharf and waterfall."

Cyrus Alger establishes a foundry in South Boston in partnership with a General Winslow. He starts his own company, the Alger Iron Works, in 1814. The company manufactures much of the weaponry used in the War of 1812, and it incorporates as the South Boston Iron Works in 1827.

 The Boston "Philo-harmonic Society" is established. Called by some the first orchestra in Boston, and possibly in the United States, it is actually more of a social organization where members meet, practice, and play music together on Saturday evenings. Founded by Gottlieb Graupner, the society performs its first concert in 1818 and continues playing until at least 1824.

1810

 Boston's population is 33,787, the fourth-largest in the United States (behind New York, Philadelphia, and Baltimore), with 1,468 classified as nonwhite. The separate towns of Roxbury, Dorchester, Charlestown, and Brighton have an additional combined population of 12,166, with 165 people classified as nonwhite.

 The Suffolk County Court House (also known as Johnson Hall), designed by Charles Bulfinch, opens on School Street. The octagonal building serves as City Hall from 1841 to 1862, then is torn down to make way for a new City Hall (now referred to as Old City Hall).

The Boylston Market, designed by Charles Bulfinch, opens at Washington and Boylston Streets. The upstairs hall becomes home to the Handel and Haydn Society for twenty-two years. The building is torn down in 1888.

Bulfinch's Colonnade Row, a series of brick town houses, is built along Tremont Street between West and Mason Streets.

 The Bunker Hill Burying Ground is established in Charlestown.

The South Burying Ground is established on Washington Street in the South End.

 The Board of Aldermen prohibits balls, according to the *Independent Chronicle*, because they are "uncongenial to the habits and manners of the citizens of this place."

 Two pirates are sentenced to be hanged at Boston Neck. A third is issued a reprieve on the gallows and later becomes a preacher.

January 10. The Park Street Church is dedicated. Designed by Peter Banner, it is the first Trinitarian-Congregationalist church in Boston. It is later called Brimstone Corner, owing either to the gunpowder stored in the basement during the War of 1812, or to the fiery sermons delivered by ministers such as Rev. Lyman Beecher. The building is restored between 1983 and 1986.

May 10. The first Promenade and Concert is held at the Exchange Coffee House. The series is performed every two weeks over the course of the summer. A new series is offered in 1811, which features the panharmonicon, described as "Wind Instruments [that] go by a most perfect mechanism, and with such exactness as to excite the greatest astonishment."

1811

February. Roxbury Town Hall opens. Thought to have been designed by Asher Benjamin, it is built on land donated by and located on the estate of Col. Joseph Dudley. The building later serves as Roxbury's city hall, then as a school. It is torn down to make way for construction of the Dudley School in 1873.

The town requires all trucks and sleds to be numbered and registered.

July. Charles Bulfinch spends a month in jail for failure to pay his bills.

February 25. Massachusetts General Hospital is chartered by the state. Its creation was sparked by Drs. James Jackson and John Collins Warren, who wrote a letter advocating construction of a hospital for "lunatics and other sick persons . . . one which would afford relief and comfort to thousands of the sick and miserable." A psychiatric hospital opens in 1816* and a general hospital in 1821.*

The first news agency in America is established in Boston. It provides news items for weekly newspapers, much of it gathered from coffeehouses where current events are discussed.

Nathaniel Dearborn introduces wood engraving to Boston.

1812

June 18. The United States declares itself to be at war with Britain, and the War of 1812 begins. News of the declaration reaches Boston on June 24.
Dorchester Heights is fortified against attack, and the British blockade Boston Harbor.
To identify true Bostonians from possible spies, guards ask soldiers and sailors what flies over Faneuil Hall, expecting the answer to be "a grasshopper."
August 30. The return of the USS *Constitution* from its victory over the British frigate *Guerrière* is celebrated.

August 13. The first captain of the Boston Night Watch is appointed. (It was previously supervised by constables.) The name of the office is changed to city marshal on May 30, 1823; to chief of police on June 24, 1852; and to superintendent in 1878.*

November 25. A petition signed by a number of residents protests the use of Boston Common for executions.

The first issue of the *New England Journal of Medicine* appears. Originally called *The New England Journal of Medicine and Surgery and the Collateral Branches of Science*, it is published by the Massachusetts Medical Society. The magazine merges with the *Boston Medical and Surgical Journal* and assumes its current title in 1828.

May 29. Oliver Barrett gives a demonstration of his new spinning machine at the State House.

March 26. The term "gerrymander" is coined. The *Boston Gazette* cartoonist Gilbert Smart draws a picture of the new state senate district in Essex County in the shape of a salamander. Because Gov. Elbridge Gerry had persuaded the legislature to create the district to favor his Republican Party, the newspaper's editor, Elkanah Tisdale, exclaims: "Better call it a Gerrymander."

1813

June 1. The British frigate *Shannon* defeats the U.S. frigate *Chesapeake* off Boston Light. The American vessel is captured despite the order issued to the crew by its captain, James Lawrence: "Don't give up the ship." Lawrence dies soon after the ship's capture.

Richmond Hall is built at today's 1111–1113 Washington Street in Dorchester.

Francis Cabot Lowell opens a textile mill on a dam across the Charles River between Newton and Waltham. A power loom begins operation in the fall of 1814. The first textile factory in the world in which all operations are carried out, it is credited with beginning the industrial revolution in America. Lowell had toured textile mills in England and Scotland in 1810, memorized their design, and worked with the mechanic Paul Moody to build this one.

March 3. The first issue of the *Boston Advertiser* appears. It is the first successful daily newspaper in Boston. William Warland Clapp is publisher, and Horatio Bigelow, editor. The newspaper is acquired by Nathan Hale in 1814, and takes over five older newspapers in 1840. The newspaper moves to Washington Street in 1883 and moves off Newspaper Row in 1902. After starting a new paper, the *American* in 1904, William Randolph Hearst purchases the *Advertiser* in 1917 and the *Record* in 1921. By 1938, the names of the three papers are changed to the *Sunday Advertiser*, the *Daily Record*, and the *Evening American*. Two of the papers merge into the tabloid *Record-American* in 1961. The *Sunday Advertiser* becomes a tabloid in 1964 and ceases publication in 1972.

1814

June 14. The Boston and Roxbury Mill Dam Corporation is incorporated. It is formed by Uriah Cotting and others to construct dams across the Back Bay to power a proposed eighty-one mills (only a few are ever built). Some oppose the plan, including a citizen who writes a column in the *Advertiser* criticizing the idea of "converting the beautiful sheet of water which skirts the Common into an empty mud basin, reeking with filth, abhorrent to the smell, and distasteful to the eye." Still seeking financing, Cotting defends the plan in a pamphlet in 1818, declaring: "ERECT THESE MILLS, AND LOWER THE PRICE OF BREAD. If the public do not have all these improvements it will not be the fault of URIAH COTTING."

The Dorchester South Burying Ground is established.

April 10. A British fleet is reportedly sighted off the coast, causing great excitement in the town. On September 16, the selectmen make plans for what to do in case of a British attack. One of the strategies calls for blowing up the four bridges that connect the town to the mainland.
December 15. The Hartford Convention opens. Attended by delegates from the five New England states opposed to the war with Great Britain (including Bostonians representing Massachusetts), secession is discussed. The Treaty of Ghent is signed, ending the war, on December 24, before the convention is adjourned on January 5, 1815.

March 22. The Home for Indigent Boys is established on Phips Place. It moves to Thompson Island in 1835.

The selectmen note "disorderly conduct . . . occasioned by a number of Spanish sailors and the sailors from the *Constitution* frigate assembling at West Boston" and request Captain Stewart "to order his men on board at sunset every evening."
The Massachusetts Social Law Library is incorporated. Established by Theophilus Parsons and others in 1804, it is initially made up of a few books collected for use by the town's handful of lawyers. Originally located in the courthouse at Court Square, the library moves to the new Old Suffolk County Court House in Pemberton Square in 1893.

The New South Church is built on Church Green. Designed by Charles Bulfinch, it is torn down to make way for a commercial building in 1868.

W. and A. Bacon opens at 2193 Washington Street in Roxbury. The oldest dry goods store in Boston by 1900, its motto is "Your Grandmother Traded Here." The Dedham Manufacturing Company opens. Built by James Read in today's Readville section of Hyde Park, it is later destroyed by fire and replaced by the current brick building, the second-oldest textile mill in the United States (after the Old Slater Mill in Pawtucket, Rhode Island). The company is later known as the Readville Cotton-Mill, the Smithfield Manufacturing Company, and then the B. B. and R. Cotton Mill.

Nathaniel Dearborn introduces a new process of printing in colors in Boston.

1815

Woodland Hills is built for Benjamin Bussey in Jamaica Plain. Located on what had been Capt. John Weld's farm, the mansion includes an 18,000-volume library. After Bussey's death in 1843, it becomes the home of Thomas Motley, brother of the historian John Lothrop Motley. Much of the grounds are bequeathed to Harvard College for what later becomes the Arnold Arboretum.

The Prison Point Bridge opens, connecting Charlestown to Cambridge from a point near the end of the Craigie Bridge.

February 13. News of the end of the War of 1812 reaches Boston, prompting a celebration in the streets. "Peace ratified; Federalists gratified; Democrats mortified" becomes a popular slogan. The celebration includes the town's first musical festival, featuring works by Handel and Haydn, on February 16, and a general illumination and peace ball on February 22.

When Charles Bulfinch fails to win reelection to the Board of Selectmen, the other members refuse to take their seats until a new election is held and he is reelected.

September 23. The Great September Gale strikes Boston.

The first naval officers' training school in the country is established in Boston. Directed by Comdr. William Bainbridge, it predates the Naval Academy at Annapolis by thirty years.

May. The first issue of the *North American Review* appears. Originally called the *North American Review and Miscellaneous Journal*, it is founded by William Tudor and others. Jared Sparks is the first editor. The premiere magazine in the United States for many years, it moves to New York in the late 1870s, suspends publication in 1940, and resumes publication at the University of Northern Iowa in 1968.

April 20. The Handel and Haydn Society is organized. The second oldest musical society in the country (after the Stoughton Musical Society) and the oldest oratorio society, it is incorporated in February 1816. In 1880 the music historian John Sullivan Dwight explains: "The membership has always been confined to the male sex. The ladies sing by invitation." The society's first concert—by a chorus made up of ninety men and ten women—is a performance of Haydn's *Creation* before a crowd of a thousand people at King's Chapel on December 24.

1816

The Greek Revival–style Dorchester Town Hall is completed in Codman (originally called Baker) Square. After Dorchester's annexation by Boston in 1870, it is used for meetings by a number of groups and for amateur theater productions. The building is torn down to make way for the construction of the Great Hall, which houses the Dorchester branch of the Boston Public Library, in 1904. After the library moves in 1975, the building is taken over by the Codman Square Health Center in 1982, and it is restored as a community meeting place in 1994.

The Hawes Burying Ground is consecrated in South Boston. It merges with the Union Cemetery in 1841.

June 8. Snow falls in Boston during what is called the "Year without a Summer," in which frost is reported in every month.
Jonathan Winship establishes a nursery in Brighton. A founder of the Massachusetts Historical Society, he expands the business and is later joined in it by his brother Francis.

The Female Society of Boston and the Vicinity for Promoting Christianity Among the Jews is founded by Hannah Adams.

October 6. McLean Hospital opens in Charlestown, in an area that today is part of Somerville. Originally the psychiatric wing of Massachusetts General Hospital, it is later named after a local merchant, John McLean, who bequeathed much of his estate to the institution. The hospital moves to a campus in Belmont designed by Frederick Law Olmsted in 1895.

January 3. The first issue of the *Boston Recorder* appears. The first anti-Catholic newspaper in Boston, it is founded by Nathaniel Willis to fight "Popery" and "Romanism." It is joined in this effort by the *Boston Watchman* in 1819.

1817

Central Wharf, designed by Charles Bulfinch, is constructed. It is described enthusiastically as "a proof of the enterprize, the wealth, and persevering Industry of Bostonians." Much of the wharf is torn down in the 1960s to make way for the New England Aquarium.
Charles Shaw's *A Topographical and Historical Description of Boston* is published.

Rev. James Davis describes the north slope of Beacon Hill, where "five and twenty or thirty shops are opened on Lord's days from morning to evening and ardent spirits are retailed without restraint . . . whole nights are spent drinking and carousing. . . . Here in this one compact section of the town, it is confidently affirmed and fully believed, there are three hundred females wholly devoid of shame and modesty."

March 13. Henry Phillips is hanged on Boston Neck for murder. The execution is described thus: "After the cap was drawn over his eyes he sang a song of three verses, dropped the handkerchief, and was launched into eternity."

William McDonough, accused of killing his wife while drunk, pleads not guilty by reason of insanity. Reportedly the first to use that defense in U.S. history, McDonough is found guilty and hanged.

Daniel Darby, a shoemaker, makes the first use of illuminating gas in Boston in his shop on Devonshire Street.

February 19. The Provident Institution for Savings opens in the Court House. The second savings bank in the United States, it was incorporated on December 13, 1816. It later moves to 30 Tremont Street, then to the former home of Thomas Perkins on Temple Place in 1856.

October. The first annual Brighton Fair and Cattle Show is held. Sponsored by the Massachusetts Agricultural Society, it continues until 1835.

December 25. Lt. Robert Massie is killed in a dual by Lt. Gustavus Drane at Fort Independence on Castle Island, following a dispute during a card game. According to legend, fellow soldiers avenge Massie's death by getting Drane drunk, placing him in chains, and walling him up inside a dungeon. The tale later inspires Edgar Allan Poe, who is stationed at Fort Independence in 1827, to write the short story "The Cask of Amontillado." In fact, Drane is court-martialed, acquitted, marries a Boston woman, and dies in Philadelphia in 1846. Massie's grave on Castle Island is later moved to Fort Devens.

1818

January. Charles Bulfinch leaves Boston after he is appointed architect of the Capitol Building by President James Monroe.

The Greek Revival Agricultural Hall is built at 54 Dighton Street in Brighton. The oldest public building in today's Brighton, it is built by the Massachusetts Society for the Promotion of Agriculture and serves as the Brighton Agricultural Fair's central exhibition hall until 1835. The building is moved to its current location at 360 Washington Street and is converted into the Scales Hotel in 1844.

(ca.) Purple windows are installed in homes on Beacon Hill sometime between 1818 and 1824. Glass shipped from England for the King's Chapel Parish House at 63–64 Beacon Street arrives with a purple hue due to a transformation of manganese oxide. Today only this house and those at 39 and 40 Beacon Street and 29A and 70B Walnut Street retain windows from that shipment of glass.

May 20. A shower of small fish falls from the sky near the Frog Pond, creating a "sensation" in the town.

July 4. St. Augustine's Chapel and Cemetery are dedicated at Dorchester and Tudor Streets in South Boston. The oldest existing Catholic church in Boston, it is built as a mortuary chapel for the remains of Father François Matignon. An enlarged chapel is built and dedicated as a parish church on October 16, 1831, and the current church is built in 1868. The cemetery is the first Catholic burying ground in New England.

(ca.) The Charles Street A.M.E. Church is established. The congregation buys the Third Baptist Church (later renamed the Charles Street Meeting House) in 1876, then moves to the former St. Angarius Church. The congregation marches together to its new church at 551 Warren Street in Roxbury in April 1939.

 Primary schools—with female instructors—for children ages four to seven are established to prepare students for the writing (elementary) schools. A Primary School Committee is established, consisting of thirty-six members (three from each ward), to supervise these schools. The committee turns over its responsibilities to the Boston School Committee in 1854.

 October. The painter Washington Allston returns to Boston from Europe. A native of South Carolina and and a graduate of Harvard, he left Boston for Europe in 1801, returned briefly about 1809–1810, and now returns to stay, declaring, "If we have any talents we owe something to our own country when she is disposed to foster them." His painting *Elijah in the Desert* is completed this year and becomes the first painting donated to the Museum of Fine Arts, in 1871.

December 25. The Handel and Haydn Society performs its first complete oratorio, the American premiere of Handel's *Messiah*. The society would perform the work annually beginning in 1854.

1819

 The Col. David Sears House, designed by Alexander Parris, is completed at 42 Beacon Street, on the site of John Singleton Copley's former home. The left half of the building and a third story are added in 1832, and the building becomes the home of the Somerset Club in 1872.

 In a letter, *North American Review* founder William Tudor is the first to describe Boston as "The Athens of America."

 August 16. Two sentries report sighting a sea serpent swim past Castle Island. Their superior, Colonel Harris, verifies the sighting, as does a resident, James Prince, who later describes the creature thus: "His head appeared about three feet out of the water; I counted thirteen bunches on his back—my family thought there were fifteen—he passed three times at a moderate rate across the bay. . . . I had seven distinct views of him from the long beach so called, and at some of them the animal was not more than a hundred yards distance."

 May 5. William Ellery Channing preaches the "Baltimore Sermon," an attempt to define Unitarian Christianity, at the installation of Rev. Jared Sparks in Baltimore.

1820

Boston's population is 43,298, the fourth-largest in the United States (behind New York, Philadelphia, and Baltimore). Of that number, 1,690 are classified as nonwhite. The separate towns of Roxbury, Dorchester, Charlestown, and Brighton have an additional combined population of 15,112, with 97 classified as nonwhite.

The Missouri Compromise is passed by Congress. In addition to admitting Maine into the Union as a free state separate from Massachusetts and Missouri as a slave state, the law prohibits slavery above thirty-six degrees, thirty minutes north latitude.

Josiah Quincy heads a state committee that recommends an end to "outdoor relief" for the poor and its replacement with almshouses.

April 26. The Siloam Lodge no. 2 is organized. The second Odd Fellows Lodge in America, it is also the second fraternal organization established in Boston, preceded only by the Masons.

June 16. The Ursuline Convent opens next to the Cathedral of the Holy Cross on Franklin Street. It later moves to Charlestown and is destroyed by a fire in 1834.*

June 30. St. Paul's Episcopal Church is dedicated. Designed by Alexander Parris and Solomon Willard for a congregation established in 1818, the church is made Boston's Episcopal cathedral in October 1912, and consecrated October 7, 1918. The building is remodeled by Ralph Adams Cram between 1913 and 1927.

April 1. The first issue of the *Euterpeiad* or *Musical Intelligencer: Devoted to the Diffusion of Musical Information and Belles Lettres* appears. The first successful music periodical in the United States, it is published by Thomas Badger, Jr., and edited by John Rowe Parker. It continues publication until June 1823.

1821

July 2. The Mill Dam Bridge connecting Charles Street to Sewall's Point in Brookline is completed. Work had begun in 1818. The road that runs across it is called Western Avenue. A toll road until December 1865, it is renamed Beacon Street on April 21, 1857 (Oliver Wendell Holmes, Sr., later described it as "the sunny street that holds the sifted few"). A smaller cross dam to Gravelly Point in Roxbury (running roughly along the route of today's Parker and Hemenway Streets) is later constructed. Although the dams enable the construction of mills, they also cause stagnant water and debris to collect and a healthy population of frogs, which one visitor described as "a foot high, and some as long as a child one year old."

The First Baptist Church in Roxbury opens; William Leverett is the first pastor. Members of the congregation are baptized in the nearby Stony Brook. The congregation becomes the Dudley Street Baptist Church and builds a new church near Warren Street in 1852. It merges with the Centre Street Baptist Church and becomes the United Baptist Church in 1967.

Looking west from the cupola of the State House toward Back Bay and the Mill Dam, 1863. (Courtesy of the Bostonian Society)

May. The English High School opens on Derne Street on Beacon Hill. The first free public high school in America, it is led by George Emerson, the first headmaster. Intended for "furnishing young men of the City who are not intended for a collegiate course of study . . . with the means of completing a good English education," it would count among its graduates the minister Louis Farrakhan, J. P. Morgan, Leonard Nimoy, and Louis Sullivan. The school moves to Pinckney Street in 1824, then to a shared building with Latin School, first on Bedford Street in 1844, then in the South End, dedicated in 1881.*

September 3. Massachusetts General Hospital's Bulfinch Pavilion opens at the corner of Blossom and Allen Streets in the West End. The third general hospital in the United States, it is now the oldest continuously used hospital building in the country. Two wings are added to the Bulfinch building in 1846. The George Robert White Memorial Building, designed by Coolidge, Shepley, Bulfinch, and Abbott and located on Fruit Street, is dedicated on October 16, 1939.

December. The Merrimack Manufacturing Company is formed by Bostonians Francis Cabot Lowell, his brother-in-law Patrick Tracy, and Nathaniel Appleton. Incorporated in February 1822, the company proceeds to build the largest dam in the world across the Merrimack River in 1848, and to construct mills in a town later named Lowell. The company also builds dormitories for its mostly female workers, who are treated so well that one, Harriet Robinson, later writes that the company introduced the notion that "corporations should have souls." However, Russell Adams later writes: "As major stockholders withdrew from active management of their companies, turning operations over to men whose primary mission was to crank out regular dividends—and never mind how—wage exploitation became common."

February 12. Edmund Kean makes his Boston debut at the Boston Theatre on Federal Street, appearing in a repertory that includes plays by Shakespeare. After a performance in *Richard III*, Kean receives what is thought to be the first curtain call in American theater history. However, when he returns to Boston in *King Lear* in May, he is displeased at the small audience and refuses to go onstage. The Boston theater audience remembers, and when he returns again in 1825, he is booed off the stage for his temperamental outburst four years earlier—and forced to flee in disguise back to New York.

1822

The city takes the area north of Broadway and east of L Street in South Boston for use as a prison, almshouse, and mental institution. The area becomes known as the City Lands.

January 7. After a number of unsuccessful attempts, Boston voters agree to apply for incorporation as a city (2,727 are in favor and 2,087 against). The Massachusetts legislature approves the measure and Gov. John Brooks signs it on February 23. Boston then votes to become a city (2,797 to 1,881) on March 4.
April 16. John Phillips is elected Boston's first mayor, receiving 2,456 of the 2,650 votes cast on the second ballot. A compromise candidate of the Federalist party, Phillips is elected after none of the original candidates (Josiah Quincy, Harrison Gray Otis, and Thomas Winthrop) received enough votes on the first ballot, on April 8.
May 1. Boston is incorporated as a city and the new charter goes into effect.
Mayor Phillips is inaugurated at Faneuil Hall. He retains his office as president of the Massachusetts Senate, spends most of his one-year term reorganizing city departments, and declines to run for reelection because of poor health.
The eight new members of the Board of Aldermen (elected at large), and forty-eight new members of the Common Council (four from each of the twelve wards) are also sworn into office at Faneuil Hall. They replace the nine selectmen who presided over the town meeting form of government.
Johnson Hall serves as City Hall until September 16, 1830; the Old State House from September 17, 1830, to March 18, 1841; Johnson Hall again from March 18, 1841, until January 9, 1863; and Mechanics Hall on Chauncy Street from January 10, 1863, until September 18, 1865.*

April. An ordinance is passed prohibiting people from smoking in the street on Sunday. The ordinance is expanded to weekdays in October 1829, but the law is not vigorously enforced until 1848.

June 20. The Boston Police Court is established. It becomes the Boston Municipal Court on July 2, 1866.
June 20. The Leverett Street Courthouse opens. It also become home to the Boston Municipal Court, which moves from School Street and then returns to Court Street in 1831.
Judge Josiah Quincy expresses an interest in "poverty, vice and crime," which he finds "little else than modifications of each other."

The Boston School Committee is reorganized. Under the new city charter, it is made up of twenty-one members (the mayor, the eight members of the Board of Aldermen, and one representative from each of the twelve wards).

The Boston Gas Light Company is founded. The second chartered gas company in a major U.S. city (after Baltimore in 1817), it opens its first gas operating plant on Copp's Hill in 1827. The company merges with several competitors to become the Boston Consolidated Gas Company in 1905, becomes Boston Gas Company in 1955, and is known as Keyspan today.

1823

The filling of the East Cove (also known as Great Cove) begins in today's Dock Square area. It is completed in 1874.

January 2. Boston's city seal is adopted. Designed by John Penniman, its motto is taken from 1 Kings 8.57: *Sicut patribus sit Deus nobis* ("God be with us as He was with our fathers"). It is followed by the inscription *Bostonia. Condita A.D. 1630. Civitatis regimine donata, A.D. 1822.*

April 14. The Federalist candidate Josiah Quincy (with 2,505 votes) defeats George Blake (with 2,180) and others to become mayor. He is a former congressman, state senator, speaker of the Massachusetts House, and judge, and would be elected to six consecutive one-year terms and later called the "great mayor." Known for rising before dawn every day to survey the city on horseback, Quincy reorganizes executive departments, leads police raids, establishes a regular sanitation and street-cleaning system, initiates the first municipal sewer system in the United States, and completes the first successful urban renewal project in 1826.*

Dr. John Collins Warren becomes president of the Massachusetts Society for the Suppression of Intemperance and persuades Mayor Quincy to prohibit the sale of alcohol in public places.

June 16. Benjamin Pollard, a Harvard graduate and lawyer, is appointed Boston's first city marshal. The police historian Roger Lane later notes that he employed "gentle tactics" in his law enforcement efforts. Pollard serves until his death in 1836.
Mayor Quincy orders dance hall fiddlers arrested and licenses taken away from taverns on Beacon Hill. The result, according to Whitehill, is that "Deprived at once of music and drink, the enemy succumbed to the authority of law without resistance."

December 1. When all the city's fire captains resign in a dispute, Mayor Quincy takes over their engines and staffs their companies with volunteers.

Boston's Catholic Bishop Cheverus is named bishop of Montauban, France. Two hundred leading citizens of Boston—all of them Protestant—protest his reassignment, declaring, "We hold him to be a blessing and a treasure in our social community, which we cannot part with, and if withdrawn from us, can never be replaced." Nevertheless, the appointment stands and Cheverus leaves Boston.

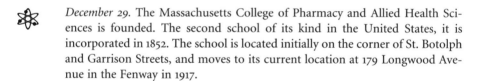

December 29. The Massachusetts College of Pharmacy and Allied Health Sciences is founded. The second school of its kind in the United States, it is incorporated in 1852. The school is located initially on the corner of St. Botolph and Garrison Streets, and moves to its current location at 179 Longwood Avenue in the Fenway in 1917.

William Austin's short story "Peter Rugg, the Missing Man" appears in an issue of the *New England Galaxy.* The story is set in 1770, and the hero is a man from Boston who, returning from Concord, is caught in a storm in Arlington and is unable to return home to his wife and daughter on Middle Road (today's Hanover Street). His ghost is reportedly sighted ever after.

Chickering and Sons Piano Company is established in a small shop on Tremont Street next to King's Chapel Burying Ground. Founded by Jonas Chickering, the company builds its first pianoforte (called "America's first gift of art to the world") this year, its first upright piano in 1830, and its first grand piano in 1833. The company later builds Chickering Hall at 152 Tremont Street, as well as a factory on Washington Street, which is replaced by a larger building in the South End in 1853.*

1824

The Boston Water Power Company is incorporated. It is given the right to purchase the water power created by the mills on the Mill Dam and acquires the mills and all the land south of the Mill Dam in 1832.

July 26. Residents vote to annex the land that would become the Public Garden to Boston Common, declaring that it would "forever after be kept open and free of buildings of any kind."

April 12. Josiah Quincy (with 3,867 votes) defeats all other candidates (with 83 votes all together) to be reelected mayor.

The Boston Female Reform Society is established. Founded for "the prevention of licentiousness," the organization later changes its name to the New England Moral Reform Society. It establishes a maternity home and hospital for unwed mothers in Jamaica Plain in 1869. Dr. Caroline Hastings becomes the hospital's first attending physician in 1871. The name is changed to the Hastings Home in 1948. It merges with the Crittenton Home in 1961.*

August 24. The Marquis de Lafayette visits Boston. Met at Boston Neck by the Boston Light Infantry and twelve hundred horsemen, he is escorted into Boston amid the firing of cannons and ringing of church bells. A number of streets, squares, and parks are named in his honor, including La Grange Street, named after his summer residence. At the same time, all the streets that make up today's Washington Street are combined under that name.

The Massachusetts Charitable Eye and Ear Infirmary is established. Founded by Drs. John Jeffries and Edward Reynolds, it is incorporated in 1826 and is located in various rented accommodations. Its first hospital building opens on Charles Street on November 1, 1849.

January 1. Russell and Company is established on India Wharf. It would handle much of the China trade that would reach Boston.
Kidder, Peabody and Company is founded by John Thayer. Henry Kidder joins in 1847, and the present name is adopted in 1865. Now the oldest private banking company in Boston, the firm receives a charter as a trust company in 1927.

December 15. The first issue of the *Norfolk Gazette* appears. The first newspaper in Roxbury, it is published by Allen and Weeks and continues until February 6, 1827.

Gilbert Stuart's painting of Mayor Josiah Quincy and Quincy Market is first exhibited.
Lydia Maria Child's *Hobomok*, a romantic novel, is published.

1825

The filling of the Church Street area begins. Carried out by individual property owners, it is completed in 1835.
Abel Bowen publishes the first plan for creating a filled-in Back Bay. His proposal calls for wide avenues and large buildings, but fails to attract significant interest.

October. The Erie Canal is completed, transforming New York into the major port in the United States, and as a result, diminishing Boston's importance. The previous February, the Massachusetts legislature had appointed a commission to "ascertain the practicability of making a canal from Boston Harbor to the Connecticut River" and "of extending the same to some point on the Hudson River . . . in the vicinity of the junction of the Erie Canal with that river." A survey is undertaken by the younger Col. Loammi Baldwin, who recommends a route from Boston through Fitchburg and the construction of a tunnel through Hoosac Mountain in the Berkshires. According to Morison, "Massachusetts wisely accepted the veto of her topography," and the idea was not pursued further.
The first street signs in Boston are erected. Most are placed on the sides of buildings at the second story level.

Dr. Caleb Snow's *The History of Boston* is published.

February 9. John Quincy Adams is elected president of the United States by a vote of the House of Representatives.
April 11. Josiah Quincy (with 1,836 votes) defeats all other candidates (with a combined 55 votes) to win reelection as mayor.

July 22. The "Beehive Riots" begins. A mob begins a weeklong series of raids on brothels in the North End, destroying property and prompting the women known as "the nymphs of Ann Street" to flee. Eventually, Mayor Quincy hires forty "truckmen" to stop the violence. Ann Street is renamed North Street in 1854.

December 12. Jonathan Houghton, a member of the Boston Night Watch, is killed responding to a robbery on State Street. He is reportedly the first law enforcement officer in Boston history killed in the line of duty.

April 7. A fire on Duane Street destroys fifty-three businesses along State, Broad, Batterymarch, Central, and Kilby Streets.

May 10. Benedict Joseph Fenwick is appointed bishop of Boston, succeeding Jean-Louis Lefebvre de Cheverus. He is installed on November 1.
May 26. The American Unitarian Association is founded in a meeting at the Federal Street Church. It is incorporated in 1847, with headquarters in Boston. Unitarianism would often be called the "Boston religion." The historian Henry Adams later writes: "Nothing quieted doubt so completely as the mental calm of the Unitarian clergy. Doubts were a waste of thought. . . . Boston had solved the universe."

There are 6,220 students in the Boston public schools—3,497 boys and 2,723 girls.

Boston ship carpenters strike—unsuccessfully—for a ten-hour workday. Ship-owners are joined by master carpenters and journeymen in opposition to their demand.
William Pendelton establishes the first lithographic press in America.

July 5. The first issue of the *Boston Traveller* appears. A twice-weekly bulletin for stagecoach schedules, it becomes a daily on April 1, 1845. It later takes over four other newspapers and begins to advertise itself as the largest evening newspaper in New England. The newspaper changes the spelling of its name to *Traveler* at the turn of the century. For years, the newspaper's office is located in the Traveller's Building at 31 State Street. It later moves to Washington Street, to Summer Street, to Tremont Street, and finally to the corner of Mason and Avery Streets. It is purchased by and merges with the *Boston Herald* on July 1, 1912, becoming first the *Traveler and Evening Herald*, and then the *Boston Traveler* on May 8, 1914. Absorbed by the *Herald*, it ceases publication in 1967.

The Brattle Book Shop opens on Cornhill Street. The oldest antiquarian bookstore in continuous operation in the United States, it is purchased by George Gloss in 1949. Forced to move numerous times as a result of urban renewal, Gloss conducts huge book giveaways prior to many of the moves. The store is currently run by his son, Ken, in a building at 9 West Street, which Gloss purchases—to avoid further moves—in 1984.

1826 to 1850

1826

S. P. Fuller designs the plan for Louisburg Square, which is developed between the mid-1830s and mid-1840s. The Louisburg Square Proprietors then form the first homeowners' association in the country. The fence around the park in the middle of the square is erected in 1846. Joseph Iasigi, a resident of no. 3, donates two statues at either end of the park, one of the Greek statesman Aristides is erected on December 1, 1849 (the first statue erected in any Boston park), and one of Christopher Columbus on August 1, 1851.

August 26. The Quincy Market complex opens. Designed by Alexander Parris, it is considered the first urban renewal project in the United States. The complex is built on land taken by eminent domain or created by filling in the Town Dock area, and the cost is soon repaid from rents, which prompts Mayor Quincy to declare that its construction "was accomplished in the centre of a populous city, not only without any tax, debt or burden upon its pecuniary resources but with large permanent additions to its real and productive property." The central market building is damaged by a fire on January 27, 1862. After the buildings deteriorate, the U.S. Food and Drug Administration recommends that the market be closed in 1950. Walter Muir Whitehill leads a preservation effort beginning in 1954, which proves successful in 1976.*

October 7. The Granite Railway is completed in Quincy. The first commercial railroad in the United States, the horse-drawn line is built by Gridley J. F. Bryant to carry granite blocks from the Quincy quarries to docks on the Neponset River in order to construct the Bunker Hill Monument. The line operates for forty years and is then taken over by the Old Colony Railroad, which opens a new line on the same route on October 9, 1871.
The first omnibus service begins in Boston. Unlike stagecoaches (which go directly from one town to another), these vehicles make several stops along their routes and the seats run lengthwise.

July 4. The fiftieth anniversary of the Declaration of Independence is marked by the raising of a liberty pole on Essex Street. Residents of Boston soon learn that John Adams died in Quincy on July Fourth and that Jefferson had died in Virginia only hours earlier.
The Massachusetts State Archives is created. One of the largest state archives in the United States, it is located initially in the basement of the State House, then moves in April 1986 to its current location, on Columbia Point, which it shares with the State Records Center and the Commonwealth Museum.

A view of Faneuil Hall Marketplace from the east. Lithograph by John Andrews. (Courtesy of the Bostonian Society)

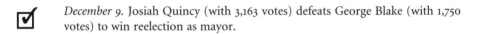

December 9. Josiah Quincy (with 3,163 votes) defeats George Blake (with 1,750 votes) to win reelection as mayor.

The Union Oyster House opens at 41 Union Street and would become the oldest restaurant in continuous operation in the United States. Daniel Webster is a regular patron, known for eating six plates of oysters at a sitting—washed down with as many brandy-and-waters. It is owned and operated today by the Milano family.

The United States Hotel opens at the corner of Lincoln and Beach Streets. Guests would include Daniel Webster and Charles Dickens. Enlarged twice, it is the largest hotel in the city, with five hundred rooms by 1859. The hotel closes in 1929 and is demolished in 1946.

The House of Reformation for Juvenile Offenders opens within the House of Correction in South Boston. It moves to a newly constructed separate building nearby in 1836, making Boston the second city in the United States to separate the youth and adult populations in corrections facilities. The institution moves to Deer Island on July 1, 1858. A separate facility for girls is constructed there in 1860. The House of Reformation moves to Rainsford Island in 1895, changes its name to the Suffolk School for Delinquent Boys in 1906, and closes in 1920.

A public high school for girls opens on Derne Street, becoming the first in the United States. There are 133 girls in the first class. Ebenezer Baily is the first master. The school is "Kept open eighteen or nineteen months, during which time not one pupil voluntarily quitted it, nor would as long as they could be allowed to stay, except in case of marriage." The cost per student is estimated at eleven dollars per year, but it closes in June 1828, when Mayor Quincy declares: "No city could stand the expense." One reason for the "expense" is that many wealthy parents, who could afford to send their girls to private school, were instead taking advantage of the free school.

In a journal entry, the Boston businessman Amos Lawrence describes his preoccupation with business: "I now find myself so engrossed with its cares, as to occupy my thoughts, waking or sleeping, to a degree entirely disproportionate to its importance."
The Boston Beer Company is founded in South Boston. The company eventually becomes the longest continually operated brewery in the United States and remains in business until 1957.

Twenty-eight newspapers, magazines, and other periodicals are published in Boston at this time.

Chester Harding assumes permanent residence in Boston and succeeds Gilbert Stuart as the most popular portrait painter in the city.
October 30. The English tragedian William Charles Macready makes his Boston debut in *Virginius* before a packed house at the Boston Theatre on Federal Street. Tickets for the performance are sold at auction.

The first collegiate gymnastics program is established at Harvard, directed by Charles Follen.

1827

The filling of the West Fourth Street area in South Boston begins. Carried out by Cyrus Alger, it is completed in 1835.

The Austin Block is erected at 92 Main Street in Charlestown.

June 16. Richard Saltonstall Greenough's statue of Benjamin Franklin, the first portrait statue in Boston, is dedicated in the Granary Burying Ground. It is later said that the sculptor captured Franklin's philosophical aspect on the left side of the statue and his comical aspect on the right side. The statue is moved to School Street in 1856.

Charging that "all offices were in the hands of the Unitarians," the Presbyterian minister Rev. Lyman Beecher organizes committees to watch for promising candidates for public office so that "the orthodox had an equal chance."
December 11. Josiah Quincy (with 2,189 votes) defeats Amos Binney (with 40) and others to win reelection as mayor.

Durgin Park restaurant opens on North Market Street. Originally a small eating place catering to workers from the docks and the market, it is soon taken over by John Durgin and Eldredge Park. Lucius Beebe later describes it as "not a restaurant [but] a dining room in the old New England manner," with waitresses "with notions of their own as to what patrons ought to eat and ideas of table service that would make the hair of a French waiter captain stand up on his head."

Papanti's dance studio opens. Founded by Lorenzo Papanti, it proves extremely popular with Boston society. Papanti builds a new studio at 23 Tremont Row in 1837, which includes the first ballroom in the country with a dance floor on springs (reportedly to accommodate one of his most generous—and generously proportioned—students, Mrs. Harrison Gray Otis). The studio continues to operate until 1899.

Robert Roberts's *House Servants Directory* is published. It is a how-to guide for those "in service."

$ The National-Boston Lead Works is established in Roxbury. It merges with the Chadwick Lead Works (established in 1862) in Fort Hill Square to form the Chadwick-Boston Lead Company in 1901.

January 12. The first issue of the *Bunker Hill Aurora* appears. The first successful newspaper in Charlestown, the weekly continues until September 24, 1870.

Sarah Josepha Buell Hale begins editing the *Boston Ladies' Magazine*. The publication merges with Philadelphia's *Godey's Lady's Book* in 1836.

 The Boston Athenaeum holds its first annual public art exhibition. The art historian William Vance later writes that until this time "only portraiture thrived" in Boston, and from this moment "art as an independent concern was finally born."

Hannah Adams becomes the first woman granted full access to the Boston Athenaeum. Described as America's first full-time professional woman author, she is locked inside the library during the staff's lunch hour "in modesty."

Samuel Griswold Goodrich's *The Tales of Peter Parley about America* is published, the first of more than one hundred children's volumes. Goodrich, a resident of Jamaica Plain, starts *Parley's Magazine for Children* in 1833.

September 24. The Tremont Theatre opens at 82 Tremont Street. Described by the *Boston Traveller* as "a new and brilliant Temple of the Muses," it has a central gallery "reserved for people of color." Performers would include Charles John Kean, Charles and Fanny Kemble, Tyrone Power, Fanny Jarman, Charlotte Cushman, and Jenny Lind. The last performance is held June 23, 1843. The building is sold to the Baptist Church in 1843.*

 July 23. Jarvis Braman opens a bathhouse at the foot of Chestnut Street at the bottom of Beacon Hill—the first swimming pool in America. He later describes the activity in the 150-square-foot saltwater pool: "The boys are safe in it and it is pleasant to see their gambols in the water." Francis Leiber teaches the first swimming classes. John Quincy Adams and John James Audubon are among the first students.

1828

September 26. The Federal Street Bridge (also called the North Bridge) to South Boston opens. A free bridge, it extends Dorchester Avenue into Boston. It is rebuilt in 1859 and again in 1873.

December 25. The Warren Street Bridge opens, connecting Boston to Charlestown at Causeway Street. Tolls are charged periodically until August 30, 1858, when it is made a free bridge. The granting of a charter for this bridge by the legislature prompted a suit by the company that had built the nearby Charles River Bridge. In what proves to be an important case, the U.S. Supreme Court rules against the plaintiffs in 1837, declaring, "the object and end of all government is to promote the happiness and prosperity of the community by which it is established." A new bridge is built as a replacement in 1884.

November 3. Andrew Jackson defeats John Quincy Adams in the presidential election.
December 15. Mayor Quincy withdraws his candidacy for reelection after failing to win on the first two ballots. Some historians attribute his loss to firefighters who are angry at Quincy's refusal to appoint their candidate chief engineer; others blame it on his closing of the high school for girls. The *Boston Patriot* later credits the "laboring class vote" for his defeat and criticizes Quincy for his "haughty anti-republican manners."
December 22. The Federalist Harrison Gray Otis (with 2,978 votes) defeats Caleb Eddy (with 1,283) to become the city's third mayor. A successful businessman, former congressman, speaker of the Massachusetts House, and president of the Massachusetts Senate, Otis suffers from gout and is sworn in at his home at 45 Beacon Street on January 5, 1829. In his inaugural address, he warns that the city must improve its planning or "the streams of our prosperity will seek other channels," but the city's economy is not strong during his administration.

The Seamen's Bethel is established at North Square. A nonsectarian parish, its first pastor, a Methodist, is Rev. Edward Taylor, a dynamic orator and the model for the preacher in Herman Melville's *Moby-Dick*. He founds the Boston Port and Seamen's Aid Society in 1847 and builds the Greek Revival–style Mariner's House at 11 North Square in the North End the same year. The building is renovated by the Boston Port and Seamen's Aid Society in 1999.

Girls are finally allowed to attend Boston's public grammar schools for the entire school year. They are also allowed to continue in school until sixteen years of age, while boys are required to leave at fourteen.

November 15. Edwin Forrest stars in *Hamlet* for the first time in Boston.

1829

January 1. The first illuminating gas streetlight is installed at Dock Square. Gas streetlights begin to replace oil lamps across the city in 1834. The last gaslights are removed in 1958 but later reintroduced in some neighborhoods.

Bowen's *Picture of Boston* is published. It is the first guidebook of the city. Many will follow.

December 14. Harrison Gray Otis (with 1,844 votes) defeats all others (with 122 combined) to win reelection as mayor.

July 4. William Lloyd Garrison makes his first antislavery speech at the Park Street Church.

September 8. An anti-Mason meeting at Faneuil Hall is attacked. The clash, according to the historian Jack Tager, is between "the anti-Masons [who] were mainly artisans, shopkeepers, and plebeians who envisioned themselves as defending democratic rights," and "the elites using direct action."

September. David Walker's *An Appeal to the Coloured Citizens of the United States* is published. Written by the African-American proprietor of a Brattle Street clothing store, it calls on slaves to fight for their freedom. When the book is distributed in the South, some of the region's governors call for Walker's arrest. After receiving numerous threats, Walker is found dead on the street on June 28, 1830. Some believe he was poisoned; others attribute his death to a seizure.

Lydia Maria Child's *The Frugal Housewife*, a guide for married women, is published.

October 16. Tremont House opens at the corner of Tremont and Beacon Streets, across from today's Parker House. Designed by Isaiah Rogers, it is the most elegant and modern hotel in America at the time. Guests can rent single rooms rather than double up with strangers, as has been the practice, and each room comes with a key, washbowl, pitcher, free soap, and gaslights. Guests would include Presidents Martin Van Buren and John Tyler, Daniel Webster, and Charles Dickens, who writes that the hotel has more "galleries, colonnades, piazzas and passages than I can remember, or the reader would believe." The building is demolished in 1895.

The Temple Club, today one of Boston's oldest social clubs, is organized. Its headquarters is at 35 West Street, which makes it convenient for the members' frequent opera and theater nights.

Boston's fire companies are made up of twelve hundred officers and men, twenty engines, one hook-and-ladder company, eight hundred buckets, and seven thousand feet of hose.

The Massachusetts Horticultural Society is founded. Gen. Henry A. S. Dearborn is the first president. The organization opens the first Horticultural Hall at 56 School Street, in 1845; the second, designed by Gridley J. F. Bryant, on Tremont Street, opposite the Granary Burying Ground, in 1865. The third and current building, designed by Wheelwright and Haven in the English Baroque style, opens on June 4, 1901.

January. The former Boston mayor Josiah Quincy succeeds John Thornton Kirkland as president of Harvard College. "If a man's in there," Quincy later says, pointing to the "Harvard Triennial Catalogue," "that's who he is. If he isn't, who is he?" Quincy is succeeded by Edward Everett (1846), Jared Sparks (1849), James Walker (1853), Cornelius Conway Felton (1860), and Rev. Thomas Hill (1862–1869*).

June 3. The Warren Institution for Savings opens. Founded by Maj. Timothy Walker, it was incorporated on February 21. It merges with the Union Institution for Savings to become the Union Warren Savings Bank in 1968.

September 5. The first issue of the *Pilot* appears. Originally the *Catholic Sentinel*, it is the first Catholic newspaper in the United States. Started by Bishop Fenwick, the paper is sold to Patrick Donahoe in 1834 and renamed first the *Boston Pilot*, then the *Pilot* in 1858. It is purchased by the Catholic Archdiocese of Boston in 1873, which appoints John Boyle O'Reilly as editor. The *Pilot* becomes the official paper of the archdiocese in 1908. Located initially at 28 State Street, it later moves to 607 Washington Street on Newspaper Row, then to the chancery in Brighton in 2002.

Boston has 34 newspapers: 6 dailies, 16 weeklies, 8 semiweeklies, and 4 published three times a week.

Robert Salmon arrives in Boston from London. He becomes the first and the foremost marine artist in the city.

The Old Corner Book Store opens. James and Richard Carter and Charles Hendee are the first proprietors. Nicknamed "Parnassus Corner" after the Greek mountain home of the Muses, it becomes the center of the town's intellectual life and a meeting place for writers such as Louisa May Alcott, Ralph Waldo Emerson, Margaret Fuller, Nathaniel Hawthorne, Oliver Wendell Holmes, Julia Ward Howe, Henry Wadsworth Longfellow, Harriet Beecher Stowe, Henry David Thoreau, and John Greenleaf Whittier. William Ticknor and John Allen take over the operation in 1832. James Fields becomes sole partner in 1854. After Ticknor's death, the company moves to 124 Tremont Street in 1864. The last bookseller leaves the building in 1903. Threatened with demolition, the building is purchased and preserved by Historic Boston, Inc. in 1960. The Globe Corner Bookstore operates there from 1982 until 1997 and the *Boston Globe* Bookstore until 2004.

August 14. The Siamese twins Chan and Eng are first exhibited in Boston. They return on August 27, 1838; April 29, 1853; and January 7, 1866.

1830

Boston's population is 61,392, the fourth-largest of any city in the United States (behind New York, Baltimore, and Philadelphia), with 1,875 described as "free colored persons." The population is nearly double what it was twenty years before. The Irish Catholic population is estimated at eight thousand, double that of five years before. The separate towns of Roxbury, Dorchester, Charlestown, and Brighton have an additional combined population of 19,076, with 136 people classified as nonwhite.

June 5. The Boston and Lowell Railroad is incorporated. The state legislature's vote for incorporation and for granting a forty-year franchise and right-of-way is the culmination of a debate between railroad and canal enthusiasts. The railroad side was strongly promoted by Nathan Hale, editor of the *Daily Advertiser*. The first to be incorporated, the Boston and Lowell Railroad is financed and built by the Perkins, Jackson, Lawrence, and Lowell families. It links the textile mills of the Merrimack Valley with Boston, and it begins operation in 1835.*

May 1. Cows are henceforth prohibited from grazing on Boston Common. Mayor Otis introduces the first municipal concerts on the Common this summer. They are supported by the Society for the Suppression of Intemperance. Sarah Josepha Buell Hale organizes a bake sale to help pay for construction of the stalled Bunker Hill Monument. Amos Lawrence offers ten thousand dollars toward completion of the project if the remaining funds can be raised, and Judah Touro, a Jewish businessman who had moved from Boston to New Orleans, matches that contribution, enabling construction to proceed.

September 17. Boston's two hundredth anniversary is celebrated at Faneuil Hall.

December 13. Harrison Gray Otis (with 2,828 votes) defeats all others (97 votes combined) to win reelection as mayor. Once again immobilized by gout, he is sworn in for the second time at his home at 45 Beacon Street.

The Cattle Fair Hotel opens on Market Street in Brighton Center. Built to accommodate those doing business with the stockyards, the hotel is later expanded. It is torn down in 1898.

March. A storm produces the highest tide in memory, flooding the Charlestown Navy Yard.

The Boston Society of Natural History is established. The first organization of its kind in New England, it is located initially in a room at the Boston Athenaeum. It moves to a new museum building designed by William Preston at 234 Berkeley Street in the Back Bay on June 1, 1864. Renamed the Museum of Science after World War II, it moves to its current site on the Charles River Dam in 1951. The Hayden Planetarium opens in 1958.

The Working Men's Party is organized. Declaring that it views that "all attempts to degrade the working classes as so many blows aimed at the destruction of popular virtue—without which no human government can long subsist," the party does poorly in the municipal elections and goes out of existence a year later.
July. The *Lintin* sails from Central Wharf for China, with seventeen-year-old John Murray Forbes aboard. He replaces Thomas Cushing, who returns to Boston as the key figure in the China trade, while his older brother, "Black" Ben Forbes, a former ship captain, handles the merchandise imported to Boston for Russell and Company.
(ca.) John Simmons manufactures the first "ready-made" suits in America. Simmons revolutionizes the clothing industry by cutting cloth in standard sizes. His suits are still hand-stitched, however, since the sewing machine has yet to be invented.

July 24. The first issue of the *Boston Evening Transcript* appears. The city's first afternoon daily is edited by Lynde Minshull Walter. Edward Clement succeeds him from 1881 to 1906. Known for its genealogy columns and for printing the text of the Constitution every Wednesday, the newspaper "reflected the atmosphere of old Boston," according to the journalist Louis Lyons. A joke is

Our Country is the World, our Countrymen are all Mankind.

The Liberator *masthead. (Courtesy of the Bostonian Society)*

told in which a Back Bay butler announces to his employer, "Three reporters are at the door—and a gentleman from the *Transcript*." Located originally on Exchange Street, the newspaper moves to 35 Congress Street on May 5, 1845, and to 322–328 Washington Street on March 26, 1860. After those offices burn in the Great Fire of 1872, the *Transcript* moves to the former *Boston Post* building at the corner of Washington and Milk Streets. Its last issue is published on April 30, 1941.

Robert Salmon's painting *The Wharves of Boston Harbor* and Michael Barry's *Savin Hill* are completed.

Sarah Josepha Buell Hale's poem "Mary Had a Little Lamb" is published in *Poems for Our Children*.

1831

December 28. The National Republican Party candidate Charles Wells (with 3,316 votes) defeats Theodore Lyman, Jr. (with 2,389), and others to win the mayoral election on the second ballot. A bricklayer, he is inaugurated on January 2, 1831. Wells later becomes president of the Massachusetts Mutual Fire Insurance Company.

January 1. The first issue of *The Liberator* appears. Published from offices at 12 Post Office Square (today's Washington Street), the weekly newspaper is founded by William Lloyd Garrison "to lift up the standard of emancipation in the eyes of the nation, within the sight of Bunker Hill, and in the birthplace of liberty." The abolitionist newspaper is later credited with helping to undermine, in the words of Charles Sumner, the symbiotic relationship between the "Lords of the Lash" (the owners of cotton plantations in the South) and the "Lords of the Loom" (the owners of textile factories in the North). It ceases publication after passage of the Thirteenth Amendment, which prohibits slavery, on December 29, 1865.

May 18. Emily Marshall marries William Foster Otis, the son of the merchant and former mayor Harrison Gray Otis. Described as one of the three most beautiful women in America at the time, she dies five years later while giving birth to the couple's third child. She is "a martyr," according to the author Cleveland Amory, "to the primitive surgery of the day."

February 3. A group of Dorchester residents organizes a protest against people being imprisoned for small debts. After a series of meetings, legislation is passed prohibiting imprisonment for debts of less than ten dollars.

The Congregational Society Church opens at 35 Bowdoin Street on Beacon Hill. Lyman Beecher, the father of Harriet Beecher Stowe, is the first pastor. Designed by Solomon Willard, the building becomes the Mission Church of St. John the Evangelist in 1883.

The S. S. Pierce Company opens at the corner of Tremont and Court Streets. Founded by Samuel Stillman Pierce to sell "choice teas and foreign fruits," it eventually takes orders for a range of specialty foods and delicacies, such as "kangaroo-tail soup, truffled lark, and reindeer tongue." The store moves in 1887 to a Victorian-style building designed by Edwin Tobey in Copley Square. The building is demolished in 1958, and the company is sold to Seneca Foods Corporation of New York in 1972.

November 9. The first issue of the *Boston Post* appears. The first inexpensive daily newspaper in Boston, it is founded by Charles G. Greene. After absorbing the *Boston Statesman*, edited by Greene's brother Nathaniel, it becomes the leading Democratic newspaper in the city. Located initially at 19–21 Water Street, the paper moves to a new building at 17 Milk Street in 1874. Its last issue appears on October 4, 1956.

July 4. The song "My Country 'tis of Thee" (also called "America"), by Samuel Francis Smith of Newton, is first sung at Park Street Church.
J. R. Anderson, an English singer, is hissed off the stage because he is believed to have spoken "disrespectfully of the American people." His manager later writes letters and sends affidavits to local newspapers claiming he "never did it."
February 27. William Pelby's American Amphitheatre opens at the corner of Portland and Traverse Streets. Renamed the Warren a few months later, it reportedly features a special third row for women of doubtful virtue. Rebuilt and renamed the National in 1832, the building burns on April 22, 1852, and reopens later as the People's National Union Concert Hall. It closes on March 24, 1863, and burns down the next day.

1832

Asher Benjamin's *Practical House Carpenter* is published.

September 10. Tremont Street opens between Boston and Roxbury. Its creation is described by the historian Francis S. Drake as "a great relief to Washington Street . . . over-crowded with country teams."

January 6. The New England Anti-Slavery Society is established. Founded by William Lloyd Garrison and eleven other white men at a meeting at the African Meeting House, it is the first antislavery organization in the country and becomes the most influential abolitionist organization in Boston. At the meeting, Garrison declares: "We have met to-night in this obscure school-house; our numbers are few and our influence limited; but, mark my prediction, Faneuil Hall shall ere long echo with the principles we have set forth. We shall shake the nation by their mighty power."

October 14. The Boston Female Anti-Slavery Society is founded by Lydia Maria Child and Maria Weston Chapman.

The siting of the town almshouse (also known as the House of Industry for "virtuous poor"), House of Correction (for "vicious poor"), and an insane asylum in South Boston prompts residents to complain that the area is being made the "dumping ground of the city."

May 30. The first Masonic Temple is dedicated at the corner of Tremont Street and Temple Place. It moves to Winthrop House at the corner of Boylston and Tremont streets, which is renamed Freemason's Hall and dedicated on December 27, 1859. After a fire destroys that building, a new temple is dedicated on June 24, 1867. This building is also destroyed by fire, and the current temple, designed by Merrill Wheelock, is dedicated on December 27, 1899.

September. Ralph Waldo Emerson resigns as pastor of the Second Church. He had been hired in January 1829. A month later, he begins a poem: "I will not live out of me/I will not see with others' eyes/My good is good, my evil ill/I would be free." Later he complains of what he calls the "corpse-cold Unitarianism of Brattle Street."

August. The Perkins School for the Blind (originally the New England Institution for the Education of the Blind) opens at 140 Pleasant Street. Six students are in the first class. It is the first school for the blind in the United States. The school is initially located in the home of its first director, Samuel Gridley Howe. Incorporated on March 2, 1829, it is renamed for Thomas Handasyd Perkins, who donates his home to the school at 17 Pearl Street in 1833. The school moves to the former Mount Washington House Hotel at Broadway and H Street in South Boston in May 1839, then to Watertown in 1912.

October 24. The Boston Lying-In Hospital opens at 718 Washington Street. Founded to care for "poor and deserving women during confinement," it moves to Springfield Street in the South End on July 12, 1855, but closes a year later because of lack of patients. The hospital reopens on January 1, 1873, on McLean Street in the West End, then moves to Longwood Avenue in 1923. It merges with the Free Hospital for Women to become Boston Hospital for Women in January 1965, and becomes part of the Affiliated Hospitals Complex with Peter Bent and Robert Breck Brigham Hospitals in 1975.

March 20. Boston ship carpenters once again strike for a ten-hour workday. Despite receiving support from other artisans, this strike, like another in 1835, is unsuccessful. The merchants and shipowners issue a petition, declaring that "labor ought always to be left free to regulate itself, and that neither the employer nor the employed should have the power to control the other." They eventually prevail.

J. S. Waterman and Sons, Inc., is established. Founded by Joseph Sampson Waterman, it is now J. S. Waterman and Sons/Eastman-Waring, the oldest continuously operated funeral service business in Boston.

Robert Salmon's painting *Shirely Gut from Deer Island* is completed. It is today the property of the Bostonian Society.

1833

April 19. The East Boston Company is incorporated. (North Boston was originally proposed as the name of the company, but the Massachusetts legislature asked that it be changed in anticipation of Charlestown's annexation to Boston.) Formed by William Hyslop Sumner and others, the company begins filling in marshes and connects Noddles, Hog, Bird, Governor's, and Apple Islands to create today's East Boston. The company continues until 1928.

The filling of South Cove begins. Undertaken by the South Cove Associates, it includes today's Tremont Street, Chinatown, and Herald Street, and is completed in 1843. The company also builds a railway station for the Boston and Albany Railroad at Beach and Lincoln Streets in 1881 and names the major thoroughfare (Albany Street) and cross streets after towns in upstate New York.

The filling of the Charles River Embankment begins in the West End. It is completed in 1888.

Municipal ferry service to East Boston begins, with two steam ferries, the *Maverick* and the *East Boston*, running between Rowes Wharf and Maverick Square. The charge for a foot passenger is set at one penny in 1887 and remains so until ferry service ends on December 31, 1952.

June 24. Drydock no. 1 is dedicated at the Charlestown Navy Yard. President Andrew Jackson attends the ceremony. Designed by Laommi Baldwin, it is the second in the United States, opening a week after one in Norfolk, Virginia.

December 9. The National Republican Party candidate Theodore Lyman, Jr. (with 3,734 votes), defeats Republican William Sullivan (with 2,009) and others to win election as mayor. Inaugurated on January 6, 1834, he is, according to the historian John Galvin, "the most intellectual mayor Boston has ever had." Lyman calls for bringing a "a copious and steady supply of pure and soft water into the City of Boston," and the engineer Loammi Baldwin is retained to develop a plan. The plan is completed a year later, but it is not implemented for another twelve years.

Lydia Maria Child's antislavery tract, *An Appeal in Favor of That Class of Americans Called Africans*, is published. Her privileges at the Boston Athenaeum are immediately revoked.

June 24. President Andrew Jackson receives an honorary degree from Harvard College. Although an overseer of the college, John Quincy Adams—who lost to Jackson in the 1828 presidential election—refuses to attend the event. He writes that he could not bear to see his college "confer her highest literary honor upon a barbarian who could not write a sentence of grammar and hardly could spell his own name." A young Josiah Quincy, whose father is the former mayor and Harvard's president at the time, does attend. He later writes that he expected Jackson to be "simply intolerable to the Brahmin caste of my native State," but finds him instead a "knightly personage," and "a gentleman" with a "high sense of honor." Quincy's use of "Brahmin" appears to predate what is generally thought to be the first use of the term, by Oliver Wendell Holmes, Sr., in his 1861 novel, *Elsie Venner*.

October 22. Henry Clay visits Boston. Touring the Brighton cattle yards, he is said, according to the historian Francis S. Drake, to have recognized some of his cattle, who "had made the tedious journey from Ashland, Kentucky, on foot."

William James Bennett's *Boston, From City Point Near Sea Street* is painted and engraved.

January 8. The Boston Academy of Music is established. Founded by the future mayor Samuel Eliot and by Lowell Mason and George James Webb, the school introduces music into the public schools. It forms an amateur chorus, and a professional orchestra conducted by Webb, which performs its first concert on November 14, 1840. Located initially in schoolrooms, the academy moves to the refurbished Boston Theatre on Federal Street, renamed the Odeon, on August 5, 1835. The school continues until 1848.

April 15. Charles Kemble and his daughter, Fanny, make their Boston debuts at the Tremont Theatre, appearing in a repertory that includes Shakespeare's *Hamlet* and *Romeo and Juliet*, and Richard Sheridan's *School for Scandal*.

April 8. "Jim Crow" Rice gives a leaping and athletic exhibition at the Tremont Theatre.

1834

March 25. Thompson Island is set off from Dorchester and annexed to Boston. The Boston Farm School opens on the island this year. It is combined with the Boston Asylum for Indigent Boys in 1835, is renamed the Boston Farm and Trade School in 1884, and then the Thompson Academy in 1955. The academy closes in 1975, and the island is leased thereafter by Thompson Island Outward Bound, which opens the Willauer School there in 1994.

Isaiah Rogers's Commercial Wharf is completed. It is renovated in 1969 and 1971.

August 9. The first ship—a ferryboat—is launched from a shipyard in East Boston. Another is launched on January 28, 1835, and the *Niagara*, a 460-ton, square-rigged sailing ship, on September 24, 1835.

May 16. The Boston and Worcester Railroad begins service as far as West Newton. Incorporated on June 23, 1831, to carry freight, it nonetheless becomes the first passenger railroad in the country, and the first to employ a steam locomotive in New England. Its route over the Back Bay passes over the so-called Dizzy Bridge. The line extends to Worcester on July 4, 1835. It operates first from a terminal on Washington Street, then opens a new terminal on freshly filled land at the corner of Lincoln and Beach Streets on November 7, 1836, and then operates from a third terminal, on Kneeland Street, which opens in September 1881 and is torn down in the 1960s.

June 11. The Boston and Providence Railroad begins service as far as the Readville section of Hyde Park. Incorporated on June 22, 1831, its terminal is at Park Square, on the site of today's Park Plaza Hotel. Its route runs over a bridge across the Back Bay, then along Stony Brook. The line is taken over by the Old Colony Railroad in 1888.

October. The Chelsea Street Bridge opens, connecting East Boston to Chelsea. Rebuilt in 1848, it becomes a free bridge on February 1, 1858.

July 2. Samuel Dewey mutilates the figurehead on the USS *Constitution*—a likeness of President Andrew Jackson—at night, during a thunderstorm. Comdr. Jesse Elliott had installed the effigy in hopes it would save the ship from decommissioning. The figurehead is repaired but later removed in 1870.

The first volume of George Bancroft's ten-volume *History of the United States (1834–1874)* is published.

December 8. Theodore Lyman, Jr. (with 4,281 votes), defeats all others (with 143 votes combined) to win reelection as mayor. In his inaugural address, he warns: "If these persons [poor immigrants from Great Britain] should actually come in great numbers, they will of course cluster in the cities, forming separate communities or colonies, detached and alienated from the general habits and associations of the people. . . . we shall have among us a race that will never be infused into our own, but on the contrary will always remain distinct and hostile."

The first waltz is danced in Boston by Mrs. Harrison Gray Otis and Lorenzo Papanti at a party in the Otis mansion on Somerset Street. Respectability comes slowly to the waltz in Boston, however. Cleveland Amory later describes a father dragging his daughter from her partner and later writing to a friend, "I can only describe the position they were in as the very reverse of back-to-back." It would be exactly one hundred years later that Mrs. E. Sohier Welch launches Boston's annual "waltz evenings," first at her home on Louisburg Square, then at the Hotel Somerset and the Copley Plaza.

August 11. The Ursuline Convent in Charlestown is burned down by a mob. Aroused by anti-Catholic feelings, the mob of teamsters from Boston and brickyard workers from Charlestown is also responding to rumors that one of the nuns was being held against her will. Neither police nor fire department officials attempt to intervene. Several men are later arrested and charged, but only one is convicted—sixteen-year-old Marvin Marcy. Sentenced to life in prison, he is pardoned a year later. The nuns attempt to start another school in Roxbury, but are unable to attract students; they move to Canada in 1838. Although the state legislature later passes a resolution deploring the crime, it refuses to reimburse the Catholic diocese for damages. The burned convent remains standing until the land is sold in 1875. The site is in today's Somerville.

Boston begins to construct its own public school buildings. Previously, schools were located in privately owned, rented buildings.

September. The Temple School opens on Tremont Street. Founded by Bronson Alcott with help from Elizabeth Peabody, it is based on the principles of Platonic thought: the goal is not so much to impart knowledge as draw it out of children. The school is closed down by authorities after Alcott publishes his educational theories, including the explanation of the process of birth that he teaches to children in *Conversations with Children on the Gospel* in 1836.

March. The Boston Trades Union is organized. A citywide union made up of various crafts, its membership eventually reaches four thousand workers. The Boston Stock Exchange opens on State Street. The third in the United States, it is founded by Peter Paul Francis Degrand and twelve other businessmen as a place to meet and trade. It moves to 53 State Street in 1891 and to its current location at 100 Franklin Street in 1908.

The Sewall and Day Cordage Company opens on Parker Street along Stony Brook. It later becomes the largest cordage mill in Boston and the source of the rigging for many of the Boston-built clipper ships.

Title page of K. N.: Six Hours in a Convent; or, The Stolen Nuns! A Tale of Charlestown in 1834, *a book about the fire at the Ursuline Convent. (Courtesy of the Bostonian Society)*

Oliver Ditson and Company is founded. Originally Parker and Ditson, the company assumes its subsequent name in 1856. Initially located on Washington Street, it moves to a new building at 178 Tremont Street in 1917. By the turn of the century the largest music publishing house in America, the company sells its catalogue in 1931.

March 13. Rose Rich, reputed to be a five-hundred-pound eight-year-old, is exhibited at the Concert Hall.

1835

May 5. The reduction of Pemberton Hill (also known as Cotton Hill) begins. Hired by the developer Patrick Tracy Jackson, a farmer, Asa Sheldon, completes the job on October 5, removing sixty-five feet from the hill's peak. The next day, house lots go on sale. By the 1850s Pemberton Square becomes a residential area similar to Louisburg Square. The fill from the project is used to create Andover, Billerica, Haverhill, Lowell, and Nashua Streets, which are completed in 1836.

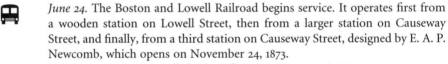

June 24. The Boston and Lowell Railroad begins service. It operates first from a wooden station on Lowell Street, then from a larger station on Causeway Street, and finally, from a third station on Causeway Street, designed by E. A. P. Newcomb, which opens on November 24, 1873.
One-horse carriages—called cabs—first come into use in Boston.

December 14. The Whig party candidate Samuel Armstrong (with 3,039 votes) defeats John James (with 1,185) and others to win election as mayor. Orphaned at thirteen and later a successful publisher of religious tracts, Armstrong is inaugurated on January 4, 1836.

October 21. William Lloyd Garrison is attacked. Prior to a scheduled speech by the British abolitionist George Thompson before the Boston Female Anti-Slavery Society at 46 Washington Street, a mob, or, according to the *Boston Commercial Gazette*, "an assemblage of fifteen hundred or two thousand highly respectable gentlemen," chases and catches Garrison, ties a rope around him, and drags him to Boston Common. Rescued by Mayor Lyman and city constables, Garrison is taken first to City Hall (now the Old State House), then to the Leverett Street Jail, for his own safety. The *Boston Transcript* later blames Garrison for the attack, because he "excited the people to such an abullition of their deeply exasperated feelings."
The New England Temperance Society of People of Color is established.

June 9. Five Spanish pirates are hanged at the Leverett Street Jail. Another is hanged on September 12, the last pirate to be hanged in Boston.

May 18. The Great Fire of 1835 burns forty buildings in the Blackstone, Pond, and Salem Street area.
August 26. Seventy buildings are burned by a fire between City Square and the Town Dock in Charlestown.

Rebecca Reed's *Six Months in a Convent* is published. The book purports to be a description of the woman's mistreatment at the hands of the Ursuline nuns.

The Boston School Committee is again reorganized. The aldermen are removed, and the board now consists of twenty-six members: the mayor, who acts as ex officio president; the president of the Common Council; and two representatives from each of the city's twelve wards.
May 3. The Abiel Smith School is dedicated on Belknap Streeet (today's 46 Joy Street). The first public primary school for African-American children in the United States, it is supported by a donation from the merchant Abiel Smith. Later boycotted by parents seeking integrated public education, the school closes after a state law prohibiting school segregation is enacted in 1855.
The Oak Square School opens at 25 Nonantum Street in Brighton. The building is replaced in 1855, and again in 1894, by a building designed by Edmund

March Wheelwright. The last wooden school building in Boston, it is converted into condominiums in 1981.

$ The Paine Furniture Company is founded. It is originally a shop run by the cabinetmaker Leonard Shearer on Blackstone Street. John Paine joins the business in 1845. It moves to Haymarket Square a few years later, then to Canal Street, then to Park Square in 1914. That building is sold in 1985.

(ca.) George Harvey's watercolor *View of the State House from the Common* is completed.
March. The Boston Brass Band is established. The first in the United States, it is founded by Edward Kimball.
Charlotte Cushman makes her stage debut in a supporting role in *The Marriage of Figaro* at the Tremont Theatre. Born in the North End and later a resident of Charlestown, Cushman becomes one of the greatest actresses of her era. Her last Boston appearance is at the Globe Theatre on May 15, 1875.
September 15. Joyce Heth appears at the Boston Concert Hall. She claims to be 161 years old and George Washington's former nurse. Admission is 25 cents for adults, and 12½ cents for children.

1836

The Charlestown Wharf Company is incorporated to develop land between the Prison Point Bridge and the Charlestown Navy Yard.

December 20. The Suffolk County Court House opens on Court Street. Also known as the Stone Court House, it is designed by Solomon Willard, and is the scene of a number of antislavery riots in the 1850s. The building is torn down in 1912 to make way for construction of the City Hall Annex.
The Alvah Kittredge House is built for the deacon of the First Parish Church near today's John Eliot Square. Later the home of Nathaniel Bradlee, it is now headquarters for the Roxbury Action Program.

December 16. An iron fence replaces a wooden one around Boston Common. Neighboring estates pay part of the cost of installing it.

December 12. The Whig Samuel Eliot (with 3,238 votes) defeats John James (with 1,007) and others to win election to the first of three terms as mayor. The father of the future Harvard president, Eliot is inaugurated on January 2, 1837, and presides over the city during a serious economic depression.

March 4. Prior to a State House hearing, Dr. William Ellery Channing makes a point of shaking hands with William Lloyd Garrison, and so publicly endorses the abolitionist cause. Witnessing the encounter, Mrs. Maria Weston describes it to the women next to her by saying, "Righteousness and peace have kissed each other."
August 11. Two runaway slaves, Polly Ann Bates and Eliza Small, are arrested, but they are ordered freed by Chief Justice Lemuel Shaw because of a defect in the arrest warrant. When the agent for the slave owner requests a new warrant,

African-American and white women riot in the courtroom and the two women escape.

April 1. Church bells are ordered rung at noon instead of 11:00 A.M., changing the city's dinner hour.

November 8. A total eclipse of the sun occurs.

West Roxbury High School opens in the Village Hall. Originally the Eliot High School, it is founded "in order to prevent the inconveniences of ignorance." The school is taken over by the newly independent town and renamed West Roxbury High School in 1855. It moves to a new building at 70 Elm Avenue in 1898, and is renamed Jamaica Plain High School in 1923. A new West Roxbury High School, designed by Samuel Glaser and Partners, opens at 1205 V.F.W. Parkway in 1976. Jamaica Plain High School moves to 144 McBride Street and merges with and becomes English High School in 1989.

May 6. The Shawmut Bank is established. Originally the Warren Bank, it incorporates as a national bank on April 7, 1864, and absorbs nine smaller banks to become the Shawmut National Bank in 1898. A new headquarters opens at 40 Water Street on May 2, 1907. The bank merges with the Fleet Financial Group in 1995.
The Boston Wharf Company is established. It would be responsible for much of the filling of the Commonwealth Flats area of South Boston.

February 16. The first issue of the *Boston Daily Times* appears. The first of the successful "pennies" (penny newspapers), its importance, according to an account in 1882, lay in "placing the daily news in the hands of the humblest and poorest citizens." Located initially on State Street, the newspaper continues publication until sold to the *Boston Herald* on April 23, 1857.

September 20. Richard Henry Dana, Jr., returns to Boston aboard the *Alert*, having left two years earlier for California on the *Pilgrim*. He later writes a book based on his adventures at sea, *Two Years before the Mast*, published in 1840.
September 19. The first meeting of the Transcendentalist Club takes place in the parsonage of George Ripley. Other original members are Bronson Alcott, James Freeman Clarke, Ralph Waldo Emerson, Converse Francis, Frederick Hedge, and Henry David Thoreau. Margaret Fuller and Elizabeth Peabody are invited to join soon after. Transcendentalism, according to William H. Channing, is "an assertion of the inalienable integrity of man, of the immanence of divinity of instinct. On the somewhat stunted stock of Unitarianism . . . had been grafted German Idealism . . . and the result was a vague, yet exalting conception of the godlike nature of the human spirit."
January 11. The Lion Theatre opens on the site of the former Lion Tavern at 543–547 Washington Street. Originally a hippodrome for equestrian performances, it is converted to a lecture and concert hall, then reopens as the Melodeon Theatre on December 29, 1839. For a time the leading concert hall in

Bird's-eye view of Boston, drawn by J. Bachman. (Courtesy of the Bostonian Society)

town, it is later called the New Melodeon and the Gaiety, and reopens as the Bijou in 1882.*

1837

The Boston Public Garden is established. The city responds favorably to a petition by Horace Gray and other amateur horticulturists for the use of twenty-four acres of marshland on which to create a botanical garden. The group incorporates on February 1, 1839, and proceeds to build a garden, greenhouse, and bird house. After Gray loses his fortune in 1847, however, the park falls into disrepair. The city reclaims the property in 1859, and following a plan by George Meacham, a landscape architect, completes the park in the early 1860s. The lagoon is completed in August 1861. The iron fence around the perimeter replaces a wooden one in 1862. The lagoon bridge, designed by William Preston, opens on June 1, 1867.

December 11. Mayor Eliot (with 3,475 votes) defeats Amasa Walker (with 1,127) and others to win reelection as mayor.

June 11. The Broad Street Riot breaks out. It begins when Irish mourners at a Catholic funeral clash with Protestant firefighters returning from a fire in Roxbury. Eventually, an estimated fifteen thousand people take part. Mayor Eliot calls out the militia and personally leads them against the rioters, getting knocked down several times in the process. Order is finally restored several hours later.

September 12. A near-riot occurs when the rest of the city's volunteer militia companies refuse to participate in the annual Fall Muster on Boston Common because of the presence of a recently formed Irish group known as the Montgomery Guards. All the guard units are soon dissolved, then reconstituted under different names, with the Montgomery Guards becoming the Columbian Artillery unit.

Harriet Martineau describes Boston in her book *Society in America*: "I know of no large city where there is so much mutual helpfulness, so little neglect and ignorance of the concerns of other classes."

James Allen's autobiography, *The Life of a Highwayman*, is published. Allen was executed for robbery, and only two copies of his book are printed. They are bound in leather made from the author's skin. One is now in possession of the Boston Athenaeum, donated by the family of a man who resisted an attack by Allen and helped bring him to justice.

July 29. The modern Boston Fire Department is established. The creation of a paid, full-time force puts an end to the problems caused by the volunteer units.

A committee finds that the Great White Oak in Brighton's Oak Square, under which John Eliot is said to have preached to the Nonantum Indians, is the largest tree in the state. Its circumference is measured at nearly thirty feet by the time it is taken down in 1855.

August 31. Emerson delivers the "American Scholar" Phi Beta Kappa address at Harvard. In it, he calls on Americans to stop imitating the "courtly muses of Europe," and declares, "Our day of dependence, our long apprenticeship to the learning of other lands, draws to a close."

Laura Bridgman, a seven-year-old blind and deaf girl from New Hampshire, arrives at the Perkins School. Her progress in learning to read, write, and perform daily chores attracts worldwide attention. She lives at the school until her death at the age of sixty. Her teacher, Anne Sullivan, later works with Helen Keller.

February 27. Dr. Sylvester Graham, the originator of the Graham cracker, is attacked and driven off the stage during his lecture by a mob of bakers, who are furious at Graham for promoting no-yeast bread, which Graham claims will enable humans to live for two centuries.

John Collins Warren's *Surgical Observations on Tumours* is published.

May 11. The Panic of 1837 forces Boston banks to stop specie (cash) payments. It is the first suspension by Boston banks. Payments resume on August 13, 1838, but eventually over one hundred banks in Boston fail, including the Franklin and Lafayette Banks in July and the larger Commonwealth in January 1838. The financial crisis causes a setback in the city's growth as a commercial and business center.

Little, Brown and Company is established. Founded by Charles Little and James Brown, the company moves to the former Cabot mansion on Beacon Street in 1909, incorporates in 1913, and opens a New York office in the 1920s. It is purchased by Time, Inc., in 1968 and moves to New York after being acquired by Warner Communications in 1989.

Orestes Brownson begins publishing the *Boston Quarterly Review*. It is later called *Brownson's Quarterly Review*. Brownson sampled so many religions that someone once remarked, "when a preacher invited to the communion table the members of all Christian churches, that Brownson was the only person in the congregation who could 'fill the bill.'"

The Harvard Musical Association is organized. Founded by John Sullivan Dwight, the organization produces concerts, establishes a library, and supports publications. Its headquarters are on Chestnut Street on Beacon Hill, where it continues operating to this day.

Charlotte Cushman makes her Boston debut in a starring role at the Tremont Theatre. Said to have "amazed the town," she appears in a repertory that includes Shakespeare's *Julius Caesar* and *Macbeth*.

June 19. The Englishman Christopher Jones dies attempting "a novel feat." After diving off the South Boston Bridge dressed as a man, he attempts to change into women's clothes before rising to the surface, but he becomes entangled in the garments and drowns.

1838

The state legislature cedes eighteen hundred acres along the Charles River in Newton to Roxbury.

The Ropewalk Building is completed at the Charlestown Navy Yard. Designed by Alexander Parris, the two-story granite building is one-quarter mile long. All the rope used by the U.S. Navy is subsequently produced there. "Way back then," the *Boston Herald* later reports, rope was "as important as nuclear fission . . . and private industry was perhaps less reliable and less capable in those days." Rope production continues in the building until 1971.

August. The Eastern Railroad begins operating between East Boston and Salem. The line is extended to Newburyport on June 17, 1840, and Portsmouth, N.H., on November 9, 1840; and into Boston on April 10, 1854. The Eastern Railroad Station is built in Boston in 1863.

The Bennington Street Cemetery is established in East Boston.

December 10. Samuel Eliot (with 3,766 votes) defeats Caleb Eddy (with 2,341) to win reelection as mayor.

Mrs. John Farrar's *The Young Lady's Friend* is published. Cleveland Amory later declares that the book "carried her idea of Proper Bostonian manners into virtually every civilized part of America of her day."

July 21. The first daytime police force is established in Boston. Under the direction of the city marshal, its six officers are issued green leather badges to be worn on the front of their hats. Although the city is now patrolled around the clock, there is no coordination between the daytime police and the Boston Night Watch.

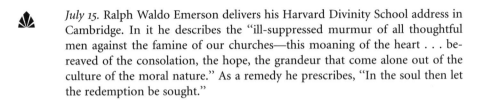

July 15. Ralph Waldo Emerson delivers his Harvard Divinity School address in Cambridge. In it he describes the "ill-suppressed murmur of all thoughtful men against the famine of our churches—this moaning of the heart . . . bereaved of the consolation, the hope, the grandeur that come alone out of the culture of the moral nature." As a remedy he prescribes, "In the soul then let the redemption be sought."

The Boston public schools adopt music as part of the curriculum, and Lowell Mason becomes the first school superintendent of music in the country. The music historian Gilbert Chase later writes, "of all musicians active in the United States during the nineteenth century, Lowell Mason has left the strongest, the widest, and the most lasting impress on our musical culture."

Benjamin Roberts begins publishing the *Anti-Slavery Herald.* Only a few issues are published before the newspaper ceases. Roberts later publishes another newspaper, *Self Elevator,* in 1853.

1839

July 18. The *Britannia* arrives in East Boston. It is the first packet of Samuel Cunard's North American Royal Mail Steam Packet Company. The company uses Boston as its only U.S. port of call. A Cunard Festival attended by thousands of people is held three days later.

December 9. Whig Jonathan Chapman (with 4,352 votes) defeats Bradford Sumner (with 3,047) to win election as mayor. The youngest mayor in Boston's history, the thirty-two-year-old lawyer, writer, and temperance advocate is inaugurated on January 6, 1840. His chief accomplishment is to reduce the city's debt.

March 9. Seventy-two Boston women petition the state legislature to repeal the law prohibiting marriage between whites and blacks.

December 15, 21, 27. The Great December Hurricanes of 1839 strike Boston. Seventy-five vessels are wrecked and approximately thirty lives are lost. The storms inspire Henry Wadsworth Longfellow to write his poem "The Wreck of the Hesperus."

The First Baptist Free Church is organized. The congregation meets initially at 31 Tremont Street, then at Congress Hall at the corner of Congress and Milk Streets. It changes its name to the Tremont Street Baptist Church (later the Tremont Temple Baptist Church) and begins to meet in the former Tremont Theatre in 1843.*
The First Lutheran Church is established at the corner of Shawmut and Waltham Streets in the South End. The congregation moves to 85 West Newton Street in 1899, then to the current church, designed by Pietro Belluschi, at 299 Berkeley Street in the Back Bay in 1957.
The Fifth Universalist Church opens at 76 Warrenton Street. Designed by Asher Benjamin in the Greek Revival style, the building becomes the Jewish

temple Ohabei Shalom, then the Scotch Presbyterian Church, then a theater in 1957.*

December 31. Edward Everett delivers the first Lowell Lecture at the Odeon Theatre on Federal Street. Endowed upon his death in Bombay in 1836 by John Lowell, Jr., the lectures prove extremely popular (some attracting as many as 10,000 applications). Later held at the Tremont Temple, the Marlboro Hotel, and Huntington Hall, they continue today in various venues throughout the Boston area.

Charles Goodyear develops the process for the vulcanization of rubber in a factory building in Roxbury. He patents the process on June 24, 1844.

E. B. Horn and Company is established. Located initially on Hanover Street in the North End, the jeweler moves to its current location at 429 Washington Street in about 1880.

The first issue of the *Boston Cultivator* appears. One of three agricultural newspapers in the city at the time, the biweekly continues publishing until 1876.

Elizabeth Peabody opens a bookstore in the parlor of her home at 13 West Street (now no. 15), which soon becomes the unofficial headquarters for the Transcendentalist Movement. Margaret Fuller holds the first of her Wednesday afternoon "Conversations" there on November 6, 1839, "so that well educated Boston women can have a place to share ideas." The series lasts for five years. Peabody's sister Sophia marries Nathaniel Hawthorne in Elizabeth's home in 1842; her sister Mary marries Horace Mann there in 1843; and Elizabeth remains there until 1850.

1840

Boston's population is 93,383, the fifth-largest of any city in the United States (behind New York, Baltimore, New Orleans, and Philadelphia). Of that number, 2,427 are described as "Free Colored Persons." The separate towns of Roxbury, Dorchester, Charlestown, and Brighton have an additional combined population of 26,873, with 173 classified as nonwhite.

February 27. Lyceum Hall is dedicated on Meeting House Hill in Dorchester. Used by the adjacent First Parish Church, it is the scene of numerous abolitionist meetings. Converted to a school in 1891, the building is demolished in 1955.

June 4. The steamship *Unicorn* arrives at the Cunard line's new pier in East Boston. Regular service between Boston and Liverpool begins in 1842. Although the line does not carry a significant number of immigrants until 1863, it spawns a number of lower-cost competitors (including Enoch Train's White Diamond Line in 1844), which is why most of the 1.5 million Irish immigrants to the United States in the next few years come through Boston. "The vast majority left their ships in East Boston," the historian Oscar Handlin later writes, "without the slightest conception of how they would earn a livelihood and with only enough money to keep them fed and sheltered for a week or two." The Cunard line uses Boston as its exclusive American port until 1848, when it begins service to New York, which becomes its principal destination by 1868.

December 14. Jonathan Chapman (with 5,224 votes) defeats Charles G. Greene (with 2,606) and others to win reelection as mayor.

September 21. A rally is held to promote the conversion of Jews to Christianity at the Clarendon Street Chapel. At the rally, an invitation is extended "to the suffering Jews of other nations, to come to this country, and [we] would now particularly invite them to our city, where we presume they might do as well as in other cities in the world, though at present we have very few with us."
The Twelfth Baptist Church is established on Phillips Street on Beacon Hill. It is formed by African Americans who wish to take a more aggressive stand on ending slavery than those at the African Meeting House. Rev. George Black is the first pastor. The congregation moves to the former Jewish temple Mishkan Tefila at 47 Shawmut Avenue in 1907, then later to its current location on Warren Avenue in Roxbury.

William C. Nell files the first suit calling for integration of the Boston public schools. Nell is joined in the suit by William Lloyd Garrison, Wendell Phillips, and others. The Boston School Committee ignores the petition, as it would another suit in 1847.
August 31. Roxbury High School for Boys opens at what is today 120 Dudley Street. It moves to a new building on today's Kearsage Avenue in 1853. A Roxbury High School for Girls opens on Kenilworth Street in September 1854. The two schools are joined in an enlarged building on Kenilworth Street in February 1861. A new Roxbury Memorial High School, designed by Bateman and Atwood, opens on Warren Street in 1885. The school moves to a building designed by Harris Atwood, at 205 Townsend Street, in 1926, and closes in 1958.

July. The first issue of the *Dial* appears. Ralph Waldo Emerson becomes its editor, and Elizabeth Peabody its publisher, in 1842. The magazine continues until 1844.

March 10. The first daguerreotype photographic likeness in America is taken in Boston.
September 7. The Austrian dancer Fanny Elssler makes her Boston debut at the Tremont Theatre. In the audience, Margaret Fuller reportedly whispers to Emerson: "Ralph, this is poetry!" He reportedly replies: "Margaret, it is *religion!*"

1841

The Sears Crescent Building is constructed. It is enlarged in 1848.
Brighton's Greek Revival–style Town Hall opens. After the town's annexation to Boston, the building serves first as a courthouse and jail, then a veteran's

Bradford House, Brook Farm, West Roxbury. (Courtesy of the Bostonian Society)

post, then headquarters of the Knights of Columbus. Seriously damaged by fire, it is torn down in 1977.

December 9. The first locomotive runs from Boston through Worcester to Albany. The Boston and Worcester, and Boston and Albany lines subsequently merge in January 1868. Although the line provides direct access to the Boston docks, it does not enable Boston to compete with Chicago as a center for the production and shipping of goods. The coming of the railroad, Charles Francis Adams, Jr., later declares, "brought to Boston the full current of modern city life—turning the large New England town into a metropolis, if a provincial one. . . . Boston became the counting house, as it were—the daily business exchange—of a vast concourse of active men having homes in every neighboring town within a limit of thirty miles."

December 13. Jonathan Chapman (with 4,608 votes) defeats Nathaniel Greene (with 3,545) and others to win reelection as mayor for a third consecutive term.

April. Brook Farm is established in West Roxbury by George Ripley, his wife, his sister, and a few friends. The goal of this experiment in communal living is "to approach more nearly the ideal of human society than any that has ever existed." Visitors come from as far away as Europe. Nathaniel Hawthorne, a member for a short time, later writes *The Blithedale Romance* based on his experience there—and also sues to reclaim $530 of his $1,000 investment. Financial difficulties, an outbreak of smallpox, and a fire force the community to close in the fall of 1847. Sold to the town of West Roxbury in 1849, the site is used as a training ground for troops during the Civil War, then as a poorhouse. Gethsemane Cemetery is established on part of the property in 1873. The remainder is used as the site of the Martin Luther German Orphans Home until 1974.

The Washingtonian Society establishes its first chapter in Boston. The organization advocates total abstinence from liquor and opens the Washingtonian Hospital, a "home for inebriates," in 1857. It becomes the nation's oldest hospital for the treatment of alcohol and drug addiction, moves to 41 Waltham Street in the South End, then to Forest Hills, and finally closes in 1981.

A shoemaker, John Augustus, becomes the town's first—and unofficial—probation officer. Impressed by the Washingtonian Society's promotion of temperance, he convinces the court to grant him custody of those convicted of drunkenness for a month, during which time he attempts to convert them to sobriety. By the time of his death in 1859, he bails out nearly two thousand men, women, and children and assists an estimated three thousand women "neglected by the world."

Davis and Palmer Jewelers is robbed of ten thousand dollars in merchandise. A Constable Clapp solves the case by using the methods of the time—convincing the thieves to turn over the merchandise in exchange for their not being prosecuted. He then returns the jewels and collects the reward offered by the jewelers.

May 19. Theodore Parker delivers a sermon, "The Transient and Permanent in Christianity," at an ordination in South Boston. In it he rejects what he calls the "supernatural elements of Christianity" and declares that "if it could be proved that Jesus of Nazareth had never lived, still Christianity would stand firm and fear no evil." As a result of the sermon, Parker is shunned by many ministers in the city, and denounced as an "infidel and blasphemer."

Brighton High School opens on Academy Hill Road. The building is replaced on the same site a number of times, until the school moves to a building designed by Edmund March Wheelwright at 20 Warren Street in 1895. The high school moves to its current building at 25 Warren Street in 1931.

June 14. The Boston Museum and Gallery of Fine Arts opens at 18 Tremont Street. Designed by Hammatt Billings, it is owned and operated by Moses Kimball. One of its first exhibits is the "Feejee Mermaid (purported to be the stuffed body of a creature half woman, half fish)," later "hired" by P. T. Barnum. The museum is first used as a theater in February 1843. It moves to a new building a few blocks away in 1846.*

February 13. The Boston Academy of Music performs Beethoven's Symphony no. 1 at the Odeon Theatre. It is the first performance of a Beethoven symphony in Boston.

1842

The Merchants Exchange Building opens at today's 53 State Street, on the site of the former Bunch of Grapes Tavern. Designed by Isaiah Rogers, it is torn down to make way for Peabody and Stearns's eleven-story Stock Exchange Building, which opens in 1891. That building is restored and joined to a forty-story glass tower, designed by the WZMH Group, and becomes Exchange Place in 1984.

December 12. Whig Martin Brimmer (with 5,084 votes) defeats Bradford Sumner (with 2,340) to win election as mayor and is inaugurated on January 2,

1843. A German-American merchant, he is Boston's first non-Yankee mayor. The author John Jay Chapman later describes him as "a little sweeter by nature and less sure he was right than the true Bostonian is."

The Underground Railroad is established in Boston. An outgrowth of the Freedom Association, it is formed by African Americans to assist fugitive slaves. It is supplanted by the Committee for Vigilance, made up of blacks and whites, in 1849.

October 20. George Latimer, a runaway slave from Virginia, is arrested. After collecting sixty-two thousand signatures on a petition to free Latimer, abolitionists buy his freedom for four hundred dollars. A year later, the General Court passes the Liberty Act of 1843, making it a crime for Massachusetts public officials to arrest or apprehend fugitive slaves or use government facilities to detain them.

April 29. Twenty-three boys and two officials from the Boston Farm School drown when their boat, the *Polka*, capsizes while returning to Thompson Island.

Nathaniel Hawthorne claims to see the ghost of Rev. Thaddeus Mason Harris at the Boston Athenaeum. In a letter written August 17, 1856, Hawthorne describes seeing Harris sitting in his accustomed chair "quite as frequently as before his death. It grew to be so common that at length I regarded the venerable defunct no more than any of the other old fogies who basked before the fire."

The first of T. W. Harris's three-volume *Insects of New England Injurious to Vegetation* is published. The next two volumes by this Dorchester native and Harvard College librarian are published in 1852 and 1862.

January 10. The revivalist Elder Knapp begins his campaign in Boston. Soon after, Stephen Allen is diagnosed as "made insane by the preaching of Elder Knapp" on January 17, and a Mrs. Tewksbury as being "made frantic by religious terrors" on January 28. Mayor Chapman calls out the militia to disperse a revival meeting on January 20.

The Gilchrist Company is established. Founded by the Scottish immigrant George Turnball, it is taken over by one of his clerks, Robert Gilchrist, and his brother John in 1855. The store moves to a building, designed by Bigelow and Wadsworth in the modern Gothic style, at 417 Washington Street in 1911. Four floors are added by R. Clipston Sturgis in 1924. The store closes in the 1970s.

Cornelia Wells Walter of the *Boston Transcript* becomes the first woman editor of a major metropolitan newspaper in the United States. She succeeds her brother, Lynde Minshull Walter, in the job.

January 22. Charles Dickens arrives in Boston on board the *Britannia*; it is the first stop of a four-month tour of the United States and Canada. Reporters go out to meet Dickens even before his ship docks, and crowds turn out to watch him disembark and proceed to his hotel, the Tremont House. During his two-week stay, he is mobbed by admirers wherever he goes, and young ladies cut pieces from his sealskin coat to keep as souvenirs. Dickens makes a number of public appearances and attends numerous private dinner parties. He also visits the Perkins School for the Blind.

1843

More than one thousand new buildings are completed this year, as the city begins a period of tremendous growth. The number increases annually for the next several years.

June 17. The Bunker Hill Monument is dedicated. Designed by Solomon Willard, the 220-foot memorial is the first major monument to be built in the United States. President John Tyler and thirteen veterans of the battle attend the event, as well as the Marquis de Lafayette and Daniel Webster, who both witnessed the laying of the cornerstone eighteen years earlier. In his speech Webster declares that the monument shall cause "from every youthful breast, the ejaculation 'thank God, I—I also—AM AN AMERICAN.'"

January 27. The Dorchester Historical Society is organized. Incorporated in 1855, it is reorganized in 1891, and rechartered by the state in 1893. Its first headquarters are in the James Blake House, which it moves to Richardson Park near Edward Everett Square in 1895.

December 11. Martin Brimmer (with 4,874 votes) defeats George Savage (with 2,237) to win reelection as mayor.

Dorothea Dix presents her talk "Memorial to the Legislature of Massachusetts," an appeal to improve the state's insane asylums, before the General Court. She describes the mentally ill as "confined in this Commonwealth in cages, closets, cellars, stalls, pens; chained, naked, beaten with rods, and lashed into obedience." Her appeal leads to improved care for the mentally ill in Boston and Worcester.

July. Margaret Fuller's essay "Woman in the Nineteenth Century" appears in the *Dial.* In it she argues that women want neither "money nor notoriety nor the badges of authority which men have appropriated to themselves . . . [but] the freedom, the religious, the intelligent freedom of the universe to use its means, to learn its secret as far as Nature has enabled them, with god alone for their guide and their judge." The essay is expanded and published as a book two years later.

Julia Ward of New York marries Samuel Gridley Howe and moves to Boston. "I was now to make acquaintance with quite another city," she later writes, "—with the Boston of the teachers, of the reformers, of the cranks, and also—of the apostles."

In *American Notes,* Charles Dickens writes of Boston: "The golden calf they worship at Boston is a pigmy compared with the giant effigies set up in other parts of that vast countinghouse which lies beyond the Atlantic, and the almighty dollar sinks into something comparatively insignificant amidst a whole

Pantheon of better gods. . . . Above all, I sincerely believe that the public institutions and charities of this capital of Massachusetts are as nearly perfect as the most considerate wisdom, benevolence, and humanity can make them. I never in my life was more affected."

June 1. The temperature drops to 30 degrees and a severe frost occurs.

April 23. William Miller and his followers don white robes and ascend to the roof of their "tabernacle" on Howard Street in Scollay Square to await the end of the world—but nothing happens. A former a sheriff in Poultney, Vermont, Miller moved his religious community to Boston in 1839, and their wooden tabernacle building was completed in 1842. He subsequently revises his doomsday prediction several times. When none comes to pass, the congregation dissolves and the building is sold. It reopens as the Howard Theatre in 1845.*

December 5. The Tremont Temple is dedicated in the former Boston Theatre at 88 Tremont Street. The Tremont Street Baptist Church is the first integrated church in America. Speakers appearing at the temple would include every president from Lincoln to Hoover, as well as Eugene Debs, Charles Dickens, Frederick Douglass, Edward Everett, William Lloyd Garrison, Rev. Billy Graham, Helen Keller, Rev. Billy Sunday, and Daniel Webster. It was after appearing at the Tremont Temple that Will Rogers commented, "I never met a man I didn't like." The building is destroyed by fires and rebuilt in 1853 and 1880. After a fire in 1893, the current building, designed by Clarence Blackall (or Blackhall) and George Newton, with murals by Edmund Tarbell, is dedicated on May 3, 1896.

A paper by Oliver Wendell Holmes, Sr., "The Contagiousness of Puerperal Fever," is published.

The New England Mutual Life Company opens at 28 State Street. Incorporated in 1835, it is the first chartered mutual life insurance company in the United States. The company is bought by Metropolitan Life and renamed New England Financial in 1996. It is located at Post Office Square from 1874 to 1941; its current headquarters at 501 Boylston Street opens in 1942.*

July 9. The painter Washington Allston dies, leaving the masterpiece he had been working on for twenty-five years, *Belshazzar's Feast*, unfinished in his studio. The painting is exhibited, however, with great success.

1844

Robert Gourlay's pamphlet "General Plan for enlarging and improving the City of Boston" is published. The author is a visiting Scotsman and an insomniac who claims to have slept only two hours in the preceding five years. Gourlay's grandiose proposal includes building one island in the middle of the Charles River and another in the middle of a new, smaller Back Bay. He correctly predicts that the city's population will reach a half million in fifty years, and presciently suggests building new residential streets across the Back Bay and also underground subway lines.

The steamship Britannia, *surrounded by ice in Boston Harbor. Drawing by J. D. King. (Courtesy of the Bostonian Society)*

July 8. The first steam packet of the White Diamond Line leaves East Boston for Liverpool. Founded by Enoch Train, the line competes with Cunard and others.

December 9. No candidate for mayor receives sufficient votes on the first ballot—or on the next six, which are held through January 1845.

February. Boston Harbor freezes as far out as Boston Light. Thousands of skaters go out on the ice, and refreshment booths are set up to serve them. The steamer *Britannia* is stuck in the ice and freed only when a ten-mile channel is cut to open water.

The Church of the Advent opens in a former Congregational church in the West End. The congregation moves to Bowdoin Street in 1864, then to its current building, designed by Sturgis and Brigham, at the corner of Mt. Vernon and Brimmer Streets on Beacon Hill in 1883. The Lady Chapel interior is designed by Ralph Adams Cram and Bertram Goodhue.

The first newsboy in Boston is employed by the *Boston Traveller*. The *Boston Post* soon joins in the practice, even putting a caricature of a newsboy on its front page. Newsboys are first licensed to sell papers on June 30, 1846.

May 20. The violinist Ole Bull is first heard in Boston at a recital at the Melodeon.
February 25. *The Drunkard, or, the Fallen Saved* opens at the Boston Museum. The melodrama proves very popular and returns to Boston year after year.

1845

The major filling of the South Bay begins. Called the South Bay Lands Project, it makes up much of today's South End and is completed in November 1862.

Henry Sturgis Grew visits the area today called Roslindale. Impressed with the topography, he purchases eight hundred acres, builds an estate in 1847, and encourages people to stroll his woods. Much of the land is later used for the Stony Brook Reservation and George Wright Golf Course.

Donald McKay opens a shipyard on Border Street in East Boston. A freelance shipbuilder in New York, Maine, and Newburyport, he launches his first ship, the *Washington Irving*, later in the year.

March 1. The first passenger train on the Fitchburg Railroad leaves Boston for Fitchburg. Incorporated in 1842, the line runs along the route proposed for a canal to the Connecticut and Hudson Rivers by the engineer Loammi Baldwin. The Fitchburg Railway Station, designed by George Dexter, opens on Causeway Street in Boston on August 9, 1848. It is torn down in 1927.

July. The Boston and Maine Railroad begins service. Incorporated in 1841, the line operates from a new station at Haymarket Square, which is torn down in 1897. Originally a branch of the Boston and Lowell, it takes over that line in 1887, and is absorbed by the New York, New Haven and Hartford in 1909.

November 8. The Old Colony Railroad, incorporated on March 16, 1844, begins service between Boston and Quincy. The line's Kneeland Street Station, designed by Gridley J. F. Bryant, opens in 1847. It absorbs the Boston and Providence Railroad in 1888, is taken over by the New York, New Haven, and Hartford Railroad in the 1890s, and ceases local operation on June 30, 1959.

Of the $130 million invested in all U.S. railroad operations, it is estimated that $30 million comes from Boston. This figure prompts the business analyst J. J. Stackpole to write: "The Boston people are certainly the only Community who understand Rail Roads. At the present time they have more money than they know what to do with."

The New England Historic Genealogical Society is organized. The first genealogical organization in the country, it begins publishing the *New England Genealogical Register* in 1847. Initially on the third floor of the City Building on Court Square, the organization moves to 18 Somerset Street in 1871, and to its current location at 101 Newbury Street in 1964.

The first volume of Richard Frothingham's *History of Charlestown* is published. Eleven volumes are eventually published, but the series is never completed.

January 6. With no mayor yet chosen, the aldermen and Common Council take office. The professions they list range from "merchant" and "lawyer" to "none."

February 21. After seven unsuccessful ballots, Thomas Davis (with 4,865 votes) defeats William Parker (with 3,341) and others on the eighth ballot to win election as mayor. Davis is a member of the Native American Party, the predecessor of the "Know-Nothings." Inaugurated on February 27, Mayor Davis resigns because of poor health on October 6 and dies November 22. Benson Leavitt, chairman of the Board of Aldermen, serves as acting mayor until the next election.

December 8. The Whig party candidate Josiah Quincy, Jr. (with 5,333 votes), defeats William Durrell (with 1,647), John Heard (1,354) and all others to win election as mayor. The son of the former mayor Josiah Quincy and a Prohibitionist, he is inaugurated on December 11. Quincy completes the effort to acquire a reservoir and provide clean water for city residents and skillfully administers city finances.

The Boston Assemblies begin. These annual society balls, run for many years by S. Hooper Hooper, are first held at Papanti's Ballroom, and later move to Horticultural Hall, the Mechanics Building, Copley Hall, and finally the Hotel Somerset.

May. Macon Allen, a licensed attorney in Maine, becomes the first African-American lawyer to practice law in Boston.
October 27. Maria Bickford is killed in a rooming house on Mount Vernon Avenue (today's Cedar Lane Way) on Beacon Hill. The lawyer for her accused killer, Albert Terrill, is Rufus Choate. He employs a number of curious arguments in his client's defense: the woman probably committed suicide, and if his client did kill her it was because she was leading him into sin, or else he killed her in his sleep. Terrill is acquitted in March 1846.

A fungus attacks the potato crop in Ireland. The resulting potato famine would force more than one million Irish citizens from their homeland over the next five years, many of them emigrating to Boston.

Elias Howe demonstrates his sewing machine at Faneuil Hall. An apprentice in Ari Davis's Boston machine shop, Howe obtains a patent on September 10, 1846, and spends the next nine years attempting to attract investors and protect his patent. In the meantime, Isaac Merrit Singer builds the first commercially successful sewing machine in the Boston shop of Orson Phelps on Harvard Place in 1851, and patents his invention on May 30, 1853. Allen Wilson later perfects the rotary shuttle mechanism. The three men subsequently combine their patent rights in what they call the "sewing machine combination" and share profits from the invention.

March 20. The Essex Company is incorporated. Founded by Abbott, William, and Samuel Lawrence, the company constructs textile mills in a town later named Lawrence.

Many of the classified notices in Boston newspapers read, "None need apply but Americans." The message is later refined to "No Irish need apply." According to recent scholars, however, the use of this wording in ads is much more rare than previously thought.

October 13. The Howard Athenaeum opens with a production of Richard Sheridan's *The School for Scandal.* During a performance of *Pizarro,* on February 25, 1846, a ball of fire representing the sun sets the scenery on fire and the building burns to the ground. It reopens in 1846.*
October 16. Edgar Allan Poe reads "The Raven" in a performance at the Lyceum Theatre. The next day, the *Boston Transcript* describes the evening as a "singularly didactic excordium" that caused the audience to walk out. Poe later

writes: "We like Boston. We were born there—and perhaps it is just as well not to mention that we are heartily ashamed of the fact."

1846

March 12. Roxbury is incorporated as a city. John James Clark is the first mayor.

The United States declares war on Mexico and the Mexican War begins. It lasts until the Treaty of Guadalupe Hidalgo is signed on February 2, 1848.

December 14. Josiah Quincy, Jr. (with 3,846 votes), defeats Charles Goodrich (with 1,319) and all others to win reelection as mayor.

September 21. The Adams House Hotel opens on the site of the former Lamb Tavern. Built for Laban Adams, it is replaced by a seven-story building with three hundred rooms in 1883. Home to Calvin Coolidge and his family for sixteen years, the hotel closes in 1927 and is torn down in 1931.

Francis Tukey is appointed city marshal. A Maine native and law school graduate, he presides over the growth of the Boston Police Department. Although his integrity is never questioned, his aggressive approach to law enforcement leads to a description of him in the *Bunker Hill Aurora* as "a terror to evildoers and some who were not evildoers." A controversial figure, he is replaced in February 1853, and leaves Boston for California.

August 16. A Boston native, John Bernard Fitzpatrick, succeeds the late Benedict Joseph Fenwick as bishop of Boston.
Theodore Parker resigns from the First Church in West Roxbury to form a new "free church," the Twenty-Eighth Congregational Society in Boston, and devotes himself to the cause of abolition.

October 16. The first successful public demonstration of ether takes place under what is later called the Ether Dome in the Bulfinch Building at Massachusetts General Hospital. The anesthetic is administered by a dentist, William T. G. Morton, to twenty-year-old Gilbert Abbot, who is having a tumor removed from his jaw. After the operation, the surgeon, John Collins Warren, exclaims: "Gentlemen, this is no humbug!" Because of the controversy over who should be credited with the discovery, no names appear on John Q. A. Ward's statue in the Public Garden celebrating the "death of pain," dedicated on June 27, 1868. The first telegraph line is strung between Boston and New York. It goes into service on June 27, 1847.

The H. P. Hood Company is established. Originally a milk route operated by Harvey Perley Hood, who had arrived in Boston two years before, the company is incorporated under the name H. P. Hood and Sons in 1890. The company opens its first plant in Charlestown in 1900, another in 1927, and its first ice-cream stand, on Beacon Street, in the early 1900s. Renamed H. P. Hood Inc. in

1972, the company is sold to Agway Inc. in 1986. Its current headquarters are in Chelsea.

 August 31. The first issue of the *Boston Herald* appears. William Eaton is the first editor. It becomes the first regular Sunday newspaper in Boston in May 1861. The company buys the *Traveler* in 1912, which serves as the evening edition of the paper until the two merge to become the *Boston Herald Traveler* in 1967. Purchased by the Hearst Corporation on June 18, 1972, it becomes first the *Record American/Herald Traveler*, then the *Boston Herald American* in January 1973. It becomes a tabloid in September 1981, is purchased by Rupert Murdoch, and is once more named the *Boston Herald* in 1982. Purchased by is current owner, Patrick Purcell, in February 1994, the *Herald* is today one of the few independently owned major metropolitan newspapers in the country. Located initially on Devonshire Street, it moves to 103 (now 241) Washington Street in 1851, to a new building at 255 Washington Street in 1878, to 171 Tremont Street in 1906, to Mason Street in 1930, and to to its current location on Herald Street in the South End in 1959.

 October 5. Isaiah Rogers's 1,360-seat, granite, Gothic-style Howard Athenaeum reopens at 34 Howard Street in Scollay Square with a production of Richard Sheridan's *The Rivals.* It is home to opera and serious drama for the next twenty years. Vaudeville is introduced in 1869, with "Lydia Thomson and Her British Blondes." At the turn of the century, the theater turns to burlesque, with performers such as Ann Corio, Sally Keith, Sally Rand, and "Tillie the Tassel." As the Old Howard, it features performers such as Abbott and Costello, Fred Allen, Jimmy Durante, W. C. Fields, Jackie Gleason, Al Jolson, Buster Keaton, Bert Lahr, Jerry Lewis, and Phil Silvers. Known for advertisements that proclaim "There Is Always Something Doing at the Old Howard," the theater is closed down in 1953.*

November 6. The second Boston Museum opens at 28 Tremont Street, next to King's Chapel Burying Ground. Designed by H. and J. E. Billings, it is owned and operated by Moses Kimball. Winsor later calls it "the most continuously successful theatre that Boston ever possessed." It closes with a performance of *Mrs. Dane's Defense* on June 1, 1903, and is torn down a few months later.

1847

The Long Wharf Immigration Station is established. Over thirty-seven thousand immigrants enter Boston during the year, most classified as "Irish labourers." Years earlier, Bishop Fenwick had advocated creating a colony for Irish immigrants in Maine, and over the next few years proposals would be made to establish such a colony in Iowa and in Canada. Edward Everett Hale later writes, "This transfer of immense bodies of people, from one climate, government, and state of society, to another wholly different is the most remarkable social phenomenon of our times."

May 29. A temporary quarantine hospital for Irish immigrants is set up at Deer Island. A permanent facility is established there in 1849.

February 22. Charlestown is incorporated as a city.

Readville (formerly the Dedham Low Plain) is named for James Read, one of the owners of Read and Chadwick, a local cotton mill.

Two summer hotels open on Spectacle Island. They operate until their illegal gambling operations are shut down by police in 1857. Nahum Ward purchases the island in 1857 and operates a rendering plant there until 1910. Taken over by the city, the island is used as a garbage dump from 1912 until 1959. It is enlarged by fill taken from the Big Dig in the 1990s, and is currently being turned into a park.

June 16. The Custom House opens. Designed by Ammi Young in the Greek Revival style, it is the most expensive government building of its time. Some of its original columns are used at the entrance of the Franklin Park Zoo, after a tower is added in 1915.*

Charles M. Ellis's *History of Roxbury Town* is published.

December 13. Josiah Quincy, Jr. (with 4,756 votes), defeats Goodrich (with 1,657) and Parker (1,547) and others to win reelection as mayor.

February 18. The Irish Famine Relief Committee is organized at Faneuil Hall in response to what Bishop John Fitzpatrick calls the "wild shrieks of famine and despair" coming from Ireland. The effort is led by both prominent Catholic and Protestant citizens. Boston subsequently sends four ships loaded with provisions to Ireland, including the *Jamestown* on March 27. The ship is on loan from the U.S. Navy and commanded by Capt. Robert Bennett Forbes—the first time a civilian is authorized to command a U.S. ship of war.

James Gately arrives in Boston from England. Later known as the "Hermit of Sally's Rock," he builds a cabin on the estate of Henry Grew in Hyde Park and dies there in 1875.

May 1. The Revere House hotel opens in Bowdoin Square, on the site of today's Saltonstall Building. Designed by William Washburn in the Greek Revival style, it is an enlargement of Charles Bulfinch's 1797 Kirk Boott House. Its guests would include Presidents Polk, Fillmore, Pierce, Johnson, and Grant; the prince of Wales; and Jenny Lind. The building burns on January 15, 1912, is rebuilt, and is then torn down in 1920.

February 2. Robert Morris is admitted to the Suffolk County Bar after becoming the first African American to pass the Massachusetts Bar examination.

January 21. One hundred buildings are destroyed in the North End in a fire, which also spreads into Charlestown.

September 6. The Josiah Quincy School opens at 90 Tyler Street in today's Chinatown. Designed by Gridley J. F. Bryant, it is dedicated on June 26, 1848. Conceived by Horace Mann, it is the first graded public middle school in the United States, and the first to assign each student to a separate seat. The first headmaster is John Dudley Philbrick, of whom it is later written, "He drastically reduced punishment by whipping, and added drawing and music to the curriculum." Destroyed by fire on December 17, 1848, the school is rebuilt and remains in operation until June 1976. Today the building serves as a Chinese community center.

September 16. Dr. Charles Putnam is the first to use anesthesia in child delivery while assisting Catherine Fisher in delivering her baby at Boston Lying-In Hospital.

The R. H. Stearns and Company department store opens on Washington Street. It moves to 140 Tremont Street in 1886, then into a new building, designed by Parker, Thomas, and Rice, on the same site in 1909. The store closes in July 1977.
Speaking of Boston businessmen, John Murray Forbes complains: "There is a class of cautious capitalists who go for 5 or 6 per cent interest with security which they can see and know all about, and you cannot touch them at all at any rate of interest [for other kinds of investment]."
Harrison Loring opens the City Point Works in South Boston. Other ironworks and machine shops in the area at this time are the Bay State Iron Works, John Souther's Globe Iron Works, Hawes and Hersey, the Gray and Woods Machine Company, and Chubbuck and Sons.
The E. Howard Watch and Clock Company is founded by Edward Howard and David Davis, former employees at the Willard Company. E. Howard Watch opens the first watch factory in the United States in Roxbury in 1850, is acquired by the Keystone Watch Case Company in 1903, and moves to Waltham in the 1930s.

April 23. Boston's first opera season opens with the American premiere of Verdi's *Ernani* by Signor Marti's Havana Opera singers.
August 27. William Warren joins the acting company at the Boston Museum, starring in Pocock's *Sweethearts.* He continues as a member until May 12, 1883, playing an estimated 575 roles and 13,000 performances. Another longtime member of the troupe is Mrs. J. R. Vincent, who joins in 1852 and is a member until her death in 1887.

1848

The Deacon House is completed at 1667 Washington Street in the South End. Designed by Gridley J. F. Bryant and Jean Lemoulnier, it is one of the most elegant residences in Boston and features the first mansard roof in the city. Sold at auction in 1871, it becomes the Massachusetts Normal School in 1873, then a dance hall. A remaining section of the building is now used as a commercial building.

October 25. A water festival is held to celebrate the opening of the aqueduct from Lake Cochituate. Construction had begun on August 20, 1846. A crowd of one hundred thousand people attend the event on Boston Common and witness a plume of water rise eighty feet into the air from the Frog Pond, followed by fireworks, cannon fire, and speeches.

A view of the Water Celebration on Boston Common. Engraving by S. Rowse, 1848. (Courtesy of the Bostonian Society)

The Beacon Hill Reservoir opens. It is demolished in 1882.

June 28. Forest Hills Cemetery opens. Designed by Gen. Henry A. S. Dearborn, it is the fourth "garden cemetery" in the country (after those in Cambridge, Brooklyn, and Providence), and it includes the first crematory in the United States. Graves would include those of James Freeman Clarke, e. e. cummings, William Lloyd Garrison, Edward Everett Hale, Eben Jordan, Reggie Lewis, Eugene O'Neill, Anne Sexton, Joseph Warren, and Jacob Wirth. The cemetery is also home to sculptures by Daniel Chester French (*Death Staying the Hand of the Sculptor*), Martin Millmore, and others.

Nathaniel Dearborn's *Boston Notions* is published.

February 23. The congressman and former president of the United States John Quincy Adams collapses and dies in the U.S. Capitol in Washington. His body is brought back to Boston, and then taken to Quincy for burial.
September 16. Abraham Lincoln speaks at a rally at Richmond Hall in Dorchester while campaigning in Massachusetts for the presidential candidate Zachary Taylor. He also appears a few days later at Tremont Temple.
December 11. The Whig candidate John Bigelow (with 5,150 votes) defeats John James (with 1,143) and others to win election as mayor. Inaugurated on January 1, 1849, he resumes the practice of granting liquor licenses, which had been stopped by his predecessor, Josiah Quincy, Jr.

December 7. Two hundred people attend a meeting at the Hanover House to discuss forming a company to look for gold in California. Prospective members are required to contribute three hundred dollars and pledge not to gamble or drink liquor. A few weeks later, on December 27, the *Sausalito* sails from Boston for California carrying passengers bound for the gold fields.

The Sisters of Notre Dame establish the first Catholic school in Boston.

Fall. Benjamin Roberts, an African American, sues the city when his five-year-old daughter, Sarah, is denied admission to the school nearest her home because of her race. Robert Morris, later assisted by Charles Sumner, argues the case, asking for "equality before the law." But in *Roberts* v. *City of Boston*, the Massachusetts Supreme Judicial Court rules unanimously against Roberts on April 8, 1850.

Charlestown High School opens on Monument Avenue. The school moves to the current building, designed by Hill, Miller, Friedlaender, Hollander, Inc., at 240 Medford Street, in 1978.

November 1. The Boston Female Medical College opens. Later called the New England Female Medical College, it is founded by Samuel Gregory, according to the medical historian Marianne Vahey, because he "feared that medicine was attracting men whose interest was not philanthropic but prurient." It becomes part of the Boston University School of Medicine in 1873.*

The Boston Society of Civil Engineers is established. It is the first engineering society in the United States.

May 1. Lee, Higginson and Company is founded by John Clarke Lee of Salem and George Higginson of Boston at 44 State Street. A private investment company, it invests heavily in New England textile mills, mining, and railroads. Henry Lee Higginson joins the firm in 1868, and James J. Storrow in 1900. The company ceases operation in 1932.*

The Massachusetts legislature imposes a 1 percent tax on goods sold at auction, despite Boston merchants' predictions that the tax will drive the China trade to New York—which is exactly what happens.

More than 120 newspapers, magazines, and other periodicals are being published in the city at this time—with a combined circulation of more than five hundred thousand.

Doll and Richards art gallery opens.

March 18. The Boston Public Library is incorporated. The first large, publicly supported, free municipal library in the United States, it is also the first to allow borrowing of books and materials. It originally opens in the Adams schoolhouse on Mason Street on March 20, 1854. The library moves to a new building by C. F. Kirby at the corner of Tremont and Boylston Streets on January 1, 1858, then to its current location in Copley Square in 1895.*

1849

Nathaniel Dearborn's *A New and Complete Map of the City of Boston 1848–1849* is published.

The Boston Board of Health describes the Back Bay as "nothing less than a great cesspool into which is daily deposited all the filth of a large and constantly increasing population."

Paul's Bridge is constructed over the Neponset River, connecting Hyde Park to Milton. Named after the family whose farm lies on the Hyde Park side of the river, it is rebuilt several times, though much of the original granite structure remains today.

December 27. The Boston Reservoir opens on Dorchester Heights in South Boston.

Francis Parkman's *The California and Oregon Trail* and George Ticknor's *The History of Spanish Literature* are published.

December 10. John Bigelow (with 4,543 votes) defeats Joseph Hall (with 705) and others to win reelection as mayor. In his inaugural address in January, he declares: "Foreign paupers are rapidly accumulating on our hands. . . . Numbers of helpless beings, including imbeciles, in both body and mind,—the aged, the blind, the paralytic, and the lunatic, have been landed from immigrant vessels, to become instantly, and permanently a charge upon our public charities."

Father Theobold Mathew, a charismatic Irish temperance priest, speaks in Boston.

Boston now has 1,200 licensed liquor dealers. Three years earlier, there had been only 850.

November 23. Dr. George Parkman disappears after leaving his Beacon Hill home after breakfast. A massive investigation follows, during which police reportedly bring in "every Irishman with a dollar in his pocket." Dr. John White Webster is subsequently arrested for murder after traces of Parkman's body are found in the drains of Harvard Medical School by a janitor, Ephraim Littlefield. The trial, before Judge Lemuel Shaw, captures national attention. Convicted and sentenced to death, Webster subsequently confesses. He is hanged on August 30, 1850, at the Leverett Street Jail, within sight of the medical school where he worked—and which is built on land donated by Parkman.

June 4. The first documented case of Asiatic cholera appears. The epidemic eventually kills over seven hundred residents of Boston, the majority of them Irish immigrants living in the crowded Fort Hill area. The author Norman Ware later recounts a doctor's visit to one cellar where thirty-nine persons were living, and another, flooded by water, where a child's body "was actually sailing about the room in its coffin."

Lewis Hayden opens a custom and ready-made clothing business on Cambridge Street. A runaway slave from Kentucky, Hayden uses his profits and products to feed and clothe fugitive slaves he harbors at his home at 66 Phillips Street on Beacon Hill, an important stop on the Underground Railroad. Hayden claims to keep two kegs of gunpowder in his basement, which he threatens to detonate if anyone attempts to search the house.

July. The Boston Athenaeum relocates to a new building at 10½ Beacon Street, designed by Edward Clarke Cabot in the Italianate style. Only the building's

Looking down Beacon Street from Bowdoin toward the Boston Athenaeum, ca. 1889. (Courtesy of the Bostonian Society)

address appears on the front door because, according to Whitehill, "of the general Boston assumption that anyone with serious business knows where things are; those who do not should inform themselves by other means than gaping at signs." Henry James later describes the library as "this honored haunt of all the most civilized," and the poet David McCord as "a kind of Utopia for books: the high-ceilinged rooms, the little balconies, alcoves, nooks and angles, all suggest sanctuary, escape, creature comfort. The reader, the scholar, the browser, the borrower is king." The organization resists an attempt to be absorbed by the new Boston Public Library in 1853 and limits the number of its proprietors to 1,049 in 1854. The building is renovated and two floors are added by Henry Forbes Bigelow in 1915, and the building is renovated again by Schwartz and Silver in 2002.

The Germania Musical Society makes its first Boston appearance. The orchestra makes Boston its headquarters for several years. The Liedertafel Club, an amateur choral group, is also established this year.

September 10. Edwin Booth makes his professional debut, playing Tressel in *King Richard III* at the Boston Museum. His father, Junius, plays the title role.

1850

Boston's population is 136,881, an increase of almost 50 percent in ten years, making it the third-largest city in the United States (behind New York and Baltimore). Of that number, 1,999 are described as "Free Colored," and 46,677 as foreign born—35,287 in Ireland. The separate towns of Roxbury, Dorchester, Charlestown, and Brighton have an additional combined population of 45,905, with 324 classified as nonwhite.

Between 1846 and 1850, 112,664 passengers came through the Port of Boston, a dramatic rise from the 36,741 in the previous five-year period. Another 117,505 enter between 1851 and 1855. The number decreases to 69,923 between 1856 and 1860 and to 42,721 between 1861 and 1865.

John Bachmann's lithograph *Bird's-Eye View of Boston* is produced.

David Sears proposes constructing a "silver lake" in the middle of the new

Immigrant arrival at Constitution Wharf, from Ballou's Pictorial. *(Courtesy of the Boston Public Library, Print Department)*

Back Bay district; George Snell suggests a "receiving basin" the length of the new Back Bay in 1859.

December. Donald McKay's *Stag Hound* is launched. The first of the fifteen-hundred-ton clipper ships, it later sets a record for sailing from Boston to the equator, in thirteen days.
Elias Haskett Derby, Jr., writes that, thanks to the expanded rail service, Boston businessmen can "reach their stores and offices in the morning, and at night sleep with their wives and children in the suburbs. No time is lost, for they read the morning and evening journals as they go and return."

August 7. Evergreen Cemetery is consecrated in Brighton.

December 9. John Bigelow (with 5,373 votes) defeats Charles Amory (with 1,169) and Goodrich (1,094) to again win reelection as mayor.

Runaway slaves William and Ellen Craft are saved from being returned to their owner when a crowd of over two thousand people threatens their owner and his slave catchers. The two later marry and are freed by the courts.
March 7. Daniel Webster delivers a speech in the U.S. Senate in which he calls for saving the Union at all cost and supports passage of the Fugitive Slave Act. The speech alienates many of Webster's followers in Boston, but the bill is signed into law by President Millard Fillmore on September 18.
October 14. An estimated six hundred people—black and white—meet at Faneuil Hall to protest and plan resistance to the Fugitive Slave Law. The Boston Vigilance Committee is organized a few days later. Chaired by Theodore Parker, the committee, which includes the former slave Lewis Hayden, raises money to assist more than one hundred runaway slaves. When another rally is held at Faneuil Hall to denounce both the Fugitive Slave Law and Daniel Webster in November, it is broken up by antiabolitionists.

A reported 2,227 Irish girls work as domestic servants in the city.

Daniel Laing and Isaac Snowden of Boston and Martin Delaney of Pittsburgh become the first African-American students admitted to Harvard Medical School. They are dismissed in 1851, after protests by white students convince the dean "that intermixing of the white and Black races . . . is distasteful to a large portion of the class and injurious to the interests of the school."

Harriet Hunt becomes the first woman to be accepted to Harvard Medical School. She is persuaded to withdraw her application, however, and the school announces soon after: "Resolved, That no woman of true delicacy would be willing in the presence of men, to listen to the discussion of the subjects that necessarily come under the consideration of the student of medicine. Resolved, That we are not opposed to allowing woman her rights, but we do protest against her appearance where her presence is calculated to destroy our respect for the modesty and delicacy of her sex."

The John Donnelly and Sons sign company is founded.

Boston has seventy-seven newspapers: twelve daily newspapers, fifty-eight weeklies, and seven semiweeklies.

Nathaniel Hawthorne's *Scarlet Letter* is published.

July 19. Margaret Fuller, her husband, and their infant son drown off Fire Island when, en route from Italy, their ship runs aground in a storm.

September 28. Jenny Lind makes her singing debut in Boston at the Tremont Temple. Seats are auctioned to the highest bidder (a common practice at the time), with Hatter Dodge reportedly paying $625 for "choice of seats." Lind's popularity is dubbed "Lindamania" by the press. When she sings again at the Fitchburg Railroad Station on October 12, a thousand people pay a dollar each for standing-room tickets, and a stampede occurs as the audience vies for the best viewing locations.

1851 to 1875

1851

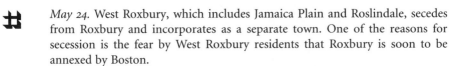

May 24. West Roxbury, which includes Jamaica Plain and Roslindale, secedes from Roxbury and incorporates as a separate town. One of the reasons for secession is the fear by West Roxbury residents that Roxbury is soon to be annexed by Boston.

Fort Warren is completed on George's Island. Begun in 1836, it is designed by Sylvanus Thayer and named for Gen. Joseph Warren, who died in the Battle of Bunker Hill. Each of the five bastions in the star-shaped structure is named for a famous New Englander. The fort is used as a prison for twelve hundred captured Confederate soldiers beginning in 1862 and as a mine and torpedo station in 1898. It is decommissioned in 1951, and turned over to the Metropolitan District Commission in 1962.

September 17. A three-day Railroad Jubilee is held to celebrate the opening of the railroad line between Boston and Canada. The event is attended by President Millard Fillmore and Secretary of State Daniel Webster.
Donald McKay's *Flying Cloud* is launched in East Boston. The naval historian Samuel Eliot Morison later describes it as "our Rheims, the *Sovereign of the Seas* [launched in 1852] our Parthenon, the *Lightning* [launched in 1854] our Amiens." The *Flying Cloud* sets a record for sailing from New York to San Francisco in eighty-nine days and eight hours in 1854.
The city's ninety-six-mile sewer system is completed.

December 14. Whig Benjamin Seaver (with 3,990 votes) defeats Dr. Jerome V. C. Smith (with 2,736) and Adam Thaxter, Jr. (1,024), and others to win election as mayor. He is inaugurated on January 5, 1852. Seaver successfully presses for the construction of a public library. In the same election, the entire Board of Aldermen is replaced, reportedly for refusing Daniel Webster use of Faneuil Hall because an abolitionist group had earlier been denied its use.

February 15. The runaway slave Shadrach Minkins is arrested at the Cornhill Coffee House (on the site of today's One Beacon Street), where he works as a waiter. Taken to the federal courthouse on Court Street one block away, he is freed by Lewis Hayden and other free African Americans, and he eventually escapes to Montreal.
April 3. The runaway slave Thomas Sims is captured in Boston. Marshal Francis Tukey prevents efforts to free him by Hayden, Thomas Wentworth Higginson, and others by running a chain around the courthouse. Under heavy guard, Sims is marched past thousands of protestors to Long Wharf on April 19, put on a ship, and returned to Georgia.

Police conveying the fugitive slave Sims to the ship that will return him to the South. Engraving from Gleason's Pictorial. *(Courtesy of the Bostonian Society)*

The Young Men's Christian Union is organized. Founded initially as a religious study group by a number of Harvard students, it is incorporated in 1852. Its High Gothic–style sandstone building, designed by Nathaniel Bradlee, opens at 48 Boylston Street in 1876. The building is added to over the years and renovated in 2003.

June 4. A Smokers' Circle is established on Boston Common, as a sanctuary from the ban on smoking in public. Those who use it whittle away at the wooden benches so "industriously" that iron benches are installed on July 27, 1847.

December 15. The Greater Boston YMCA is organized. The first in the United States, it is located initially at 228 Washington Street on March 11, 1852, moves to the Tremont Temple a year later, and then to a building at the corner of Tremont and Stuart Streets in 1872. It moves to a building designed by Sturgis and Brigham at the corner of Boylston and Berkeley Streets on November 14, 1883, then to its current building, designed by Shepley, Rutan, and Coolidge, at 312–320 Huntington Avenue in 1912.

The feminist Amelia Bloomer, wearing her eponymous trousers, speaks out for women's rights on Boston Common.

Abner Forbes and J. W. Green's pamphlet "The Rich Men of Massachusetts" is published. It lists five hundred residents of Suffolk County thought to be worth more than one hundred thousand dollars.

April 23. Marshal Tukey and the Boston police stage the "Ann Street Descent" on the red-light district in the North End. Nine men are arrested as "tipplers, vagabonds, pipe players, etc." and sixty women as "keepers of brothels, noisy and disorderly houses, violators of the license and Sunday laws, etc." Many of the women are given suspended sentences, then proceed to hire themselves out as domestic servants. Another 150 are arrested a week later.

The Boston police institute a "rogues gallery." Pickpockets, burglars, and streetwalkers, although not under arrest, are required to present themselves before the police force weekly so they might be identified later. When they leave the station, they are set upon by citizens who tear at their clothes and mark their backs with crosses in chalk. According to Marshal Tukey, there are 227 houses of prostitution and 26 gambling dens operating in the city, along with 1,500 shops selling liquor—900 of them run by Irishmen.

September. Barney McGinniskin becomes the first Irish American appointed to the Boston police force. Reporting to work on November 3, McGinniskin declares himself "fresh from the bogs of Ireland," although he had been in this country for twenty-two years. His appointment was opposed by Marshal Tukey, and former mayor Bigelow described it as "a dangerous precedent to appoint a foreigner to stations of such trust," but Mayor Seaver orders that McGinniskin be kept on the force. There are nearly forty Irish-American police officers by 1869 and forty-five by 1871.

November 24. The Charles Street Jail opens. Designed by Gridley J. F. Bryant, it is expanded in 1901 and 1920. After the Federal District Court judge W. Arthur Garrity spends a night there, he orders it closed on July 20, 1973, but it remains open until the South Bay Correctional Facility opens on December 20, 1991. The old jail is currently being converted into a luxury hotel.

The position of superintendent of the Boston public schools is created. The authority of the superintendent is increased somewhat in 1898, then substantially in 1906.

January 20. The Jordan Marsh Company opens at 129 Milk Street. Founded by Eben Jordan and Benjamin Marsh, it incorporates on May 17, 1901. The store moves to Pearl Street in 1854, to Winthrop Square in 1859, and to Devonshire Street in 1861. The first retail sale is made by Eben Jordan, Jr.—a yard of cherry-colored ribbon. A new building, designed by S. J. F. Thayer, opens at 450 Washington Street in 1880. An addition, designed by Perry, Shaw, and Hepburn, opens in 1951, and the current building opens in 1978. The store is sold and the name is changed to Macy's on January 11, 1996.

May 26. The Union Boat Club is organized, and is now the second-oldest rowing association in the United States. Its boathouse at the foot of Charles Street on Beacon Hill is built in 1870.

1852

July. The state legislature appoints the Commission on Boston Harbor and Back Bay Public Lands (later the Harbor and Land Commission). The commission subsequently recommends filling in the Back Bay and adopts a plan by the architects Arthur Gilman and George Snell, as well as the landscape architects Copeland and Cleveland, for developing a residential area of long, wide, French-style boulevards (named by 1857) and cross streets (named beginning in 1859). The urbanologist Lewis Mumford later calls the plan for the Back Bay one of the the outstanding achievements in American city planning in the nineteenth century. The architectural historian Bainbridge Bunting later declares that it "expressed [Boston's] will to assume a place among the great cities of the world."

June 24. The Mount Hope Cemetery is dedicated on Canterbury Street in Roslindale.

William C. Nell's *Services of the Colored Americans in the Wars of 1776 and 1812* and Josiah Quincy's *The Municipal History of the Town and City of Boston* are published.
The first volume of Samuel G. Drake's *History and Antiquities of Boston* is published. The last is published in 1856.

December 13. Benjamin Seaver (with 6,018 votes) defeats Dr. Jerome V. C. Smith (with 5,021) and others to win reelection as mayor.

March 20. Harriet Beecher Stowe's *Uncle Tom's Cabin* is published by John Jewett of Boston. The daughter of the former Boston minister Lyman Beecher, Stowe wrote the novel while living in Maine. In its time it becomes the most popular book in the history of the United States. Henry Wadsworth Longfellow complains that every evening "we read ourselves into despair in that tragic book. . . . It is too melancholy, and makes one's blood boil too hotly."
The Massachusetts legislature passes a state Prohibition law. The ban on the private sale of alcohol proves difficult to enforce, especially in Boston, and is repealed in 1868.

April 28, noon. The first electric fire alarm in the world is rung from what is now Box 1212 for a fire on Causeway Street. Created by Dr. William Channing and Moses Farmer, the system consists of forty miles of wire, forty-five signal boxes, and sixteen alarm bells. Police officers and members of the Boston Night Watch are given keys to the locked boxes to enable them to turn in alarms. Part of the system is still in use today.

March 26. Temple Ohabei Shalom is dedicated on Warren (later Warrenton) Street. It is the first synagogue in Boston and the third in New England (after those in Newport and New Haven). The congregation was formed by Jewish immigrants from Poland on May 24, 1843. It meets initially in rented quarters, purchases the Universalist church building across the street, then moves to the former Congregational church at 11 Union Park Street in the South End. The synagogue moves to the corner of Shawmut Avenue and Madison Street in 1898, then several more times until reaching its current location on Beacon Street in Brookline in 1929.

Dorchester High School opens with fifty-nine students in the first class. It moves to Codman Square in 1895, then to a building designed by Harris Atwood at 9 Peacevale Road in 1925.
September. Girls High School opens in the Adams School building on Mason Street. The first successful public high school for girls in the country, it merges with the Normal School in 1854 and becomes Girls High and Normal School.

It moves to West Newton Street in 1870. The high school becomes a separate school from the teachers' college in 1872.

The *Boston Pilot* complains: "Our little boys scoff at their parents, call their fathers by the name Old Man, Boss, or Governor. The mother is the Old Woman. The little boys smoke, drink, blaspheme, talk about fornication, and so far as they are physically able, commit it. Our little girls read novels . . . quarrel about their beaux, uphold Woman's Rights."

May 13. Edward Capen is named the first librarian (chief executive) of the Boston Public Library. The title is later changed to superintendent, back to librarian, to director, and finally, in 1934, to director and librarian. Capen is succeeded by Charles Coffin Jewett (1858), Justin Winsor (1868), Samuel Green (1877), Mellen Chamberlain (1878), Theodore Dwight (1892), Herbert Putnam (1895), James Whitney (1899), Horace Wadlin (1903), Charles Belden (1917), Milton Lord (1932), Philip McNiff (1965), Liam Kelly (1983), Arthur Curley (1985), and Bernard Margolis (1997 to the present).

October 1. Joshua Bates donates fifty thousand dollars to the Boston Public Library for the purchase of books. Born in Weymouth, Bates worked at a countinghouse in Boston at fifteen and later moved to England, where he became a senior partner at Baring Brothers. In making the contribution, he describes "my own experience as a poor boy . . . having no money to spend and no place to go, not being able to pay for a light or fire in my own room, I could not pay for books." He imposes two stipulations on his gift: that the library be a building the city will be proud of and that it contain a reading room big enough to accommodate more than one hundred people. Bates later donates another fifty thousand dollars to buy more books. Bates Hall, the library's main reading room, is later named after him.

Margaret Fuller's *The Memoirs of Margaret Fuller Ossoli* and Nathaniel Hawthorne's *Blithedale Romance* are published.

February 5. The singer Jenny Lind marries her accompanist, Otto Goldschmidt, in the home of the banker Samuel Gray Ward at 20 Louisburg Square.

April. The first issue of *Dwight's Journal of Music* appears. For many years the only music journal in Boston, it is published by John Sullivan Dwight and continues until September 1881.

November 20. The Boston Music Hall opens on Hamilton Place with a concert by the Musical Fund Society and the Handel and Haydn Society. The hall is designed by George Snell and since its opening, M. A. De Wolfe Howe later writes, "it was unnecessary to ask a visiting Jenny Lind to sing in the Fitchburg Railroad Station." The "great organ," the largest in the United States, is dedicated there on November 2, 1863. The final scene of Henry James's 1886 novel, *The Bostonians,* is set here. In it the hero declares, "even when exasperated, a Boston audience is not ungenerous." After 1900 the building becomes Lowe's Family Vaudeville House, then the Empire. Substantially renovated by Thomas Lamb, it becomes the Orpheum, the city's first movie theater, in 1915.

A dramatization of *Uncle Tom's Cabin* by H. J. Conway is performed at the Boston Museum. Harriet Beecher Stowe and her father, Rev. Lyman Beecher, attend one of the performances.

Boston Music Hall at 6½ Hamilton Place, ca. 1898 (Courtesy of the Bostonian Society)

 August 3. Harvard defeats Yale in crew on Lake Winnipesaukee in New Hampshire in what is considered the first intercollegiate athletic contest held in the United States.

1853

The Hyde Park Land Company begins developing land in what was then part of Dorchester and is now Hyde Park. The area had been called *Tist* by the Indians.

October 4. Donald McKay's clipper ship *Great Republic* is launched before thirty thousand cheering spectators in East Boston. Because the shareholders are temperance advocates, it is christened with a bottle of water from Lake Cochituate. It is McKay's largest ship and the largest on the seas at the time. Schools and businesses are closed to celebrate the event. With the development of steamships, the clipper shipbuilding industry in Boston begins to wane after 1856. McKay sells his shipyard in 1869, and it closes in 1875.

December 12. No mayoral candidate receives sufficient votes on the first ballot, or on the second ballot held on December 27, so the election is postponed until January 1854.*

February 2. Emma Snodgrass, demonstrating for women's rights, causes a sensation by strolling through the streets of Boston dressed in men's clothing.
May 17. The maximum hours of labor are fixed by law at twelve hours during the summer and ten hours in winter.
Sarah Redmond of Salem, a free African American, buys an orchestra seat to a show at the Howard Athenaeum by mail. When she attempts to attend the performance, she is asked to sit in the balcony. After refusing and being denied entrance, Redmond goes to court and wins five hundred dollars in damages from the theater.

The mayor and the aldermen are jointly authorized to appoint the chief of police, a practice that continues until 1878.

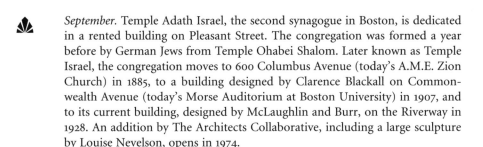

September. Temple Adath Israel, the second synagogue in Boston, is dedicated in a rented building on Pleasant Street. The congregation was formed a year before by German Jews from Temple Ohabei Shalom. Later known as Temple Israel, the congregation moves to 600 Columbus Avenue (today's A.M.E. Zion Church) in 1885, to a building designed by Clarence Blackall on Commonwealth Avenue (today's Morse Auditorium at Boston University) in 1907, and to its current building, designed by McLaughlin and Burr, on the Riverway in 1928. An addition by The Architects Collaborative, including a large sculpture by Louise Nevelson, opens in 1974.

Girls Trade School opens in the South End. Originally the Industrial School for Girls, it is founded by the Massachusetts Association of Women Workers. Later taken over by the Boston School Committee, it becomes the first public industrial school for females. The school moves to Dorchester, then to a building at the corner of Hemenway Street and Westland Avenue in the Fenway in 1904.

The R. H. White Company is established. The retail store moves into a building designed by Peabody and Stearns on Washington Street in 1877 and is absorbed by Filene's in 1929.

Fitz Hugh Lane's *View of Boston Harbor, 1853* and John White Allen Scott's *Boston Harbor, 1853* are completed.
The Chickering Piano Factory opens at 791 Tremont Street in the South End. Designed by Edwin Payson, it is said to be the second-largest building in the United States (after the Capitol Building). The company moves to Rochester in 1928, and in 1974 the building becomes the Piano Craft Guild, an artists' housing and studio cooperative.

1854

September 26. The Commission on Boston Harbor and Back Bay Public Lands reaches an indenture agreement concerning property ownership in the Back Bay with the Boston and Roxbury Mill Dam Corporation and the Boston Water Power Company. Each company has conducted some filling over the previous thirty years. New filling begins in May 1855.

January 9. Dr. Jerome Van Crowninshield Smith (with 6,840 votes) defeats John Wilkins (with 3,171) and others to win the mayoral election. A member of the Native American (Know-Nothing) Party, he is later described by Richard Henry Dana, Jr., as being "raised by accident to a mayoralty." Inaugurated the next day, Smith had formerly been Boston's port physician and lived on an island in Boston Harbor. He had also written a book, *The Ways of Women*, in which he claimed that if women were elected to public office, "they would have too much self-respect to . . . foist their imbecile relatives into office or vote to raise their own pay at the expense of the people overburdened by taxation."
Voters approve changes in the mayor's office through a revision in the city charter. The changes give the mayor qualified veto powers, but excludes the

mayor from the deliberations of the Board of Aldermen, which still must approve appointments and initiatives. Membership on the Board is increased from eight to twelve.

December 11. Dr. Jerome V. C. Smith (with 6,429 votes) defeats George Upton (with 4,409) and others to win reelection as mayor.

May 24. The runaway slave Anthony Burns is captured in Boston. Brought before the fugitive slave commissioner, Edward Greely Loring, and defended by Richard Henry Dana, Jr., he is tried, found guilty, and ordered returned to his master in Virginia. Burns's supporters riot and James Batchelder, a courthouse guard, is killed on May 26. Fifty thousand demonstrators line State Street as 2,000 militia, police, and federal soldiers escort Burns to the steamer *John Tyler*, which takes him back to the South on June 2. Burns's freedom is subsequently purchased by members of the Twelfth Baptist Church, and he returns to Boston a year later. He eventually becomes a minister and moves to Canada.

May 30. Congress passes the Kansas-Nebraska Act. The law effectively repeals the Missouri Compromise and allows each new state to decide the slavery issue for itself. Its passage prompts the Bostonian Amos Lawrence to declare, "We went to bed one night, old-fashioned, conservative, compromise, Union Whigs, and waked up stark mad Abolitionists."

June 2. The first Women's Rights Convention is held in Boston.

May 26, 6:00 P.M. The Boston Police Department is established. Authorized by state legislation enacted three days before, the force combines the daytime police and the Boston Night Watch into one department, which is modeled after the London police force. There are 260 paid officers. Located initially in an office in the courthouse, the police headquarters moves to the Old City Hall in 1865, to 37 Pemberton Square in 1883, to 154 Berkeley Street in 1926, and to 1199 Tremont Street in Roxbury in 1997.

Breck's Nursery is established at 35 Nonantum Street in Oak Square, Brighton by Joseph Breck, later the editor of the *New England Farmer* and president of the Massachusetts Horticultural Society.

April. The "Angel Gabriel," a self-ordained Protestant preacher whose real name is John Orr, fans anti-Catholic sentiments in Boston. Described by the historian Edward Savage as a "poor, illiterate, half-breed Scotchman with more impudence than brains," Orr leads a mob that steals a cross from a Catholic church in Chelsea on May 7. He incites more disturbances in June and July, is arrested and fined in August, and disappears soon after.

The Boston School Committee is again reorganized. Under the revised city charter, it now consists of seventy-four members (the mayor, the president of the Common Council, and six representatives from each of the twelve wards). A third of them are elected annually for three-year terms.

June 11. Another cholera outbreak provokes great alarm in the city.
Two Boston-area gunsmiths, Horace Smith and Daniel Wesson, announce they have developed a fast-firing revolver.

April 28. The Boston Board of Trade is established in order to organize the business interests in the city, especially with regard to the operation of the Port of Boston.

May 1. The Boston Five Cents Savings Bank opens in a storefront on School Street. Its declared goal is "to induce the young and industrial classes to make a beginning to save by encouraging deposits as small as five cents, and to give minors the right to withdraw their money in person without a guardian." A new bank building opens is 1858. It is replaced by one designed by Parker, Thomas, and Rice at 10–32 School Street in 1926. An addition, by Kallmann and McKinnell, is completed in 1972.

Beacon Press is established. Originally the Book Fund Project of the American Unitarian Association, it seeks to remedy the problem, described by the AUA's president, Samuel Eliot, that "books that appeal to the higher instincts do not command as a rule a higher circulation and cannot, therefore, be handled by publishing houses that are primarily commercial." The press is located today at 41 Mt. Vernon Street.

The Boston Art Club is formed. Initially made up of twenty artists who meet in one another's studios, it opens up its membership to nonartists in 1870 and soon reaches its limit of eight hundred members. Only one in eight is an artist, however, and it becomes more of a social club where, according to one of its founders, Samuel Gerry, "the palette and the palate seem to thrive together." The club holds annual juried exhibitions of contemporary art and several other exhibitions each year. After renting a house at 64 Boylston Street, it moves to a new building, designed by William Ralph Emerson, at 270 Dartmouth Street in 1882 (today's Snowden International High School).

Mason and Hamlin Company is established. Founded by Henry Mason and Emmons Hamlin, it makes one-fourth of all reed organs in the United States by 1865, and begins making pianos in 1883. The organ business is later purchased by the Aeolian Company in 1911, and the piano company is sold and the plant moved to Rochester in 1932.

September 11. The second Boston Theatre opens at 539 Washington Street with a production of Sheridan's *The Rivals* and a farce, *The Loan of a Lover*. Designed by Edward and James Cabot and Jonathan Preston, the 3,600-seat theater is the largest and most luxurious of its day. It also features a lobby with the first refreshment counter in a theater in the United States, which serves ice cream and nonalcoholic "temperance drinks." Renamed the Boston Academy of Music between 1860 and 1862, it later reassumes its original name. The building is taken over by B. F. Keith and used for vaudeville beginning in 1909, becomes the Keith Boston Theater in 1914, and is torn down to make way for the Keith Memorial Theatre in 1925.

1855

May 21. Washington Village (now called Andrew Square) is annexed to Boston from Dorchester.

The filling of the Back Bay in Roxbury begins. It continues until 1894.

The Fairmount Land Company and Twenty Associates, led by Alpheus Blake, purchase land from the town of Milton and begin to build houses for themselves and for sale along today's Fairmount Avenue. The area is named Hyde Park by Rev. Henry Lyman, after "the beautiful and aristocratic suburb of London."

 The Boston and New York Central Railroad is completed to its terminal near today's South Station. Offering service as far as Putnam, Connecticut, it is later called the Boston, Hartford, and Erie, and then the New York and New England Railroad.
June. The *Merrimack* is launched at the Charlestown Navy Yard. It is later converted into an ironclad ship for the Confederate Navy.
The Mount Washington Bridge is completed across the Fort Point Channel, connecting Boston with the main wharf of the Boston Wharf Company.

 William C. Nell's *The Colored Patriots of the American Revolution with Sketches of Several Distinguished Colored Persons to Which Is Added a Brief Survey of the Condition and Prospects of Colored Americans* is published.

 December 10. Alexander Hamilton Rice (with 7,401 votes) defeats Dr. Nathaniel Shurtleff (with 5,800) and others to win election to the first of three terms as mayor. Inaugurated on January 7, 1856, Rice is Boston's first Republican mayor. The historian John Galvin later describes the man who was also a three-term governor as "the most successful politician-businessman Boston has ever known."

 October 5. The Parker House opens at today's 60 School Street. Designed by Gridley J. F. Bryant, it is originally called Parker's and is an outgrowth of Parker's Restaurant (established in 1832). The restaurant becomes known for its Boston Cream Pie and Parker House rolls and for coining the term "scrod" for the white-fleshed catch of the day. Regular diners would include James Michael Curley, Isabella Stewart Gardner, and John F. Kennedy. Guests would include Willa Cather, Charles Dickens, Generals Grant and Sherman, and the actors Sarah Bernhardt and Edwin and John Wilkes Booth. Employees would include Malcolm X and Ho Chi Minh. After expanding into a number of adjoining buildings, the complex is replaced by the current building, designed by G. Henri Desmond, on May 12, 1927. The rooftop terrace opens in 1935, then closes in 1969 after taller buildings block the view. Today called the Omni Parker House Hotel, it is the oldest continuously operated hotel in the United States.
Boston's first B'nai B'rith organization is founded.

 According to the historian Roger Lane, "in most years before the middle of the 1850's, no homicides at all were reported for Suffolk County."

 September 3. The Boston public schools are the first of any major city in the United States to be integrated. African-American children begin attending their local schools after a law passed on April 18, 1854, by the Massachusetts legislature prohibits exclusion on account of "race, color, or religious opinions."

$ Despite Boston's loss of primacy in the China trade, Edward Cunningham, a partner in Russell and Company, predicts: "China will become in the course of time, our most important commercial connection, if no untoward event intervenes."

The Saturday Club is founded by Horatio Woodman. Charter members include Louis Agassiz, Richard Henry Dana, Jr., John Sullivan Dwight, Ralph Waldo Emerson, Ebenezer Rockwood Hoar, James Russell Lowell, John Lothrop Motley, Benjamin Peirce, Samuel Gray Ward, and Edwin Pierce Whipple. Henry David Thoreau declines to join and later writes: "They have got a club, the handle of which is in the Parker House at Boston, and with this they beat me from time to time, expecting to make me tender or

The Parker House at 60 School Street, ca. 1892. (Courtesy of the Bostonian Society)

minced meat. . . ." The group meets initially in a private dining room at the Parker House on the last Saturday of each month (with summers off), switches from dinner to lunch in 1898, and relocates to the Union Club in 1902. It continues today.

The Olympic Club of Boston, organized the year before, beats the newly formed Elm Tree Club in the first baseball game ever played in Boston on Boston Common. The teams play the "Massachusetts Game," also called the "New England Game," which involves a smaller ball and closer bases than today's game.

1856

December 11. The Tripartite Agreement is reached among the Boston Water Power Company, the state, and the city over development in the new Back Bay. The city receives two and three-quarter acres for an addition to the Public Garden.

March 26. A horsecar line begins regular service between Bowdoin Square in Boston and Cambridgeport. The first in New England, it is operated by the Cambridge Street Railroad Company. The next line to operate runs between Scollay Square and Roxbury. A Dorchester line opens in 1857, and Charlestown and South Boston lines in 1858. The number of horsecars in the city eventually reaches an estimated eight thousand before they are replaced by electric streetcars. The last horsecar run is made along Marlborough Street from Arlington Street to Massachusetts Avenue on December 24, 1899.
The Meridian Street Bridge opens, connecting East Boston to Chelsea.

May 22. U.S. Senator Charles Sumner, of Boston, is beaten with a walking stick by U.S. Representative Preston Brooks of South Carolina on the floor of the Senate in Washington. Three days before, Sumner had denounced Brooks's uncle, Senator Andrew Butler of South Carolina, for supporting the Kansas-Nebraska Bill and attacked the "slavocracy" of the South. Sumner is welcomed back to Boston by a large crowd of people on November 3. After a long recovery, he returns to the Senate.

December 8. Alexander Hamilton Rice (with 8,714 votes) defeats Jonathan Preston (with 2,025) and others to win reelection as mayor.

 The winter of 1856–1857 is the harshest in forty years.

 Louis Prang's Art Publishing House opens in Roxbury. A German immigrant, Prang introduces chromolithography—the process of reproducing oil paintings—to Boston.

Francis Parkman's *Vassall Morton* is published.

January 25. The Boston-born opera singer Elise Hensler debuts in her hometown.

1857

 A state legislative committee decries that there is "a palpable lack of room for dwelling-houses in and near the city of Boston . . . rents are enormously high,—and it is becoming a serious problem where the people whose business draws them to the metropolis of New England and the capital of the State, shall be accommodated."

 Le Voyageur de la Mer is launched by Holden and Gallagher in East Boston. Built for the pasha of Egypt, it is the first large steam vessel made of iron built in the United States. The ironclad *Wide Awake* is also launched this year.

 Thomas Simonds's *A History of South Boston* is published.

 December 14. The Republican and Citizens party candidate Frederick Lincoln, Jr. (with 8,110 votes), defeats Charles Hall (with 4,193) and others to win election as mayor. A distant relative of the future president, he is inaugurated on January 5, 1858. Lincoln serves a record seven terms as mayor and becomes known for visiting saloons and gambling houses in disguise to check for lawbreaking, and, during the Civil War, aggressively recruiting for the Union cause.

The Hotel Pelham opens at the corner of Tremont and Boylston Streets. Designed by Alfred Stone, it is one of the first apartment houses in the United States and introduces the "French flat" to Boston—a kind of residential hotel in which separate apartments share a central kitchen in the basement. The building is later moved to allow Boylston Street to be widened and is torn down to make way for construction of the Little Building around 1917.

The first chapter of the Ancient Order of Hibernians is organized in Boston.

January. Temperatures plunge to as low as 13 degrees below zero and Boston Harbor again freezes. An eight-mile passage in the ice is cut to allow the Cunard steamer *America* to sail back to England.

After a severe winter, a thaw raises the level of the Neponset River, sweeping the Fairmount footbridge away.

The Boston Farm and Trade School on Thompson Island forms the first school band in America. The band first parades in Boston in 1859.

The Panic of 1857 occurs. Boston banks stop specie payments for sixty days. Although few banks fail, their investments diminish. The depression particularly damages Boston's shipbuilding industry, and, together with the Civil War, diminishes Boston's standing as a commercial and business center for years to come.

October 27. The first issue of the *Atlantic Monthly* appears. The magazine is founded by members of the Magazine or Atlantic Club (most of whose members belong to the Saturday Club); it is published by James Fields from an office in the Old Corner Book Store. It moves to Arlington Street in 1920 and today is located at 77 North Washington Street. James Russell Lowell, the first editor, declares the magazine will be "free without being fanatical," its pages "open to all available talents of all shades of opinion." He is succeeded by James Fields (1861), William Dean Howells (1870), Thomas Bailey Aldrich (1881), Horace Scudder (1890), Walter Hines Page (1898), and Bliss Perry (1899 to 1909*).

The Flemish dealer Gambert brings French paintings to Boston for sale. He returns with more paintings in 1860. The French dealer Cadart follows in 1865.

1858

May. The major filling of the Back Bay begins. The state, and later the Boston Water Power Company, contract the work to Norman Munson and George Goss. They build a nine-mile railroad to a gravel quarry in West Needham, and run thirty-five-car trains, loaded with gravel, every hour, twenty-four hours a day, six days a week, until 1863 (then less frequently after that). The filled land reaches Clarendon Street by 1860, Exeter Street by 1870, and is completed in the Back Bay by 1886. It reaches the Fens by 1890, and is completed there in 1894. The first houses are built in 1859; construction peaks when eighty-nine houses are built in 1868. Though Henry James later decries "a tract pompous and prosaic," Lewis Mumford declares that it was "in the Back Bay that Boston first established itself as one of the centers of world culture in the arts and sciences."

August 2. The first street letter boxes are erected around the city. Mail can be deposited in them for collections at 9:00 A.M. and 3:30 and 7:00 P.M.

The first volume of John Gorham Palfrey's eventual five-volume *History of New England 1858–1890* and Gen. William H. Sumner's *History of East Boston, with Biographical Sketches of Its Early Proprietors* are published.

Engraving by an unknown artist prior to the filling in of the Back Bay. (Courtesy of the Bostonian Society)

December 13. Frederick Lincoln, Jr. (with 6,298 votes), defeats Moses Kimball (with 4,440) and others to win reelection as mayor.

October 11. Jefferson Davis defends slavery in a speech at Faneuil Hall. He receives what the *Boston Post* describe as "a cordial greeting to the honored guest from Mississippi."

Boston police officers begin to wear uniforms: a double-breasted, dark-blue frock coat, a tall hat, and, in summer, a silk vest. Intended to help citizens recognize police, the uniforms are criticized for making officers look like "popinjays" and for exposing them to criminals. White cotton gloves are issued as part of the uniform in 1861.
October 22. The second Ann Street Descent occurs. In another attempt to close the brothels in that area, police arrest fifty-one people, mostly women from small towns throughout New England. Forty-seven receive suspended sentences and are sent back home.

Temple Mishkan Israel is established. Founded by East Prussian Jews who have left Temple Adath Israel, the congregation initially meets in an apartment on Oswego Street in the South End. Later the first Conservative congregation in the city, it moves to a number of other locations in the South End, joins with Shaaray Tefila to form Mishkan Tefila in 1895, moves to the former Immanuel Congregational Church on Moreland Street in Roxbury in May 1907, then to Seaver Street in Roxbury in 1925.*

Carter's Ink Company is established. It is located initially on Water Street and then on Batterymarch Street. The company opens a new plant at 162–172 Columbus Avenue in 1884, then moves to Cambridge in 1910. The Columbus Avenue building is later converted into office and retail space, then into the Back Bay Raquette Club in 1980.

In his column "The Autocrat of the Breakfast-Table" in the *Atlantic Monthly*, Oliver Wendell Holmes, Sr., declares: "the Boston State-House is the hub of the solar system. You couldn't pry that out of a Boston man if you had the tire of all creation straightened out for a crowbar."

W. S. Hatton's painting *Washington Street and the Old Corner Book Store, 1858* is completed.
H. R. Hunt's painting *Skating on Jamaica Pond* is completed.

September 8. The Trimountain Club loses to Portland, Maine, 47–42 in the first "New York" baseball game ever played in Boston, on Boston Common. Organized the year before, the Trimountains play the "New York," or "National," game, which is closer to modern baseball.

1859

The Allen House is completed at 1682 Washington Street in the South End. Designed by John McNutt in the Italianate and French Empire styles, it is built for the wealthy furniture dealer Aaron Hall Allen and is the most elaborate surviving example of a Victorian town house in Boston. It is currently being renovated.

April 1. The announcement of the discovery of a cave on Boston Common attracts a number of people, who pay admission at a small tent erected there— only to find they are victims of an April Fool's prank.
July 7. An elephant, owned by Sam Rice, bathes in the Frog Pond on Boston Common.

December 12. Frederick Lincoln, Jr. (with 5,932 votes), defeats Joseph Wightman (with 4,208) and others to win reelection as mayor.

May. John Brown, an antislavery agitator who wishes to instigate a slave rebellion, visits Boston to consult with supporters. His raid of the federal arsenal at Harper's Ferry, Virginia, takes place on October 16 and is reportedly financed in part by the "Secret Six" (a group of five New Englanders, Thomas Wentworth Higginson, Samuel Gridley Howe, Theodore Parker, Franklin Sanborn, and George Stearns, and one New Yorker, Gerrit Smith). Brown is captured by troops led by Robert E. Lee and hanged on December 2.
Harriet Tubman visits Boston. "We have had the greatest heroine of the age here," Thomas Wentworth Higginson writes. "Harriet Tubman, a black woman, and a fugitive slave, has been back eight times secretly and brought out in all sixty slaves with her, including all her own family. . . . Her tales of adventure are beyond anything in fiction and her ingenuity and generalship extraordinary."

April 7. The Boston Aquarial Gardens opens at 21 Bromfield Street. Called by some the first freestanding, public aquarium in the United States, it moves to Central Court (near today's Lafayette Mall) in 1860, and closes in 1863. The building is used later for balls and fairs, and it reopens as the Theatre Comique in 1865, then the New Adelphi Theatre in 1869. It burns down on February 4, 1871.

February 27. Henry Morgan rents the Boston Music Hall and delivers his first sermon in Boston. Morgan soon after becomes the first pastor of the Union Mission Society, renamed Morgan Memorial in 1895.

March 7. Ten-year-old Thomas Whall refuses to say the Protestant version of the Lord's Prayer. A Catholic student at the Eliot School in the North End, he had been warned against repeating the King James version of the prayer by his priest at the nearby St. Mary's Church. After refusing again a week later, Whall is beaten by his teacher. Hundreds of other Catholic students join in his protest, and they are all expelled. Whall subsequently receives praise and tributes—including gold medals —from Catholic parishes and schools around the country.

The Boston Lunatic Hospital opens in South Boston. Its mission is to serve the poor and those assigned by the probate judge of Suffolk County. The institution is moved to the Retreat for the Insane at Austin Farm near Forest Hills in 1884. Renamed the Boston Insane Hospital in 1897, it is later taken over by the state and renamed Boston State Hospital in 1908. The institution closes in 1981.

The First National Bank of Boston is established. Originally called the Safety Fund Bank, it is chartered on February 1, 1864, and is the first Boston bank to become a national bank under the National Banking Law of 1863. The bank merges with the Massachusetts Bank in 1903 and opens a new headquarters at 70 Federal Street in 1908. It opens branches in Argentina in 1917 and Havana in 1923. Later renamed the Bank of Boston, it merges with Fleet Bank and becomes FleetBoston in 1999 and is acquired by Bank of America in 2004.

February. Thomas Wentworth Higginson's "Ought Women to Learn the Alphabet" appears in the *Atlantic Monthly.*

Curtis Guild begins publishing the *Commercial Bulletin.* He is soon joined by his son, the future Massachusetts governor Curtis Guild, Jr. The weekly covers business, financial, and manufacturing news.

Winslow Homer's engraving *Scavengers in Back Bay* is completed.

1860

Boston's population is 177,840, the fifth-largest of any city in the United States (behind New York, Philadelphia, Brooklyn, and Baltimore). Of that number, 2,261 are described as "Free Colored," 63,791 are foreign born, and an estimated 1,000 to 2,300 are Jewish. The separate towns of Roxbury, Dorchester, Charlestown, Brighton, and West Roxbury have an additional combined population of 69,656, with 300 classified as nonwhite.

The filling of Charlestown begins and continues until 1896.

The filling of the flats around Massachusetts General Hospital begins. It is completed in 1870.

The twin Gibson Houses, designed by E. C. Cabot, are completed at 135–137 Beacon Street. No. 137 opens as a museum on June 11, 1957, as a result of a bequest by its last owner and occupant, the poet and society man Charles Hammond Gibson.

October 25. A large rally in Ward 7 around Fort Hill, attended mostly by Irish Americans, is held for the presidential candidate Stephen Douglas. He had also campaigned in Boston in July.

November 2. Abraham Lincoln is elected president. He carries ten of the twelve wards in Boston, losing only in the heavily Irish-American wards 1 and 7.

December 13. Joseph Wightman (with 8,834 votes) defeats Moses Kimball (with 5,674) and others to win election as mayor. Boston's first Democratic party mayor, he is inaugurated on January 7, 1861.

William C. Nell is appointed a U.S. postal clerk, becoming the first African American to hold a federal civilian job in Boston.

April 10. Isabella Stewart of New York marries John Gardner of Boston. Her father, David Stewart, builds a house for the couple at 152 Beacon Street in 1861, and the adjoining house is added to it in 1880.

October 18. A daylong celebration is held to honor the visiting prince of Wales (Lord Renfrew, the future Edward VII). A military review is held on Boston Common in the morning, a musical festival at the Music Hall in the afternoon, and then a ball at the Academy of Music in the evening. Eleven hundred tickets are printed for "ladies and gentlemen," and an additional 525 for "ladies only." Supper is served at midnight and the dancing continues until 4:30 A.M. the next morning.

November 6. Young's Hotel, founded by George Young, opens at the corner of Court Street and Court Square. An addition is built in 1882. Guests would include presidents Ulysses S. Grant, William Howard Taft, and Calvin Coolidge. Room 16 becomes the scene of as many as three hundred weddings per year for couples who receive their marriage licenses at nearby City Hall. The ceremonies are performed by the assistant city registrar "Judge" James O'Fallon. The hotel closes in 1927 and is torn down in 1936.

Six night patrolman are found to have been stealing cigars and other items from the shops along their beat. It is the first scandal in the history of the newly formed Boston Police Department.

Christ Church is established, the first Episcopal church in Hyde Park. The congregation moves to a new church building, designed by Ralph Adams Cram, in 1894.

October 13. James Black of Boston takes the first successful aerial photograph in America. The photos are shot from *Queen of the Air*, a balloon tethered twelve hundred feet above the city. Only one of the twelve exposures is successful, however.

Benjamin Franklin Sturtevant's "pegger" is introduced to the shoe manufacturing industry. Although Sturtevant loses the patent rights to that invention, he develops others and founds the B. F. Sturtevant Company in 1863. Located initially in a machine shop on Sudbury Street, the company moves to a small factory in Jamaica Plain, then to one of the largest factories in New England, in Hyde Park, in 1901.

 William Dean Howells first visits Boston. "I came," he later writes, "as a passionate pilgrim from the West approached his Holy Land in Boston." He returns to live in Boston in 1866.
Henry Wadsworth Longfellow's "Midnight Ride of Paul Revere" is published.
December 30. The local singer Adelaide Phillips makes her debut with the Handel and Haydn Society in the *Messiah.*

1861

 The extension of Albany Street begins. The filling is completed in 1868.

 April 12. Confederate troops attack Fort Sumter in Charleston, S.C., and the Civil War begins.
Fort Warren and George's Island are used as a prison for captured Confederate soldiers, including the Confederate commissioners to England and France, James Murray Mason and John Slidell. They are later ordered set free by President Lincoln to avoid an international incident. Legend has it that the island is also the scene of the tragedy involving "the Lady in Black." The wife of a prisoner, Samuel Lanier, dressed as a man, rows out to the island and tries to free her husband, but she accidentally kills him when she tries to shoot the prison commander, Col. Justin Dimmick. She is hanged, wearing black clothes, and is alleged to haunt visitors to the island.

 December 9. Joseph Wightman (with 6,765 votes) defeats Edward Tobey (with 5,795) and others to win reelection as mayor.

 January 20. Wendell Phillips's speech "On Disunion," delivered at the Music Hall, creates a near-riot. Four days later, the Massachusetts Anti-Slavery Society's annual meeting at Tremont Temple is broken up by opponents. The police do not intervene in either event, reportedly because Mayor Wightman is a Democrat and slavery sympathizer.

 Anthony Trollope visits Boston and later writes: "I became very enamored of Boston at last. Beacon Street was very pleasant to me, and the view over Boston Common was dear to my eyes. Even the State House, with its great yellow painted dome, became sightly; and the sunset over the western waters that encompass the city beats all other sunsets that I have seen."

 January 12. The *Pilot* declares, "We Catholics have only one course to adopt, one line to follow: Stand by the Union; fight for the Union; die by the Union."
December 12. The Arlington Street Church opens. Designed by Arthur Gilman, it is the first new church in the Back Bay.

 The Studio Building, a center for dealers and art supplies, is completed at the corner of Tremont and Bromfield Streets. Many of Boston's best-known artists maintain studios here, including Appleton Brown, John Enneking, William Morris Hunt, and Elihu Vedder. It is later described as containing "a delightful flavor of not indecorous bohemianism at a time when the town's atmosphere was more rigidly puritanical than at present." It becomes a commercial building in the 1880s and is torn down in the 1990s to make way for Suffolk University Law School.

Oliver Wendell Holmes, Sr.'s *Elsie Venner* is published. The novel contains what is generally regarded as the first uses of the term "Boston Brahmin," including "He comes of the Brahmin caste of New England. This is the harmless, inoffensive, untitled aristocracy"; also, "Boston Brahmins . . . with their houses by Bulfinch, their monopoly of Beacon Street, their ancestral portraits and Chinese porcelains, humanitarianism, Unitarian faith in the march of the mind, Yankee shrewdness, and New England exclusiveness."

Harriet E. Jacobs's *Incidents in the Life of a Slave Girl* is published.

Edward Weston of Boston walks to Washington, D.C., a distance of 478 miles, in 208 hours. The Union Army reportedly considers Weston's feat in determining how far troops can be ordered to go on a forced march.

1862

September. Camp Meigs is established on the former Ebenezer Paul Farm in the Readville section of Hyde Park. It is initially a military training camp, but the Readville General Military Hospital opens there as well in June 1864. After the war, the land is used as a racetrack and for warehousing. Most of the site is purchased for the creation of the Neponset River Fowl Meadow Reservation in 1899.

August 27. A "Great War Meeting" is held on Boston Common. The next day, the *Advertiser* reports: "On no occasion which the war has given rise to has the expression of the people been so general and so marked by patriotic fervor as in the grand celebration of yesterday."

September 17. Oliver Wendell Holmes, Jr., is wounded at the Battle of Antietam. His father travels to Virginia in search of his son, and describes the battlefield as being "like the table of some hideous orgy left uncleared."

December 11. Louisa May Alcott leaves Boston to serve as a nurse in a hospital in Washington, D.C. She later describes "feeling as if I was the son of the house going to war."

December 8. Frederick Lincoln, Jr. (with 6,352 votes), defeats Joseph Wightman (with 5,287) to again win election as mayor. He is inaugurated on January 5, 1863.

The New England Hospital for Women and Children, the first hospital in the United States run and staffed by women, opens on Codman Avenue in Roxbury. Its mission is "to provide for women medical aid of competent physicians of their own sex." Dr. Marie Zakrzewska is the first director. Incorporated in 1863, it becomes the Dimock Community Health Center in 1969.

$ *April 21.* The John Hancock Mutual Life Insurance Company is incorporated. George Sanger is the first president. Albert Murdock is the company's first agent and policyholder. The company converts from a mutual to a stock company on January 27, 2000, and is purchased by and merged with Manulife of Canada in 2004. Located initially at 41 State Street, it moves to the Sears Building in July 1869. Its first headquarters building, designed by Shepley, Rutan, and Coolidge, opens on Franklin Street in 1907; its second, at 197 Clarendon Street, on April 1, 1923; and its third, in 1947.*

⚭ The Universalist Publishing House is established.
February. Julia Ward Howe's "The Battle Hymn of the Republic" is published in the *Atlantic Monthly.*

♫ William Morris Hunt settles in Boston. After attending Harvard and then living abroad, he returns to become an important painter and art teacher.
January 7. The Charlestown Public Library opens in the Warren Institution for Savings building. It moves to the new City Hall in 1869, then, as a branch of the Boston Public Library, to Monument Square in 1913. The current branch library opens at 179 Main Street in 1970.
Patrick Sarsfield Gilmore writes "When Johnny Comes Marching Home."

1863

♯ It was in this year that the main character of William Dean Howells's *The Rise of Silas Lapham* is said to have "bought very cheap" a house in the South End from "a terrified gentleman of good extraction who had discovered too late that the South End was not the thing."

🏛 William Robert Ware and Henry Van Brunt begin informal architecture classes in their Boston office. Ware later forms the first architectural school in the United States at the Massachusetts Institute of Technology in September 1867.

🍎 *October 1.* The Deer Park opens on Boston Common. In addition to deer, peacocks are introduced in May 1864. The park closes in 1884.

▣ *May 28.* The Massachusetts Fifty-Fourth Regiment goes to war. The first African-American company from the North to fight for the Union, it is led by twenty-six-year-old Col. Robert Gould Shaw. In offering Shaw the command, Gov. John Andrew told him, "I know not, Mr. Commander, where in all human history to any given thousand men in arms there has been committed a work at once so proud, so precious, so full of hope and glory." The regiment marches past the State House to Battery Wharf while a crowd estimated at 20,000 looks on.
July 8. A public draft lottery is instituted. Names are placed in a large copper sphere, which is revolved and mixed after each drawing. The *Boston Daily Advertiser* reports the names and comments that, for once, people "were very anxious NOT to see their names in the newspapers."
July 14. An antidraft riot breaks out in the North End, two days after the *Boston Herald* declared, "The draft is received in this State without the faintest show

Robert Gould Shaw and the 54th Regiment Memorial *on the Boston Common, by Augustus Saint-Gaudens. (Courtesy of the Bostonian Society)*

of opposition, so far as we have learned," and one day after a much larger draft riot in New York. In Boston thousands of mostly Irish immigrants take part.

July 18. The Fifty-Fourth Regiment attacks Fort Wagner in Charleston Harbor, South Carolina. Shaw, two other officers, and thirty-one soldiers are killed. When a request is made that Shaw's body be returned, the Confederate reply is reported to be "We've buried him with his niggers." After the battle, the remainder of the Fifty-Fourth Regiment goes on fighting—for both the Union and justice. For eighteen months, the soldiers refuse to accept a salary lower than that paid to white soldiers, until Congress finally increased their pay, retroactively.

November 19. Edward Everett delivers a two-hour oration at the dedication of the new cemetery at Gettysburg. After Everett is finished, President Lincoln delivers the brief remarks that we know today as the Gettysburg Address. The next day, Everett writes to Lincoln: "I should be glad, if I could flatter myself, that I came as near to the central idea of the occasion in two hours, as you did in two minutes."

December 14. Frederick Lincoln, Jr. (with 6,206 votes), defeats Thomas Rich (with 2,142) and others to win reelection as mayor.

January 1. A celebration to mark the implementation of the Emancipation Proclamation is held at the Boston Music Hall. It is attended by both blacks and whites. Emerson recites the "Boston Hymn," which he composed for the occasion; it includes the lines "To-day unbind the captive./So only are ye unbound;/Lift up a people from the dust./Trump of their rescue, sound!"

April 9. The Union Club is founded by John Murray Forbes and others upset at the Somerset Club's lack of support for the Lincoln Administration. Its first president is Edward Everett. The club's headquarters are in the former homes of Abbott Lawrence and John Amory Lowell at 7 and 8 Park Street.

May 28. The curtains of the Somerset Club are said to be drawn so members—many of them Confederate sympathizers—do not have to witness the Fifty-Fourth Regiment march past the building. This story is later refuted, however, in a 1951 history of the club.

An etiquette pamphlet published in Boston advises: "The perfect hostess will see to it that the works of male and female authors be properly separated on her bookshelves. Their proximity unless they are married should not be tolerated."

Sarah Josepha Buell Hale of Boston helps convince President Lincoln to declare Thanksgiving a national holiday.

Dr. George Winship displays his "lifting machine" in his new office in the basement of the Park Street Church. Called the "Roxbury Hercules" for his prodigious strength, Winship, a graduate of Harvard and Harvard Medical School, has "strength seekers" flocking to his office from around the country to try his weight training equipment.

June 9. Carney Hospital opens on the former Howe estate on Telegraph Hill in South Boston. Named for the clothing merchant Andrew Carney, an early benefactor, it is founded "to afford relief to the sick poor" and is incorporated in 1865. The hospital moves to its current location on Dorchester Avenue on December 1, 1953.

The Boston Eight Hour League is established. It is founded by Ira Steward, who later writes: "Men who labor excessively are robbed of all ambition to ask for anything more than will satisfy their bodily necessities, while those who labor moderately have time to cultivate tastes and create wants in addition to mere physical comforts."

July 7. The correspondent Charles Carleton Coffin's account of the Battle of Gettysburg appears in the *Boston Journal*. Coffin left the battle and traveled directly to Boston. The night the newspaper appears, thousands gather around his South End home to hear the story of the battle directly from his lips.

May 12. Walt Whitman and Ralph Waldo Emerson stroll back and forth along the Beacon Street Mall of Boston Common as Emerson attempts to persuade Whitman to remove the sexual passages from *Leaves of Grass*. Whitman later writes: "Each point of Emerson's statement was unanswerable, no judge's charge ever more complete or convincing. I could never hear the points better put—and then I felt down in my soul the clear and unmistakable conviction to disobey all, and pursue my own way." The two men then retire to the American House for what Emerson later describes as a "bully good dinner." *Leaves of Grass* is banned in Boston in March 1882, with Thomas Wentworth Higginson leading the campaign against the book.

Edward Everett Hale's short story "The Man without a Country" appears in the *Atlantic Monthly*.

Louisa May Alcott's *Hospital Sketches* and Henry Wadsworth Longfellow's *Tales of a Wayside Inn* are published.

March 9. Tom Thumb and his wife make their first appearance in Boston.

November 7. The first football game takes place on Boston Common. The local team was organized in 1862 as the Oneida Football Club by "Gat" Miller and other students from Mr. Dixwell's private school on Boylston Place. Members wear red handkerchiefs as uniforms. The team takes its name from a lake near Miller's hometown of Peterboro, New York. They continue playing their games on Boston Common, and the team's goal line is not crossed for three years.

1864

December 12. Frederick Lincoln, Jr. (with 6,877 votes), defeats Thomas Amory (with 3,732) and others to win reelection as mayor.

Boston City Hospital Administration Building, ca. 1865–1875. (Courtesy of the Bostonian Society)

January 10. The United Hebrew Benevolent Society is established. Founded by Nathan Strauss and others, the organization moves its office to the Municipal Charity building at the corner of Chardon and Hawkins Streets in 1883.

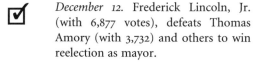

The first annual "Schoolboy Parades" are held in Boston. Begun a year after the state legislature recommends making military drills part of the school curriculum for boys over twelve years old, the parades of high school military marching bands attract as many as three hundred thousand spectators and continue until 1960.

May 26. Five safes on Commercial Street are blown open by explosives in one night.

Elizabeth Palmer Peabody opens a kindergarten school on Pinckney Street on Beacon Hill. The first successful kindergarten in the United States, it is modeled after the "children's garden" movement promoted by the German educator Friedrich Fröbel.

September 5. Boston College opens on Harrison Avenue and James Street in the South End. Incorporated on April 1, 1863, the school is founded by Rev. James McElroy of the Society of Jesus (S.J.). John Bapst is the first president. He is succeeded by Robert Brady (1869), Robert Fulton (1870), Jeremiah O'Connor (1880), Edward Boursaud (1884), Thomas Stack (1887), Nicholas Russo (1887), Robert Fulton (1888), Edward Devitt (1891), Timothy Brosnahan (1894), W. G. Mullan (1898), William Gannon (1903), and Thomas Gasson (1907). Initially sharing quarters with Boston College High School, the college moves to Chesnut Hill in 1913.*

March 1. Rebecca Lee graduates from the New England Female Medical College in the South End. The first African-American woman doctor in the United States, she serves as a nurse during the Civil War, then establishes a practice with her husband, Dr. Arthur Crumpler, at their home at 67 Joy Street on Beacon Hill.

May 24. Boston City Hospital, designed by Gridley J. F. Bryant, is dedicated at 818 Harrison Avenue in the South End. Its construction was authorized by the state legislature in 1858 in the wake of a cholera epidemic. The hospital's stated mission is to serve "the honest, temperate and industrious poor." Except for accident or emergency, the trustees direct that no patient "be admitted to the Hospital who cannot give a satisfactory reference as to character when requested to do so." A new hospital building opens in 1994.*

December. The first issue of the *Boston Daily Evening Voice* appears. It is reportedly the only labor newspaper that advocates including freed slaves in the ranks of organized labor.

The Holton Library opens at 40 Academy Hill Road in Brighton. Supported by a bequest from James Holton, it contains ten thousand volumes and is one of the largest in the area. It merges with and becomes home to the Brighton branch of the Boston Public Library in 1874. The current branch library building, by The Architects Collaborative, opens on the same site in 1969.

Beacon Park racetrack opens on the east side of lower Cambridge Street in Brighton. The site becomes the Boston and Albany rail yard in the 1890s.

1865

(ca.) The filling of the east side of the South Bay begins. It is completed in 1868.

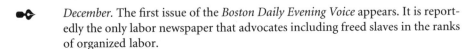

September 18. The building today known as Old City Hall is dedicated on School Street. Designed by Gridley J. F. Bryant and Arthur Gilman in the French Second Empire style, it is built on the foundation of Johnson Hall. Twenty thousand people attend the official opening in December. In *The Last Hurrah*, Edwin O'Connor later describes the building as "a lunatic pile of a building: a great, grim resolutely ugly dust-catcher." It is converted to commercial uses in 1971.

The French Second Empire–style Harrison Loring House is built at 789 East Broadway in South Boston.

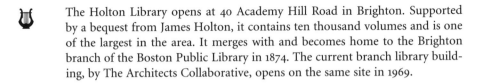

April 10. News of Gen. Robert E. Lee's surrender to Gen. Ulysses S. Grant, ending the Civil War, reaches Boston, prompting a celebration that includes the ringing of church bells, waving of flags, and firing of cannons on Boston Common.

April 15. News of President Lincoln's assassination the day before reaches Boston, resulting in an outpouring of grief. Theaters are closed until April 20, and Boston Harbor is closed while the manhunt is conducted for John Wilkes Booth. He had visited Boston on April 5 and 6, staying at the Parker House and reportedly practicing his shooting at Rold Edwards Pistol Gallery on to-day's School Street. On the night he assassinated the president in Ford's The-atre in Washington, his brother, Edwin, was appearing at the Boston Theatre on Federal Street in *The Iron Chest* and *Don Cesar de Barzan*.

John Gorham Palfrey's *History of the Revolution* and the first volume of Francis Parkman's *France and England in the New World (1865–1892)* are published.

December 11. Frederick Lincoln, Jr. (with 4,520 votes), defeats Dr. Nathaniel Shurtleff (with 3,690) and others to win reelection as mayor.

The New England Home for Little Wanderers opens in the North End. An orphanage, it is today located on South Huntington Avenue in Jamaica Plain.

December. The Crawford House opens at the corner of Court and Brattle Streets, and is substantially enlarged in 1874. The hotel later houses a nightclub that features the stripper Sally Keith, known as the "Queen of the Tassels." Its well-known theatrical bar remains after its four upper floors are removed in January 1950. The building is later demolished to make way for Government Center in 1962.

The Boston lawyer John Swett Rock becomes the first African American to practice law before the U.S. Supreme Court and the first to speak before the U.S. House of Representatives.

June 12. The Bussey Woods murders take place. Two children—fifteen-year-old Isabella Joyce and her eight-year-old brother John—go on a picnic and are later found murdered in the Bussey Woods. A vagrant named Scratch Gravel is suspected, but no one is ever convicted of the crime. Another suspect, Henry Johnson Brent, later claims to see an apparition near the site of the murders and writes an account of the murders entitled *Was It a Ghost?*

February 20. Massachusetts Institute of Technology (MIT) opens, with a class of fifteen students. Incorporated on April 10, 1861, it is known as Boston Tech for the first fifty years of its existence. William Barton Rogers is the first presi-dent. He is succeeded by John Daniel Runkle (1870), serves again as president (1879), and is succeeded by Francis Amasa Walker (1881), James Crafts (1897), Henry Pritchett (1900), Arthur Noyes (1907), Richard Maclaurin (1909), Ernest Fox Nichols (1921), Samuel Stratton (1923), Karl Compton (1930), James Killian (1948), Julius Stratton (1959), Howard Johnson (1966), Jerome Wiesner (1971), Paul Gray (1980), Charles Vest (1990), and Susan Hockfield (2004). The first class meets in rented rooms at 16 Summer Street. The school's first new build-ing, named the Rogers Building for the college's first president, opens on Boyl-ston Street in the Back Bay in 1865 (on the site of today's New England Life building). The school moves to Cambridge in 1916.

Ferdinand and Company, a household furnishings store, is established at the corner of Washington and Warren Streets in Dudley Square, Roxbury. A new building by John Lyman Faxon called the Blue Store opens in 1895 and is enlarged in the 1920s.

Boston has eight daily newspapers, forty-nine weeklies, and five semiweeklies.

Thomas Bailey Aldrich's book of poems *Blue and Gold* and James Russell Lowell's "Commemoration Ode" are published.
The Harvard Musical Association concerts begin. Performed by a newly formed orchestra under the direction of Carl Zerrahn, the series includes all nine symphonies of Beethoven, twelve by Haydn, and six by Mozart. The concerts continue until 1882.
May 25. A dramatization of Oliver Wendell Holmes, Sr.'s *Elsie Venner* begins a brief run.

1866

October 15. The leveling of Fort Hill begins. It is completed in July 1872, and the fill is used to create Atlantic Avenue and raise the Bay Village area. The project is as much a slum clearance operation as an expansion of the city. In the 1840s a committee studying the area had declared: "Here is a density of population surpassed, probably, in few places in the civilized world."

The L Street Bath House opens in South Boston. The first free municipal public baths in America, the facilities are initially reserved for men and boys. Facilities for women and girls open in 1899. The current Art Deco building opens in 1931 and is renovated in 1989.

All "repentant rebels" in Boston are required to take an oath of allegiance to the United States.

December 10. The Republican Otis Norcross (with 5,662 votes) defeats Dr. Nathaniel Shurtleff (with 4,755) and others to win election as mayor. Norcross is later described as "a man who abhorred any increase in the city indebtedness and stood firmly against vague enterprises." Inaugurated on January 7, 1867, he later becomes the first mayor to be defeated in an attempt to serve a second term.
Edwin Garrison Walker of Charlestown and Charles Lewis Mitchell of Boston become the first African Americans elected to the Massachusetts legislature. Other African-American legislators elected soon after include John Smith (1868), George Ruffin (1870), and Lewis Hayden and Joshua Smith (1873).

The Young Women's Christian Association (YWCA) opens at 23 Chauncy Street. Established "to care for the temporal, moral and religious welfare of young women," it would be criticized by those who thought that women should not live "independently." In defense, one of the founders, Mrs. Henry Durant, later declares, "There will always be young women dependent on their own exertions for support." The organization moves to 40 Berkeley Street in the South End, a building that includes one of the first gymnasiums in the country designed specifically for women, in 1885. It moves to 410 Stuart Street in 1929.

Deputy Chief Edward H. Savage's *Chronological History of the Boston Watch and Police* is published.

March 8. Pickpockets are caught "at work" at a town meeting. After being beaten, they are sent to jail.

November 14. Although astronomers had predicted a meteor shower and a large crowd assembles on Boston Common to watch, the meteors do not appear.

February 13. John Joseph Williams succeeds the late John Bernard Fitzpatrick as the Catholic bishop of Boston. He is installed on March 11, and appointed the first archbishop of Boston on May 2, 1875.

The Calumet and Hecla Consolidated Copper Company is formed to develop a copper mine discovered by Edwin Hulbert in Michigan. Quincy Shaw is the first investor. Alexander Agassiz soon fires Hulbert and takes over as director. The mine soon produces half the copper in the United States and tremendous profits for investors—most of whom are among Boston's leading families. Hulbert later writes: "In my younger days, I became strangely, confidently, and I may add, foolishly, impressed, [with] the significance of an oft quoted phrase, which read, in this way, 'The solid men of Boston.'"

August 24. With the completion of the Atlantic Telegraph cable, Boston newspapers begin reporting the previous day's European news.

Phillips Brooks writes "O Little Town of Bethlehem."

The Boston Yacht Club is organized, and it is incorporated two years later. Its founders include August and Charles Russ. The club opens its first clubhouse at City Point in South Boston in 1874 and later moves to Marblehead.

1867

The eastern part of Brighton is named Allston, after the painter Washington Allston, who lived in nearby Cambridgeport. It is reportedly the only community in the United States named for a painter.
D. A. Sanborn's *Insurance Map of Boston* is published.

The Boston Society of Architects is formed.

Cedar Grove Cemetery in Dorchester is laid out by Luther Briggs, Jr.

Francis Parkman's *The Jesuits in North America* is published.

December 9. The Democrat Dr. Nathaniel Shurtleff (with 8,383 votes) defeats Otis Norcross (with 7,867) and others to win election as mayor, and is inaugurated on January 6, 1868. After leaving office he writes the first topographical history of Boston.
Patrick Collins is elected state representative from South Boston. A year later, he, Thomas Gargan, Michael Cunniff, Patrick Maguire, and others form the

Young Men's Democratic Club to enlist Irish Catholics in the Democratic Party. Collins becomes the first Irish Catholic elected to the Massachusetts State Senate in 1870. He is elected chairman of the Board of Aldermen in 1878.

 Spring. The Radical Club is formed. It is a discussion rather than a dinner club. A journalist once declared the club's primary distinction was that it survived for years without a kitchen.

November 19. Charles Dickens makes his second visit to Boston. He reads *A Christmas Carol* in the United States for the first time at the Tremont Temple on December 2. A year later, in *American Notes*, he describes Boston this way: "the city is a beautiful one, and cannot fail, I should imagine, to impress all strangers very favorably. The private dwelling-houses are, for the most part, large and elegant; the shops are extremely good; the public buildings handsome."

 September 30. The Boston School Committee requests that schoolbooks be furnished free of charge to all public school students.

 February 11. The Boston Conservatory is established; Julius Eichberg is the first president. He is succeeded by Agida Jacchia (1920), Albert Alphin (1932), George Brambilla (1967), Dale DuVall (1979), William Seymour (1981), and Richard Ortner (1998 to present). The music school moves to the former Boston Medical Library building at 8 The Fenway in 1936.

February 18. The New England Conservatory is moved to Boston. It was founded by Eben Tourjee and initially located in Providence. Tourjee is succeeded as director by Carl Faelten (1890) and George Whitefield Chadwick (1897). Located first in rented rooms in the Boston Music Hall, the school moves to the former St. James Hotel in the South End in 1882, and then to its current location on Huntington Avenue in 1902.*

1868

 January 6. Roxbury is annexed to Boston, adding 2,450 acres to the city.

April 22. Hyde Park is incorporated as a separate town, made up of land ceded by Dedham, Dorchester, and Milton.

July. The raising of over two hundred buildings in the Church Street area begins. Undertaken to solve drainage problems caused by the filling of the Back Bay, it is completed in October 1869. The raising of hundreds of buildings in the Suffolk Street (today's Castle Square) area begins in October 1870 and is completed in 1872.

The filling of Atlantic Avenue begins. It is completed in October 1870.

 August. Curtis Hall, the town hall for West Roxbury, opens on Centre Street in today's Jamaica Plain. The building is damaged by fire and repaired in 1907. It is rebuilt in 1912 and today serves as a community center.

October 26. The 37.5-acre Lawrence Basin Reservoir opens at Chestnut Hill. Purchased by Boston College and filled in during the 1950s, it is now the site of the college's Alumni Stadium. The 87.5-acre Bradlee Basin Reservoir opens

in 1870 and is still in existence. The High Service Station, designed by Arthur Vinal in the Romanesque style, opens in 1888. The Low Service Station, designed by Shepley, Rutan, and Coolidge in the Beaux Arts style, opens in 1901.

December 14. Dr. Nathaniel Shurtleff (with 11,005 votes) defeats Moses Kimball (with 9,156) and others to win reelection as mayor.

The New England Women's Club is organized. Founded by Caroline Severance (its first president), Julia Ward Howe (its president for more than forty years), and others to promote civic involvement, it is located initially on Park Street and later moves to Boylston Street.
November 19. The New England Woman Suffrage Association is organized. Julia Ward Howe is the first president.
The Common Council appropriates several thousand dollars for distribution of soup to the poor by the Boston Police. The program continues until budget constraints brought on by the Panic of 1873 cause it to be ended, but only after much debate. The Common Council ultimately decides that "police work is one thing and work of charity is another."

April 21. The St. James Hotel opens at 11 East Newton Street in the South End. Designed by M. M. Ballou in the French Second Empire style, it is one of the most luxurious hotels in Boston. It becomes home to the New England Conservatory of Music in 1882, the Franklin Square House (a home for women) in the 1910s, and housing for the elderly in 1976.
Jacob Wirth's restaurant opens at 31–39 Stuart Street. It becomes noted for its German food and waiters, and is still in operation today.

March 31. The Massachusetts Society for the Prevention of Cruelty to Animals is founded by George Angell. The first organization of its kind in the United States, it brings a complaint against Peter Hines of Dorchester on October 20, for abandoning his cow in a salt marsh (the animal remained mired for a whole day until its rescue).

St. Elizabeth's Hospital opens. Founded as a hospital for poor women by five laywomen who are members of the Order of St. Francis, it is incorporated in 1872. It is located initially at 78 Waltham Street in the South End, then moves to a new Spanish Mission–style building in Brighton Center in 1914. That building is demolished to make way for the current building in 1983.
March. Eighteen-year-old Thomas Edison arrives in Boston. Working in the shop of Charles Williams at 109 Court Street, he devises and later patents his first invention, a vote-recorder machine. He later develops a stock ticker for the Boston Stock Exchange at 53 State Street, but, after failing to enlist investors, moves to New York in 1869.

January. In an article in the *North American Review*, Charles Francis Adams bemoans Boston's failure to continue to grow as a commercial center. "The merchant and the manufacturer were no longer to move forward with equal steps," he complains. "Boston . . . in spite of her wealth and prestige, her intrinsic worth and deserved reputation, her superficial conceit and real cultivation, failed to solve the enigma—did not rise to the height of the great argument. . . . She is not better known. She does not bear that proportional influence with the country now that she did then. She has lost much of her influence and all of her prestige."

Louisa May Alcott's *Little Women* (Part I) is published. The novel sells thirteen thousand copies in the first two weeks.

1869

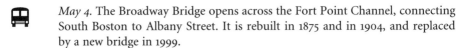

May 4. The Broadway Bridge opens across the Fort Point Channel, connecting South Boston to Albany Street. It is rebuilt in 1875 and in 1904, and replaced by a new bridge in 1999.

December 2. In an editorial in the *Boston Adviser,* Robert Morris Copeland outlines a municipal and metropolitan park system connected by boulevards. On December 4 and 8, Uriel H. Crocker, first in a letter to the *Boston Advertiser,* then to the Joint Special Committee of the legislature, proposes a system of parks, joined by parkways, along both sides of the Charles River out to the Chestnut Hill Reservoir. The legislature later grants Boston authority to purchase land for parks, but the city's attempt to create a park commission with four members appointed by the governor and four by the Common Council is not approved by Boston voters.

December 13. Dr. Nathaniel Shurtleff (with 13,054 votes) defeats George Baldwin (with 4,790) and others to win reelection as mayor.

November 21. The Boylston National Bank on Washington Street is robbed of $320,000, mostly in government bonds and securities, in the biggest robbery in the city's history to date. The robbers had rented a room in a building adjoining the bank and tunneled through a twenty-inch brick wall. The bank is robbed again in 1897.*
Between 1860 and 1869, seventy homicides are recorded in Suffolk County.
George Ruffin becomes the first African American to graduate from Harvard Law School.

September 8. A storm flattens the temporary Coliseum in Copley Square, uproots trees in the Public Garden, and topples church steeples.

The German Sons of St. Alphonsus (later called the Redemptorists) establish a mission on the former site of Artemus Ward's Revolutionary War headquarters and the Dearborn estate on Parker Hill. Joseph Wissel is the first pastor. A wooden church is built in 1871, and it is replaced in 1878.*

The Horace Mann School for the Deaf opens on Warrenton Street in the South End. It moves to a new building at 20 Kearsage Avenue, on the former site of Roxbury Latin School, in 1920.
The first evening high school in Boston opens. Critics are afraid it will give underprivileged boys and girls "upstart notions."

Hyde Park High School opens at the Fairmount School. It moves to rented rooms in Liberty Hall in 1870, to the new Grew School in 1872, and to the Everett School building in 1874. It moves to a building by Loring and Phipps at Harvard and Everett Streets (later the William Barton Rogers School) in 1902, then to its current building, designed by McLaughlin and Burr, at 655 Metropolitan Avenue, in 1929.

May 19. Charles W. Eliot succeeds Thomas Hill as president of Harvard. He would be credited with "professionalizing" the school—and American higher education—by instituting an "elective system" for undergraduates and creating specialty graduate schools and research centers. He serves in office until 1909.*

May. Boston University is incorporated. Founded in April 1839 by the New England Friends of Improved Theological Training by Methodists, the school was initially located in various places in northern New England, then opened in Boston as the Boston Theological Seminary in 1867. William Warren becomes the university's first president in 1872. He is succeeded by William Huntington (1903), Lemuel Murlin (1911), and Daniel Marsh (1926). The school becomes the first university to admit women to all of its departments in 1873. Located initially on Beacon Hill, then in various parts of the city, the school moves to the Charles River campus in 1948.*

July. Children's Hospital opens at 9 Rutland Square in the South End. The third children's hospital in the United States (after those in Philadelphia and Chicago), it is founded by Drs. Francis Henry Brown and William Ingalls. The hospital moves to a new building at 1583 Washington Street in 1870, and to Huntington Avenue (on the site of today's Symphony Hall) in 1882. The current building, designed by Shepley, Rutan, and Coolidge, at 300 Longwood Avenue in the Fenway, opens in 1914. The Children's Hospital Medical Center, an alliance with other hospitals in the city serving children, is established in 1959. The current Children's Hospital complex is begun at 300 Longwood Avenue in 1959 and substantially completed in 1971.

November 9. In a letter to his sister, Pamela Clemens Moffett, Mark Twain writes: "Tonight I appear for the first time before a Boston audience—4,000 critics."

June 15. Patrick Sarsfield Gilmore's National Peace Jubilee opens in the specially built Coliseum in today's Copley Square. The first concert, by a thousand-member orchestra, accompanied by a ten-thousand-voice choir and one hundred Boston firemen beating anvils, is later said to have attracted "the largest audience ever before gathered in America." The five-day event attracts an estimated sixty thousand spectators daily, including President Ulysses S. Grant, Adm. David Farragut, and other distinguished guests.

June 10–12. The renowned Red Stockings of Cincinnati play a series of exhibition baseball games in Boston, beating the Lowells (29–9), the Trimountains (40–12), and the Harvards (30–11) in games played in a specially constructed stadium erected on the parade grounds on Boston Common.

The National Peace Jubilee, from a stereograph of the interior of the Coliseum in Copley Square. (Courtesy of the Bostonian Society)

1870

Boston's population is 250,526, the seventh-largest of any city in the United States (behind New York, Philadelphia, Brooklyn, St. Louis, Chicago, and Baltimore). Of that number, 3,496 are described as "Colored," including 12 Indians and 5 Japanese, and 87,987 are classified as foreign born. The separate towns of Charlestown, Brighton, West Roxbury, and Hyde Park have an additional combined population of 46,109, with 259 classified as nonwhite and 12,419 as foreign born.

January 3. Dorchester is annexed to Boston. The annexation, which includes today's Mattapan, adds 5,600 acres to the city.

March 15. Roslindale is named. It was originally a part of Roxbury and then the "South Street" district of West Roxbury. The name is reportedly suggested by John Pierce, an Englishman, who claims the area resembles the historic town of Roslin, Scotland.

November 4. The Kenmore Square area, formerly part of Brookline, is annexed to Boston.

The Back Bay begins to supplant the South End as a desirable place to live, as is illustrated by Oliver Wendell Holmes, Sr.'s eventual move to a house built at 296 Beacon Street. Of his move from Beacon Hill, Holmes declares that he is committing "justifiable domicide."

The Hyde Park Town Hall is moved—in sections—from Boston and reassembled at the corner of Gordon Avenue and River Street. Destroyed by fire on March 8, 1883, it is replaced by a new building at the corner of Harvard Avenue and River Street in February 1891.

May 23. The first through transcontinental train leaves Boston for San Francisco. Eight specially built Pullman cars take members of the Boston Board of Trade and their families on a trip that lasts thirty-nine days.

December 12. The Democrat and Citizens party candidate William Gaston (with 10,836 votes) defeats George Carpenter (with 7,836) to win election as mayor. The former mayor of Roxbury, Gaston is inaugurated on January 2, 1871. He is later elected governor; afterward, he is one of the founding partners of the Boston law firm of Gaston, Snow, and Ely Bartlett.

March 8. Led by the abolitionists and women's rights advocates Angelina and Sarah Grimké, forty-four Hyde Park women cast the first votes by women in the United States. Their ballots are later discarded.
(ca.) Lucy Stone moves to Boston, settling with her husband and daughter on Boutwell Street in the Pope's Hill area of Dorchester. With others, she founds the *Woman's Journal*, the weekly newspaper of the American Woman Suffrage Association, with offices at 5 Park Street. Two years later, Stone becomes editor, a position that she, her husband, and eventually her daughter, Alice, hold for the next forty-seven years.

The St. Cloud Hotel opens at 567 Tremont Street in the South End. Designed by Nathaniel Bradlee, it is today considered the oldest remaining hotel building in Boston.

February 15. Boston's Aldermen dismiss police chief John Kurtz and replace him with Edward Savage. A career police officer, Savage ends the practice of the police accepting rewards for the return of stolen goods and encourages a more benevolent approach to dealing with social crimes. He steps down in 1878, then writes a number of books about Boston and Boston Police history.

According to census figures, there are 207 churches in Boston. The most common are Congregational (30), followed by Catholic, Methodist, and Unitarian (28 each), Baptist (25), and Episcopal (24).

The Boston public schools open a free, public kindergarten on Somerset Street. Mary Peabody Mann, Elizabeth's sister and the widow of Horace Mann, is director. Several more kindergartens are soon established, but their closings are announced in 1879 because of lack of funds. Pauline Agassiz Shaw steps in to support them privately and more than thirty are operating by 1883. The Boston public schools resume operation of the kindergartens in 1887.

The Boston Fruit Company is established. Founded by Lorenzo Baker (who introduces bananas to Boston this year) and others, it joins with Minor Keith's Costa Rican company to form United Fruit Company in 1899. The company later merges with Cuyamel Fruit Company of New Orleans.

John Boyle O'Reilly arrives in Boston. A British soldier convicted of treason for trying to recruit other Irish-born soldiers like him to join the cause of Irish independence, O'Reilly was sentenced to prison in Australia, but he made a daring escape in 1869. Arriving in Boston, he is befriended by Patrick Collins, who finds him a job as a reporter for the *Pilot*.

February 4. The Museum of Fine Arts is incorporated. Gen. Charles Loring becomes the first curator in July, and the first director in April 1887. He is succeeded by Edward Robinson (1902), Arthur Fairbanks (1907), Edward Holmes (1925), George Edgell (1934), Perry Rathbone (1955), Merrill Rueppel (1973), Jan Fontein (1975), Alan Shestack (1987), and Malcolm Rogers (1994 to the present). Operating initially on the top floor of the Boston Athenaeum, the museum moves to a new building near Copley Square in 1876.*

Louisa May Alcott's *An Old-Fashioned Girl* is published.

The East Boston Branch Library opens. The first branch public library in America, it is initially located in the Lyman School; it later moves to the Austin School, then to its present location at 276 Meridian Street in 1914.

Thomas Bailey Aldrich's *Story of a Bad Boy* is published. Of Boston, Aldrich would write: "The people of Boston are full-blooded readers, appreciative, trained. The humble man of letters has a position here which he doesn't have in New York. To be known as an able writer is to have the choicest society opened to you."

1871

July. The contractors retained by the city to fill in Atlantic Avenue are found selling the same dirt to ship owners for use as ballast. Of the dirt one alderman declares that a "large portion had been carried everywhere [except] where it was wanted."

May 18. The demolition of the Scollay Building is completed, leaving a triangular space that comes to be called Scollay Square.

The *Nation* editor E. L. Godkin declares, "Boston is the one place in America where wealth and the knowledge of how to use it are apt to coincide."

December 11. William Gaston (with 9,838 votes) defeats Newton Talbot (with 6,231) and others to win reelection as mayor.

The Hotel Vendome, designed by William Preston in the French Second Empire style, opens at 160 Commonwealth Avenue. An addition by Ober and Rand in 1881 makes it the largest hotel in the city. Guests would include Presidents Ulysses S. Grant and Grover Cleveland, P. T. Barnum, Sarah Bernhardt, John Singer Sargent, Mark Twain, and Oscar Wilde. It is the first building in the United States lit by electricity, and the installation is personally inspected by Thomas Edison in 1882. The hotel closes on June 1, 1970, and the building is heavily damaged by a fire in 1972.*

April. Timothy Lynch dies after being arrested by the Boston Police. A member of a crowd that gathered when police attempted to arrest another man in East Boston, Lynch is taken into custody and reportedly injured in the process. Found unconscious in his cell the next morning, he dies a few hours later at Boston City Hospital. The coroner's jury exonerates the police, citizens protest, and the case fades from public attention—but not before a judge calls on the Massachusetts Supreme Judicial Court to define "reasonable force."

Crowds at the South End Grounds watching the Boston Nationals baseball club. (Courtesy of the Bostonian Society)

The Massachusetts Horticultural Society holds its first annual spring flower show. The event continues today.

The Boston Weather Bureau is established and begins recording data.

The Massachusetts Homeopathic Hospital opens. Incorporated in 1855, it becomes the largest homeopathic hospital in the United States. Located initially in a house at 14 Burroughs Place in the South End, it moves to a new hospital designed by William Ralph Emerson on East Concord Street in May 1876. The hospital later departs from the homeopathic tradition and is renamed the Massachusetts Memorial Hospital in 1929. It joins with the Boston University School of Medicine to form the Boston University Medical Center in July 1962.

Louisa May Alcott's *Little Men* and William Dean Howells's *A Chance Acquaintance* are published.

May 16. The Boston Red Stockings lose to the Troy Haymakers, 29–14, in their first home game at the South End Grounds, near today's Ruggles MBTA station. A member of the new, loosely organized National Association, the team wins the championship every year from 1872 until 1875, when the league disbands.

1872

The Mount Hope Cemetery area of West Roxbury is annexed to Boston.

October 14. The filling of the twenty-five-acre section of the South Boston Flats (today's Fan Pier) begins. Undertaken by the Boston Wharf Company, it is completed on January 7, 1878.

The Boston and Providence Railroad Station, designed by Peabody and Stearns, opens in Park Square. At the time it is the longest railroad station in the world. It is torn down soon after South Station opens in 1898.

Robert Morris Copeland's *The Most Beautiful City in America: Essay and Plan for the Improvement of the City of Boston* is published. It contains a proposal for a system of large parks, linked by boulevards, and an improved sewage system in the Back Bay.

The Arnold Arboretum is established by Harvard University. The first in the United States, it is supported by a monetary gift from the New Bedford businessman and horticulturist James Arnold and a gift of 210 acres of land from the scientific farmer Benjamin Bussey. Charles Sprague Sargent, a "gentleman landscape gardener," becomes the first director in 1873. Harvard turns the property over to the city on December 30, 1882, leasing it back for one thousand years at one dollar per year, with an option to renew under the same terms. The site now covers 265 acres and contains more than sixty-five hundred living plants.

December 10. Republican Henry L. Pierce (with 8,877 votes) defeats William Gaston (with 8,798) and others to win election as mayor, after 400 votes for Gaston in the North End are judged to have come in after the polls had closed. The *Transcript* later reports that the votes were "apparently manufactured to meet the emergency [in a] ward that has always been noted for its elastic majorities." The owner of the Walter Baker Chocolate Factory, Pierce is inaugurated on January 6, 1873. Wendell Phillips later remarks that if Diogenes came to Boston searching for an honest man that year, he would find him in the mayor's chair.

Fall. The "torso murder" of Abijah Ellis occurs. After a body is found floating in a barrel in the Charles River, Boston police find the killer by employing a chemist—reportedly for the first time—to identify bloodstains on the accused man's clothes.

November 9. The Great Boston Fire occurs. The blaze starts in the basement of a dry goods store at 83–85 Summer Street near the corner of Kingston Street. Firefighters from as far away as New Hampshire and Maine are called for assistance. The fire burns for four days, kills fourteen (including seven firefighters), destroys 776 buildings on 65 acres, and causes $75 million in damage. The contents of many bank vaults in the area are reduced to ash, prompting Oliver Wendell Holmes, Sr., to comment: "I saw the fire eating its way straight toward my deposits." Four hundred fifty people are later jailed for looting. Afterward Mayor Pierce rejects suggestions to take the opportunity to redraw streets in a more cohesive pattern, declaring: "such a plan would not only involve enormous expense, but seriously interfere with the business interest of the city." The cause of the fire is suspected to be the steam engine in the basement of the building on Kingston Street, which operated the elevator. The

Ruins on Beacon Street after the Great Boston Fire, 1872. (Courtesy of the Bostonian Society)

calamity forces insurance companies to reorganize and prompts adoption of more stringent building code regulations.

April. As part of the leveling of Fort Hill, the Church of St. Vincent de Paul (built in the 1820s as a Unitarian Church) is disassembled, the stones are loaded on barges, and the church is reconstructed in South Boston.

The Boston Normal School opens as a separate institution from Girls High School. A teacher training school, it moves to the Rice School on Dartmouth Street in 1876, and to a new building on Huntington Avenue in 1907. Renamed the Teachers College of the City of Boston in 1924, the State Teachers College at Boston in 1952, and Boston State College in 1960, it becomes part of the University of Massachusetts at Boston in 1982.

The New England Baptist Hospital for Women and Children opens the first training school for nurses in America. It is founded by Dr. Susan Dimock. The first graduate, in 1873, is Linda Richards. The Boston Training School for Nurses, affiliated with the Massachusetts General Hospital, opens a year later. *October.* An outbreak of equine influenza catarrh, popularly called "the epizooty," strikes horses in Boston. The epidemic brings transportation and business almost to a halt, and it limits the ability of Boston's fire department to fight the Great Boston Fire.

The Crédit Mobilier scandal rocks State Street. The corporation was set up in 1864 to let contracts for construction of the Union Pacific Railroad. U.S. Representative Oakes Ames and his brother Oliver are the biggest investors. When it is revealed that some elected officials were allowed to buy stock at favorable prices and some people were excluded from purchasing stock, control of the railroad passes out of the hands of Boston investors, and many reputations are tarnished.

March 4. The first issue of the *Boston Globe* appears. It is founded by Eben Jordan and five other businessmen; Maturin Ballou is the first editor. Charles H. Taylor becomes publisher in August 1873 and editor in 1880. The first *Sunday Globe* appears on October 14, 1877. One of the newspaper's early editorial policies is to print the name or picture of every resident in Greater Boston at least once during the year. The paper moves from offices at 236–238 Washington Street to the old *Advertiser* building at 246–248 Washington Street in 1902, and to Morrissey Boulevard in Dorchester in 1958.

James T. Fields's *Yesterdays with Authors* and Oliver Wendell Holmes, Sr.'s *The Poet at the Breakfast-Table* are published.
June 17. A twenty-day World Peace Jubilee is held in the specially built Coliseum near today's Copley Square. Produced by Patrick Sarsfield Gilmore to celebrate the end of the Franco-Prussian war, it is less successful than the jubilee held three years before. The highlight is the performance of Verdi's *Il Trovatore* by a twenty-thousand-member orchestra, conducted by Johann Strauss, Jr., and one hundred assistants, accompanied by a two-thousand-voice chorus.

1873

Brighton, Charlestown, and West Roxbury residents vote for annexation to Boston, but Brookline voters reject the proposal by a two-to-one margin. A Brookline newspaper later proclaims, "we will not be Suffolk-kated."
In John P. Marquand's *The Late George Apley*, set during this year, the eponymous character's father explains the family's move back to Beacon Hill this way: "Your grandfather had sensed the approach of change; a man in his shirt sleeves had told him that the days of the South End were numbered."

The first U.S. Post Office building in Boston, designed by Alfred Mullett, opens in what is today called Post Office Square. Its construction led to the rediscovery of the Great Spring of Boston, which began flowing again. The building is replaced after only ten years of use, and it is replaced again, by the Boston Post Office and Federal Building, designed by Cram and Ferguson, in 1933. It is named the John W. McCormack Post Office and Courthouse in 1972.

Samuel A. Drake's *The Old Landmarks and Historic Personages of Boston* is published.

November 28. Mayor Pierce resigns after he is appointed to fill a vacancy in Congress on November 6, 1873. Leonard Cutter, chairman of the Board of Aldermen, is appointed to serve out his term as acting mayor.
December 9. The non-partisan candidate Samuel Cobb (with 19,187 votes) defeats Henry Cushing (with 572) and others to win election to the first of three consecutive terms as mayor. Inaugurated on January 5, 1874, Cobb opposes creating jobs for the unemployed during the Depression of 1873–1878, declaring

the idea "subversive to our whole social fabric, tending directly to communism in its worst form."

Bailey's Candy Store is established at 43–45 West Street, the former home of the scientist Louis Agassiz. The company later opens a number of other shops in downtown Boston.

December 5. Bridget Landergan becomes the first victim in what the press calls the "belfry murders." After Mabel Young is murdered in the Warren Avenue Church on May 23, 1875, the church sexton, Thomas Piper, is arrested. He confesses in jail and is hanged on May 26, 1876.

May 30. A fire breaks out in the same area as the Great Boston Fire of the previous November. It destroys 105 businesses, including the Globe Theatre on Washington Street, Chickering's piano warerooms, and the Chauncy Hall School, and causes one million dollars in damage.

Four women (Ann Adeline Badger, Lucretia Crocker, Abigail Williams May, and Lucia Peabody) are elected to the Boston School Committee. They are not allowed to take office, however, because the School Committee rules prohibit women from serving on the board. The Massachusetts Supreme Judicial Court upholds the ban, but the state legislature soon after enacts a law that makes women eligible to serve on school committees across the state, beginning in 1874.*
The Boston School Committee first appoints truant officers.
Ellen Swallow Richards becomes the first woman graduate of MIT and the first woman in the United States to receive a degree in chemistry. Admitted as a special student, she later teaches at the college and becomes a pioneer in the field of sanitary engineering.

The first ambulance in Boston is put in service at Massachusetts General Hospital. A one-horse vehicle capable of carrying two patients and three attendants, it remains in use for fifteen years.
November 5. Boston University School of Medicine is established. The first coeducational medical school in the United States, it is created through a merger with the Female Medical College. The school later merges with the Massachusetts Memorial Hospital and becomes the Boston Medical Center in July 1962.

September 20. The Boston Stock Exchange closes and the Depression of 1873–1878 begins. Boston banks lose eight million dollars during the next two weeks; savings banks are particularly affected. Investment halts and workers' unions dissolve.
The Abattoir opens in North Brighton, operated by the Butchers' Slaughtering and Melting Association. Its creation and the consolidation of all the various stockyards were ordered by the state legislature in 1870 because of public health and safety concerns. More than twenty slaughterhouses move their operations there, including one owned by Gustavus Swift, which becomes the largest in the country before moving to Chicago. The Abattoir closes in 1956.

Massachusetts College of Art is founded. Originally the Massachusetts Normal Art School, it is created to train the art teachers needed to meet the demands of the May 1870 state Industrial Drawing Act, which required that all children in public schools be taught to draw. It is the only public art school in the country; Walter Smith is the first director. The school begins in rented rooms in Pemberton Square and on School Street, moves to a newly constructed building at the corner of Exeter and Newbury Streets in 1887, to Brookline Avenue in 1930, and to its current location, at 621 Huntington Avenue, in 1983.

1874

January 5. Brighton (2,664 acres), Charlestown (424), and West Roxbury (8,075)—including Jamaica Plain and Roslindale—are annexed to Boston.
May 5. The Massachusetts legislature awards the city a strip of land along Commonwealth Avenue, formerly belonging to Brookline, to enable a geographic connection with Brighton. Boston refuses to annex Chelsea, however, reportedly because of that community's poor economic situation.

The Dorchester Municipal Building, designed by George Clough, opens at the corner of Adams and Arcadia Streets.

June 24. Ernest Bowditch, an associate of the late Robert Morris Copeland, publishes a plan for a park system. The plan includes many of Copeland's ideas and calls for connecting already publicly owned sites with boulevards. He publishes a refined version of the plan in a pamphlet, "Rural Parks for Boston," in early 1875.
November 2. The Parker Hill Reservoir is opened to receive water. Built on the former Parker estate, the facility is closed and the city sells the land in 1918.

December 15. Samuel Cobb (with 17,874 votes) defeats Francis Hayes (with 835) and others to win reelection as mayor.

Because of the recent annexations, the Boston School Committee now consists of 116 members.
The four women elected to the School Committee the previous year but not allowed to serve are "reelected," along with three others.

St. Margaret's Hospital is established. Originally St. Mary's Asylum for Infants, it is located on Jones Hill in Dorchester and is noted for obstetrics and gynecology. One of every two births in Boston is said to take place here during the 1940s and 1950s. The hospital merges with St. Elizabeth's and moves to Brighton in 1993.

November 19. The Cecilia Society (originally the Cecilia) performs its first concert at the Music Hall. Selections include Mendelssohn's *Walpurgisnacht,* with Carl Zerrahn conducting. Initially part of the Harvard Musical Association, the society becomes independent on April 20, 1876. Although it is founded as an a cappella chorus, an orchestra is employed in the 1878–1879 season.

May 14–15. Harvard beats McGill University of Canada, 3–0 at Jarvis Field (the site of today's Harvard Law school) in Cambridge. It is the first intercollegiate football game in history; the two schools play a tie game the next day.

1875

The first Chinese community is established in Boston in today's Ping On Alley in Chinatown. It is made up of Chinese workers, living in tents, who were brought from California to break a strike by workers in North Adams and who later move on to Boston in search of work. The community expands south of Kneeland Street when the Atlantic Avenue elevated line is taken down in 1942.

Charles Davenport's "New Boston and Charles River Basin" plan is published. It proposes to dam the Charles River and create a "water park" similar to the Alster Basin in Hamburg, Germany.

The Hayden Building opens at 681 Washington Street. Designed by H. H. Richardson, it is built for his father-in-law and today is the architect's only remaining commercial structure in Boston.
The Gasometer (later known as the Roundhouse Building) of the Roxbury Gaslight Company opens on Massachusetts Avenue in Roxbury.

The Congress Street Bridge, spanning the Fort Point Channel, is completed. It is rebuilt in 1930.
The Boston, Revere Beach, and Lynn Railroad begins service to East Boston.

July 8. A three-member Boston Park Commission is established. Charged with establishing a park system and solving the drainage and sewage problem in the Back Bay, the commission releases a report on April 24, 1876, which recommends the creation of a series of parks, connected by parkways and accessible "for all classes of citizens," and serves as the basis for today's parks system. By March 1878 land is purchased and a design competition held for the first park—the Back Bay Park (renamed the Back Bay Fens in 1888).

December 14. Running as the candidate of the Citizens Party, Samuel Cobb (with 14,932 votes) defeats Halsey Boardman (with 12,178) and others to win reelection as mayor.

The Chinese Consolidated Benevolent Association is established to preserve ties between Chinese immigrants and China and promote positive relations with Americans.
The first Young Men's Hebrew Association in Boston is organized at Temple Ohabei Shalom.

January 1. The drawing for the Steaming Kettle Contest is conducted by the recently opened Oriental Tea Company on Court Street. Contestants were asked to guess the capacity of the kettle hanging outside. A crowd estimated at fifteen thousand turns out to witness the results. After eight boys and a man in a tall silk hat climb out of the kettle, eight people are declared winners for

Cathedral of the Holy Cross, 1400 Washington Street, ca. 1875. (Courtesy of the Bostonian Society)

correctly guessing the exact capacity of the pot: 227 gallons, 2 quarts, 1 pint, and 3 gills. They share the first prize—a chest of forty pounds of tea.

December 8. The Cathedral of the Holy Cross is dedicated at 1400 Washington Street in the South End. Designed by Patrick Keeley (or Keely), it is one of the largest Gothic cathedrals in the world. The basement chapel contains the altar from the original cathedral on Franklin Street, and the arch separating the vestibule is made of bricks from the ruins of the Ursuline Convent in Charlestown. Two towers that were part of the original design are never built.

December 15. The Third Church (also called the new Old South Church), on the corner of Boylston and Dartmouth Streets in the Back Bay, is dedicated. Its design is by Cummings and Sears in the Italian Gothic style. The church's tower is rebuilt in 1940.

Mary Baker Eddy's *Science and Health with Key to the Scriptures* is published.

May 19. The Boston School Committee is again reorganized. By a special act of the state legislature, it is reduced to twenty-four members (one-third elected at large, two-thirds by ward). The mayor continues to serve as chairman, ex officio, until 1885, when the committee would elect its own chairman.

Dr. James Still becomes the first African American elected to the Boston School Committee. He serves for a single one-year term. The second African American on the committee, Dr. Samuel Courtney, is elected in 1897 and serves a full three-year term.

October 14. The Free Hospital for Women opens. Founded by Dr. William Henry Baker, it operates initially from a rented house at 16 East Springfield Street, moves to 60 East Springfield Street in 1877 and then to Pond Avenue in

Brookline on January 1, 1895. It merges with the Boston Lying-In Hospital to form the Boston Hospital for Women on May 2, 1966.

June 1. The Boston Safe Deposit and Trust Company opens. It becomes the Boston Company in 1964, and is acquired by Shearson, Loeb, Rhodes in 1981. That company is in turn acquired by American Express to become Shearson Lehman/American Express.

The printer Louis Prang introduces the first mass-produced Christmas card in the United States, a year after the cards first appeared in England. The earliest cards contain a picture of a Christmas scene, designed by Mrs. E. O. Whitney of Boston, but no message.

Boston has eight daily newspapers, four weeklies, and sixty-seven semiweeklies.

Henry Bacon's *The Boston Boys and General Gage, 1775* is first exhibited. The painting dramatizes an incident in which boys protested that British soldiers were interfering with their sledding, prompting General Gage to remark, "the very children here draw in a love of liberty with the air they breathe."

October 25. Tchaikovsky's *Piano Concerto no. 1,* performed by Hans von Bülow, receives its world premiere at the Music Hall.

Charles Waite, first base man for a Boston amateur team, uses the first baseball glove. The invention is not immediately popular with other players, who hesitate to join what would be derided by newspapers as the "kid glove aristocracy."

November 13. Harvard beats Yale 4–0 at Hamilton Park, in Springfield, before two thousand spectators in the first football game played between the two schools.

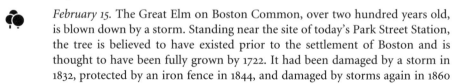

1876 to 1900

1876

February 15. The Great Elm on Boston Common, over two hundred years old, is blown down by a storm. Standing near the site of today's Park Street Station, the tree is believed to have existed prior to the settlement of Boston and is thought to have been fully grown by 1722. It had been damaged by a storm in 1832, protected by an iron fence in 1844, and damaged by storms again in 1860 and 1869.

July 4. A centennial celebration crowd estimated at between fifty and one hundred thousand gathers to see fireworks on Boston Common, but the display is spoiled by high winds.

The original Old South Church is saved from demolition through an effort led by Mrs. Mary Hemenway. Whitehill later describes it as "the first instance in Boston where respect for the historical and architectural heritage of the city triumphed over considerations of profit, expediency, laziness and vulgar convenience."

Leopold Morse is elected to serve in the U.S. House of Representatives, the first Jew from Boston to do so.

The number of wards in the city is increased to twenty-five, and the number of members of the Common Council to seventy-five.

December 12. Democrat Frederick Prince (with 16,582 votes) defeats Republican Nathaniel Bradley (with 13,782) to win election as mayor. Prince is backed by the ward boss Patrick J. Maguire, "the only city-wide boss Boston ever had," according to John Galvin, and for the next twenty years, "party decisions were made in the back rooms of Maguire's real estate office."

John Smith becomes the first African American elected to the Common Council. At least one African American serves on the council every year until 1895.

March 10. Alexander Graham Bell invents the telephone at 5 Exeter Place (near the corner of today's Harrison Avenue and Lafayette Place). A member of Boston University's faculty, he was on sabbatical and had set up a lab in a boardinghouse to work in secrecy. After accidentally spilling acid on his clothes, he transmits the first intelligible speech ("Mr. Watson, come here. I want you") to his assistant, Thomas Watson, in another room. Bell, who had been granted a patent three days before, had transmitted sounds, but not a distinguishable human voice, in Charles Williams's shop at 109 Court Street (on the site of today's JFK Plaza) on June 2, 1875.

July 3. The Museum of Fine Arts, designed by John Sturgis and Charles Brigham in the Italian Gothic style, opens on St. James Avenue. The art historian

The Museum of Fine Arts at Copley Square, in a photograph taken between 1876 and 1890. (Courtesy of the Bostonian Society)

Arthur Dexter later describes it as a "beautiful and characteristic edifice . . . which no intelligent person, seeing it for the first time, could possibly take for anything but a museum." Immediately popular with the public, the museum attracts 158,000 visitors in 1877—most of them, however, on Saturdays and Sunday afternoons, when admission is free. A second wing opens July 1, 1879, and a third on March 18, 1890. The museum moves to its current site in the Fenway in 1909.*

Rachel Washington becomes the first African-American graduate of the New England Conservatory of Music. She later becomes the organist and choir director at the Twelfth Baptist Church in Boston and a music teacher in Boston's African-American community.

 April 29. The Boston team in the new National League loses to Hartford 3–2 in ten innings in its first home game at the South End Grounds. Champions in 1877, 1878, 1883, 1891–1893, and 1897–1898, the team is known as the Red Caps (1876–1882), the Beaneaters (1883–1906), the Doves (1907–1910), and the Rustlers (1911), the Braves (1912–1935), the Bees (1936–1940), then the Braves again in 1941. The stadium is renovated after the 1887 season into the first double-decked ballpark in the United States, topped by distinctive, twin towers resembling witch's hats.

1877

 The Swan Boats are introduced to the Public Garden by Robert Paget, who had previously operated rowboats on the lagoon. They are inspired by Richard Wagner's opera *Lohengrin.*

 December 11. Republican Henry Pierce (with 25,090 votes) defeats the incumbent Democrat, Frederick Prince (with 22,892), and all others to win election

Swan Boats on the lagoon in the Public Garden, in a photograph taken in 1941. (Courtesy of the Bostonian Society)

as mayor. Inaugurated on January 7, 1878, Pierce is a former mayor and congressman who declines to run for reelection.

The Women's Educational and Industrial Union is established. Founded by Dr. Harriet Crisby, Louisa May Alcott, Julia Ward Howe, and others "to promote the educational, industrial, and social advancement of women," it provides free legal advice to poor workers in 1878, opens an employment bureau soon after and the first credit union in the United States in 1913. It opens a retail shop in 1905, which closes in 2004. Originally located at 4 Park Street, it moves to Boylston Place, Byron Street, and then to its longtime location at 356 Boylston Street.

Gilchrist's hires the first woman store clerk in a Boston department store. A newspaper later reports that "passers-by came in to view the curiosity of a young lady who was not busy with domestic, social or teaching responsibilities."

January 28–May 27. The evangelist preacher Dwight Moody and the organist and singer Ira Sanky begin a religious revival campaign in a six-thousand-seat tabernacle constructed at Tremont Street and Warren Avenue.

February 9. Trinity Church in Copley Square is dedicated; Phillips Brooks is the first pastor. Designed by H. H. Richardson in the Romanesque style, the church is built on filled land and rests on 4,502 wooden piles, which must be kept from drying out. The interior design is by John LaFarge. The porch and front towers are completed after Richardson's death by Hugh Shepley in 1897. The literary critic Van Wyck Brooks later describes the building's significance as "the break of the Boston mind with its Puritan past."

Parker Bailey becomes the first African-American graduate of Boston Latin School. He goes on to graduate from Harvard and become a high school teacher in Washington, D.C.

Helen Magill White becomes the first woman in the United States with a doctorate when she receives her degree from Boston University.

May 17. E. T. Holmes opens the first telephone exchange at 342 Washington Street. Six subscribers are provided with daytime service only. Miss Emma Nutt becomes the first female telephone operator on September 1, 1878. She is hired after complaints are made that the male operators are too gruff.

January 2. The School of the Museum of Fine Arts, originally called the School of Drawing and Painting, opens in the basement of the museum at Copley Square. Eighty students are enrolled in the first classes. The school moves with the museum to the Fenway in 1909, first to a temporary building, then to its current building in September 1927, enlarged by an addition designed by Graham Gund in 1987. The school becomes affiliated with Tufts University in 1945. Charles Follen Adams's *Leedle Yawcob Strauss* is published.
February 9. The Footlights Drama Club opens with a performance of *A Scrap of Paper* at the German Theatre on Boylston Street in Jamaica Plain. The oldest community theater in the United States, it is founded by Caroline Morse. The company moves to Eliot Hall at 74 Eliot Street in 1878. When that building is threatened with demolition, the drama club members purchase it in 1889.

The Longwood Cricket Club is organized. Formed to promote cricket, it soon becomes more of a tennis club. It is located initially on the David Sears estate, called Longwood (the name of Napoleon's home in exile on St. Helena), which is today the campus of the Winsor School. The club moves to its current location on Hammond Street in Chestnut Hill in 1922.
April 12. Harvard's James Alexander Tyng becomes the first baseball player to use a catcher's mask. The device is invented by Fred Thayer, who adapts a fencing mask for the purpose and patents his invention the following year.

1878

December. The Boston Park Commission engages Frederick Law Olmsted as an adviser in developing what becomes known as the "Emerald Necklace," a nine-mile, eleven-hundred-acre chain of parks. In his *Notes on the Plan of Franklin Park and Related Matters* in 1885, Olmsted declares: "the beauty of the park should be . . . the beauty of the fields, the meadow, the prairie, of the green pastures, and the still waters. What we want to gain is tranquillity and rest to the mind." Olmsted's contract is terminated in 1885, but his firm is retained periodically thereafter, even after Olmsted's retirement in September 1895.

Francis S. Drake's *The Town of Roxbury, Its Memorable Persons and Places* is published.

December 10. Frederick Prince (with 19,676 votes) defeats Charles Codman (with 18,003) and others to again win election as mayor.

The New England Watch and Ward Society is established. Originally called the New England Society for the Suppression of Vice, it is incorporated in 1891 for "the protection of family life in New England." Praised by Robert Wood Johnson as "a sort of Moral Board of Health" in 1903, it is later denounced by the former Massachusetts attorney general Herbert Parker as including "detested types of procurers and falsifiers lingering within the somewhat withered vineyards of the Massachusetts moral prohibitory laws." The organization reaches the peak of its power between 1913 and 1926, when, through an arrangement with the Boston Board of Retail Book Merchants, it bans "indecent" books, including Theodore Dreiser's *An American Tragedy*, Sinclair Lewis's *Elmer Gantry*, John Dos Passos's *Manhattan Transfer,* and Ernest Hemingway's *The Sun Also Rises*. Unable to ban Kathleen Winsor's *Forever Amber* in 1948, the organization's power wanes thereafter.

June 27. A three-member Boston Police Commission is appointed by Mayor Pierce, with the approval of the Common Council. Authorized by the legislature on May 15, the commission does away with the position of chief of police, names former Chief Savage probation officer, and appoints Samuel Adams the first superintendent.

The Church of Our Lady of Perpetual Help (commonly called Mission Church), designed by Schickel and Ditmar in the Romanesque style, opens at 1525 Tremont Street. It is constructed from Roxbury pudding stone taken from Coleman's Quarry across the street. Its 250-foot twin towers, designed by Joseph Franz Joseph Untersee, are added in 1910. The church is named a basilica in 1954.

February 9. Girls Latin School opens on West Newton Street in the South End. John Tetlow is the first headmaster. The school expands to a building in Copley Square in 1898, shares a building with the Boston Normal School on Huntington Avenue in 1907, and moves to the former Dorchester High School for Girls in Codman Square in 1955. The school becomes coeducational and changes its name to Boston Latin Academy in 1972. It moves to 141 Ipswich Street in the Fenway in 1981, then to its current location at 205 Townsend Street in Roxbury in 1991.
East Boston High School is established. The school moves to a building designed by John Lyman Faxon on Marion Street in 1901, then to its current building, designed by the John Gray Company, at 86 White Street in 1926.

The first telephone directory in Boston is distributed. It is a single sheet of paper containing twenty-two names and no numbers. Callers must signal the central office ("Hello, Central") and announce the name of the party to whom they wish to speak.

February 12. The New England Telephone and Telegraph Company is incorporated by Alexander Graham Bell, Gardiner Greene Hubbard, and Thomas Sanders (two of Bell's financial backers and the fathers of two of his students at the school for the deaf). It later relocates to 125 Milk Street, then to Bowdoin Street in 1930.

Two Boston merchants, Caleb Chase and James Sanborn, make the first-ever shipment of coffee in cans.

July 14. The Boston Central Labor Union is established. Originally the Workingmen's Central Union, it is organized three years before the American Federation of Labor. Its goals are "to encourage all legislation for the benefit of working men; aid in the enforcement of present laws in the interest of labor which are evaded or carried out in a loose or improper manner; watch all proposed legislation in the councils of the city or state; and use its best efforts for the promotion of the general good."

 William Morris Hunt's *Talks about Art* is published.

Portrait of Frederick Law Olmsted. (Courtesy of the National Park Service, Frederick Law Olmsted National Historic Site)

November 25. Gilbert and Sullivan's *H.M.S. Pinafore* receives its American premiere at the Boston Museum and is very well received.

 February 11. The Boston Bicycle Club is established by G. B. Woodward and others. The first bicycle club in the country, it adopts a uniform consisting of a gray jacket, shirt, breeches, and stockings and a blue cap; it operates out of a clubhouse at 87 Boylston Street.

1879

 Construction begins on Boston's new park system, beginning with the 113-acre Back Bay Fens. Completed in 1894, it is redesigned by Arthur Shurcliff in the 1930s. The 527-acre West Roxbury Park (later called Franklin Park) is added to the park system in 1884 and completed in 1896. The 28-acre Riverway is added in 1890. Creation of the 120-acre Jamaica Pond Park begins in 1891 and is completed in 1894. The boathouse and bandstand are added in 1912. The entire system is considered finished when Marine Park is completed in 1895, although work continues in various parks for a number of years.

The City of Chicago attempts to purchase the Old State House and move it to the "Windy City." William Whitmore and others form the Boston Antiquarian Club in an effort to save and preserve the building. Incorporated as the Bostonian Society on December 2, 1881, the organization purchases the building, retains the architect George Clough to restore it, and begins to operate it as a museum in July 1882. The building is renovated again, by Joseph Chandler in 1907, by Perry, Shaw, and Hepburn in 1943, and by Goody, Clancy and Associates in 1992.

Thomas Wyman's *The Genealogies and Estates of Charlestown* is published.

April 10. Women are given the right to vote in Massachusetts—but only in school committee elections.

December 9. Frederick Prince (with 18,697 votes) defeats Solomon Stebbins (with 16,083) and others to win reelection as mayor. In his inaugural address on January 12, 1880, he declares: "Boston occupies a high position among the cities of the country. It is in some respects regarded as a model city, as it receives constant applications for information touching its management of municipal matters and its administrative methods."

December 3. An Omaha Indian, Suzette LaFlesche, speaks out against the cruelties of the American Indian reservation system at Faneuil Hall.

The Hong Far Low Restaurant opens at 36½ Harrison Avenue. The first Chinese restaurant in Boston, it is first listed in the city directory in 1896. The restaurant closes in 1960.

A total of 107 homicides are reported during the 1870s.

April 12. The Church of Christ, Scientist, founded by Mary Baker Eddy, is organized in Boston. The congregation meets in various rented rooms until moving to what comes to be called the "Mother Church," designed by Franklin Welch and dedicated on January 6, 1895. The building is later referred to as the "chapel." The "basilica" opens in 1906.

The Copley Society is organized. The oldest art association in the United States, it is originally called the Boston Art Students' Association and is open only to graduates of the School of the Museum of Fine Arts. The organization opens up its membership and assumes its current name in 1901.

Good Friday. An orchestra led by Georg Henschel and the Handel and Hayden Society perform Bach's *St. Matthew Passion* at the Music Hall. The work is performed in two parts on the same day, before capacity audiences.

April 14. The Park Theatre opens at 117 Washington Street with a production of *La Cigale,* starring the theater's owner, Lotta Crabtree. It becomes Minsky's Park Burlesque in the 1930s and features performers such as Gypsy Rose Lee. The theater later becomes the Trans-Lux and then the State movie theater.

April 10. Arthur Soden, president of the Boston Red Caps baseball team, introduces the "reserve clause" in player contracts. The clause becomes an integral part of major league baseball until withdrawn as part of an agreement between the owners and the players' union in 1976.

1880

Boston's population is 362,839, the fifth-largest of any city in the United States (behind New York, Philadelphia, Brooklyn, and Chicago). As a result of annexation and immigration, it is more than double what it had been twenty years before. A total of 6,013 are described as "Colored" (including "Chinese, Japanese and civilized Indians"), and of those, 5,873 are African American. The number of foreign born is 114,796, including 64,793 from Ireland. An estimated

4,000 to 5,000 are Jewish. The separate town of Hyde Park has an additional population of 7,088, with 149 classified as "Colored" and 1,703 as foreign born.

 (ca.) The three-decker tenement begins to appear in Boston. Built on a small plot, it allows good light for all three units and provides the homeowner with rental income. New housing regulations, which prohibit building houses so close to one another, end construction of the traditional three-decker after 1926.

 September 17. Boston celebrates its 250th birthday. Two parades are held—one during the day, one at night. The former is four and a half miles long, lasts three and a half hours, and includes 14,500 marchers, 325 vehicles, and numerous floats. The nighttime parade includes a thousand torch bearers and sixteen tableaux representing events in the city's history. Speaking at the Old South Church, Mayor Prince declares: "Scarcely a feature of the landscape remains to tell us how nature looked before she was subdued by civilization. The sea has been converted into land; the hills have been leveled—the valleys filled up, the sites of the Indian wigwams are now those of the palaces of our merchant princes, and where 'the wild fox dug his hole unscared,' art has reared her beautiful temples for the worship of God and the dissemination of learning."

 December 14. Frederick Prince (with 21,112 votes) again defeats Solomon Stebbins (with 20,531) and others to be reelected mayor.

 January 3. The St. Botolph Club meets for the first time; Francis Parkman is the first president. Soon after the social club is organized, Rev. Edward Everett Hale feels forced to resign because the club refuses to prohibit "the use of wines and liquor" when asked to do so by the Women's Christian Temperance Union. Meeting initially in a home at 2 Park Street, the club moves into rented quarters at 85 Boylston Street in 1880, to 2 Newbury Street in 1887, to 115 Commonwealth Avenue in 1941, then to its current location at 199 Commonwealth Avenue.

In his essay "The Perfect Brahmin," John Jay Chapman describes the social scene of the era: "Evening receptions were regarded as a natural form of amusement; people stood in a pack, and ate and drank, and talked volubly till midnight. And they enjoyed it too. There was a zest in it. I don't know why the world has become so dull of recent years, and society is so insipid. People in Boston in the Eighties knew how to enjoy themselves."

 Emerson College is established. It is originally called Emerson College of Oratory, later changes its name and becomes a liberal arts college, and is authorized to grant bachelors' degrees in 1919. Charles Emerson is the founder and first president. He is succeeded by William Rolfe (1904), Henry Southwick (1908), Harry Ross (1932), Boylston Green (1945), S. Justus McKinley (1953), Richard Chapin (1967), Gus Turbeville (1975), Allen Koenig (1979), John Zacharis (1991), and Jacqueline Liebergott (1993 to present). Located initially at 13 Pemberton Square, the school moves to 36 Bromfield Street in 1886, to the Odd Fellows Hall at the corner of Tremont and East Berkeley Streets in 1891, to Chickering Hall at 235 Huntington Avenue in 1901, to the Huntington

Chambers in 1911, and to Beacon Street in the Back Bay in 1932. The school moves to the Boylston and Tremont Street area of downtown Boston beginning in 1993.

Archbishop John Williams announces the establishment of a separate Catholic school system.

 The Adams Nervine Asylum opens on the former J. Gardiner Weld estate at 990 Centre Street in Jamaica Plain; it is supported by a bequest from Seth Adams, a Boston sugar merchant. The asylum's purpose—according to *King's Handbook*—is to serve "indigent, debilitated, nervous people, inhabitants of the State, who are not insane." The hospital closes in 1976 and is later converted into condominiums.

 Houghton Mifflin Company is established. Formed by the merger of the former Ticknor and Fields and the Riverside Press (established in 1852), it is incorporated in 1908. In addition to trade books and textbooks, the company publishes children's books, including H. A. and Margaret Rey's *Curious George* series. It is purchased by Vivendi Universal in 2001, then by a consortium of investment firms on January 1, 2004. Located initially at 4 Park Street, the Boston office moves to 222 Berkeley Street in the 1990s.

 M. Steinert and Sons piano sellers opens its Boston store. Founded originally in New Haven by Morris Steinert, the company moves its headquarters to Boston in 1883. Steinert Hall, designed by Winslow and Wetherell, opens at 162 Boylston Street in 1896, and is today the oldest music retail location in the United States. The company is acquired by Jerome Murphy and partners in 1934.

Lucretia Peabody Hale's *The Peterkin Papers* is published. A sequel, *The Last of the Peterkins,* is published in 1886.

1881

 The Immigrant House is established in East Boston. It is described by the historians Michael Price and Anthony Mitchell Sammarco as "a detention center for immigrants who were ill upon arriving . . . or whose papers were not in order. Young, single, immigrant women were required by the authorities to remain at the house until claimed by family members or their fiancés."

 Justin Winsor's work *The Memorial History of Boston, Including Suffolk County, Massachusetts: 1630–1880* is published.

 December 13. The Republican and Citizens Party candidate Samuel Green (with 20,429 votes) defeats Albert Palmer (with 19,724) and others to win election as mayor. A former city physician and a temperance advocate, Green successfully expands the park system.

 Clark's Boston Blue Book is published. Subtitled *The Elite Private Address and Carriage Directory, Ladies Visiting and Shopping Guide for Boston, Brookline, Cambridge, Jamaica Plain and Charlestown District,* it is published annually thereafter. Edward Clark also begins publishing *The Boston Club Book*, which lists the membership of Boston's men's clubs, beginning in 1888.

Oliver Wendell Holmes, Jr.'s *The Common Law* is published. Based on a series of lectures he delivered, the book contains this passage: "The life of the law has not been logic; it has been experience. . . . The law embodies the story of a nation's development through many centuries, and it cannot be dealt with as if it contained only the axioms and corollaries of a book of mathematics."

September 6. The air is clouded as a result of forest fires in Michigan and Canada, and the temperature reaches 102 degrees, one of the hottest days in the city's history. It is dubbed "Yellow Day."

March 1. The combined Latin School/English High School is dedicated on Warren Avenue (Latin) and Montgomery Street (English) in the South End. Designed by George Clough, it is described as "the largest [building] in the world used as a free public school." Latin moves to the Fenway in 1922,* and English in 1954.*
The North Bennet Street School is purchased by Pauline Agassiz Shaw and other women. It is turned into a vocational training school for the poor and immigrants, which opens in 1885.
Lelia Robinson graduates from the Boston University School of Law and later becomes the first woman admitted to the Massachusetts Bar.

Filene's department store opens at 10 Winter Street. The first Boston store owned by William Filene (he opened one in Salem in 1852), it moves to 445–447 Washington Street in 1890, to 453–463 Washington Street in 1907, and to the current Beaux Arts building at 426 Washington Street, designed by Daniel Burnham, on September 3, 1912. Filene's Basement opens in a separate building in 1908, initiates the automatic markdown system in 1911, and moves into the basement of the current building in 1912. Edward Filene takes over management of the company from his father in 1891. He establishes the first employees' credit union in the United States, promotes consumer cooperatives, and is subsequently ousted after trying to transform the company into an employees' cooperative. Filene's is now owned by Federated Department Stores, Filene's Basement by Retail Ventures Inc.

The Vose Galleries opens in Boston. Originally an art supply store run by the artist Ransom Hicks in Providence, Rhode Island, it is purchased a few years later by Joseph Vose. His son, Seth, opens the gallery in Boston. Located in the Studio Building by the end of the nineteenth century, it moves to 559 Boylston Street in the 1920s, then to its current location, the Vose family's former town house at 238 Newbury Street, in 1962.
October 22. The Boston Symphony Orchestra makes its debut performance at the Boston Music Hall. It is founded by Maj. Henry Lee Higginson to provide "the best music at low prices, such as may be found in all the large European cities, or even in the smaller musical centres of Germany." Georg Henschel is named the first conductor. He is succeeded by Wilhelm Gericke (1884), Arthur

Nikisch (1889), Emil Paur (1893), Wilhelm Gericke (1898), Karl Muck (1906), Max Fiedler (1908), and Karl Muck again (from 1912 to 1918*).

March 28. Sarah Bernhardt makes her Boston debut, performing in French.

Austin and Stone's Dime Museum opens at the corner of Howard Street and Tremont Row in Scollay Square. Performers would include Tom Thumb, the Bearded Lady, the Dog-Faced Boy, and the Witch of Wall Street. It closes in 1911, is torn down, and is replaced by Scollay's Olympia Theatre, one of the first buildings in Boston constructed with steel-reinforced concrete.

September. Richard Sears of Boston becomes the first U.S. National Lawn Tennis singles champion. He retains the title for the next six years. Playing with Dr. James Dwight of Boston, he goes on to win six national doubles championships as well.

1882

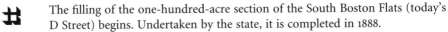

The filling of the one-hundred-acre section of the South Boston Flats (today's D Street) begins. Undertaken by the state, it is completed in 1888.

A New York immigration organization, the British Mansion House, sends a ship carrying 415 Russian Jews from New York to Boston. Boston's primarily German Jewish community—and its Hebrew Emigrant Aid Society—declares it is unable to provide the necessary help, and the ship is sent back to New York.

Fall. The first electric (incandescent) streetlights are installed in Boston.

Upon the death of Edward Ingersoll Brown, an eponymous fund is established by a Boston attorney "for the adornment and benefit of [his] native city."

Patrick Collins becomes the first Irish American from Boston elected to the U.S. Congress. Reelected twice, he later declares: "In practice, the Congressman is an errand boy. He must secure places for the men who gave him their support." Collins also warns, "if we continue our present course, wealth will control all the avenues to honest political distinction."

December 12. Democrat Albert Palmer (with 21,713 votes) defeats Samuel Green (with 19,575), in a reversal of the previous election, to be elected mayor. Despite backing from the Democratic ward boss Patrick J. Maguire, Palmer leaves office after only one term to return to private business.

F. J. Doyle's Tavern opens at today's 3484 Washington Street in Jamaica Plain. Founded by two brothers, Francis and Barney Doyle, it is expanded in 1907 to include the Braddock Café. The Doyle brothers' nephew Bill sells the business to Ed Burke in 1971, who continues to operate it today.

December 5. Oliver Wendell Holmes, Jr., is appointed to the Supreme Judicial Court of Massachusetts, where he serves until 1902.*

The *Jewish Watchman* begins publication. It is the first Jewish periodical in Boston.

Patrick J. Maguire begins to publish the *Republic*, to promote "all things Irish" and to condemn "all things Republican as anti-Irish." It is the first Irish newspaper in Boston.

Thompson's Spa opens at 219 Washington Street along Newspaper Row. It becomes one of the most popular lunch restaurants in the city and a center for newspaper gossip.

January 31. Oscar Wilde lectures at the Music Hall. An editor at the *Boston Transcript* later explains the less-than-warm reception Wilde's words and manner receive by writing, "There are some things that can be done in New York that cannot be done in Boston."

December 11. The renamed Bijou Theatre opens on Washington Street, with a production of Gilbert and Sullivan's *Iolanthe.* Family-oriented, live entertainment, called vaudeville, is soon offered, including the comedy team of Weber and Fields.

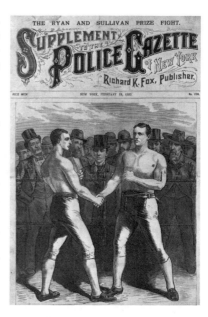

Ryan and Sullivan prize fight, from the cover of the Supplement to the Police Gazette. *(Courtesy of the Bostonian Society)*

February 7. John L. Sullivan ("the Boston Strong Boy") knocks out Paddy Ryan in the ninth round to win the U.S. bare-knuckles heavyweight boxing championship in Mississippi City, Mississippi. He beats Jake Kilrain in a seventy-five-round fight in Richburg, Mississippi, to win the last undisputed bare-knuckles heavyweight championship fight on July 8, 1889. Then he loses the heavyweight championship to James J. Corbett in a twenty-one-round fight in New Orleans in the first title fight in which gloves are worn on September 7, 1892.

September 6. The Boston Bicycle Club Meet takes place. Seven cyclists complete a 102.5-mile course from Worcester to Boston in twelve hours and six minutes, with frequent stops for rest and repairs.

1883

George Bromley's *Atlas of the City of Boston* is published.
T Wharf is completed.

The Calf Pasture Pumping Station opens at 435 Mt. Vernon Street on Columbia Point. Designed by the city architect George Clough, it is the first sewage pumping station in the city. It becomes part of a waterfront park dedicated on June 14, 1992.

February 21. Art Square is renamed Copley Square. The city acquires the property by purchasing land from the state, MIT, and the Museum of Fine Arts.

F. J. Doyle's Tavern, Jamaica Plain, today. (Photograph by Richard Tourangeau)

The square is redesigned by Sasaki Dawson in 1969, then by Clarke and Rapuano and Dean Abbott in 1990.
Charlesbank and Marine Park are added to the city's park system. The filling of both parks begins this year. The filling of Charlesbank is completed in 1888 and of Marine Park in 1893.

Edwin M. Bacon's *King's Dictionary of Boston* is published.

December 11. The Republican and Citizens Party candidate Augustus Martin (with 27,494 votes) defeats Hugh O'Brien (with 25,950) to win election as mayor. A Maine native and Civil War hero, General Martin is backed by Protestant ministers who declaim from their pulpits against "rum and Romanism." As mayor, he supports passage of a civil service law covering city employees.

The Clover Club is organized. Founded by a group of Irish Americans for "the social enjoyment of its members," the club operates without a headquarters and becomes known for its annual dinners, at which parodies of popular songs are performed.

George Ruffin of Boston becomes the first African-American judge in Massachusetts when he is appointed to the Charlestown Municipal Court by Gov. Benjamin Butler.

Antiseptic techniques are introduced to reduce infection after childbirth at Boston Lying-In Hospital, greatly reducing the number of maternal and infant deaths.

September. The Foreign Exhibition of the New England Manufacturers and Mechanics Association is held, featuring artists such as Edouard Manet, Claude Monet, Camille Pissarro, Auguste Renoir, and Alfred Sisley. The art critic Trevor Fairbrother later describes the show as "the first important display of such paintings in America."

Boston-born Childe Hassam holds his first solo exhibition of watercolors at Williams and Everett's Gallery.

Julia Ward Howe's *Biography of Margaret Fuller* and William Dean Howells's *A Woman's Reason* are published.

The Metropolitan Opera Company of New York begins making annual visits to Boston, performing at the Boston Theatre.

The Gaiety Museum opens on Washington Street on the site of the former Lane Tavern. It is operated by Benjamin Keith and Edward F. Albee. Its first attractions include a midget named Baby Alice and a stuffed "mermaid."

January. A Dark Secret is performed at the Howard Athenaeum. The *Boston Post* later describes the production as "a thrilling tale of the Thames Valley, with Marvellous Aquatic Scenes—the Henley Regatta, presented with real sailboats, Rowboats, Racing Shells, and Steam Engines, the Stage Being Flooded with 5,000 Cubic Feet of Water."

October 1. The Count of Monte Cristo, starring James O'Neill, opens at the Globe Theatre. O'Neill performs in the play thousands of times during his career; he serves as the model for the father in the play *Long Day's Journey into Night*, written by his son, Eugene.

1884

January 1. The Main Drainage System begins operation. The city's new sewage system, it includes lines connected to a pumping station at Moon Island and is the most modern system of its time. Construction began in 1878.

Franklin Park is added to the city's park system.

December 9. Democrat Hugh O'Brien (with 27,494 votes) defeats Republican Augustus Martin (with 24,168) to be elected mayor. Inaugurated on January 5, 1885, O'Brien becomes Boston's first Irish-born and first Catholic mayor. He pleases—and surprises—the Yankee business establishment with his moderation.

The first branch of the Salvation Army opens at the corner of Washington and Warren Streets.

The Tavern Club is established. William Dean Howells is the first president. Initially located in rented rooms at 1 Park Square, the club purchases and moves to 4 Boylston Place a few years later. The building is damaged by fire in 1957 and then restored.

March 27. A long-distance telephone line between Boston and New York opens.

Carroll Wright's study *Working Girls of Boston* is published by the Massachusetts Bureau of Labor Statistics.

September 3. The first issue of the daily *Boston Evening Record*, the evening edition of the *Advertiser*, appears. Joseph Edgar Chamberlin is the first editor. The *Record* becomes the city's first tabloid in December 1920. It is purchased

The Cyclorama Building on Tremont Street in the South End. (Courtesy of the Bostonian Society)

by William Randolph Hearst and merges with the *Advertiser* in 1921, and merges with the *American* to become the *Record-American* in 1961. The paper moves to One Winthrop Square from 1924 to 1972, when it ceases publication.

 The Cyclorama Building opens at 505 Tremont Street in the South End. Designed by Cummings and Sears, it is built by the Chicago businessman Charles Willoughby to house the 50-by-400-foot mural *The Battle of Gettysburg* by the Parisian artist Paul Dominique Philippoteaux (it later moves to Gettysburg). The round brick building later houses a carousel, roller skating, carnivals, boxing matches, and an automobile manufacturing plant. The Cyclorama becomes home to the Boston Flower Exchange in 1923 and to the Boston Center for the Arts in 1970. Although common in its time, it is now one of only three such buildings remaining in North America.

As You Like It, starring Maurice Barrymore and Helena Modjeska, is performed at the Globe Theatre. Georgie Drew, Barrymore's wife, is also in the cast, and inserts a line of dialogue ("Be sure 'tis but sighing you do, lest it lead to deeper things") to warn the Polish actress to keep away from her husband offstage.

1885

 The filling of Miller's River and Charles River Bay are completed in Charlestown.

In *The Lodging-House Problem in Boston*, Albert Wolfe later writes: "By 1885 the South End had become dominantly a lodging house section."

 December 15. Hugh O'Brien (with 26,690 votes) defeats Clark (with 17,992) to be reelected mayor with the largest majority in any citywide election in Boston's history.

W. W. Bryant is appointed deputy sealer of weights and measures. He is thought to be the first African-American municipal official in Boston's history.

December 20. The Hendricks Club is established in the West End. Founded by Martin Lomasney (known as "the Mahatma") and others, it becomes one of the most powerful Democratic organizations in the city. Lomasney later declares: "The great mass of people are interested in only three things—food, clothing, and shelter. A politician in a district such as mine sees to it that his people get these things. If he does, then he doesn't have to worry about their loyalty and support." Other ward bosses in the city at the time include Matthew Keany (North End), Thomas Flood (South Boston), P. J. Kennedy (East Boston), Joe Corbett (Charlestown), Joseph O'Connell (Dorchester), "Smiling" Jim Donovan (South End), and P. J. "Pea Jacket" Maguire, and later "One-Armed" Peter Whalen (both in Roxbury).

October. The Ellis Memorial Foundation (originally the Ellis Club) is founded by Ida Eldredge to provide educational and recreational programs for children. It is named after Rev. Rufus Ellis, pastor of the First Church of Boston. Located initially in an empty storefront on Tremont Street, it moves to Providence Street in the South End, then to Carver Street in 1900, and to its current location on Berkeley Street in 1924.

The Algonquin Club is founded by Gen. Charles H. Taylor. Augustus Martin is the first president. The club moves to its current headquarters, designed by Charles Follen McKim, at 217 Commonwealth Avenue in 1888.
The first annual Hunt Ball is held at the Odd Fellows Hall.

July 24. The Republican-dominated state legislature takes away the power to appoint the three-member Boston Police Commission from the now Democrat-dominated city administration and gives that authority to the governor. The commission is reduced to a single commissioner, appointed to a five-year term, in 1906. The power to appoint the Boston Police commissioner is not returned to the mayor of Boston until April 1962.

The First Spiritualist Temple opens at Exeter and Newbury Streets. Designed by Hartwell and Richardson, it is built for the Working Union of Progressive Spiritualists. The congregation later moves downstairs, and the upstairs is converted to the Exeter Street movie theater (the only one that proper Boston women are said to patronize) in 1914. The building is converted to retail use in 1985.

The Boston School Committee is again reorganized. An amendment to the city charter removes the mayor as an ex officio member and calls for a committee of twenty-four members elected at large.

William Dean Howells's novel *The Rise of Silas Lapham* is published.
July 11. The Boston Symphony Orchestra performs its first Boston Pops concert at the Music Hall, described as "light music of the best class." The Promenade Concerts of the Boston Symphony Orchestra was the original title of the series; the name "Pops" comes from a popular march tune ("The Pops") performed at the first concert. Liquid refreshments are served at this May through June series. Adolph Neuendorff is the first music director.

Skating on Jamaica Pond, from Ballou's Pictorial. *(Courtesy of the Bostonian Society)*

The Boston Music Company is established. It becomes a leading publisher and seller of musical publications.

Twenty Days, or Buffalo Bill's Pledge, starring William Cody, is performed at the Howard Athenaeum.

1886

 Jamaica Pond is purchased by the city.

 December 14. Democrat Hugh O'Brien (with 23,426 votes) defeats Republican Thomas Hart (with 18,685) and others to be reelected mayor.

 Oliver Wendell Holmes, Sr., writes a smug paean to comfortable Bostonians: "What better provision can be made for mortal man than such as our own Boston can offer its wealthy children? A palace on Commonwealth Avenue or on Beacon Street; a country-place at Framingham or Lenox; a seaside residence at Nahant, Beverly Farms, Newport, or Bar Harbor; a pew at Trinity or King's Chapel; a tomb at Mount Auburn or Forest Hills; with the prospect of a memorial stained-glass window after his lamented demise,—is not that a pretty programme to offer a candidate for human existence?"

 February. The Stony Brook Flood occurs. Three days of rain, along with melting snow, combine to flood sixty-three acres of land to a depth of three feet. Nearly two hundred houses are damaged in an area of Roxbury bordered by Shawmut Avenue and Lenox, Tremont, and Roxbury Streets.

November. H. E. McCurdy is killed near the Chestnut Hill Reservoir in what is reportedly the first fatal bicycle accident in the Boston area.

 Cooking is introduced into the elementary school curriculum by Mary Hemenway, making Boston the first school system in the United States to offer such courses.

Dr. R. H. Fitz of Massachusetts General Hospital first describes and recommends surgery as a treatment for appendicitis.

The first visiting nurse service in the United States is established in Boston.

February 20. Boston Edison begins operation, with Thomas Edison throwing a switch sending current to light the nearby Bijou Theatre on Washington Street. Originally called the Edison Electric Illuminating Company, it is incorporated on December 26, 1885, and operates the first electric generating station in Boston, a seventy-five-horsepower engine and two dynamos. A new station is set up in a former stable at the corner of Haymarket Place and Bumstead Court in 1887.

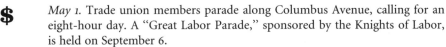

May 1. Trade union members parade along Columbus Avenue, calling for an eight-hour day. A "Great Labor Parade," sponsored by the Knights of Labor, is held on September 6.

The Hatters Union is established. The oldest women's union in Boston, it joins the Knights of Labor later in the year. The Women Bookbinders Union and the Laundry Union are organized in 1896, the Women Tobacco Strippers in 1899, and several branches of the garment trade unions in 1901 and 1902.

Four important paintings are completed: Childe Hassam's *Rainy Day, Boston* and *Boston Common at Twilight*, Winslow Homer's *Lost on the Grand Banks*, and John Singer Sargent's *Carnation, Lily, Lily, Rose*.

Henry James's *The Bostonians* is published. In it a Mrs. Luna announces that the motto for Bostonians is: "Whatever is, is wrong." Later, James writes to his brother, William: "I shall be much abused for the title." He declares that he "hadn't a dream of generalizing," and promises to write another book, entitled *The Other Bostonians*—but he never does.

1887

November 12. Henry Whitney's West End Street Railway Company absorbs the Metropolitan Railroad, the South Boston Railroad, and the Boston Consolidated Street Railway, and, a week later, the Cambridge Railroad. Authorized by the West End Consolidation Act passed earlier in the year by the Massachusetts legislature, the takeovers enable Whitney to create the largest streetcar system in the world.

The Allston Depot opens at 353 Cambridge Street. Designed by Shepley, Rutan, and Coolidge, it is originally a station for the Boston and Albany Railroad and is later converted to a restaurant.

March. The Hyde Park Historical Society is established.

December 13. Hugh O'Brien (with 26,636 votes) defeats Thomas Hart (with 25,179) to be reelected mayor. For the first time in the city's history, the mayor, chairman of the aldermen, president of the Common Council, City Clerk, and chairman of the School Committee are all Irish Catholics.

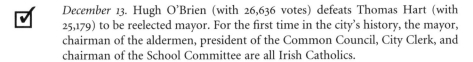

May 10. Queen Kapiolani and Princess Liliuokalani of the Kingdom of Hawaii visit Boston. The queen later claims to posses English blood "because my grandfather ate Captain Cook."

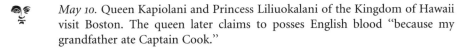

March 14. The Bussey Bridge disaster takes place. In the worst railroad accident up to that time in the United States, twenty-three are killed and more than one hundred are injured when a commuter train from Dedham derails on the Bussey Bridge at South Street and Archdale Road in Roslindale.

 September 5. After the state legislature makes it an official holiday, Labor Day is celebrated as twenty thousand workers march through Boston. The *Boston Globe* later describes the holiday as "a veritable festival of joy . . . recognized by the people of Boston and vicinity."

 Samuel Warren donates a Greek terra-cotta statue to the Museum of Fine Arts, which was purchased by his brother, Ned. It is the first original classical sculpture acquired by the museum and is, according to Whitehill, "followed by companions who routed the plaster casts that had seemed so all-important in the museum's first decade." Ned Warren begins a long association with the museum, purchasing and donating art on its behalf. "I have always said and believed that it was hate of Boston that made me work for Boston," he later admits. "The collection was my plea against that in Boston which contradicted my [pagan] love."

The Club of Odd Volumes is organized. Originally a dinner club that meets in restaurants and other clubs, it rents buildings at 50 and 54 Mount Vernon Street, then buys its current headquarters at 77 Mt. Vernon Street in 1936.

Dr. Jekyll and Mr. Hyde, starring Richard Mansfield, is given its American premiere at the Boston Museum. Mansfield is later suspected of being the real-life Jack the Ripper.

 Boston Latin beats Boston English 16–0 in the first meeting of the schools' football teams. In the oldest continuous school sports rivalry in the country, the games are played at Harvard Stadium from 1903 to 1970, at Boston University Field from 1971 to 2001, then back at Harvard Stadium beginning in 2002.

March 15. The Boston Athletic Association (BAA) is organized. Robert Clark is the first president. The first Boston Athletic Association track and field competition is held in 1891. The organization's clubhouse at the corner of Exeter and Blagden Streets opens on December 29, 1888, and closes, owing to a decline in membership and financial difficulties, on August 3, 1935. The club's headquarters are currently located at 131 Clarendon Street.

1888

 A member of the Common Council suggests that they "inquire into and report what negligence if any, is attached to [East Boston] ferry employees, that admits of so many accidents and suicides by falling and jumping from boats."

The Iron Bridge to Head Island in Pleasure Bay in South Boston opens. It is destroyed by the Great New England Hurricane of 1938 and replaced. A dike is built enclosing the body of water that becomes known as the "Sugar Bowl" in 1959.

The Romanesque Revival–style Mount Bellevue water tower is constructed. It is replaced by a granite structure in 1916. The current metal tank is built in 1956. Bellevue Hill (325 feet above sea level) is the tallest in Boston, followed by Green Hill in Jamaica Plain (305), Metropolitan Hill in Roslindale (246), Peters Hill in Jamaica Plain (235), and Mission Hill in Roxbury (220).

December 11. Republican Thomas Hart (with 32,712 votes) defeats Democrat Hugh O'Brien (with 30,880) to be elected mayor and deprive O'Brien of a fifth consecutive term as mayor. A successful businessman, Hart consolidates a number of city departments.

August 28. The German socialist Friedrich Engels visits Boston and his nephew Willie, who works for the Boston and Providence Railroad. Engels writes in his diary: "Boston is just a village, sprawling far and wide, more human than New York City."

March 11. The Great Blizzard of '88 strikes. Winds reach a reported sixty miles per hour, and the storm lasts for three days.

The first Christian Science reading room opens in the lobby of the Hotel Boylston.

Wheelock College is established. Originally called the Wheelock School at Chauncy Hall, it is founded by Lucy Wheelock. The first class consists of six students studying the "new education," as the kindergarten movement is then called. Wheelock is the first president. She is succeeded by Winifred Bain (1940), Frances Mayfarth (1955), James Connor (1962), Henry Callard (acting, 1965), Margaret Merry (1966), Donald Cruickshank (1971), William Irvine (acting, 1972), Gordon Marshall (1973), Daniel Cheever, Jr. (1983), Gerald Tirozzi (1991), Marjorie Bakken (1993), and Jackie Jenkins-Scott (2004 to the present). Located initially in Copley Square, the school moves to 200 The Riverway in 1914.

June. The Boston Electric Light Company is organized. It builds an alternating current generating station on L Street in South Boston and is taken over by the Edison Company on February 5, 1902.

John Singer Sargent holds his first solo exhibition at the St. Botolph Club. Sargent, who had first visited Boston the previous year, includes in the show a portrait of Isabella Stewart Gardner that is considered so shockingly sensual that her husband, Jack Gardner, orders it to be removed from public view. Although it is hung at Fenway Court, Mrs. Gardner prohibits it from being shown until after her death.

1889

The creation of the Bay State Road area is begun by the Riverbank Improvement Company from fill created by the dredging the Charles River. Many fine homes are built there, but the area is developed just as the demand for such residences begins to wane.
The filling of a seventy-acre section of the South Boston Flats (today's Northern Avenue) begins. It is completed in 1895.

Electric trolley cars on Tremont Street, 1895. (Courtesy of the Bostonian Society, Boston Elevated Collection)

The Ames Building opens on Court Street. Designed by Shepley, Rutan, and Coolidge in the Romanesque style, it is the tallest building in New England (14 stories and 190 feet), and is built just prior to the introduction of steel-framed construction.

December 11. The Boston Architectural Center opens. Originally called the Boston Architectural Club, it provides atelier-style training in various offices. The school moves to a building designed by Ralph Adams Cram at 16 Somerset Street on Beacon Hill in 1911, then to its current building, designed by Ashley, Meyer and Associates, at 320 Newbury Street, in 1966. Richard Haas's trompe l'oeil painting is added to the exterior in 1975.

January 1. The first electric trolley car in Boston goes into operation. The initial run is made from the Allston car barn, via Coolidge Corner in Brookline, to Park Square. After first investigating the cable power system, representatives of the West End Street Railway traveled to Richmond, Virginia, and decided to adopt the kind of electric motors developed there by Frank Sprague. Boston becomes the first major city in the United States to electrify its entire system when it is completed on September 30, 1896. By the 1890s seventy-one different lines operate, with color codes denoting the various routes (green, Roxbury; purple, Dorchester; scarlet, South Boston; pale blue, Brookline; brown, Brighton; maroon, Somerville and Charlestown; and there was even a plaid line).

May 24. Sparked by the interest in "horseless carriages," the Back Bay Cycle and Motor Company opens the first public garage in Boston. It is advertised as a "stable for renting, sale, storage and repair of motor vehicles."

Dr. Dudley Sargent of Harvard designs the first "open air gymnasium" in the United States, a ten-acre park for men on the Charlesbank in the West End. A women's gymnasium, screened by shrubbery to provide "the seclusion desirable for the sex," opens in 1891.

The Bostonian Society votes to admit women members. One Boston newspaper applauds the move, declaring, "If Minerva knows more on certain subjects than Jupiter, give Minerva fair play and a chance."
John Fiske's *The Beginnings of New England*, and Solomon Schindler's *Israelites in Boston: A Tale Describing the Development of Judaism in Boston* are published.

December 10. Republican Thomas Hart (with 31,133 votes) defeats Democrat Owen Galvin (with 25,673) and others to be reelected mayor.
The Australian ballot, with its secret voting procedures, is adopted in Boston and throughout Massachusetts.

Vida Scudder and others establish the Rivington Street Settlement House. Several other settlement houses are soon established in the city. Andover House (later called the South End House) is founded at 20 Union Park by the theology professor William Jewett Tucker and is run by Robert Woods in 1891. Emily Balch founds the Denison House at 93 Tyler Street in South Cove in 1892; it later moves to Dorchester. The North End Union is founded in 1892, the Elizabeth Peabody House opens at 156 Chambers Street in the West End in 1896, the Little House in Dorchester is founded in 1906, and Dorchester House is incorporated in 1909.
The Hecht House is established. Originally called the Hebrew Industrial School for Girls, it is founded by Mrs. Jacob (Lina) Hecht. Located initially on the second floor of a building on Hanover Street, it moves to its own building on Bulfinch Place in the West End in 1922, then to the former Home for Jewish Children, at 160 American Legion Highway in Dorchester, on January 19, 1936. The building is sold to the Lena Park Housing Development Corporation on December 22, 1970.

October 16. Helen Keller enters the Perkins School for the Blind. Left blind, deaf, and mute by illness when she was nineteen months old, Keller learns to read and speak. She later attends the Horace Mann School for the Deaf and graduates from Radcliffe College in 1904.

Boston has ten daily newspapers. There would be eleven in 1891, and twelve in 1901.

The "Boston School" of painting is formed with the appointment of Frank Weston Benson and Edmund Tarbell to the faculty of the School of the Museum of Fine Arts. Joseph DeCamp, Philip and Lillian Westcott Hale, and William and Elizabeth Paxton are also members of this group at some point. At about this time, however, Boston loses two painters, Dennis Bunker and Childe Hassam, to New York.
October 12. The second Tremont Theatre opens at 176 Tremont Street with a performance of *David Garrick*, starring the English actor Charles Wyndham.

Damaged by a fire on January 23, 1916, the theater is remodeled and renamed the Astor in 1949.

 December 2. Harvard's John Cranston, Arthur Cummock, and James Lee are named to Walter Camp's first all-American collegiate football team.

1890

 Boston's population is 448,477, the sixth-largest of any city in the United States (behind New York, Chicago, Philadelphia, Brooklyn, and St. Louis). Of that number, 8,590 are described as "Colored," including 8,125 who are African American; 158,172 are foreign born, including 71,441 from Ireland. An estimated 5,000 are Italian, and 20,000 are Jewish. The town of Hyde Park has a population of 10,193, with 98 classified as "Negro" and 2,808 as foreign born.

 Deer Island Light is erected in 1890. Fort Dawes is built there at the beginning of World War II. The island is connected to Winthrop, first by a bridge in 1937, then by sand deposited by the Great New England Hurricane of 1938.

 (ca.) The philanthropist Robert Treat Paine and his Workingman's Building Association constructs one of the first subsidized single-family housing developments in the United States on Round Hill Street in Jamaica Plain.

 Castle Island is transferred by the federal government to the city and added to the Boston park system. A wooden causeway opens on July 29, 1892, connecting Castle Island to Marine Park in South Boston, and a roadway opens in 1932. Reactivated during World War II as a facility to demagnetize ship hulls so German mines would not be attracted to them, Castle Island is deactivated in 1947.
The Riverway and Olmsted Park are completed.

 James Cullen's *History of the Irish in Boston* is published.

 December 9. Democrat Nathan Matthews, Jr. (with 32,210 votes), defeats Moody Merrill (with 19,957) and others to become mayor for the first of four consecutive terms. A graduate of Harvard and Harvard Law School and a lecturer in municipal government there, he is later described by John Galvin as "the most astute student of city government to hold the office."

 Harriet Smith becomes the first African-American teacher in the Boston public school system. She teaches at the Sharp School on Beacon Hill until 1917.
Physical education is introduced as a systemwide program in the Boston public schools.

 The *Chinese Monthly News* begins publication.

 The William S. Haynes Company of Boston is established. The custom flute manufacturer is currently located at 12 Piedmont Street in Bay Village.

November 22. Harvard beats Yale 12–6 to finish 11 and 0 and win its first national collegiate football championship. Harvard also wins the championship in 1898, 1899, 1912, and 1913.

September 25. The Boston Reds baseball team loses 10–4 to Cleveland in the last game of the season, but wins the championship in its only year in the Players League.

1891

The "composer streets" are laid out in Hyde Park, in an area formerly called Gypsy Hill. Brahms, Haydn, Liszt, and Mendelssohn Streets become public ways in 1929.

Fall. The Harvard Bridge opens, connecting West Chester Park in Boston with Harvard Bridge Avenue in Cambridge. The bridge and both streets are renamed Massachusetts Avenue in 1894.

Dorchester Park and Wood Island Park are added to the Boston park system.

The Bostonians Jacob Askowith and his son, Charles, design what becomes the Jewish flag. Created for the local B'nai Zion Educational Society, the flag consists of two blue horizontal stripes on a white background and an inscribed Star of David.
The Dorchester Historical Society is established.

December 15. Nathan Matthews, Jr. (with 34,708 votes), defeats Horace Allen (with 19,532) and others to be reelected mayor.
Congressman Henry Cabot Lodge writes: "Immigration is making its greatest relative increase from races most alien to the body of the American people and from the lowest and most illiterate classes among those races. In other words, it is apparent that, while our immigration is increasing, it is showing at the same time a marked tendency to deteriorate in character."

November 10. The Women's Christian Temperance Union holds its first world convention at Faneuil Hall. The group pledges to work for "the annihilation of the trade in beverage alcohol."

The Boston *Social Register* list of eight thousand families includes fewer than a dozen Catholic families and one Jewish family, that of Louis Brandeis.

The Vincent Memorial Hospital is established. Founded by friends of Mary Ann Vincent, an actress and Beacon Hill resident who died in 1887, its mission is to provide health care for women. The site of the development of the Pap Smear test, the hospital becomes part of Massachusetts General Hospital in 1940, and is now its Women's Care Division.

July 1. The State Street Safe Deposit and Trust Company opens; its name is shortened to the State Street Trust Company in 1897. The company merges with the National Union Bank (established 1792) in 1925.

The Anti–Tenement House League is organized. It is founded by George Mc-Neill and others to combat sweatshops and substandard housing.

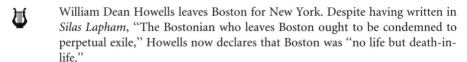

January 4. The *Boston Globe* begins publishing mild-mannered editorials signed "Uncle Dudley." The practice continues until January 5, 1966, when the signature is dropped and the newspaper begins to take stronger editorial positions.

Edwin Grozier buys the *Boston Post.* A former aide to Joseph Pulitzer, he improves news coverage, initiates a series of promotional stunts, and increases circulation to over six hundred thousand in 1919, the largest of any newspaper in the United States.

According to the newspaper historian Herbert Kenney, there are nine daily newspapers, four semiweeklies, six Sunday-only, five fortnightly, and seventy-five monthly publications in Boston this year.

William Dean Howells leaves Boston for New York. Despite having written in *Silas Lapham,* "The Bostonian who leaves Boston ought to be condemned to perpetual exile," Howells now declares that Boston was "no life but death-in-life."

The Cecilia Society begins a series of Wage Earners' Concerts, designed to introduce a new audience to choral music. Tickets are distributed to employers for their employees. Despite some abuse, the series continues for twenty years. (According to Cecilia's historian, William Carroll Hill, "many citizens, fully able to pay regular subscription prices, began using the wage earners tickets with a consequent diminishing of the support for the regular concerts.")

February 9. The Bostonian Charles Hoyt's *A Trip to Chinatown* opens at the Boston Theatre for a two-week run before going to New York for 657 performances. Hoyt initiates the practice of using Boston as a tryout town, and later serves as a "play doctor" for many productions.

September 25. The Boston Reds beat Baltimore 6–2 in Baltimore to win the American Association baseball championship in the team's only year in the league. Begun in 1882, the league disbands at the end of this season.

1892

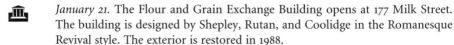

(ca.) Mystic Wharf is completed in Charlestown.

After receiving state approval, the city establishes a height limit of 125 feet for all downtown buildings, excluding the spires of churches. A seventy-foot limit is established along the edges of parks and playgrounds in 1895, and a ninety-foot limit around three sides of Copley Square (100 feet on the north side) in 1898. The downtown height limit is increased to 155 feet in 1923.

January 21. The Flour and Grain Exchange Building opens at 177 Milk Street. The building is designed by Shepley, Rutan, and Coolidge in the Romanesque Revival style. The exterior is restored in 1988.

The Lawrence Model Lodging Houses are completed at 79–109 East Canton Street. Designed by Kirby and Goodwin, the development is funded by a bequest of Abbott Lawrence, "to be let to poor, temperate, industrious families

. . . at reasonable rents." They are the oldest existing units of philanthropic, affordable housing in the city.

The L (later called the Summer) Street Bridge opens across the Reserve Channel in South Boston.
Electric streetcar lines begin operating in South Boston. They continue until 1953.
A garbage processing plant opens on Moon Island. It is moved to Spectacle Island in 1912 and closed in 1959.

Olmsted's Charlesbank Park is completed along the Charles River. Designed "to offer a variety of recreational facilities for the poor in the crowded tenement district of Boston's West End," it is considered to be the first public playground in the city.
The Arborway is completed from Jamaica Pond to Franklin Park, becoming part of the park system. Franklin Field is completed.

Francis Parkman's *A Half Century of Conflict* and Solomon Schindler's *History of the Jews of Boston and New England* are published.

December 13. Nathan Matthews, Jr. (with 39,986 votes), defeats Homer Rogers (with 26,671) and others to be reelected mayor.
John F. Fitzgerald is elected as one of the youngest members of the Massachusetts Senate. Upon the death of Matthew Keany, he also becomes ward boss of the North End.
Martin Lomasney is elected to the Board of Aldermen, his first public office. He serves here, in the Massachusetts House of Representatives, and in the Massachusetts Senate for much of the next thirty-five years.

The Women's Era Club is formed by Josephine St. Pierre Ruffin to improve conditions for the "Negro race" in general and "Negro women" in particular.
The first Knights of Columbus lodge in Boston is organized in Charlestown.
September 8. "The Pledge of Allegiance" is first published in the *Youth's Companion* magazine, located at 201 Columbus Avenue. Written by Francis Bellamy and edited by James Upham, the pledge is part of an issue celebrating the four hundredth anniversary of Columbus's discovery of America.

The Vincent Club is organized, with a clubhouse at 71 Brimmer Street. A women's club, its members produce an annual theatrical production to benefit the Vincent Memorial Hospital. Initially it is a series of tableaux vivants, but later productions are musicals, which include a precision dance routine known as the "Vincent Drill." Until 1916 the only males allowed to view the show are firemen, required by city ordinance to be on the premises. The show is replaced as a fund-raiser by the Gardenia Ball in 2003.

Nine inmates at Charlestown State Prison escape. They are dubbed "the Sewer Gang" for the route they took out of the prison. Only five of the inmates are later recaptured.

April 10. Eight boys and one official from the Boston Farm School drown when their boat capsizes while returning to Thompson Island. The accident occurs almost fifty years to the day after a similar tragedy claimed twenty-five lives.
July 4. Two men are killed and a third is saved when their balloon plunges into Boston Harbor. An estimated hundred thousand on Boston Common—and one million more throughout the area—had watched the balloon take off minutes earlier from the Common.

The Long Island Chronic Disease Hospital opens. It eventually absorbs the almshouse on the island and is today primarily a homeless shelter.

Cabot, Cabot and Forbes Company is established. Founded by George Cabot as a financial management company, it is incorporated in 1904 and becomes a real estate development company in the 1950s.

October 10. The *Boston Globe* prints a story by the reporter Henry Trickey implicating Lizzie Borden in the August 4 murder of her parents in Fall River. The paper is forced to issue a retraction the next day when it turns out the story was based on false information provided by a private detective. Borden is subsequently found not guilty of the crimes on June 20, 1893.

(ca.) Childe Hassam's painting *Charles River and Beacon Hill* is completed.
January 31. Speaking at the Boston Music Hall, Oscar Wilde declares that Boston is "the only city to influence thought in Europe," and that "in Boston are the elements of a great civilized city: a permanent intellectual tradition."
George William Curtis's *From the Easy Chair* is published.
Amy Beach's *Mass in E-flat Major* is premiered by the Handel and Haydn Society. It is the first work by a woman performed by the organization.

1893

The filling of the Dorchesterway (today's Columbia Road) and the Strandway (now Day Boulevard) begin. They are completed in 1903.

The Winthrop Building is completed at 276–278 Washington Street (on the site of the Great Spring). Designed by Clarence Blackall in the Renaissance Revival style, it is Boston's first entirely steel-framed skyscraper. Originally the Carter Building, it is renamed in 1899 for Gov. John Winthrop, whose home was nearby.

The New York, New Haven, and Hartford Railroad completes its Shore Line route between Boston and New York by leasing the Old Colony Railroad track between Boston and Providence.

A one-hundred-foot-wide promenade is completed along the Charles River in the Back Bay.

December 12. Nathan Matthews, Jr. (with 36,354 votes), defeats Thomas Hart (with 31,255) and others to be reelected mayor.

Patrick Collins is appointed consul general to London by President Grover Cleveland. He accepts this "lesser" post, in which the salary is augmented by fees for services, because he could not afford to serve as either a cabinet secretary or an ambassador.

The Boys Club of Boston opens its first clubhouse in Charlestown. A Roxbury clubhouse opens in 1910 and a South Boston clubhouse in 1938. Girls are admitted as members and the organization's name is changed to the Boys and Girls Clubs of Boston in 1981. A Dorchester/Mattapan clubhouse opens in 1995.

Alfred Shurtleff, a Harvard Divinity School student, begins one Beacon Hill Christmas tradition when he places a lit candle in the window of his parents' West Cedar Street home. Ralph Adams Cram begins another tradition in 1907, when he and some friends begin caroling on Chestnut Street. Both practices continue to this day.

The Boston terrier is first enrolled on the American Kennel Club's official stud list. The breed began sometime after 1865 with a dog named Judge (a cross between an English bulldog and a white English terrier).

Mechanic Arts High School opens. Later one of the city's three competitive "exam schools," it becomes Boston Technical High School in 1944 and moves to the former Roxbury Memorial High School building at 205 Townsend Street in 1959. It moves to New Dudley Street in 1987, merges with Mario Umana Technical High School in 1989, and is renamed the John O'Bryant High School of Mathematics and Science in 1992.

June. The New England Baptist Hospital opens in a house at 47 Bellevue Street in the Longwood area of Boston. Originally called the Boston Baptist Hospital, it is founded by Dr. Francis Fremont Whittier. The hospital moves to the former Bond Mansion on Parker Hill in 1896, constructs a new building there in 1924, purchases the adjacent Robert Breck Brigham Hospital in 1969, and erects another new building next door to that in 1986.
August 22. Tufts School of Medicine is established. The first classes are held at 188 Boylston Street on October 4. The school moves to several sites, including 416 Huntington Avenue, before moving to its current location on Harrison Avenue in the South Cove in 1950.

The greatest financial panic since 1873 occurs. The economy does not rebound for four or five years.

Edward Simmons's painting *Boston Public Garden* and Frank Benson's portrait *Thomas Wentworth Higginson* are completed.
Louise Imogen Guiney's collection of poetry *A Roadside Harp* is published.
April 7. The Bostonian Margaret Ruthven Lang's *Witichis* is performed by the Boston Symphony Orchestra, with Arthur Nikisch conducting.

1894

April 12. F. Gordon Dexter applies to the Board of Street Commissioners to develop the Mission Hill area. He chooses Indian names for many of the new streets, possibly because Allegheny Street had already been laid out, in 1845.

The (Old) Suffolk County Court House is completed at Pemberton Square. It is designed by George Clough in the German Renaissance/French Second Empire style, and a two-story mansard roof is added in 1910. Renamed the John Adams Court House, it is being renovated and is scheduled to reopen in 2004.

January 24. Five Corners in Dorchester is renamed Edward Everett Square.
July 2. The Boston Elevated Railway Company is established. It is created by the Massachusetts legislature to build and operate an elevated subway line when the West End Railway is unable to raise the capital needed to construct such a system. The state's first public authority, it begins leasing all West End Railway properties in December 1897.
Union Station opens. Designed by Shepley, Rutan, and Coolidge, it is torn down to make way for the construction of North Station and the Boston Garden in 1927.

Smith Playground in Brighton and West Roxbury Parkway are added to the city's park system.

April 19. Patriots Day becomes a legal holiday in Massachusetts.

March 7. Alderman Martin Lomasney is shot in the leg outside the mayor's office in City Hall by James H. Duncan, a constituent who had recently been ordered to vacate his home on Billerica Street by the Board of Health.
December 11. Republican Edwin Upton Curtis (with 34,982 votes) defeats Democrat Francis Peabody (with 32,425) and others to be elected mayor. A former city clerk, Curtis later becomes police commissioner.
John F. Fitzgerald is elected to Congress for the first of three consecutive terms. He is the only Catholic in the U.S. House of Representatives at the time.

The Immigration Restriction League of Boston is organized by young Brahmins and Harvard graduates. Its efforts are supported by Congressman Henry Cabot Lodge, who later declares: "The lowering of a great race means not only its decline, but that of civilization."
The New Era Club for African-American Women is organized. Founded by Josephine St. Pierre Ruffin, it is part of the African-American women's club movement started by Ida B. Wells. Its headquarters are at 103 Charles Street, on Beacon Hill.
November 26. In a rally at Faneuil Hall, Julia Ward Howe and others speak out against the recent massacre of two hundred thousand Armenians by the Turks.

Locke-Ober restaurant opens. Originally called the Winter Place Tavern, it results from the merger of Frank Locke's wine bar (established 1892) with Louis Ober's French restaurant (established 1868). It is given its current name by

Emil Camus, the first manager and later the owner, in 1901. Famous for its Sweetbreads Eugénie and Lobster Savannah, the restaurant excludes women from the downstairs dining room until 1970 (except on New Year's Eve and the evening of the Harvard-Yale football game—*if* played in Cambridge and *if* Harvard wins). The restaurant is also known for a painting of a nude woman, *Yvonne* (whose upper torso is covered *if* Harvard loses its game with Yale or the New York Yacht Club loses the America's Cup).

 The Boston Fire Department headquarters opens off Albany Street in the South End. Designed by the Boston architect Edmund March Wheelwright, it is modeled after Florence's Palazzo Vecchio. The building becomes the Pine Street Inn, a homeless shelter, in 1980.

 All Boston public school students are given medical examinations. Boston is the first city in the United States to institute this practice.
July 25. The Boston Floating Hospital first sails. Founded by Rev. Rufus Tobey, it operates initially from the *Clifford*, a rented barge that docks at various spots around Boston Harbor during the summer months, where staff members treat children and instruct parents on health care. A larger ship is purchased in 1905, but is destroyed by fire at its North End dock on June 1, 1927. A land-based hospital is built at 800 Washington Street in the South Cove in 1931, becomes part of Tufts–New England Medical Center in 1965, and moves to its current location, designed by Perry, Dean, Rogers and Partners, at 750 Washington Street, in 1982.

 February 20. A mob of unemployed men, led by Herbert Casson and Morrison Swift, storm the State House, demanding state assistance and public works jobs. They later join "Coxey's Army," a group led by Jacob Coxey that attempts an unsuccessful march on Washington to demand federal action to end the national problem of unemployment.

 Grundmann Studios opens on Clarendon Street, on the site of today's Hancock tower. A former roller skating rink, it is leased by the Boston Art Students Association, and converted into the group's headquarters, exhibit halls, and thirty-four studios. Named for Otto Grundmann, former director of the School of the Museum of Fine Arts, the building is torn down in 1917.
March 24. B. F. Keith's New Theatre opens on Washington Street. It is the first in what becomes a chain of four hundred vaudeville theaters across the country, owned and operated by Keith and his partner, E. F. Albee. The three-thousand-seat theater is connected with the existing eight-hundred-seat Bijou. It closes in 1928, reopens as the Shubert Apollo Theatre in 1929, and is renamed the Shubert Lyric Theatre in 1930. It becomes a movie house in 1935—first the Normandie and then the Laff Movie—and is torn down in 1952.
November 12. The Castle Square Theatre opens at the corner of Tremont and Chandler streets in the South End. Actors who began their careers here include Alfred and Mary Young Lunt and William Powell. Later called the Arlington, it closes in 1927 and is torn down in 1932.

May 16. A fire breaks out during a baseball game at the South End Grounds, burning down the stadium along with more than two hundred other buildings.

The ballpark is rebuilt, then demolished when the Braves move to a new stadium in 1915.*

May 30. Boston beats Cincinnati 20–11 at the Congress Street Grounds, as Bobby Lowe becomes the first player in major league baseball history to hit four home runs in one game.

1895

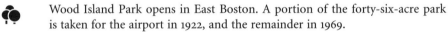

Wood Island Park opens in East Boston. A portion of the forty-six-acre park is taken for the airport in 1922, and the remainder in 1969.

The Headhouse opens at Marine Park on City Point in South Boston. Designed by Edmund March Wheelwright, it is destroyed by fire in December 1942.

Arnold Arboretum and Bussey Park are added to the Boston park system.

Brooks Adams's *The Law of Civilization and Decay* is published.

Boston's charter is revised. The mayor is given authority to appoint and supervise city department heads (except police). His term is extended to two years, and he is no longer a member of the twelve-member Board of Aldermen (who are now to be elected by ward instead of at large) or the Boston School Committee.

December 10. Democrat Josiah Quincy (with 40,300 votes) defeats Republican Edwin Curtis (with 35,864) and others to be elected mayor. A grandson and great grandson of earlier mayors, Quincy establishes an informal Board of Strategy (to receive input from ward bosses), and a Merchants' Municipal Committee (to hear from the business community). He implements a number of public works projects but is less successful at providing services for the poor.

July 4. The "Little Red School-house Riot" breaks out in East Boston. Violence occurs after the American Protective Association drives a float in a parade through a Catholic area of East Boston. John Willis, a Catholic longshoreman, is killed. His is reportedly the only death attributed to anti-Catholic activity in Boston history.

The Combined Jewish Philanthropies is founded. Originally called the Federation of Jewish Charities, it is the first organization of its kind in the United States. For many years, it is located at 72 Franklin Street.

The first Morgan Memorial Goodwill thrift store opens in the South End. It is founded by Rev. Edgar Helms.

William Monroe Trotter graduates magna cum laude from Harvard. The year before, he had become the first African American elected to Phi Beta Kappa.

March 19. The Boston Aeronautical Society is established. The first such organization in the United States, it is founded to encourage aerial experiments.

March 11. The Italian Renaissance–style Boston Public Library opens in Copley Square. Designed by McKim, Mead, and White, it is described by Oliver Wendell Holmes, Sr., as "a palace for the people." Later known as the McKim Building, it features bronze doors by Daniel Chester French, carved panels and

Boston Public Library at Copley Square, ca. 1895 (Courtesy of the Bostonian Society)

two lions by Louis Saint-Gaudens, staircase murals on the first and second floors by Puvis de Chavannes and Edwin Austin Abbey, and the magnificent Bates Hall reading room. The two statues in front—*Art* and *Science*—are by Bella Pratt. The building also contains the first children's library in the United States. John Singer Sargent's unfinished third floor murals, *The Triumph of Religion*, are installed between the 1890s and 1919. Philip Johnson's addition opens on December 11, 1972.

January 20. The violinist Eugene Ysaÿe makes his first Boston appearance.

1896

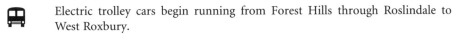

Electric trolley cars begin running from Forest Hills through Roslindale to West Roxbury.

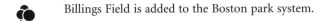

Billings Field is added to the Boston park system.

The Florence Crittenton Home opens at 37 Green Street, part of a national network of shelters founded by Charles Crittenton of New York. Its mission is soon changed from the "rescue and redemption of prostitutes" to "residential and maternity care for unmarried mothers." The Crittenton Home and Hospital is built near Oak Square in Brighton in 1924. It merges with the Hastings Home in 1961.*

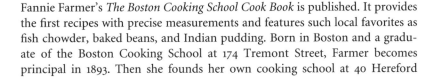

Fannie Farmer's *The Boston Cooking School Cook Book* is published. It provides the first recipes with precise measurements and features such local favorites as fish chowder, baked beans, and Indian pudding. Born in Boston and a graduate of the Boston Cooking School at 174 Tremont Street, Farmer becomes principal in 1893. Then she founds her own cooking school at 40 Hereford

Street in 1902. The Fanny Farmer Candy Company is established in 1919, but only after agreeing to change the spelling of Farmer's first name.

The Massachusetts Audubon Society is established. The oldest state Audubon Society in the country, it is an outgrowth of efforts by Harriet Hemenway and Mina Hall to save the snowy egret, hunted for plumes to decorate women's hats. The organization's headquarters is eventually located at 273 Clarendon Street.

May 18. In *Plessy v. Ferguson*, the U.S. Supreme Court upholds segregation by allowing "separate but equal" public schools. In its decision, the court cites the Massachusetts Supreme Judicial Court decision in *Roberts v. City of Boston* in 1848.

February 5. The New England Deaconess Hospital is dedicated. An outgrowth of the New England Deaconess Home and Training School, it is initially located at 691 Massachusetts Avenue. It relocates to a new building on Pilgrim Road on April 15, 1907.
The photographer Walter Dodd produces the first X-ray image taken in the United States at Massachusetts General Hospital, thirty days after the technique is discovered in Europe. Dodd later goes on to graduate from medical school and returns to work at Massachusetts General Hospital, but within five years contracts cancer—probably due to overexposure to the X rays.
Samuel Langley of Roxbury produces a one-quarter-sized scale model of a steam-driven, heavier-than-air flying machine. Five years later, he builds a full-size "aerodrome." Initially unsuccessful, it is adapted by Glen Curtis and makes a number of flights at Lake Keuka in New York in 1914.

July 11. Unwilling to endorse the Democratic presidential candidate William Jennings Bryan, the *Boston Globe* announces it will no longer make any political endorsements—a policy it finally abandons beginning with the Boston mayoral race of 1967.*

July. Charles Follen McKim attempts to donate Frederick MacMonnies's statue *Bacchante with Infant Faun* to the Boston Public Library. The joyfully nude figure is installed in the courtyard, but after it is denounced by the Watch and Ward Society as "the glorification of that which is low and sensual and degrading," the library trustees ask McKim to take it back. He does, donating it to New York's Metropolitan Museum of Art instead. A bronze replica of the sculpture is subsequently installed in the library courtyard, but not until the late 1990s.
Isabella Stewart Gardner obtains Titian's *The Rape of Europa* (1562). Later called one of the greatest works of art in Boston, the painting, which Mrs. Gardner had never seen, is purchased for her by Bernard Berenson soon after he failed in his attempt to help her obtain Gainsborough's *The Blue Boy*.
Maurice Prendergast's painting *South Boston Piers* is completed.
October 30. Amy Beach's *Gaelic Symphony*, opus 32, receives its premiere performance by the Boston Symphony Orchestra. It is the first symphony com-

posed by an American woman to be performed by the orchestra. Born in New Hampshire, Beach was brought up and educated in Boston.

April 6. James Brendan Connolly of South Boston wins the first event in the modern Olympics in Athens, Greece—and the first in fifteen centuries. A Harvard freshman forced to drop out of college to compete, he wins the hop, step, and jump (later called the triple jump) and finishes second in the high jump and third in the long jump.

August 25. The Readville Trotting Park opens in the Stony Brook Reservation in Hyde Park. The first two-minute mile by a pacer is run here in 1897, and the first by a trotter is run here in 1903. The course is converted exclusively to auto racing in the 1930s and closes on May 31, 1937. It is later demolished, and the property is used for warehouses.

The Franklin Park Golf Course opens. Originally called Abbotswood Golf Course, the nine-hole course, designed by Willie Campbell, is the second public golf course in the country (after New York's Van Cortland Park). An unofficial, six-hole layout by a clerk in George Wright's sporting goods store had been opened earlier. The present Donald Ross–designed eighteen-hole course opens in 1922, first as the Scarboro Golf Club, then as the Franklin Park Golf Course. It is named for William J. Devine, a former Boston parks commissioner, on August 17, 1967. Closed after the clubhouse burns down in 1975, the grounds are kept open and golfers are allowed to play for free for a number of years. It is restored in the mid-1980s.

1897

A state commission is appointed to investigate the "wants of the port of Boston for an improved system of docks and wharves and terminal facilities." Following the commission's recommendations, the state takes fifty-seven acres of Noddles Island by eminent domain, begins to fill that area, and makes plans to build a pier on the South Boston Flats.

The First Corps of Cadets Armory (today's Park Plaza "Castle") opens in Park Square. Designed by William Preston, it is built as headquarters for volunteer militia units, which were often called upon to preserve order. Today it houses an exhibit and function hall for the Park Plaza Hotel and a restaurant.

September 1. The Boston subway opens. It is the first major subway in the United States and fourth in the world (after London, Budapest, and Glasgow). The head houses at Park Street are designed by Edmund Wheelwright. Today's Green Line, the first section, runs between Park Street and Boylston Stations, and an estimated hundred thousand people line up to pay the five-cent fare for the ride. The line is extended to North Station on September 3, 1898, to Lechmere via the East Cambridge viaduct on July 10, 1912, and to Kenmore Square, via the Boylston Street tunnel, on October 3, 1914.

May 31. The *Robert Gould Shaw and the 54th Regiment Memorial* is dedicated. It is created by the sculptor Augustus Saint-Gaudens. He had initially been hired to create a statue only of Shaw—but the family demanded that Shaw's

Construction of the Boylston Street subway station, 1896. (Courtesy of the Bostonian Society, Boston Elevated Collection)

troops be included. Speakers at the ceremony include Booker T. Washington and William James, whose brothers Robertson and Wilkie were officers in the regiment. Robert Lowell describes the event in his 1964 poem "For the Union Dead": "at the dedication, / William James could almost hear the bronze Negroes breathe. / Their monument sticks like a fishbone / in the city's throat." Originally, only the names of the white officers killed in battle appear on the monument. The names of the slain African-American infantrymen are added in 1984.

 December 21. Josiah Quincy (with 39,984 votes) once again defeats Edwin Curtis (with 35,947) to be reelected mayor.

 September 8. The Hotel Touraine opens at the corner of Boylston and Tremont Streets (on the site of the former home of John Quincy Adams). Guests would include Presidents Theodore Roosevelt, Taft, McKinley, and Coolidge, as well as Enrico Caruso and Jenny Lind. It closes in September 1966 and is later converted into an office building.

 May 19. The Boylston National Bank on Washington Street is robbed again— this time by a bank messenger who flees with $30,940.35. He is apprehended three days later in Farmington, Maine, and all of the money is recovered— minus $130, which the man had spent.
The Domestic Relations Court of Boston is established.

 March 4. A gas explosion during construction of the subway kills ten people and injures more than thirty.

A. H. Murray becomes the first African American to serve on the regular force of the Boston Fire Department.

September 24. Commercial courses are introduced into Boston public high schools.

Harvard College builds its athletic facilities along the Charles River on Soldiers Field in Allston, on land donated by Col. Thomas Henry Higginson in memory of six friends (Edward Barry Dalton, Charles Russell Lowell, James Jackson Lowell, Stephen George Perkins, James Savage, Jr., and Robert Gould Shaw) killed during the Civil War.

Solomon Carter Fuller graduates from Boston University School of Medicine and becomes the first African-American psychiatrist in the United States.

"The Ten" is formed. The group of Boston and New York artists includes Frank Benson, Joseph DeCamp, Childe Hassam, and Edmund Tarbell. Its members withdraw from the Society of American Artists and the National Academy of Design to protest the organizations' conservative tastes and large shows. The group holds smaller exhibitions of its members' works beginning a year later and continuing for the next twenty years.

(ca.) Maurice Prendergast's *Franklin Park, Boston* is completed.

The first Society of Arts and Crafts in America is founded in Boston.

Louise Imogen Guiney's *Patrins*, a collection of prose, is published.

April 19. John McDermott wins the first Boston Marathon in a time of 2:55:10. The second marathon run in the United States (after a Stamford, Connecticut, to New York City race run six months before), it is the first to become an annual event. The original course (from Metcalf's Mills in Ashland to the Irvington Oval in Boston) measures 24.5 miles. The starting line is moved to Hopkinton in 1924 and the distance is increased to the Olympic distance of 26 miles and 385 yards in 1927, with the finish line at the Exeter Hotel, then the Prudential Center, and today at the Boston Public Library. Only fifteen runners enter the first race; the field is limited to ten thousand today. Originally a race for amateurs, prize money is awarded beginning in 1986.

July. Star Pointer sets a pacing world record of 1:59 for a quarter-mile race at the Readville track.

George Tuohey's *A History of the Boston Base Ball Club* is published.

1898

Chestnut Hill Park in Brighton is added to the city's park system.

A metropolitan water system is established and the Sudbury Reservoir replaces Lake Cochituate as the source of Boston's water.

In response to the growing demand for outdoor athletic recreation, Mayor Quincy initiates legislation to create at least one playground in every ward of the city.

April 25. The United States declares war on Spain. A peace treaty is signed on December 10, 1898.

September 8. The Massachusetts Ninth Regiment ("the Fighting Ninth") returns from Cuba to Boston's Park Square railroad station. Although few casualties were sustained in battle, many of its members fell victim to malaria and other diseases.

September 27. The first full illumination of the State House takes place. Alice Clement, who proposed the idea, presses the button that turns on 498 electric bulbs.

Robert Woods's *The City Wilderness* is published. A study of the South End, it is considered the first social survey to be published in the United States. In it Woods lists some of the goals of the settlement houses: "[to] reestablish on a natural basis those relations which modern city life has thrown into confusion . . . to rehabilitate neighborhood life and give it some of that healthy corporate vitality which a well-ordered village has . . . and to furnish neutral grounds where separated classes, rich and poor, professional and industrial, capitalist and wage-earning, may meet each other on the basis of common humanity."

An ordinance is passed prohibiting men and women from wearing hats in places of public amusement.

November 26–27. The Portland Gale strikes. The storm is named for the steamship *Portland*, which sinks soon after leaving Boston Harbor. All 192 aboard, including the largely African-American crew, drown in the worst maritime disaster in the city's history. The wreck of the ship is found off Stellwagen Bank in July 2002.

The state legislature enacts a law allowing the Boston School Department to establish its own budget, separate from other city departments. The law devotes a specific share of the city's taxes to the schools, thereby making them more financially independent.

October 3. Northeastern University is founded. Originally called the Department of Law of the Boston YMCA's Evening Institute for Young Men, it holds the first classes in the YMCA building at the corner of Berkeley and Boylston Streets. Frank Palmer Speare is the college's first president. A day college is added, and the College of Engineering first implements the cooperative plan of education, subsequently adopted by all the school's colleges, in 1909. The school moves to the current YMCA building on Huntington Avenue in 1912. Renamed Northeastern College in 1916, then Northeastern University in 1935, the school formally separates from the YMCA in 1944. It moves to its current location on Huntington Avenue in 1938.*

The Joslin Diabetes Clinic is established. A new facility at 1 Joslin Place in the Fenway opens in 1976.

January 9. The *Boston Post* begins a serialized publication of H. G. Wells's *War of the Worlds*, but it is altered so that it is set in and around Boston.

Howard Pyle's painting *The Battle of Bunker Hill* is completed.

January 19. Brown defeats Harvard 6–0 in the first intercollegiate hockey game.

July 3. Joshua Slocum returns to Boston on the thirty-seven-foot sloop *Spray* after completing the first solo trip around the world. He left from East Boston on April 24, 1895.

1899

The Queen Anne–style Washington Building is built in Brighton Center. The adjoining Imperial Hotel is built in 1909.
The Cobleigh Block (later the Central Building) is built in Roslindale Square.

January 1. South Station opens. Designed by Shepley, Rutan, and Coolidge in the Classical Revival style, it was dedicated on December 30, 1898. Originally called South Union Terminal, it would be the busiest in the world until 1913. The train shed, the largest in the world at the time, is torn down in 1930, and the wings attached to the head house are removed in the 1970s. Slated for demolition in 1975, the building is instead preserved and renovated in 1989.
September 10. Back Bay Station opens. It burns down on April 15, 1928, and is replaced with a smaller station, which opens on July 1, 1929. That one is re-placed by a third station, which opens for subway trains in May and for commuter trains in October 1987.

Cleary Square is dedicated in Hyde Park. It is named for John Cleary of Hyde Park, a member of the Seventh Regiment, who was killed in Santiago during the Spanish-American War.
McConnell Park in Savin Hill and Rogers Park in Brighton are added to the city's park system.

Julia Ward Howe's *Reminiscences* and Frank Parsons's *The City for the People* are published.

December 10. Republican Thomas Hart (with 40,838 votes) defeats Democrat Patrick Collins (with 38,557) to win another term as mayor.
James Michael Curley wins his first election, as one of three representatives from Roxbury's Ward 17 to the seventy-five-member Common Council. He is elected state representative in 1901, and a member of the Board of Aldermen in 1903.

The first Animal Rescue League in the country is incorporated in Boston.

The first Greek Orthodox congregation in Boston is established. Meeting ini-tially in rented halls, it moves to a new church on Winchester Street in 1907, then to the Greek Orthodox Cathedral of New England at 514 Parker Street in 1923, designed by Hachadoor Demoorjian. The interior is by Ralph Adams Cram and Kenneth Conant, and the stained glass windows are by Charles Connick.

January. The Boston public schools establish the first special class for mentally retarded children.

September 11. The Charles River Speedway opens in Brighton. A harness track located along what is now Soldiers Field Road, it is part of a larger park designed by Olmsted. The track closes in the 1950s.

December 12. The Boston dentist Dr. George Franklin Grant receives a patent for the golf tee. The device is meant to replace the mound of sand that players had used to elevate the ball when driving. The second African-American graduate of Harvard Dental School and the first on its faculty, Dr. Grant is a regular golfer at Franklin Park.

1900

Boston's population is 560,892, the fifth-largest of any city in the United States (behind New York, Chicago, Philadelphia, and St. Louis). Of that number, 12,809 are described as "Colored," including 11,591 who are African American. Of the 197,129 listed as foreign born, 70,147 are from Ireland, 47,374 are from English Canada, 14,995 are from Russia, and 13,738 are from Italy. An estimated 40,000 are Jewish. The separate town of Hyde Park has a population of 13,244, with 128 classified as "Colored," including 116 classified as "Negro" and twelve Chinese; 3,805 are foreign born.

The Old Colony Railroad Bridge is built across the Fort Point Channel. It is a Scherzer rolling lift bridge, the first to be built in the United States outside Chicago, and the largest in the world at the time.

The Summer Street Bridge is completed.

The Port of Boston is the second-busiest in the United States. It falls to sixth in 1920.

Brooks Adams's *America's Economic Supremacy* is published.

December 31. The Dawn of the New Century is celebrated. Just before midnight, the State House is illuminated, the Handel and Haydn and Cecilia Societies perform, and Rev. Edward Everett Hale reads the Nineteenth Psalm on the steps of the State House, asking God to "teach us to number our days that we may apply our hearts unto wisdom." Afterward, Hale declares, "I do not think they thought of it as a religious service when they came, but they all did when they went away."

When Mayor Hart attempts to reduce the city's workforce, Common Councilor James Michael Curley complains: "Men are being discharged indiscriminately for their political belief and nothing else. . . . I live in a district . . . composed largely of working people, who have large families of six or eight; and I have seen those same families in actual want or suffering during the last month or two, due to no other reason than the men were Democrats."

July 13. Youths from East Boston and Chelsea battle with fists, rocks, and clubs on the bridge between the two communities. The fight reportedly starts over a romantic entanglement. Police arrive to break up the fight. They arrest some of the participants, but others escape by jumping from the bridge and swimming away.

Symphony Hall on Huntington Avenue, as shown on a postcard. (Courtesy of the Bostonian Society)

March 3. The Trustees of Boston University announce that men and women may not dance together on university property and that no man may enter the "sanctum sanctorum" of the women's gymnasium.

The National Negro Business League is founded in Boston by Booker T. Washington. Its goal is "to bring the colored people who are engaged in business together for consultation, and to secure information and inspiration from each other." The organization holds its annual convention in Boston in 1915, and its diamond anniversary convention here in 1975.

May. The Colored Magazine begins publication.

(ca.) Maurice Prendergast's *West Church, Boston* is completed.
October 15. Symphony Hall opens with the Boston Symphony Orchestra, Wilhelm Gericke conducting. The orchestra performs Bach's chorale "Grant us to do with zeal our portion whatsoever" and Beethoven's *Missa Solemnis.* The building is designed by Charles Follen McKim in the Italian Renaissance style, and the acoustic engineering is by the Harvard physics professor Wallace Clement Sabine. Originally called the new Music Hall, the building seats 2,625 for the symphony and 2,371 for the Pops. The proscenium arch was to be inscribed with the names of nine famous composers, but the directors could agree on only one name—Beethoven. The statues surrounding the hall are copies of originals by Pietro Caproni. The original pipe organ, by the Hutchings Organ Company, is replaced by an Aeolian Skinner organ by G. Donald Harrison, dedicated on October 7, 1949. The symphony's Friday afternoon

concerts soon become a Boston institution, which, according to the author Lucius Beebe, "assume the aspect of holy days dedicated to the classics and a vast craning of necks to be certain that the Hallowells and Forbeses are in their accustomed stalls." The author Eleanor Early describes how Boston spinsters attend: "They will arrive in the family's old car. . . . And they will smile gently at the men who did not marry them. And their shabbiness will be in the traditional manner. For this is the Boston legend."

December 20. The Colonial Theatre opens at 106 Boylston Street with a production of *Ben Hur*, starring William Farnum and W. S. Hart. The play features a cast of 350 and a dozen horse-drawn chariots. The *Boston Globe* declares the next day, "Nothing so beautiful, pictorial and mechanical has ever been seen before on a Boston stage." Performers at the 1,700-seat theater designed by Clarence Blackall would include Fred and Adele Astaire, Ethel Barrymore, Fanny Brice, Eddie Cantor, W. C. Fields, Henry Fonda, Julie Harris, Helen Hayes, Katharine Hepburn, Bob Hope, James Earl Jones, Gertrude Lawrence, Frederick March, Ethel Merman, Paul Muni, Laurence Olivier, Cole Porter, Paul Robeson, Will Rogers, Ethel Waters, Ed Wynn, and the Ziegfeld Follies.

 August 8–10. The United States beats Britain in the first Davis Cup tennis championship, played at the Longwood Cricket Club.

1901 to 1925

1901

June 10. The Washington Street elevated subway line, today's Orange Line, opens from Sullivan Square to Dudley Square. Construction began on March 30, 1899. The line is extended to Forest Hills on November 22, 1909, and to Everett on March 15, 1919. The elevated is replaced from Haymarket to Malden on December 27, 1975, and from Chinatown to Forest Hills on May 4, 1987.
August 22. The elevated Atlantic Avenue loop opens. It is discontinued on October 1, 1938, and torn down in 1942.

The Strandway and Columbus Park are added to the Boston parks system.

March 17. The first Evacuation Day Parade is held from City Point to Faneuil Hall. Although St. Patrick's Day parades were held since at least 1876, this is the first year that the day is declared a city holiday—officially to commemorate the day the British were driven out of Boston by the Continental Army. The state legislature makes the day a Suffolk County holiday in 1938.

December 10. Democrat Patrick Collins (with 52,035 votes) defeats Republican Thomas Hart (with 33,196) to win election as mayor. Irish-born, a Harvard Law School graduate, and a fiscal conservative, Collins is inaugurated in the Common Council Chambers on January 4, 1902. As mayor he would preach "caution, prudence and economy."

December 17. The first execution in the electric chair in Massachusetts takes place at Charlestown State Prison. Sixty-four men are electrocuted there, the last two on May 9, 1947. For a time, the Boston Edison Company refuses to provide electricity for the executions, which forces the prison to construct its own power plant.

July 21. The *Sunday Globe* presents an editorial symposium entitled "Can prayer bring rain?" Seven local clergymen are asked the question, and vote 4–3 in the affirmative.
The play *Pilate's Daughter*, by Rev. F. L. Kenzel, is performed for the first time at St. Alphonsus Hall on Mission Hill. The annual production draws large audiences from all over New England and continues until the late 1960s.

South Boston High School, designed by Herbert Hale, opens at 95 G Street. Divided into three individual schools, it is renamed the South Boston Educational Complex in 2003.

November. A number of cases of smallpox are reported. The city responds with an aggressive—some say coercive—smallpox vaccination effort, which inoculates four hundred thousand.

 King Gillette invents the safety razor with a disposable blade in an apartment at 64 Westland Avenue in the Fenway. A traveling salesman from Wisconsin, he teams with William Nickerson, an engineer, and soon opens the Gillette Safety Razor Company above a fish store at 424 Atlantic Avenue. The Gillette factory opens on West First Street in South Boston in 1906.

 November 9. The first issue of the *Guardian* appears. Founded by William Monroe Trotter and others, it is published by Trotter. In 1911 he writes: "This is the home of abolition, of equal rights. It leads in these principles the rest of the country. Reaction is setting in. Any compromise in Boston will doubly damage the cause." After Trotter's death in 1934, his sister, Maude, and her husband, Dr. Charles Steward, continue to publish the newspaper until 1957.

 The first of the Boston Pops "College Nights" is held. During these private concerts for graduates and alumni, various colleges competed in the early years of the series to see which group could be the rowdiest.
February 8. Chickering Hall opens on Huntington Avenue near Massachusetts Avenue. Renamed the St. James Theatre in 1912, it becomes the Uptown movie house in 1929. It closes and is demolished in 1968.
October. Beautiful Jim Key, a performing horse, appears at the Boston Food Fair. Promoted by Albert Rogers as being able to read, write, and compute, the horse is the subject of a study conducted by Harvard professors, which concludes that the act is not a hoax.

 May 8. The Boston baseball team in the new American League beats Philadelphia 12–4 in its first home game at the new Huntington Avenue Grounds (on the site of today's Northeastern University campus). Known unofficially as the Americans, the team officially becomes the Red Sox in 1907 and moves to a new stadium in the Back Bay Fens in 1912.*

1902

 The social scientist Robert Woods writes: "There are actually streets in the West End where, while Jews are moving in, Negro housewives are gathering up their skirts and seeking a more spotless environment."

 Chestnut Hill Park, Beacon Street, and Commonwealth Avenue are added to the Boston park system.

 Robert Woods's *Americans in Process*, a study of settlement houses in the North and West Ends, is published.

 December 8. Oliver Wendell Holmes, Jr., Chief Justice of the Massachusetts Supreme Judicial Court, is nominated to the U.S. Supreme Court by President Theodore Roosevelt. He serves for thirty years, becoming most known for his

dissenting opinions, as in *United States v. Rosika Schwimmer*, in which he defended "Free thought—not free thought for those who agree with us but freedom for the thought we hate."

September 7. An explosion of eighteen thousand pounds of gunpowder stored in Fort Winthrop on Governor's Island rocks the city. Two men are killed, but hundreds of Sunday sightseers on the island somehow escape injury. The men who died were initially thought to have caused the blast by carelessly smoking their pipes near the gunpowder. It is later suspected, however, that the blast was caused by a group of boys from East Boston who detonated the powder as a prank.

October 9. Simmons College opens. It was incorporated on May 24, 1899, and is supported by a bequest from the Boston merchant John Simmons. Henry Lefavour becomes the first president in 1901. He is succeeded by Bancroft Beatley (1933), William Park (1955), William Holmes (1970), Jean Dowdall (1993), and Daniel Cheever, Jr. (1996 to present). The school moves to a campus designed by Peabody and Stearns at 300 The Fenway in 1904 and is today the last remaining women's college in Boston.

January 9. The Aero Club of New England is organized. Its is the first aeronautical club in the United States, and Professor A. Lawrence Rotch is the first president. The organization soon purchases two balloons, the *Boston* (35,600 cubic feet) and the *Massachusetts* (65,000 cubic feet). Members' interest shifts to airplanes, however, after 1910.

May 21. Jewish women riot in the West End to protest high prices being charged for kosher meat by the wholesaler Solomont and Sons. A similar riot takes place on June 24, 1912.
The first automobile insurance policy in the United States to cover a car as property is written in Boston.
The Mt. Sinai Dispensary opens at 105 Chambers Street in the West End. Offering only outpatient services, it moves to 17 Staniford Street from 1903 to 1916. It becomes Beth Israel Hospital and moves to the former Dennison Estate at 59 Townsend Street in Roxbury on October 22, 1917, then moves to Brookline Avenue in the Longwood area on August 1, 1928.

The first issue of the *Jewish Advocate* appears. Originally called the *Mt. Sinai Monthly*, it is published from offices at 170 Summer Street. The newspaper later becomes the *Jewish Home Journal*, the *Boston Advocate*, and finally the *Jewish Advocate* in 1905. The newspaper moves to Causeway Street in 1917 and later to School Street. It merges with the London *Jewish News* in 2004.

Helen Winslow's *Literary Boston of Today* is published.
September 18. The New England Conservatory relocates to a new building, designed by Wheelwright and Haven, at 290 Huntington Avenue. George Whitefield Chadwick is succeeded as director by Wallace Goodrich (1931), Quincy Porter (1942), and Harrison Keller (1947), who then serves as president beginning in 1953. He is succeeded by James Aliferis (1958), Chester Williams (1962),

Gunther Schuller (1967), J. Stanley Ballinger (1977), Laurence Lesser (1983), Robert Freeman (1997), and Daniel Steiner (2000 to the present).

The L Street Brownies are organized in South Boston and hold their first annual winter swim. The organization's name is derived from the deep tan of its members, the result of swimming in Boston Harbor all year round.

Sam Langford fights for the first time in Boston. An African American from Nova Scotia, he is nicknamed the "Boston Tar Baby." Some call him the "greatest non-champion" in the history of boxing. Partially blind from childhood, Langford engages in an estimated 650 official and unofficial fights in his twenty-five-year career, including an exhibition fight against Jersey Joe Wolcott at the Old Howard Theatre.

1903

The Boston Elevated Railway takes over street railway lines in West Roxbury, and the Blue Hill Avenue electric streetcar line is extended from Grove Hall to Mattapan Square.

M. A. De Wolfe Howe's *Boston: The Place and the People* and Lillian Whiting's *Boston Days* are published.

February. The Good Government Association (some call its members "Goo-Goos") is established by the Boston Chamber of Commerce, the Massachusetts Bar Association, the Merchants Association, the Associated Board of Trade, and the Fruit and Produce Association. Its goal is to reduce corruption and inefficiency in government and support candidates of talent and integrity for elective office.

September 24. James Michael Curley and Thomas Curley (no relation) are convicted of having taken a postal service exam for two Irish immigrants on December 4, 1902. Sentenced on November 7, 1904, to serve sixty days in the Charles Street Jail, they are released on January 6, 1905.

December 15. Patrick Collins (with 48,745 votes) defeats George Swallow (with 22,369) and others to win reelection as mayor, carrying every ward in the city except East Boston.

Despite his recent fraud conviction, Curley wins election to the Board of Aldermen, running on the slogan "I did it for a friend."

July 30. The so-called Boston Riot occurs at the Columbus Avenue A.M.E. Zion Church. Booker T. Washington's talk is interrupted by William Monroe Trotter and others, who are critical of what they believe is Washington's accommodationist approach to civil rights. Trotter presents nine provocative questions, the last of which is "Are the rope and the torch all the race is to get under your leadership?" Police are called and several people are arrested, including Trotter, who spends a month in Charles Street Jail, where he reads W. E. B. Du Bois's *The Souls of Black Folk*.

The Catholic Charitable Bureau is organized.

July. The Boston Police Department employs the first automobile used as a police cruiser in the United States. A Stanley Steamer, it is driven by a chauffeur, while a uniformed police officer rides in back on a seat high enough "to allow him to look over the back fences."

The Boston Legal Aid Society is founded to provide legal advice and aid to the poor.

October 2. A laundry owner, Wong Yak Chong, is shot and killed on Harrison Avenue in Chinatown. Two Chinese men, allegedly hired killers, are arrested for the murder. Fearing a "tong war" between Chinese gangs, police arrest an estimated 250 to 300 Chinese men (approximately one-third of the city's Chinese population) ten days later for not being able to produce immigration papers; 50 are subsequently deported and the rest are released a few days later.

Fisher College is established. Located today at 118 Beacon Street, the school is authorized to grant associates' degrees in 1957 and bachelors' degrees in 1999.

March. Faulkner Hospital opens. Incorporated in 1900, it is founded by Dr. George Faulkner and his wife as a memorial to their invalid daughter, Mary, who died at age thirty-seven in 1896.

September 8. The first escalator in Boston begins operation at R. H. White's department store.

March. The United Drug Company is incorporated. Founded by Louis Liggett at 43 Leon Street, the company first manufactures and delivers drugs to pharmacists, then opens its own chain of Liggett retail drugstores and purchases the Rexall chain of drugstores in 1910.

Alvan Fuller opens his car dealership in the Motor Mart building in Park Square. Initially a Packard and then a Cadillac dealership, it eventually moves to 808 Commonwealth Avenue in 1928, the first large building on what would become Boston's "automobile row." The business closes on March 1, 1978, and the building is later sold to Boston University.

November 14. The National Women's Trade Union League is established at a meeting in Faneuil Hall by the Bostonians Mary Kenney O'Sullivan, William Walling, Mabel Gillespie, and others. Mary Morton Kehew is the first president. While not a union, it is affiliated with the American Federation of Labor and its goals are to organize and support working women.

January 1. Isabella Stewart Gardner's Fenway Court opens at 280 The Fenway. Guests at the New Year's night party, including Edith Wharton and William James, are served Champagne and doughnuts and are entertained by fifty members of the Boston Symphony, with Wilhelm Gericke conducting, and a nine-member choral group. Although the building was officially designed by William Sears, Mrs. Gardner was involved with every detail of the design, construction, and decoration of the Venetian-style palazzo. Henry Adams later describes the building and garden as "peace, repose or dream, rather like opium." The building opens to the public for two weeks each spring and fall. Visitors are charged one dollar for admission to ensure they appreciate the experience. After Mrs. Gardner's death in 1924, it becomes the Gardner Museum, operating under the stipulation in her will that all the objects continue to be exhibited just as they are—or else everything is to be sold at auction, with the proceeds going to Harvard College.

October 20. Jordan Hall opens at 30 Gainsborough Street with a performance of George Whitefield Chadwick's *Melpomene* by the Boston Symphony Orchestra. Designed by Wheelwright and Haven, with acoustics by Wallace Clement Sabine, the 1,019-seat hall is a gift from Eben Jordan to the New England Conservatory of Music. The hall is renovated by Ann Beha Associates, with Kirkegaard and Associates responsible for the acoustics, in 1995.

February 16. The Majestic Theatre opens at today's 219 Tremont Street with a performance of the "musical fantasy" *The Storks.* Designed by John Galen Howard in the Beaux Arts style for Eben Jordan, the 1,700-seat theater houses opera, theater, and vaudeville. Performers would include W. C. Fields, George Burns and Gracie Allen, Uta Hagen, and Gertrude Lawrence. Transformed into the Saxon movie house in 1956, it is purchased by Emerson College and renamed the Emerson Majestic in 1983. It is restored and officially reopens as the Cutler Majestic on October 30, 2003.

 October 1. The Boston American League team, known as the Americans, loses 7–3 to the Pittsburg (*sic*) Pirates of the National League at the Huntington Avenue Grounds, in the first-ever World Series game. Boston beats the Pirates 3–0 in game 8 in Boston to win the best-of-nine series on October 13.

November 14. Harvard loses to Dartmouth 11–0 in the first football game played at Harvard Stadium. Designed by McKim, Mead, and White, it is the world's first massive, reinforced-concrete building, and the country's first large collegiate stadium. The initial seating capacity of 22,000 is later increased to as much as 58,000, and is currently 37,000.

1904

 Boston adopts comprehensive limits on building heights, the first city in the United State to adopt this form of zoning. Boston's code establishes different heights for commercial and residential structures and is expanded over subsequent years.

 The Great Hall opens at 6 Norfolk Street in Dorchester. Designed by Charles Bateman as a branch library, it becomes the Codman Square Health Center in 1982, then the Codman Square Municipal Building in 1995.

 December 30. The subway line to East Boston opens. Today's Blue Line, it runs initially from Court Street to Maverick Square, through the first underwater transit tunnel in the country. The line is extended to Scollay Square Under and Bowdoin Square on March 18, 1916, then to Wonderland in Revere on January 19, 1954.

 Dorchester Day is established by the Dorchester Historical Society. An annual celebration of the founding of the town, it features the Dorchester Day Parade.

 The Harriet Tubman Settlement House opens. Founded by six African-American women to "assist working girls [from the South] in charitable ways," it becomes part of the Federation of South End Settlements in 1950, which in turn becomes the United South End Settlements in 1959. Located originally at 37 and then at 25–27 Holyoke Street in the South End, it moves to its current headquarters at 566 Columbus Avenue in 1976.

April 5. Wentworth Institute is incorporated as a school of mechanical arts. Chartered in 1911, the school is supported by a bequest from the Boston merchant Arioch Wentworth, who died in 1903. The Wentworth Institute complex, designed by Kilham and Hopkins, opens at 360 Ruggles Street (today's 550 Huntington Avenue) in 1913. Arthur Williston becomes the first president in 1911. He is succeeded by Frederick Dobbs (1924), H. Russell Beatty (1953), Edward Kirkpatrick (1971), and John Van Domelen (1990 to the present).
July. Girls Trade High School opens at 676 Massachusetts Avenue. Originally privately run, it is taken over by the Boston School Department in 1909. It later moves to Hemenway Street and closes in 1973.
November 2. A riot involving students from MIT occurs in front of the school on Boylston Street. Several Boston police superior officers are later demoted because men under their command use excessive force against the students.

April. The Italian Laborers Union is established. It is founded by Domenic D'Alessandro, an immigrant and North End banker, to combat the exploitation of Italian immigrants by *padroni*—labor agents hired by construction companies to recruit cheap manual labor.

March 21. The first issue of William Randolph Hearst's *Boston American and New York Journal* appears. It becomes the *Boston Evening American* on April 15, 1905. Hearst buys the *Advertiser* in November 1917, and the *Record* in 1921, so that he has morning, evening, and Sunday newspapers in Boston. The *Boston American* becomes a tabloid in 1921, and merges with the *Record* in 1961. Located originally at 82 Summer Street, it moves to 309 Washington Street, and then to 5 Winthrop Square and ceases publication in 1972.
Horticulture magazine begins publication. Originally a trade journal, it is purchased by and becomes a publication for the Massachusetts Horticultural Society in 1923. It becomes a national magazine in the 1970s and is sold by the society in 1981 and is now owned by F & W Publications.

April. The art critic William Howe Downes's "Boston as an Art Centre" appears in *New England Magazine.* In this reply to Herbert Croly's "New York as an American Metropolis" published the previous year, Downes boasts of "an army of professional artists" in Boston and declares that the city is "an art centre of importance, and shows no signs of ceasing to be such."
November 11. A fire at the Harcourt Building destroys the life's work of many of Boston's most accomplished artists, including William Worcester Churchill, Joseph DeCamp, Mary Brewster Hazelton, William Paxton, Elizabeth Vila Taylor (later Watson), and Theodore Wendel. On the day after the fire, DeCamp reportedly walks into the St. Botolph Club and announces: "I have a family to support. I'll paint anybody's portrait for $100."

October 10. The Boston Americans beat the New York Highlanders 3–2 in the first game of a doubleheader in New York on the last day of the season, to repeat as the American League champions. However, the National League champions, the New York Giants, refuse to play in a World Series.

1905

The Boston-Worcester streetcar begins service. It is discontinued in 1930.

September 14. Mayor Patrick Collins dies suddenly while on vacation in Hot Springs, Virginia. Common Council president Daniel Whelton is appointed the next day to finish the term.
Democrat John F. Fitzgerald (with 44,171 votes) defeats Frothingham (with 36,028) and Dewey (11,608) for mayor. Inaugurated in the Common Council chambers on January 1, 1906, Fitzgerald is the first American-born, Irish Catholic mayor. In his inaugural address, he promises "a bigger, better, busier Boston."

January. The Boston School Committee is again reorganized. By a special act of the legislature, it is to consist of five members elected at large for staggered three-year terms. The committee's duties are to set educational policy, and it is instructed to yield other powers to school department officials.

May. The Harvard University/Museum of Fine Arts Archaeological Expedition to Egypt is organized. Responsible for the acquisition of numerous pieces, it continues until the sites are turned over to the Egyptian government in 1947.
November 21. Parker and Douglas Thomas's Arts and Crafts/Beaux Arts–style Fenway Studios opens at 30 Ipswich Street. Residents would include Joseph DeCamp, Philip Hale, William Paxton, Lila Cabot Perry, John Singer Sargent, and Edmund Tarbell. The building contains forty-six studios, but no central exhibition space. According to the *Boston Sunday Globe:* "Late suppers and noisy revelers, associated from long since with studio life, are here rare. It is a Boston atmosphere that one finds in the building, of respectability and quiet, yet an atmosphere of art withal." The building becomes a resident artists' co-operative in 1981.

April 1. Harvard loses to Haverford 1–0 at Soldiers Field in the first intercollegiate soccer game in the United States.

1906

The Brookline Street Bridge, connecting Brighton to Cambridge, opens. It is replaced by the Cottage Farm Bridge in 1927, which is renamed the Boston University Bridge on May 7, 1949.
The Wachusett Reservoir opens, providing Boston with drinking water. When it fills in 1908, it is the largest reservoir in the world.

Albert Wolfe's *The Lodging House Problem in Boston* is published.
October 25. The West End House is dedicated at 9 Eaton Street. It was founded originally as the Bootblack League, then the Excelsior Club, for the "Mental, Moral and Physical Advancement of Its Members" in 1903. James Jackson Stor-

First Church of Christ, Scientist, on Massachusetts Avenue, ca. 1906. (Courtesy of the Bostonian Society)

row (described at the time as "Boston's most useful citizen") is the first chairman of its board. The club moves to 45 Chambers Street in 1912, then 16 Blossom Street in the West End in 1929, closes temporarily in 1966, then moves to its current location at 105 Allston Street in Allston in 1971.

H. G. Wells visits Boston. In *The Future America*, he later writes: "Boston presents a terrible, terrifying unanimity of aesthetic discriminations. There broods over the real Boston an immense sense of finality. One feels in Boston, as one feels in no other part of the States, that the intellectual movement has ceased. . . . The capacity of Boston, it would seem, was just sufficient but no more than sufficient, to comprehend the whole achievement of the human intellect up, let us say, to the year 1875. Then an equilibrium was established. At or about that year Boston filled up."

September 1. Irene Shannon (Mrs. Chester Jordan), a dancer at the Old Howard, is murdered by her husband. He cuts up her body, stores it in a trunk, and is arrested a few days later in a rooming house at 7 Hancock Street on Beacon Hill as he prepares to flee to New York. Tried and convicted, he is electrocuted in September 1912.
The Boston Juvenile Court is established. Harvey Baker is the first judge.

June 10. First Church of Christ, Scientist, is dedicated. The church is designed in the Italian Renaissance style by Brigham and Beman; its auditorium seats five thousand and contains the largest pipe organ in the western hemisphere, an Aeolian Skinner with 13,595 pipes, which was made in Boston. The church complex is expanded with additional buildings and a reflecting pool, designed by I. M. Pei, in 1973.

September 19. Suffolk Law School opens. Founded by Gleason Archer, it is located initially in his home on Alpine Street in Roxbury; it later moves to the Tremont Temple and then to 45 Mount Vernon Street on Beacon Hill. The

Archer Building, the school's first new building, opens in 1920. The school expands to become Suffolk University in 1937. Archer is the first president. He is succeeded by Walter Burse (1948), Robert Munce (1954), Dennis Haley (1960), John Fenton (1965), Thomas Fulham (1970), Daniel Perlman (1980), and David Sargent (1989 to present).

The Harvard Medical School complex, designed by Shepley, Rutan, and Coolidge, opens on the former Francis estate on Longwood Avenue in the Fenway. The Boston Sanatorium for Consumptives is established on River Street in Mattapan. Built to house patients quarantined with tuberculosis, it is later renamed the Boston Specialty and Rehabilitation Hospital and closes on October 1, 1996.

The *Boston Post* establishes the *Post* Santa, publishing stories and soliciting gifts for the needy at Christmastime. When the *Post* goes out of business in 1956, the *Boston Globe* assumes the tradition with its *Globe* Santa.

June 16 and 19. Aeschylus' *Agamemnon* is performed at Harvard Stadium, complete with chariots and live horses.
The Théâtre Comique opens in Scollay Square. The 350-seat theater is the first built specifically to show films.

1907

The Boston Society of Architects solicits suggestions for developments to improve the city. The suggestions eventually would include construction of a boulevard along Arlington Street, a civic center at Arlington Street and Commonwealth Avenue, a man-made island in the Charles River, nine hundred mile-long piers extending out to Thompson Island, a new City Hall on Beacon Hill, and an "Inner Boulevard" and an "Outer Boulevard" connecting Boston with surrounding communities.

Henry Adams's *The Education of Henry Adams* is published privately, and then commercially after his death in 1918. The book wins the Pulitzer Prize for biography. It contains a number of descriptions of Boston, including this one: "Boston had solved the universe; or had offered and realized the best solution yet tried. The problem was worked out."

July. The Boston Finance Commission (FinCom) is created by the Republican-dominated legislature to scrutinize the financial practices of the Democrat-dominated city government. Composed of five members appointed by the governor and chaired by the former mayor Nathan Matthews, Jr., the commission holds a number of hearings. Then it issues a four-volume report, which includes charges that "administrative offices are given out as a reward for party work; and the number and the salaries are increased beyond the requirements of the service." The FinCom continues to analyze city finances today.
December 10. Republican George Albee Hibbard (with 38,112 votes) defeats Democrat John F. Fitzgerald (with 35,935) to be elected mayor. Another Democrat, John Coulthurst, ran as an independent and captured 17.6% of the votes.

The former Boston postmaster, Hibbard reduces the municipal workforce, cuts the cost of street maintenance in half, and reduces the city's deficit.

The Robert Gould Shaw House is founded as a social service agency for African-American residents of Boston.

February 23. President Theodore Roosevelt visits Boston.

August 30. William Henry O'Connell succeeds the late John Joseph Williams as Catholic archbishop of Boston. Nicknamed "Gangplank Bill" for his frequent sea cruises, and "Number One" for his influence, he establishes, according to the author Paula Kane, a "triumphalist, separatist Catholic subculture . . . sacred but equal, separate but integrated." He is elevated to cardinal, the first in Boston and third in the United States, on November 27, 1911.

Commerce High School is established. It opens in a new school building on Avenue Louis Pasteur in 1915 and closes in 1954.
The High School of Practical Arts opens in Lyceum Hall on Meeting House Hill in Dorchester. It moves to Perrin Street in Roxbury in 1910, then to the corner of Winthrop and Greenville Streets in Roxbury in 1914. The all-girls high school offers courses for students who do not plan to attend college. It closes in 1954.
Evrio Hebrew School is opened by the Jewish People's Institute. The first successful Hebrew school in Boston, it becomes coeducational in 1915.

Albert Champion, a former French bicycle racer, invents the AC spark plug in his shop in the Cyclorama Building in the South End.

March 1. Debussy's *La Mer* receives its American debut by the Boston Symphony Orchestra, Karl Muck conducting, before "an audience," the music historian Nicolas Slonimsky later writes, "of easily discomfited dowagers, quiet academically minded New England music lovers, and irascible music critics."
April 12. Richard Strauss's opera *Salome* is performed, despite protests by the New England Watch and Ward Society that it is indecent. Called on by the group to ban the production, Mayor Fitzgerald writes: "The mayor's office does not interfere as a rule with the productions of Boston theaters . . . [but trusts] no theater manager will fly in the face of public opinion." Fitzgerald's successor, George Hibbard, however, does ban a production of the opera two years later, after receiving a phone call from a woman who had attended a New York performance and found it to be scandalous.
Florenz Ziegfeld produces the first of his *Ziegfeld's Follies* in Boston, before taking the production to New York. The show plays Boston annually until 1932.

June. Margaret Curtis of Boston wins the first of three U.S. women's amateur golf championships. She also wins in 1911 and 1912.

1908

The Northern Avenue Bridge is completed across the Fort Point Channel, connecting Rowes Wharf to Fan Pier. Closed to automobile traffic today, it is one of the few remaining swing bridges in Massachusetts. It is replaced for automobile use by the Evelyn Moakley Bridge, which is dedicated on October 14, 1996.

September 16. Upon his death, George Francis Parkman leaves his house at 33 Beacon Street, built in 1825, to the city. He also leaves a substantial bequest "to be applied to the maintenance and improvement of the Common and parks now existing, but is not to be used for the purchase of additional land for park purposes." Parkman had lived with his mother and sister in seclusion in the house since the murder of his father, Dr. George Parkman, in 1849.

George Hiram Walker's "Boston and Surroundings" is published.

November 10. Voters approve revisions to the city charter that had been proposed by the Finance Commission. Effective in 1909, the changes call for a "strong mayor," elected to a four-year term; abolition of the seventy-five-member Board of Aldermen; and replacement of the forty-eight-member Common Council, elected by district (and composed at the time, according to one newspaper, of "incompetents and nobodies, with a mixture of convicts and notorious grafters"), with the nine-member Boston City Council, elected at large. Nonpartisan preliminary and final elections are also established.

February 23. The Ford Hall Forum holds its first lecture at Ford Hall on Beacon Hill. The oldest continually held lecture series in the United States, it is founded by the businessman George Coleman, in affiliation with the Boston Baptist Social Union, to provide "moral and intellectual stimulus, without prejudice to race, creed or class." Speakers would include Winston Churchill, Clarence Darrow, W. E. B. Du Bois, Alexander Kerensky, Dr. Martin Luther King, Jr., Henry Kissinger, Norman Mailer, Reinhold Niebuhr, Linus Pauling, Eleanor Roosevelt, Ayn Rand, Elie Wiesel, and Malcolm X. One feature of the program is to allow one hour for questions from the audience. The forum becomes independent from the Baptist Social Union in 1928, and the lectures continue today in various venues around the city.
The Women's Municipal League of Boston is established by Katharine Bowlker to promote women's involvement in civic affairs and to improve the city's sanitation, social, and educational services.

Giuseppe Parziale introduces pizza to Boston at his shop on Prince Street in the North End.
Moseley's-on-the-Charles nightclub opens in West Roxbury.

Three men rob a Jamaica Plain bar and are chased to the Forest Hills Cemetery by police. After holding off three hundred police officers for two days and wounding nine people, one of the robbers is finally killed and the other two are captured.

April 12. The Great Chelsea Fire occurs. Fifty people are killed, 492 acres are destroyed, and more than seventeen thousand people are left homeless by the fire, which causes an estimated twenty million dollars in damages. Many of the Jewish residents displaced from Chelsea move to the Boston neighborhoods of Roxbury, Dorchester, and Mattapan.

October 28. The Boston archdiocese celebrates its centennial with a weeklong series of events. It has grown from two priests serving 2,000 parishioners to 1,500 priests serving over 1.5 million people. Delivering the centenary sermon at Holy Cross Cathedral, Archbishop O'Connell declares: "The Puritan has passed, the Catholic remains. The city where a century ago, he came unwanted, he has made his own. . . . It is time for Catholic manhood to stand erect, square its shoulders, look the world in the eye and say, 'I am a Roman Catholic citizen; what about it?' "

The Oak Square School opens in Brighton. Designed by Edmund March Wheelwright, it is now the only wooden schoolhouse remaining in Boston. It is converted to condominiums in the 1980s.
September 28. The Franklin Institute opens in a building designed by R. Clipston Sturgis at 41 Berkeley Street in the South End. Supported by part of the bequest by Benjamin Franklin to the city of Boston, it provides technical training in various crafts and sciences. The school is renamed the Benjamin Franklin Institute of Technology in 1961 and is authorized to grant bachelors' degrees in 1995.
Harvard's Graduate School of Business opens in Allston. McKim, Mead, and White's group of buildings on the campus is completed in 1927.
Portia Law School opens. Founded informally when an attorney, Arthur MacLean, begins tutoring two women in his Beacon Hill office, it becomes the first and only law school in the country exclusively for women. The school admits men in 1930 and changes its name to the New England School of Law in 1972. It moves to its current location at 154 Stuart Street in 1980.

November 25. The first issue of the *Christian Science Monitor* appears. Founded by Mary Baker Eddy, the newspaper declares its missions are to cover "the daily activities of the entire world," and "to injure no man but to bless all mankind." Archibald McLellan is the first editor.

Charles Frederick White's *Plea for the Negro Soldier, and One Hundred Other Poems* is published.
November 23. The Gaiety Theatre opens at 659 Washington Street, on the site of the former Boylston Museum and Lyceum Theatre. Designed by Clarence Blackall, the 1,700-seat theater is one of the few that present African-American entertainers and produce shows for racially integrated audiences in the 1920s. Performers would include Milton Berle, the Marx Brothers, Red Skelton, and an eight-year-old Sammy Davis, Jr. The building is purchased by E. M. Loew and turned into a movie theater in the 1940s, renamed first the Victory and then the Publix, before closing in 1983.

The Austrian Alois Anderle wins the first annual Boston Light Swim, although he is later disqualified for walking across an exposed sandbar at Nix's Crag.

The ten-mile race from Boston Light on Little Brewster Island to L Street in South Boston is held every year until the outbreak of World War II, then resumes in 1978.

1909

March 30. Edward Filene, Louis Brandeis, and others announce the formation of the "New Boston 1915" campaign to develop a comprehensive physical and social plan for the metropolitan Boston area. The organization publishes a magazine, *New Boston*, in 1910, but dissolves in 1912. Toward the end of its existence, critics began to call the year 1915 the "Filennium."

The landscape architect Arthur Shurtleff's "Map of the Existing and Proposed Circumferential Thoroughfares and of the District and Their Connections, 1909" is published by the state's Metropolitan Improvement Commission. The study proposes the construction of radial highways out from the center of the city and a circumferential road around it.

The Dana Avenue Bridge is completed over the Neponset River in Hyde Park. It is the oldest surviving reinforced arch bridge in Boston and one of the earliest built in the United States.

Savin Hill Park is added to the Boston park system.

The first Joe and Nemo's hot dog stand opens in Scollay Square. Founded by Joseph Merlino and Anthony Calogerre, it becomes a restaurant on Howard Street, then expands onto nearby Stoddard Street. Additional restaurants are opened beginning in 1955, until there are twenty-seven in the Boston area and Florida by the early 1960s. The Scollay Square restaurant closes in June 1963. A new restaurant opens on Cambridge Street in 2003.

J. J. Foley's Café is established on Dover (now East Berkeley) Street in the South End. Founded by Jeremiah Foley, the tavern is currently owned and operated by his grandson of the same name.

December 25–26. The Christmas Storm causes millions of dollars in damage and creates the highest tides since 1851.

May 19. A. Lawrence Lowell succeeds Charles W. Eliot as president of Harvard. He presides over the university's greatest period of physical expansion. It is Lowell's secretary who, according to Boston legend, explains his absence to a visitor by saying: "The president is in Washington, seeing Mr. Taft." He serves until 1933.*

Professor Gaetano Lanza constructs the first wind tunnel in the United States at MIT. Comdr. J. C. Hunsaker constructs the first modern wind tunnel there in 1914.

Ellery Sedgwick succeeds Bliss Perry as editor of the *Atlantic Monthly;* Edward Weeks succeeds him from 1938 to 1966.* During the tenure of these two men, the magazine becomes one of the most influential in the English-speaking

The Museum of Fine Arts on Huntington Avenue, as shown on a postcard. (Courtesy of the Bostonian Society)

world. Its contributors include Felix Frankfurter, Carl Jung, Walter Lippmann, André Malraux, Jean-Paul Sartre, Edmund Wilson, Virginia Woolf, and W. B. Yeats.

In another of the publisher Edwin Grozier's promotions, the *Boston Post* delivers 431 gold-headed canes to 431 towns in five of the six New England states (all but Connecticut). The canes are to be presented—on loan—to the community's oldest living male resident, and then to his successor. Women are made eligible in 1930. The practice is still continued in some of the towns.

November 15. The Museum of Fine Arts opens its current facility, designed by Guy Lowell, in the Fenway, on the former site of circus and rodeo grounds. Cyrus Dallin's sculpture *Appeal to the Great Spirit* is installed in the forecourt in 1913. John Singer Sargent's murals in the dome are unveiled in October 1921 and in the stairwell in November 1925. The Evans Wing opens in 1915, the Decorative Arts Wing in 1928, the George Robert White Wing in 1970, the West Wing in 1981, and Kinsaku Nakane's Japanese garden in 1988.

Judge Robert Grant's novel *The Chippendales* is published.

November 8. The Opera House opens at 343 Huntington Avenue, with a performance of Amilcare Ponchielli's *La Gioconda*. Designed by Parkman Haven for Eben Jordan, the 2,750-seat hall is home to the Boston Opera Company, which lasts only three seasons. Jordan then rents it out to touring opera companies. The building is sold to the Shubert Company in 1916 and converted to a theater. It closes on September 25, 1957, is purchased by Northeastern University, and torn down to make way for a dormitory in 1958.

The Boston Licensing Division is established. It was created by legislation the year before to license "theatrical exhibitions, public shows, public amusements, and exhibitions of every description." Its three members are appointed by the governor. The first director is John Casey, who, acting as de facto "city censor," uses his authority to prompt theater managers to change the text of hundreds of plays and musicals for the next twenty-eight years.

Hazel Hotchkiss Wightman wins the national women's tennis singles, doubles, and mixed doubles championship—a feat she repeats in 1910 and 1911. A Bostonian since marrying George Wightman and moving to Chestnut Hill, she wins a total of forty-four national titles, as well as the Wimbledon and Olympic doubles titles in 1924.

1910

Boston's population is 670,585, the fifth-largest of any city in the United States (behind New York, Chicago, Philadelphia, and St. Louis). Of that number, 14,889 are described as Negro (including 13,564 who are African American), Indian, Chinese, Japanese, and "All Other." A total of 243,365 are foreign born: 66,041 from Ireland, 41,892 from Russia, and 31,380 from Italy. An estimated 60,000 are Jewish. The separate town of Hyde Park has an additional population of 15,507, with 103 classified as "Colored," including 87 classified as "Negro" and 16 as Indian, Chinese, or Japanese; and 4,442 are foreign born.

(ca.) "The Grove" community begins as a group of summer camps in West Roxbury.

The Thayer House is built at 84 Beacon Street. Designed by Ogden Codman, it becomes a small hotel called the Hampshire House during World War II. After it is purchased in 1969 by Thomas Kershaw and a partner, the upper floors are transformed into a restaurant and the basement into the Bull and Finch Pub, the inspiration for the setting of a television series that first airs in 1982.*

The Charles River Dam is completed. Built on the site of the former Craigie Bridge, it replaces a temporary dam completed in October 1908. The dam alleviates the sanitation problems at low tide that the Board of Health had described as "an atmosphere of stench so strong as to arouse the sleeping, terrify the weak, and nauseate and exasperate nearly everybody. . . . It visits the rich and poor alike." The dam also transforms the water behind it from brackish to fresh and enables construction of the Esplanade. A new dam is completed behind North Station on the site of the former Warren Street Bridge in 1978.

The Society for the Preservation of New England Antiquities is established. Founded by William Sumner Appleton, its headquarters is located today in Bulfinch's first Harrison Gray Otis house at 141 Cambridge Street. The society changes its name to Historic New England in 2004.

M. A. De Wolfe Howe's *Boston Common: Scenes from Four Centuries* is published.

Dr. John Collins Bossidy writes his ode to Boston. An updated version of a toast delivered at a Holy Cross reunion, it includes the lines "And this is dear old Boston,/The home of the bean and the cod,/Where the Lowells talk only to Cabots,/And the Cabots talk only to God."

C. Grahame-White at the Harvard-Boston Aero Meet, 1910. (Courtesy of the Bostonian Society)

January 11. Democrat John F. Fitzgerald (with 47,177 votes) narrowly defeats Republican James Jackson Storrow (with 45,775) (with the incumbent, Republican George Hibbard, running as an independent, drawing only 1,614 votes) to again win election as mayor. It is one of the closest mayoral elections in city history—and the first for a four-year term. Fitzgerald campaigned on the slogan "manhood against money" and put up posters showing a large photo of City Hall under which was inscribed, "NOT FOR SALE MR. $TORROW." Storrow's slogans included: "For Better Streets! For Better Schools!" Fitzgerald is inaugurated in Faneuil Hall on February 7.

James Michael Curley is elected to the U.S. House of Representative for the first of two consecutive terms.

The first annual Feast of the Madonna del Soccorso ("Fisherman's Feast") is held in the North End, and has since become the oldest of the neighborhood's summer festivals. Others would include the feasts of St. Agrippina di Mineo (1914), St. Anthony (the largest), St. Domenic, St. Joseph, St. Jude, St. Lucia, St. Rocco, St. Rosalia, Madonna del Grazie, and Madonna della Cava.

The Chilton Club is organized. Named for Mary Chilton, the only passenger on the *Mayflower* to move from Plymouth to Boston, it is the first female counterpart to the city's many exclusive men's clubs. Soon after its founding, the club acquires its headquarters at 150–152 Commonwealth Avenue, a building reportedly with three entrances (one for members only, one for members with guests, and one—in the alley—for servants).

September 2–12. The Harvard-Boston Aero Meet is held at Squantum Airfield. The first aviation meet in the eastern United States, it attracts an estimated 250,000 paying spectators. More than one million people gather along the shore and on boats, which fill Boston Harbor, to witness the flight by Claude

Grahame-White around Boston Light and back on September 12. Subsequent meets are held in 1911 and 1912.*

$ Daniel Crawford opens the Eureka Co-Operative Bank in Boston. It is described as "the only bank in the East owned and operated by 'Colored People.'"
December 7. The Industrial Credit Union opens. Now the oldest credit union in Boston, it was authorized under first-in-the-nation state legislation in 1909 and incorporated on July 26.

January 24. The Shubert Theatre opens at 265 Tremont Street with a production of *The Taming of the Shrew*, starring E. H. Southern and Julia Marlowe. The building is designed by Thomas James. Those performing here would include Julie Andrews, John Barrymore, Richard Burton, Maurice Evans, John Gielgud, and Laurence Olivier.
Waldron's Casino Theatre opens at 44 Hanover Street in the North End. The theater initially features musical comedies, minstrel shows, and operettas, then in later years, burlesque. It closes in 1962 and is torn down to make way for Government Center.

December. The Boston Arena opens. The oldest artificial-ice arena in the United States, it is built and operated by the city. Speakers at nonsporting events would include Presidents Coolidge, Hoover, and Franklin Roosevelt; Gov. Al Smith; and Charles Lindbergh. Nearly destroyed by a fire on December 18, 1918, it is rebuilt. It is purchased by Northeastern University in 1977, and is renovated and reopened as Matthews Arena on November 14, 1982.

1911

July 4. The temperature reaches 104 degrees, the hottest ever recorded in Boston.

Harriet Quimby of Boston becomes the first woman in the United States to obtain an airplane pilot's license. Dubbed the "Dresden China Aviatrix" by the press, she becomes the first woman to fly solo across the English Channel, on April 16, 1912.

September 23. The Plymouth Theatre opens at 131 Stuart Street, with a repertory performance by the Abbey Theatre Company of Dublin in its American debut. At the performance of J. J. Synge's controversial *Playboy of the Western World* on October 16, the director Lady Augusta Gregory and her partner, William Butler Yeats, hire several Harvard graduates for protection against protestors. The theater becomes the Gary movie theater in 1958.

April 19. Clarence DeMar, twenty-one, of Melrose, wins the first of his record seven Boston Marathons. He also wins in 1922, 1923, 1924, 1927, 1928, and 1930. The Bostonian Eleonora Sears wins the first of four national doubles tennis titles between 1911 and 1917. She is also singles runner-up in 1911, 1912, and 1916. The Franklin Field Speedway opens. Constructed by the Dorchester Gentlemen's Driving Club, the track is used for harness racing. Mayor Fitzgerald is a participant and wins one of the races in 1912.

1912

 Mary Antin's *The Promised Land* is published; it is a memoir based on her experience as a Russian Jewish immigrant who came to Boston.

January 1. Hyde Park is annexed to Boston, adding 2,869 acres to the city.
The Woodbourne residential community begins near Forest Hills in Jamaica Plain. It is developed by Robert Winsor, a director of the Boston Elevated Railway, through the Boston Dwelling House Company. The purpose is to provide affordable homes for company workers. Over the next thirty years, 381 homes are built. The community is later declared a National Historic Landmarks District.

March 23. The subway line from Park Street to Harvard Square, today's Red Line, opens. Its construction began on August 12, 1909. The line is extended to Washington Street, via the Dorchester Tunnel, on April 4, 1915; to South Station on December 3, 1916; to Broadway on December 15, 1917; to Ashmont on September 1, 1928; to Quincy Center on September 1, 1971; to Braintree on March 22, 1980; and to Alewife on March 30, 1985.
The Boston Fish Pier is completed. The largest in the world at the time, it can accommodate eighty vessels. Henry Keyes's Greco-Roman–style buildings on the pier are completed in 1914. The pier is purchased by the Massachusetts Port Authority in 1972 and renovated in 1985.

The Parkman Bandstand is dedicated on Boston Common. Designed by Derby, Robinson, and Shepard, it is built on the former site of the Cow Pond, and filled in 1838 after the pasturing of cattle is prohibited.
Angell Memorial Fountain and Park opens in Post Office Square. Designed by Peabody and Stearns, it is named for the Boston lawyer George Thorndike Angell, one of the founders of the Society for the Prevention of Cruelty to Animals. The park is renovated in 1982.
November 28. The Boston Aquarium opens in Marine Park, in South Boston. Designed by William Downes Austin, it closes on September 30, 1954, and is torn down thereafter.
Ronan Park in Dorchester is added to the city's park system. Originally called Mt. Ida Park, it is later named for Father Peter Ronan, who presided over the construction of St. Peter's Church.

M. A. De Wolfe Howe's *Boston: The Place and the People* is published.

The Boston branch of the National Association for the Advancement of Colored People (NAACP) is founded. The first official branch in the United States, it is initially made up mostly of older white men. Butler Wilson becomes the first African-American president in 1926.

The Italian Renaissance–style Copley Plaza Hotel, designed by Blackall and Hardenberg, opens in Copley Square, on the former site of the Museum of Fine Arts. The Merry-Go-Round Lounge opens in 1933.

The first municipal Christmas Eve celebration is held on Boston Common. Ten thousand people join Mayor Fitzgerald at the ceremony, which includes the lighting of a thirty-five-foot tree with two thousand lights and a performance by a Navy band and a choir.

July 1. The Harvard-Boston Aero Meet ends in disaster. The Boston pilot Harriet Quimby and her passenger, William Willard, die when they are thrown from their Bleriot monoplane and plunge one thousand feet into Dorchester Bay—only two hundred feet from shore, where a crowd of five thousand spectators watch in horror. The plane then glides down into the water and is barely damaged.

March 18. Boston (originally called Boys) Trade High School opens. Located initially in the Brimmer School on Common Street, it moves to a new building on Parker Street on Mission Hill in 1917. Additions to the building are completed in 1926 and 1939, but the school closes in 1973.

George Santayana resigns his teaching position at Harvard and sails to Europe, never to return to Boston or the United States.

June 24. The Boston Psychopathic Hospital opens on Fenwood Road in the Longwood area. Originally the Psychopathic Department of the Boston State Hospital, it is founded, according to Dr. Vernon Briggs's 1922 history, because "confused and mentally ill persons continued to be arrested on the streets of Boston." It is renamed the Massachusetts Mental Health Center in May 1956.

June 7–August 19. Boston Elevated Railway workers go on strike. After thirty-eight hundred workers walk off the job, violence occurs when two thousand scabs are hired as replacement workers. After the strike spreads to adjoining towns, Mayor Fitzgerald and the City Council press for a resolution of the dispute, which is accepted by Local 589 of the Amalgamated Transit Union.

The Art Institute of Boston is established. The school merges with Lesley University in 1998.

January 1. The Toy Theatre opens on Lime Street on Beacon Hill. The first "little theater" in the United States, it is organized by Mrs. Lyman Gale. After attempting to produce the kind of experimental plays being written and performed in Europe, it closes the following year.

April 20. The Red Sox beat the New York Highlanders 7–6 in eleven innings before twenty-seven thousand spectators in the first official game played at Fenway Park. (The Red Sox had beaten Harvard 2–0 in an exhibition game on April 9.) James McLaughlin is the architect, and John I. Taylor is the team owner.

October 16. The Red Sox beat the New York Giants 3–2 in ten innings of game 8 (game 2 was a tie) at Fenway Park to win the World Series.

1913

The South Boston Municipal Building opens on the former site of the Perkins School for the Blind in South Boston.

Hibernian Hall is built in Dudley Square in Roxbury. Owned and operated by the Ancient Order of Hibernians until 1960, the building later serves as headquarters for Opportunities Industrialization Center, a job training program. It is scheduled to reopen as the Roxbury Center for Arts, Culture, and Trade in 2004.

Commonwealth Pier opens. The largest on the East Coast at the time, it is built by the state to accommodate large ocean liners. It is later renovated into a meeting and convention facility, reopening as the World Trade Center in 1986.

The Franklin Park Zoo opens. Granite entrance columns from the Custom House are added in 1917, and from the former Post Office in 1929. Daniel Chester French's statues *Commerce* and *Industry* are added in 1929, and the aviary opens in 1931. Annual attendance reaches one million visitors in the 1930s and 1940s. Operated initially by the city, it is taken over by the Metropolitan District Commission in 1958. After a special legislative commission declares conditions "intolerable" and "deplorable," the zoo is taken over by the Boston Zoological Society in December 1970. The African Tropical Forest Pavilion opens in 1989.

The Boylston fish weir is discovered during the construction of the Boylston Street subway station. The weir was built by Indians over much of the Back Bay as early as 2000 B.C. and made up of some 6,500 stakes. Sections are later discovered during construction of many of the high-rise buildings in the area.

December 18. Mayor Fitzgerald withdraws from his campaign for reelection, claiming poor health—but only after his opponent, James Michael Curley, threatens to deliver a series of lectures, including "Great Lovers from Cleopatra to Toodles" (a reference to Fitzgerald's alleged affair with a twenty-three-year-old "cigarette girl," Toodles Ryan). "Politics and holiness are not always synonymous," Curley later declares. "There are times . . . when, if you wish to win an election, you must do unto others as they wish to do unto you, but you must do it first."

The Harvard Club of Boston, designed by J. Harleston Parker, opens at 374 Commonwealth Avenue.

December 20. The Women's City Club of Boston is founded by a group led by Helen Osborne Storrow "to promote a broad acquaintance among women through their common interest in the welfare of the City of Boston and the Commonwealth of Massachusetts." Its membership tops five thousand in the 1920s. The club first rents its headquarters at 39–40 Beacon Street, then buys it in 1919. The club sells the building in 1992 and proceeds to share space with the Union Club on Park Street.

December 3. Twenty-seven people are killed and eighteen injured in a fire that destroys the Hotel Acadia.

May 2. The Boston School Committee approves Superintendent Jeremiah Burke's proposal to establish intermediate (junior high) schools.

March. Boston College moves to the former farm of A. A. Lawrence in Chestnut Hill. The first building to open is Recitation (now Gasson) Hall. Thomas Gasson, S.J., is succeeded as president by Charles Lyons (1914), William Devlin (1919), James Dolan (1925), Louis Gallagher (1932), William McGarry (1937), William Murphy (1939), William Keleher (1945), Joseph Maxwell (1951), Michael Walsh (1958), W. Seavey Joyce (1968), J. Donald Monan (1972), and William Leahy (1996 to the present). The school becomes coeducational by 1970.

January 27. Peter Bent Brigham Hospital opens on the site of the former Francis estate in the Fenway. Construction had begun in 1911. Incorporated in 1902, the hospital was endowed by and named for a Boston restaurant owner and real estate mogul who died in 1877. The hospital merges with two others in 1980.*

Ida M. Cannon's *Social Work in Hospitals* is published.

August 4. The *Boston Post* conducts its most outlandish promotion. Joseph Knowles, a forty-four-year-old illustrator at the newspaper, is sent into the woods of northern Maine for sixty days—with no food or water, unarmed, and naked. Living on roots, berries, and game, he is allowed no contact with any human being, and files stories and drawings describing his experience by means of charcoal markings on birch bark. Emerging from the woods two months later near Megantic, Quebec, Knowles is taken by private train to Boston and met by a crowd estimated at between 150,000 and 400,000 people on Newspaper Row. He later appears on B. F. Keith's vaudeville circuit and repeats the stunt for a Hearst newspaper in California some years later.

The Connick Studios open at 9 Harcourt Street. The company would furnish stained-glass windows to more than five thousand churches, schools, and hospitals around the world and continue operating until 1986.

Spring. The Copley Gallery hosts the first all-women-artist exhibition in Boston, "a show," according to the *Boston Evening Transcript*, "in which no mere man has any part."

April 28. The Armory Show opens at Copley Hall in Boston. Because of limited space, fewer than one-fourth of the twelve hundred objects shown in New York and Chicago are displayed. While the show is credited with launching "modern art" in America, it is panned in Boston. The *Christian Science Monitor* critic calls it "an insult to art," and F. W. Coburn, of the *Boston Herald*, writes, "the art of European painting has degenerated from banality into buffoonery."

M. A. De Wolfe Howe's *Letters of Charles Eliot Norton* is published.

The eight-hundred-seat Modern Theatre, designed by Clarence Blackall in the High Victorian style, opens at 523 Washington Street. The acoustics are by Wallace Clement Sabine. It is renamed the Mayflower in 1949 and closes in the early 1980s. A proposal is currently being made to preserve the building.

The Children's Museum opens in Jamaica Plain. The second-oldest children's museum in the United States (Brooklyn opened one in 1899), it moves to Pinebank in the 1920s, to the former Morse/Milton estate on Burroughs Street in March 1936, and to a building designed by Cambridge Seven Associates on Museum Wharf in 1979.

September 20. The American amateur Francis Ouimet beats the English professionals Ted Ray and Harry Vardon in a three-way, eighteen-hole playoff to win the U.S. Open golf tournament at The Country Club in Brookline. The son of a gardener, Ouimet grew up across the street from and caddied at the club. His victory is regarded by many as the biggest upset in golf—and sports—history.

1914

January 27. The Boston Planning Board is created. Authorized by state legislation passed the previous year, it is one of fourteen in the country at the time. The city ordinance declares the board "shall consist of five members, one of whom at least shall be a woman."

May 22. City Hall Annex, designed by Edward Graham in the Classical Revival style, opens.

Smith Pond Playground, in Hyde Park, is added to the city's park system.

January 11. James Michael Curley engages in what his biographer Jack Beatty describes as "the single most recounted" story of his colorful career. Reciting the Lord's Prayer at a campaign rally in front of St. Augustine's Church in South Boston, Curley intones, "Give us this day, our daily bread and forgive us our trespasses . . ." Then, noticing someone reaching into his car, he shouts: "Get that sonuvabitch, he's stealing my coat!" Curley then quickly resumes, "as we forgive those who trespass against us. . . ."
January 13. Democrat James Michael Curley (with 43,262 votes) defeats Thomas Kenny (with 37,522) to win the first of his four terms as mayor. Curley would be called "Mayor of the Poor" and initiate numerous job-producing public works projects that led to the construction of roads, bridges, beaches, municipal buildings, neighborhood health clinics, and a rebuilt Boston City Hospital. He would also be known for antagonizing the Yankee business establishment, ignoring ward bosses, and, as Thomas O'Connor later writes, "claiming the people as his only constituency."

In a meeting with President Woodrow Wilson at the White House, William Monroe Trotter and other civil rights leaders present a petition signed by twenty thousand people protesting the segregation of African Americans in the federal workforce. When the discussion becomes heated, they are asked to leave.

October 7. The daughter of former mayor John Fitzgerald, Rose, marries the son of the East Boston ward boss P. J. Kennedy, Joseph Patrick Kennedy, in a wedding officiated by Cardinal O'Connell in the cardinal's private chapel.
Brigham's Ice Cream Company is established. It results from the merger of the Durand Candy Company, founded by the Symmes brothers in Post Office

Square, and a store selling homemade ice cream, established by Edward Brigham in Newton Highlands.

Robert Breck Brigham Hospital for Incurables opens at 125 Parker Hill Avenue. Incorporated in 1903, the hospital was endowed and named for the nephew of Peter Bent Brigham and was built on the former site of the Parker Hill Reservoir.

November. The Forsyth Dental Infirmary for Children, designed by Edward T. P. Graham, opens at 140 the Fenway. The bronze doors are sculpted by Roger Burnham. Endowed by a Scottish family that settled in Roxbury, the clinic provides "nearly free treatment" for children (for years, each child is charged a nickel). It becomes the Forsyth Dental Center in 1962 and the Forsyth Institute in 1999.

November 16. The Boston branch of the Federal Reserve Bank opens. It moves to a building designed by R. Clipston Sturgis, with murals by N. C. Wyeth, in Post Office Square in 1922. It moves to another building in Post Office Square in 1953, then to its current location at 600 Atlantic Avenue, a building designed by Hugh Stubbins and Associates, in 1976.

The Economy Grocery Store opens in the Grove Hall section of Roxbury. The first store in what later becomes the Stop and Shop supermarket chain, it is founded by brothers Irving, Norman, and Sidney Rabinovitz.

February 21. In an article in the *Boston Globe*, Lincoln Steffens states: "Boston is the case of a failure of government by good people. Boston is paved with good intentions. So is Hell. . . . Boston is a common city of superior people. It has all the good things that other cities think, if they had them, would make impossible political corruption. Yet Boston has always had the good things and has always had political corruption."

April 19. The Colonial Revival–style Wilbur Theatre opens at 246 Tremont Street, with a production of *Romance*. Designed by Clarence Blackall and built by the Shubert brothers, it is named for their friend, the theater manager A. L. Wilbur. According to the architectural historian Douglass Shand-Tucci, "The auditorium is in its chaste way the handsomest of any Boston playhouse."

March. Teresa Weld of Boston wins the first of six U.S. national figure skating championships in New Haven, Connecticut. She also wins from 1920 to 1924, and teams up with Nathaniel Niles, also of Boston, to win the pairs championship in 1918 and again from 1920 to 1927.

July 4. Harvard beats the Union Boat Club of Boston to become the first American crew to win the Challenge Cup at the Royal Henley Regatta in England.

October 13. The Braves beat the Philadelphia Athletics 3–1 in game 4 to sweep all four games and win the World Series. Because their new stadium is under construction, the team (called the "Miracle Braves" for winning the pennant after being in last place on July 19) plays games 3 and 4 at Fenway Park.

1915

The state begins filling the East Boston Flats to construct a shipping terminal. The filling continues until 1923, is resumed by the city to construct Boston

Airport in 1930–31, and is resumed again to expand Logan Airport in the 1940s, 1960s, and 1970s.

 January 18. The Custom House tower opens. Added to the original building, the 32-story, 496-foot tower, designed by Peabody and Stearns, makes it the tallest in Boston until 1947. The tower's construction is allowed only because federal buildings are not subject to the city's 125-foot height limit. The federal government moves out of the building in 1987, and it is converted into time-share condominiums, reopening on August 6, 1997.

December 30. The Commonwealth Armory is dedicated. It is later sold to Boston University, used as a track facility, then torn down to make way for the construction of a new arena.

The Curley House opens at 350 The Jamaicaway. It is designed by Joseph McGinnis in the Georgian Revival style and decorated with furnishings from the Henry Rodgers House in Fairhaven, Massachusetts. Curley displays his Irish pride—and annoys his Yankee neighbors—by having shamrocks carved in the window shutters. Hollywood recreates the interior of the house in the movie version of *The Last Hurrah.* Curley sells the home to the Oblate Fathers in August 1956. The George Robert White Fund purchases it for the city in 1988.

The Custom House tower after its completion, 1916. (Courtesy of the Bostonian Society)

 William S. Rossiter's *Days and Ways in Old Boston* is published.

 The Permanent Charities Fund of Boston is established. Founded by Charles Rogerson, president of the Boston Safe Deposit and Trust Company, his son, Charles H., and James Longley, it later becomes the Boston Foundation.

The Angell Memorial Hospital is established to care for animals.

Shortly before his death this year, Charles Francis Adams, Jr., writes: "I have known, and known tolerably well, a good many 'successful' men—'big' financially—men famous during the last half-century; and a less interesting crowd I do not care to encounter. Not one that I have ever known would I care to meet again, either in this world or the next."

April 17. D. W. Griffith's *The Birth of a Nation* opens at the Tremont Theatre. Despite minor changes made at the request of Mayor Curley, the movie sparks protests, led by William Monroe Trotter, because of the way it portrays African Americans. The film continues to be screened, however, for the next six and a half months. Trotter and others successfully persuade authorities not to allow a return engagement in 1921.

December 20. The Fenway Theatre opens at 136 Massachusetts Avenue. Designed by Thomas Lamb, it is the first "uptown" theater built for movies. Closed in 1959, the building is purchased first by the Bryant and Stratton Commercial School, then by Berklee College of Music, and reopens as the Berklee Performance Center on April 5, 1976.

The Brighton Theatre opens at 400 Market Street. Known as "the Barn," it is the first theater in Brighton. It closes in the early 1930s.

George Bernard Shaw's *Pygmalion*, starring Mrs. Patrick Campbell, for whom the role of Eliza Doolittle was written, is performed at the Colonial Theatre.

 August 18. The Braves beat St. Louis 3–1 in the first game played at the new Braves Field, before a crowd estimated at fifty thousand (ten thousand more than the park's capacity). Built on the site of the former Allston Golf Club, the stadium becomes known for its "jury box" bleachers (so named after a sportswriter counts only twelve people sitting there at a game), and the railroad tracks and Charles River running behind, beyond left field.

October 13. The Red Sox beat the Phillies 5–4 in Philadelphia to win game 5 and the World Series. Because of its larger seating capacity, the Red Sox played games 2 and 3 at the new Braves Field.

1916

 Robert Shackleton's *The Book of Boston* is published.

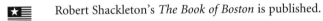 *November 14.* Republican Henry Cabot Lodge defeats Democrat and former Boston mayor John F. Fitzgerald for the U.S. Senate.

Aloy Soong becomes, according to the *Boston Post*, the "First Chinaman to Get a City Position." He is hired as assistant bacteriologist.

 January 28. Louis Brandeis is appointed to the U.S. Supreme Court by President Woodrow Wilson. He is the first Jew in history to be named to the nation's highest court. With Holmes, he becomes known for issuing liberal, dissenting opinions.

 November 7. A trolley plunges off an open drawbridge on Summer Street into the Fort Point Channel, killing more than forty people in the worst tragedy in terms of loss of life to this point in the city's history.

 November 12. The Evangelist Billy Sunday preaches to an estimated fifty-five thousand people in a tabernacle erected on Huntington Avenue, and another fifteen thousand are turned away. A former major league baseball player, Sunday calls himself "the Lord's third base coach—trying to get the sinners home." His ten-week crusade in Boston attracts an estimated one and a half million people.

 The Boston public schools introduce a cooperative system of manual training in high schools, under which students alternate weeks of classroom study with shop work. Each high school offers a specialty. Brighton offers woodworking, then auto mechanics; Charlestown, electricity; Dorchester, woodworking; East Boston and Hyde Park, machine shop; Jamaica Plain, agriculture; Roxbury, printing; and South Boston, sheet metal.

 Boston's first neighborhood health center opens on Blossom Street in the West End.

 La Notizia begins publication. Boston's first Italian newspaper has its offices at 30 Battery Street.

 Edmund Tarbell's *Girl Crocheting* is sold for sixteen thousand dollars, a record price for a work by a living American artist. He leaves Boston a year later for Washington, D.C.

The Horn Book is published by the Union Book Shop. It would be credited with elevating children's literature.

Roland Hayes makes his singing debut at Jordan Hall. After moving to Boston to study in 1911, Hayes spends—and loses—his life savings of two hundred dollars to produce the concert. Later he is one of the first African-American singers to perform with major symphony orchestras and tour internationally. He first performs at Symphony Hall on November 15, 1917; he continues to perform until 1950.

The Longy School of Music is established in Boston. It is founded in the style of the French conservatory by Georges Longy, who is the first oboist for the Boston Symphony Orchestra until he resigns after a dispute with Serge Koussevitzky in 1921. The school later moves to Cambridge.

 October 9. The Red Sox beat the Brooklyn Dodgers 2–1 in fourteen innings at Braves Field in the longest World Series game in history, behind the complete-game pitching of Babe Ruth. The Red Sox win the series in the fifth game on October 12, also at Braves Field. After the season, thirty-six-year-old Harry Frazee buys the team.

1917

 The filling of Old Harbor Beach in South Boston begins. It is completed in 1919.

 January 30. The official Boston city flag is adopted. It comprises the city seal displayed in the official city colors—Continental blue and Continental buff.

April 6. The United States declares war on Germany and enters World War I. The war lasts until the armistice is signed on November 11, 1918.

Boston Harbor is mined and a net is stretched across it to guard against submarine attack.

July 1. A peace parade by socialist groups on Boston Common turns into a "patriotic riot" when police and some of the estimated twenty thousand onlookers attack the marchers.

November. Two thousand people attend a rally in support of the Balfour Declaration at the Tremont Temple.

December 18. Democrat Andrew Peters (with 37,923 votes) defeats James Michael Curley (with 28,848) and James Gallivan (19,427) to be elected mayor. Although endorsed by the Good Government Association, as mayor Peters is criticized for paying more attention to yachting, golf, and his teenage mistress, Starr Faithful, than to running the city or discouraging corruption.

Harry Gardiner, known as "the Human Fly," scales the exterior of the New England Life Building on Milk Street to raise money for the Red Cross.

Blinstrub's Village opens at West Broadway and D Street. Owned and operated by Stanley Blinstrub, the seventeen-hundred-seat restaurant and nightclub becomes a popular spot with politicians and entertainers. It is destroyed by a fire on February 8, 1968.

March 17. Two men are killed when a bomb explodes in a second-floor corridor of the old Suffolk County Court House in Pemberton Square. The perpetrators are never caught. A similar bombing takes place in 1976.*

December 6. A collision between a munitions ship and a steamship in Halifax Harbor causes an explosion that kills more than two thousand people and destroys much of the city. A train containing medical personnel and supplies, food, clothing, and $750,000 in donations leaves Boston that night. In appreciation, the province of Nova Scotia begins a practice—which continues today—of sending a Christmas tree to Boston as an annual gift to the city.

February 13. Rat Day is held. Sponsored by the Women's Municipal League of Boston to encourage the depletion of the city's rodent population, prizes are awarded to citizens who bring in the most dead rats.
April 9. The Judge Baker Foundation for the Study of Juveniles is established. Named for Harvey Baker, the first judge of Boston's Juvenile Court, the foundation is located initially at 38 Beacon Street, moves to 3 Blackfan Circle in the Longwood medical area, and to Parker Hill Avenue on Mission Hill in 2004.

April 17. The federal government orders its first monoplanes from the Pigeon Hollow Spar Company of East Boston. The planes are assembled in Swampscott.

April 30. The first annual Exhibition by Boston Woman Artists opens. Sponsored by Robert Vose, Sr., the show contains sixty-three paintings by fifty artists. In a review, the critic F. W. Coburn later writes, "the feeling is still strong and is presumably justified, that to be an artist and a woman subjects one to a somewhat lower rating."
Josiah Benton dies, leaving more than a million dollars to the Boston Public Library.
October 2. The Boston Symphony Orchestra holds its first recording session with the Victor Talking Machine Company in Camden, New Jersey. The first piece recorded is the finale to Tchaikovsky's Fourth Symphony.

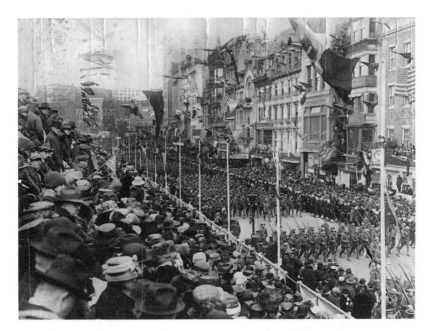

A parade down Tremont Street for returning Word War I soldiers. (Courtesy of the Bostonian Society)

1918

The Roslindale Municipal Building is built at 6 Cummins Highway.

January 1. A 7-cent subway fare is established. It is increased to 10 cents on July 10, 1919; 15 cents beginning November 10, 1951; 20 cents on April 12, 1954; 25 cents December 1, 1968; 50 cents on June 27, 1980; 85 cents on August 21, 1991; $1.00 on September 9, 2000; and $1.25 on January 3, 2004. Tokens are first used in 1918, discontinued, then reintroduced on November 10, 1951.
July 1. The state takes over the operation of the Boston Elevated Railway.

November 11. The signing of the armistice ending World War I prompts rejoicing throughout the city. At 3:15 A.M., a whistle blows and the ringing of church bells soon follows.

March 25. The state legislature enacts a law prohibiting the mayor of Boston from succeeding himself in office. Aimed at curtailing the power of James Michael Curley, the law remains in effect until May 10, 1938.

February 4. Charles Jennings, a lighthouse keeper, rescues the entire twenty-four-man crew of the USS *Alacrity*, which ran aground near Boston Light.
February 21. Thirteen boys escape across the ice of Boston Harbor from the Suffolk School for Delinquent Boys on Rainsford Island. They are all eventually returned to the school.

The legislature enacts a law separating Boston's school taxes from the rest of its municipal taxes, and requiring the city to petition the legislature every year for an annual tax limit.

The Hebrew College opens at 14 Crawford Street in Roxbury. Originally called the Hebrew Teachers Training School, its first class graduates in 1925. The college is granted the power to confer undergraduate and graduate degrees in 1927, moves to the former Wightman estate in Brookline in 1951, and to Newton in 1996.

August 27. Sailors on board the receiving ship at Commonwealth Pier begin reporting to sick bay. Three days later, over sixty are diagnosed with Spanish influenza. On September 3, the first civilian flu casualties are admitted to Boston City Hospital. Eventually, tents are set up on the hospital grounds to accommodate the large number of flu patients. Between September and December, the flu kills 4,794 people in the city; by mid-March 1919, 6,225 flu deaths are reported in Boston. Over half a million people would die across the United States.

January 17. The Museum of Fine Arts makes admission free for the duration of World War I. When the war ends in November, the free admission policy is continued until 1966.

March 25. Karl Muck, the German-born conductor of the Boston Symphony Orchestra, is arrested as an enemy alien. Muck is interned for the remainder of the war at Fort Oglethorpe, Georgia, and sent back to Germany after the war. By the end of the year, twenty-nine members of the orchestra—seventeen of them German Americans—would leave. Henri Rabaud replaces Muck as conductor. He is succeeded by Pierre Monteux in 1919, who remains until 1924.*

November 11. The Strand Theatre opens at 543 Columbia Road in Dorchester. Designed by Funk and Wilcox, it is later described as "Boston's first great movie palace." Performers who appear at the fourteen-hundred-seat theater would include Fred Allen, Jack Benny, Milton Berle, Fanny Brice, Tommy Dorsey, and Ray Bolger. The building closes in 1960, is taken over by the city in 1975, and reopens as the M. Harriet McCormack Center for the Arts in 1979.

September 11. The Red Sox beat the Chicago Cubs 2–1 at Fenway Park to win game 6 and the World Series. It is the team's third World Series win in four years.

1919

June 10. The South Boston Army Base opens on the South Boston waterfront. The adjacent South Boston Naval Annex opens soon after. Both military bases close in the 1970s. The property becomes the Boston Marine Industrial Park in 1977. The Boston Design Center opens in the former army warehouse on February 19, 1986.

The Chinese Merchants Association building opens at 2 Tyler Street. A remodeled tenement, it is replaced by a new building at 20 Hudson Street, designed by Edward Chin Park and topped by a Chinese pagoda, which opens on October 1, 1951. Part of the building is demolished to make way for construction of the Central and Surface Arteries in 1953.

The Metropolitan District Commission (MDC), an outgrowth of the Metropolitan Parks Commission, is created. Its mission is to coordinate water, sewer, and park administration in metropolitan Boston. It merges with the Department of Environmental Management in 2003.
September. The City Planning Board recommends Columbus Park in South Boston as the "most suitable and available" site for construction of a new airport.

February 24. President Woodrow Wilson pledges to fight for creation of a League of Nations in a speech at Mechanics Hall. A few days earlier, a crowd of two hundred thousand greeted him as he arrived in Boston Harbor on his return from signing the Treaty of Versailles, formally ending World War I.
March 19. A. Lawrence Lowell (for) and Henry Cabot Lodge (against) debate President Wilson's proposal to establish a League of Nations at Symphony Hall. Seventy-two thousand people applied for tickets to the event.
Arthur Crews Gilman, a wealthy, eccentric Back Bay recluse, begins the 155-volume, 177-million word diary he keeps until his death in 1963.

October 10. The Home for Italian Children is established. Founded in the North End to care for children orphaned by the 1918 flu epidemic, the home moves to 1125 Centre Street in Jamaica Plain on September 16, 1928.

October 8. Harvey Yates becomes the first African American appointed to the Boston police force. (There is, however, an unconfirmed report that the first "colored" police officer is appointed on July 1, 1879.) Other African-American officers appointed in the next few weeks are Frederick Mayor, Joshua McClain, and Charles Montier. More than thirty African-American officers are appointed by 1923.

January 15. The Great Molasses Flood occurs. At 12:30 P.M., a tank 50 feet high and 90 feet in diameter, owned by the Purity Distilling Company at 529 Commercial Street in the North End, collapses, releasing a fifteen-foot wave containing over two million gallons of molasses. The flood kills 21 people and injures more than 150. The *Boston Herald* later describes how "a muffled roar burst suddenly upon the air," and the *Boston Post* reports, "horses were blown about like chips, houses torn asunder, and the heavy section of the Elevated railroad structure smashed like an eggshell." Although anarchists are initially suspected of sabotage (the molasses was to be used in the production of munitions), the cause is later attributed to expansion of the molasses due to unusually warm weather and the shoddy construction of the tank.

Anshe Vilna Temple, known as the "Vilna Shul," opens on Phillips Street on Beacon Hill. Designed by Max Kalman, it is built on the site of the former African Methodist Church and is the first home for a congregation of Lithuanian Jews founded in the West End in 1893. By 1985 only one member remains.

The Boston Post *headline following the Molasses Flood, 1919. (Courtesy of the Bostonian Society)*

A nonprofit Vilna Center for Jewish Heritage is formed in 1989 to preserve the building.

The Quong Kow School opens at 16–18 Oxford Street. It is founded by Chinese businessmen to preserve Chinese language, history, and cultural traditions. Emmanuel College opens in buildings designed by Maginnis and Walsh at 400 The Fenway. The first Catholic women's college in New England, it is founded by the Sisters of Notre Dame de Namur. The school becomes coeducational in 2001. Sister Janet Eisner, SND, is the current president.

Charles Jackson, an African-American mechanic in Boston, invents the diving suit. Jackson's device sets a new world record for deep-sea diving in 1920, when John Turner uses it to reach a depth of 360 feet.

January. The Boston Trade Union College is established. Organized by the Boston Central Labor Union, it is "based on the conviction that organized labor must develop its intellectual resources if it is to realize its hopes in the coming social and industrial order." It is thought to be the first college operated by a labor union in the United States. Classes are held initially at the High School of Practical Arts, then at the Abraham Lincoln School, then at private offices.

April 15–21. The Boston Telephone Operators' Union goes on strike. Led by president Julia O'Connor, the strike paralyzes phone service in New England and leads to higher wages and improved working conditions.

May 1. The May Day Riot occurs. A parade sponsored by the Lettish Socialist Workmen's Society, which also includes suffragists, turns into a riot. Scores are injured and two hundred are arrested.

July 17–20. Street railway workers strike. Garment workers, fishermen, and actors also strike during the next few months.

September 9. The Boston Police Strike takes place. Over 1,100 of the city's 1,544 officers turn in their badges and walk off the job, protesting low salaries (frozen since 1898) and the administration's refusal to allow them to form a union. Three days of rioting and looting follow, which the historian Francis Russell later describes as a scene "that made respectable middle-class observers think back uneasily to *A Tale of Two Cities,* read long ago in school. For a few moments, the lid was off their stratified social structure, and the glimpse they had of what lay underneath was cold and cruel, something they did not like to think about." Nine people are killed and twenty-three wounded. After initially refusing, Gov. Calvin Coolidge calls out the Massachusetts National Guard; he replies to a telegram from Samuel Gompers with the words some later say made him president: "There is no right to strike against the public safety by anybody, anywhere, anytime." Order is generally restored by September 12. Though the strikers' demands are subsequently met, none of them is ever rehired.

 M. A. De Wolfe Howe's *The Atlantic Monthly and Its Makers* is published.

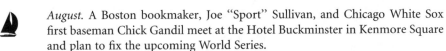 *August.* A Boston bookmaker, Joe "Sport" Sullivan, and Chicago White Sox first baseman Chick Gandil meet at the Hotel Buckminster in Kenmore Square and plan to fix the upcoming World Series.

December 26. The Red Sox sell Babe Ruth to the New York Yankees for $125,000 and a $300,000 loan; the transaction is announced on January 5, 1920. Contrary to popular belief, the money was *not* used to finance Red Sox owner Harry Frazee's production of *No, No, Nanette* (which didn't open on Broadway until September 16, 1925). The transaction did spark outrage, however. One Boston newspaper featured cartoons of Faneuil Hall and the Boston Public Library with "For Sale" signs on them. Ruth is also not the only Red Sox player sold or traded to the Yankees. Two years later, New York wins the World Series with eleven former Red Sox players, and Frazee sells the Red Sox in July 1923.

1920

Boston's population is 748,060, the seventh-largest of any city in the United States. Of that number, 17,575 are described as Negro (including 16,350 African Americans), Indian, Chinese, Japanese, and "All Other." A total of 242,619 are foreign born: 57,011 from Ireland, 38,021 from Russia, and 38,179 from Italy. An estimated 80,000 are Jewish.

The Federal Immigration Station opens at 287 Marginal Street in East Boston. It replaces a rented facility on Long Wharf.

January 2. Federal agents raid radical and suspected communist organizations in and around Boston, arrest four thousand people, and detain them on Deer Island.

November 2. John McCormack is elected state representative from South Boston. He is elected to the state senate in 1922 and wins a special election to the U.S. House of Representatives in 1928. He is elected Speaker of the House in 1962, and is the first Catholic to hold the post. After serving in the post for four terms, he retires in 1971.

Members of the Boston Police Department with confiscated alcohol during Prohibition. (Courtesy of the Bostonian Society)

January 15. On the eve of the day Prohibition goes into effect, a mock funeral is held in Boston for "John Barleycorn." Hotels are packed, waiters wear black, and empty liquor bottles are placed in coffins.

August 18. The Nineteenth Amendment, granting universal suffrage, is ratified.

April 15. Armed men rob a South Braintree shoe factory, kill a paymaster and guard, and escape with $15,765. Two Italian immigrants, Nicola Sacco and Bartolomeo Vanzetti, are arrested in Bridgewater on May 5 and later charged with the crime. They are convicted by a jury in a trial presided over by Judge Webster Thayer at Dedham Courthouse on July 14, 1921, and are imprisoned until all of their appeals are exhausted in 1927.*

July 24. The *Boston Post* begins a series exposing the pyramid scheme of Charles Ponzi. An Italian immigrant, Ponzi opened an office at 27 School Street the previous December and began promising investors a 50 percent return in forty-five days and 100 percent in ninety days. After attracting an estimated fifteen million dollars in investments, Ponzi is arrested on fraud charges, pleads guilty on November 30, and is imprisoned. Released three and a half years later, he is tried and convicted on other charges in other states, jumps bail, is recaptured twice, jailed, and finally deported to Italy in 1931. He dies in a hospital for paupers in Rio de Janeiro in 1949.

The *Boston Chronicle* begins publication. Described as "New England's Largest Negro Weekly Newspaper," it continues until 1967.

January 1. Harvard beats Oregon 7–6 in the Rose Bowl to win its seventh national collegiate football championship—and the last to date.

May 1. The Boston Braves and Brooklyn Dodgers play to a 1–1 tie in twenty-six innings at Braves Field in the longest game in major league baseball history. Boston's Joe Oeschger and Brooklyn's Leon Cadore both pitch complete games.

Charles Francis Adams, nephew of the historian, skippers the *Resolute* to victory over Sir Thomas Lipton's *Shamrock IV* to win the America's Cup.

1921

The filling of South Bay west of Dorchester Avenue in South Boston begins. Undertaken by the New York, New Haven, and Hartford Railroad, it is completed in 1929.

Charles Street is widened by an additional ten feet. Some buildings along the west side of the street—including the Charles Street Meeting House—are moved, others cut back.

Samuel Eliot Morison's *The Maritime History of Massachusetts, 1783–1860* is published.

December 13. Democrat James Michael Curley (with 74,261 votes) beats John Murphy (with 71,791) to win his second term as mayor. The *Boston Herald* describes Curley as winning "without the assistance of a single political leader of either party, and with every machine of recognized standing against him." He is inaugurated in January before twelve thousand people at Mechanics Hall.

Six women are appointed to the Boston police force.

Frances Greely Curtis wins election to the Boston School Committee with 79,139 votes, more than either of the two mayoral candidates.

Harvard University segregates the residence of its five African-American freshmen from the rest of the incoming class. William Monroe Trotter, W. E. B. Du Bois (both alumni), and others protest. Du Bois writes that the time has come "when the grandson of a slave has to teach democracy to a president of Harvard."

September 19. Radio station WBZ makes its first broadcast, live from the Eastern States Exposition in Springfield. Granted the first radio station license in Boston on September 15, WBZ has its first studio in a Westinghouse plant in Springfield. An affiliated station in Boston, WBZA, begins broadcasting from a studio at the Hotel Brunswick in Boston in 1924, then switches call letters with the Springfield station to become WBZ in March 1931.

1922

The Colonial Filling Station is completed on Massachusetts Avenue in the South Bay. Designed by Coolidge and Carlson, the round, domed building is later converted to a fruit stand.

February 24. The first bus route in Boston is established. Replacing a streetcar line, the route runs along North Beacon Street from Union Square to the North Beacon Street Bridge.

June 10. The Boston Elevated Railway Company officially takes over the West End Railway and becomes responsible for all Boston transit lines and stations.

 January 27. Upon his death, the businessman George Robert White bequeaths $5.5 million "for creating works of public utility and beauty for the use and enjoyment of the inhabitants of the City of Boston." Daniel Chester French's statue of George Robert White is installed in the Public Garden in 1924.

 M. A. De Wolfe Howe's *Memories of a Hostess* is published.

 November 7. Susan Walker Fitzgerald is elected state representative from Jamaica Plain. She is the first woman Democrat elected to the state legislature; the first woman Republican, Sylvia Donaldson, a state representative from Brockton, is elected at the same time.

 Latin School moves to a new building, designed by James McLaughlin, at 78 Avenue Louis Pasteur in the Fenway. Dedicated on May 17, 1923, the building is enlarged in 1933, and renovated and expanded in 1989 and again in 2002.

When the incoming freshman class is 21 percent Jewish, Harvard's President Lowell calls for imposing a quota on the number of Jewish students admitted. The Board of Overseers, however, rules against excluding students on the basis of race or ethnic background in April 1923.

 Jack's Joke Shop opens on Hanover Street. Reportedly the first novelty and joke store in the United States, it later moves to 197 Tremont Street, then to 38 Boylston Street.

December 23. The *Boston Globe* mourns the demise of "fakirs' row," where street peddlers set up along Tremont Street every Christmas, selling toys, games, and other gifts.

 October 23. Mayor Curley bans Isadora Duncan from further performances in Boston. The mayor takes the action because of complaints about Duncan's transparent dancing costume and her onstage declaration of support for the Soviet regime and for her husband, the Soviet poet Sergei Yesenin.

1923

 September 8. Boston Airport officially opens in East Boston; it was previously called East Boston Airport and was operated by the U.S. Army. Those using the new municipal airport must be ferried there from the mainland. The first passenger service begins in 1927, and the first regularly scheduled passenger service to New York on April 15, 1929. The state takes over operation from the city in 1941, and the airport is renamed for Maj. Gen. Edward Logan of South Boston, a commander of the Yankee Division in World War I (who reportedly had never been in an airplane) in 1943. The State Airport Management Board assumes authority in 1948 and the Massachusetts Port Authority in 1959. Over

the years, the airport is expanded by more than fourteen hundred acres through filling and the takeover of Governor's Island in 1942, Apple and Bird Islands in 1948, and Wood Island Park in 1969.

The G & G Delicatessen opens at 1106 Blue Hill Avenue in Dorchester. Owned and operated by Irving Green and Charlie Goldstein, the restaurant is the social and political center for the predominantly Jewish neighborhood. The author Mark Mirsky later writes: "On the tables of the cafeteria, talmudic jurisprudence sorted out racing results, politics, the stock market, and the student could look up from his 'desk' to leer at the young girls sipping cream soda under the immense wings of their mothers; watch the whole world of Blue Hill Avenue revolve through the G & G's glass gate."

In *The Boston Public Schools Past and Present*, Thornton Apollonio writes: "The relationship between City Hall and the School Committee, or in other words, between the mayor and the School Committee, has varied from time to time. . . . Some mayors have attempted what the School Committee considered to be unwarranted interference in the administration of the schools, and such effort has always met with prompt and vigorous opposition."

Hindy, the *Boston Post* cat, dies. After arriving in the newspaper's office a few years earlier, the cat first wins fame through stories by the reporter Herb Baldwin. Eventually, a column appears under Hindy's byline and more than one hundred thousand photos are sent to people who request them. The cat is buried in an animal cemetery in Methuen; the inscription on its tombstone reads: "Here Lies/HINDY/the Boston Post's/Famous Cat."

The Moscow Art Theater, directed by Constantin Stanislavsky, makes its only Boston appearance at the Opera House. The group performs a repertory that includes Chekhov's *The Cherry Orchard* and a version of *The Brothers Karamazov* called *In the Claws of Life*.
The psychic Margery, the Canadian-born wife of Dr. Le Roi Goddard Crandon, a lecturer at Harvard Medical School, begins holding seances in her home at 10 Lime Street on Beacon Hill. Mrs. Crandon's psychic powers are consulted by fashionable Bostonians, investigated by *Scientific American* magazine, and doubted by Harry Houdini.

1924

Old Colony Parkway is completed. It is renamed the William Morrissey Boulevard, after the former chairman of the Massachusetts District Commission, in 1951.
September 6. Six U.S. Army officers making the first around-the-world flight land at Boston Airport. They are greeted by a crowd estimated at more than one million people.

Almont Street Park in Mattapan is added to the city's park system.

November 4. Republican Alvan Fuller (with 650,000 votes) defeats Democrat James Michael Curley (with 490,000) for governor.

The state revises Boston's charter again, replacing the nine-member at-large City Council with a twenty-two-member City Council, with one councilor elected from each ward of the city. The city's ward boundaries are redrawn to their present boundaries. The change is the result of special state legislation, effective January 1, 1926.

The Aristo Club is organized by Wilhelmina Crossen and others. Its goal is to teach African-American history in the community and in the Boston schools. The club sponsors the first official Negro History Week program in Boston in 1926 and remains active into the 1970s.

The Boston Fire Department retires its last fire horse.

The Boston School Committee is reorganized by an amendment to the city charter; its five members are to be elected for staggered, four-year terms.

The Boston stockbroker L. Sherman Adams introduces the Massachusetts Investors Trust. The first mutual fund ever offered, it is initially called a "Boston fund." Adams's company is today MFS Investment Management.

M. A. De Wolfe Howe's *Barrett Wendell and His Letters* is published.
Serge Koussevitzky succeeds Pierre Monteux as conductor of the Boston Symphony Orchestra. Considered one of the great figures in twentieth century music—as musician, conductor, composer, music publisher, teacher, and promoter of new music and musicians' rights—he is named to the newly created post of music director in 1947 and serves until 1949.*

December 1. The Boston Bruins beat the Montreal Maroons 2–1 at Boston Arena, in the team's first home game in its first year in the National Hockey League. The Bruins lose to the Montreal Canadiens 1–0 in their first game in the new Boston Garden, on November 20, 1928.

1925

Mayor Curley declares, "The port of Boston, which for more than a century occupied the first place commercially . . . and a harbor once alive with the shipping of the nations of the world is today merely a port of call."

Frances Greely Curtis becomes the first woman to run for mayor of Boston. A thirteen-year member of the Boston School Committee, she declares: "With women in office, there will be no graft. Women will not stand for graft." Curtis, however, fails to collect enough signatures to get her name on the ballot.
November 3. Malcolm Nichols (with 64,492 votes) defeats Theodore Glynn (with 42,687), John O'Neil (31,888), Daniel Coakley (20,144), and others to be elected mayor. The last Republican mayor of Boston, Nichols is a former regional head of the Internal Revenue Service. Ironically, his administration would be criticized for allowing corruption.

The Women's Municipal League's *Our Boston* is published.

The Eliot Hotel opens at 370 Commonwealth Avenue. Originally built as an adjunct for the Harvard Club, it becomes a residential hotel in 1940s, and then a luxury "boutique" hotel in the 1980s.

July 4. Shortly before 3:00 A.M., the Dreyfus Hotel at 12 Beach Street collapses, killing forty-four people. The collapse is attributed to dancers doing the Charleston in the second-floor Pickwick Club, but the building had been damaged by a fire just ten weeks before.

September 13. Temple Mishkan Tefila is dedicated on Seaver Street in Roxbury. The congregation moves to Newton in 1957, and the building is sold first to a Lubavitcher Hasidim congregation in 1958, then to the Elma Lewis School of Fine Arts in 1968.

The Lahey Clinic opens at 605 Commonwealth Avenue. Founded by Dr. Frank Lahey, it specializes in surgery but has no inpatient facilities, utilizing those of other Boston hospitals instead. The clinic builds its own hospital and moves to suburban Burlington in 1980.

Amy Lowell's book of poetry *What's O'Clock* is published. It wins a Pulitzer Prize in 1926.
October 16. The Metropolitan Theatre opens at 270 Tremont Street. Designed by Clarence Blackall as a "movie palace" several years before New York City's Radio City Music Hall is built, it is New England's largest theater, with more than thirty-eight hundred seats. An estimated twenty thousand people attend the first night celebration, and the *Boston Advertiser* describes them "rubbing their eyes and wondering if it was all a dream." Performers would include Jack Benny and George Burns and Gracie Allen. It becomes the Music Hall in 1958, the Metropolitan again in 1980, and the Wang Center for the Performing Arts in 1983.
November 10. The Huntington Theatre opens at 264 Huntington Avenue, with a performance of Sheridan's *The Rivals.* Designed by J. William Beal and Sons, the Georgian Revival–style building is originally called the Repertory Theatre and is home to a short-lived professional repertory company. It closes in 1930, then reopens first as the Esquire movie theater, then the Civic Repertory Theatre, featuring out-of-work actors as part of the federal WPA project. It becomes the Boston University Theatre in 1958, and later assumes its current name.

1926 to 1950

1926

The Senator John W. Weeks Footbridge over the Charles River opens, connecting Allston and Cambridge.

A. M. Leahy and Dr. Charles G. Lutts, employees at the Charlestown Navy Yard, invent the Die-Lock Chain. Quickly adopted by the U.S. Navy, it helps to restore the Navy Yard's place as a center for research and refitting of navy ships.

Amelia Earhart applies for job placement assistance at the Women's Educational and Industrial Union. On her application it is noted, "Holds a sky pilots license!" She subsequently gets a job teaching English to immigrant children at a settlement house in Chinatown.

Roslindale High School opens at 110 Poplar Street. The school closes in 1976, and the building is later converted to housing for the elderly.

April 5. H. L. Mencken's *Mercury* magazine is banned in Boston. After selling a copy of it to J. Frank Chase, secretary of the Watch and Ward Society, on Boston Common, Mencken is charged with purveying obscenity, arrested, then released on his own recognizance. The next day, Judge James Parmenter dismisses the case. Mencken celebrates by going to lunch at the Harvard Club with Professor Zachariah Chafee and Felix Frankfurter. But the day after, at the urging of the Watch and Ward Society, the post office bars the *Mercury* from using the mail.

April 13. The Red Sox lose to the Yankees 12–11 in their home opener at Fenway Park. In the first radio broadcast of a Red Sox game, Gus Rooney is the announcer on WNAC. Other Red Sox radio and television broadcasters would include Jim Britt (1940–1950), Curt Gowdy (1951–1965), Ned Martin (1961–1992), Ken Coleman (1966–1974 and 1979–1989), and Joe Castiglione and Jerry Trupiano (1983 to the present).

April 21. The Braves beat the Phillies 2–1 in their home opener, the first of the team's games to be broadcast, also by Gus Rooney on WNAC.

1927

Resentful at being excluded from Boston society, Joseph Kennedy moves his family to Riverdale in the Bronx, New York. "I was born here," he reportedly declares. "My children were born here. What the hell do I have to do to be treated like an American?"

May 18. The Ritz-Carlton Hotel opens. It is designed by Strickland, Blodgett, and Law for Edward Wyner, the owner. Telephone reservations are not accepted, and all guests must be approved by Wyner, who bases his judgment on their social standing. Those guests would include Winston Churchill, John F. Kennedy, Charles Lindbergh, and numerous actors, playwrights, and composers.

March 10. The Statler-Hilton Hotel and Office Building (today's Park Plaza Hotel and Towers) opens in Park Square. It is the first hotel in the city to have bathrooms, telephones, and radios in every room.

July 22. Charles Lindbergh visits Boston on his way home from his historic flight across the Atlantic on May 20–21. After landing at Boston Airport, he is given a ticker-tape parade, speaks at Boston Arena, and is celebrated with fireworks at Boston Common.

Kelly's Landing opens in a former boathouse between Carson Beach and Castle Island in South Boston. The restaurant is owned and operated by Larry and Maizie "Ma" Kelly and their children. The building is destroyed by Hurricane Carol and a subsequent fire in 1954. The restaurant later reopens in a new building nearby, and continues to operate until 1974. A new restaurant, named The Original Kelly's Landing and operated by the Kellys' grandchildren, opens at L and East Fourth Street in 2004.

August 23. At 12:03 A.M., Sacco and Vanzetti are executed at Charlestown State Prison. They were sentenced to death by Judge Webster Thayer on April 9, but the execution was delayed until a review of the trial was completed by the so-called Lowell Committee (made up of Harvard President A. Lawrence Lowell, MIT President Samuel Stratton, and Judge Robert Grant). The committee released a report on August 7 that concluded that the two men had received a fair trial. On August 21, Governor Alvan Fuller spent the entire day in his office receiving all the numerous protestors who came to Boston, including Edna St. Vincent Millay, whose poem "Justice Denied in Massachusetts" appeared that day in the *New York Times.* Before he is executed, Vanzetti declares: "That last moment belongs to us. That agony is our triumph." The funeral is held on August 28. Fifty thousand begin the march to the Forest Hills Cemetery, while two hundred thousand line the route, standing in the rain. The bodies of the two men are cremated, and their ashes are today stored in a locked vault in the Boston Public Library.

The Catholic archbishop's residence is completed at 2101 Commonwealth Avenue in Brighton. Construction of the Italian Renaissance–style villa was supported by a bequest from the theater magnate Benjamin F. Keith. The building and grounds are sold to Boston College in 2004.

May. After a bookstore clerk is arrested for selling Upton Sinclair's book *Oil!* because it contains a single reference to birth control, Sinclair comes to Boston. He attempts to sell the book himself to a policeman, then parades through the streets, wearing a fig leaf–shaped sandwich board and trying to sell the book—minus the offending passage. Other books banned this year include *Elmer Gantry, The Sun Also Rises, Manhattan Transfer*, and *An American Tragedy*.

January 28. Aaron Copland's *Concerto for Piano (in One Movement)* is given its world premiere by the Boston Symphony Orchestra, Serge Koussevitzky conducting and Copland as soloist, at Symphony Hall. Boston music critics call it "insulting" and a "shocking lack of taste" (the *Herald*), "concatenation of meaninglessly ugly sounds" (the *Post*), and a "harrowing horror from beginning to end" (the *Transcript*).

February. Ridgley Torrence's *The Rider of Dreams* is performed by the Boston Stage Society. It is said to be the first play about African Americans to attract a wider audience in Boston.

April 13. The Bruins lose to the Ottawa Senators 3–1 in the fourth and final game of the Stanley Cup finals.

1928

August 30. The Sears, Roebuck and Company building opens on Park Drive in the Fenway. Designed by George Nimmons in the Art Moderne style, it closes in 1986 and reopens as the Landmark Center in 2000.

November 14. North Station is dedicated on Causeway Street. President Calvin Coolidge throws a switch in the White House to turn on the lights in the station via telegraph.

October 18. Boston police draw up a "deadline" around Chinatown, refusing to let anyone enter as they search for what the *Boston Herald* describes as ten "out of town gunmen" suspected of involvement in a three-day "tong war" between the Hip Sing and the On Leong Chinese gangs.

October 12. An artificial respirator is first used at Children's Hospital. Credit for the idea of the so-called iron lung is given to the Harvard researchers Philip Drinker and Louis Agassiz Shaw.

Upton Sinclair's *Boston* is published. Based on the Sacco and Vanzetti trial, the novel is immediately banned by the New England Watch and Ward Society. The society's action prompts Edward Weeks to lead a campaign that results in the modification of the state's obscenity laws in 1930. Under the new law, books cannot be banned for containing obscene passages, only for being obscene in and of themselves. A law making the sale of obscenity by booksellers a civil rather than criminal matter is passed in 1945.

October 29. The B. F. Keith Memorial Theatre opens at 539 Washington Street. Designed by Thomas Lamb in the Beaux Arts style, it is built by E. F. Albee in honor of his late partner, who became known as the "father of vaudeville." The 2,300-seat theater is later renamed the Savoy, then, after it is purchased by the Opera Company of Boston in 1978, the Opera House. It closes in 1990, is restored, and reopens with a performance of *The Lion King* on July 16, 2004.

November 17. Boston Garden opens, built by George Lewis ("Tex") Rickard. The first event in the 14,890-seat arena is a benefit boxing match in which local featherweight Dick ("Honey Boy") Finnegan beats the welterweight champion André Routis in a nontitle bout. Boston Garden closes with a grand finale night of entertainment on September 29, 1995, and is demolished in May 1998.

November 29. East Boston High School beats South Boston High School on Thanksgiving Day, as Ralph Colson scores a record twelve touchdowns.

1929

The Hyde Park Municipal Center is built at 1179 River Street.

Nicola Sacco and Bartolomeo Vanzetti. (Courtesy of the Boston Herald)

August 26. The trolley line opens from Ashmont through Cedar Grove in Dorchester to Mattapan Square. Still in use, it is reportedly the only mass transit line in the United States that runs through a cemetery.

November 5. Democrat James Michael Curley (with 117,084 votes) defeats Frederick Mansfield (with 96,626) and others to win a third term as mayor. Inaugurated on January 6, 1930, at Symphony Hall, Curley promises "work and wages." His early support for Franklin Delano Roosevelt is reportedly not rewarded with significant New Deal federal assistance for Boston.

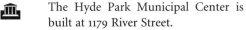

The Napoleon Club opens at 52 Piedmont Street. Boston's most popular gay nightclub of the era, it closes in 1998. The building is later turned into luxury condominiums.

January 1. Legislation goes into effect requiring all Boston public school teachers to possess a college degree as of January 1, 1934.
Boston College Law School opens.

September 6. Letitia Campfield and Frances Harris become the first two African-American women admitted to the School of Nursing at Boston City Hospital. Dr. John Hall II becomes the first African-American intern to train at Boston City Hospital in 1931.
The Jewish Memorial Hospital and Rehabilitation Center opens at 59 Town-

A concert at the Hatch Shell, 1943. (Courtesy of the Bostonian Society)

send Street in Roxbury. Originally called the Greater Boston Bikur Cholim Hospital, it opens in the former Beth Israel Hospital, and is expanded over the years.

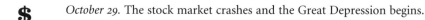

$ *October 29.* The stock market crashes and the Great Depression begins.

 July 4. The Boston Pops, Arthur Fiedler conducting, performs its first annual free, open-air concert on today's Esplanade in a wooden "shell" constructed by the Metropolitan District Commission. A second, metal shell is built in 1934. The third and current building, the Edward A. Hatch Memorial Shell designed by Richard Shaw, is dedicated on July 2, 1940. A gift from Maria Hatch in memory of her brother, the shell undergoes a renovation by Notter, Finegold, and Alexander, completed on July 2, 1991.

September 30. Eugene O'Neill's *Strange Interlude*, scheduled to be performed at the Hollis Street Theatre, is banned in Boston by Mayor Nichols, who had seen the play in New York. It is subsequently performed in Quincy and attended by that city's Mayor McGrath.

The Egyptian Theatre opens at 326 Washington Street in Brighton Center. Built as a movie house, the seventeen-hundred-seat theater closes in 1959.

April 22. The Ringling Brothers and Barnum and Bailey Circus performs for the first time at Boston Garden.

January 26. The first Knights of Columbus Track Meet is held at Boston Garden. The Olympic champion Pavo Nurmi of Finland wins the two-mile race in nine minutes and twelve seconds.

March 29. The Bruins beat the Rangers 2–0 at Madison Square Garden in the first Stanley Cup competition between two U.S. teams. The Bruins sweep the two-game series and win the team's first Stanley Cup.

1930

Boston's population is 781,188, the ninth largest of any city in the United States. Of that number, 22,432 are described in the U.S. Census as "Negro and Other Races," including 20,574 who are African American. The census reports 233,687 are foreign born: 43,932 from Ireland, 31,359 from Russia, and 36,274 from Italy. An estimated 85,000 are Jewish.

The Boston Planning Board issues its "Report on a Thoroughfare Plan for Boston." It contains recommendations for construction of a central artery, a tunnel to East Boston, and a system of "radial highways." Similar recommendations are later made by the state in 1948.*

February 19. The United Shoe Machine Building opens at 160 Federal Street. Designed by Parker, Thomas, and Rice in the Art Deco style, it is the first building to conform to the 1928 "pyramid" amendment to the city's zoning code, which allows buildings to exceed the height limit provided their upper floors are set back from the street. The building is renovated and renamed the Landmark in 1987.

July 20. The first traffic light in the city is installed at the intersection of Stuart and Tremont Streets.

October 12. Columbus Park is dedicated in South Boston. It is renamed for U.S. Representative J. Joseph Moakley in 2001.
Roberts Playground in Dorchester is added to the city's park system.

Mary Caroline Crawford's *Famous Families of Massachusetts* is published. The book begins with Oliver Wendell Holmes, Sr.'s definition of family: "Four or five generations of gentlemen and gentlewomen; among them a member of his Majesty's Council for the Province, a Governor or so, one or two Doctors of Divinity, a member of congress, not later than the time of long boots with tassels."
Samuel Eliot Morison's *Builders of the Bay Colony* and *Growth of the American Republic* (written with Henry Steele Commager) are published.
September 14–20. "Boston Week" caps a summerlong celebration of the city's tercentenary. Events include a 10,000-person "town meeting" in the Public Garden and an eight-hour parade featuring 40,000 marchers, 108 units, and 200 floats, which are watched by an estimated one million people. At Faneuil Hall, Mayor Curley places a letter in a time capsule, to be opened in 1980, in which he expresses the hope "that the career of the Mayor of 1980 would not be as tempestuous" as his had been.

August. The Hotel Manger opens next to North Station. Renamed the Hotel Madison in 1958, it closes in 1976. The building is imploded on May 15, 1983.

Tufts–New England Medical Center is established in the South Cove.

May. The Edward Kirstein Business Branch Library, designed by Putnam and Cox, opens at 20 City Hall Avenue. Modeled after the arch of Bulfinch's Tontine Crescent, the building is donated to the city by the businessman Louis Kirstein, in honor of his father.

 May 7. Arthur Fiedler becomes the eighteenth conductor of the Boston Pops Orchestra. The first American to hold the post, he continues until his death in 1979.
December 19. Igor Stravinsky's *Symphony of Psalms* is given its American premiere by the Boston Symphony Orchestra. The piece was commissioned by the BSO for its fiftieth anniversary.

 April 3. The Bruins lose to the Canadiens 4–3 in Montreal in the second and final game of the Stanley Cup championship.

1931

 The gangster Frank Wallace, leader of the Gustin Gang, is shot and killed while attending a meeting with Joe Lombardi in the North End. Wallace is reportedly killed either because he was trying to expand his organization's activities beyond South Boston or as a show of strength by the emerging Boston chapter of the Mafia.

 January 27. An exhibit of modern paintings by "Pavel Jerdanowitch" is held at the Vose Galleries. Although the "art" had previously won critical acclaim in New York, Chicago, and Paris, the show is later revealed to be a hoax perpetrated by Paul Jordan Smith and abetted in Boston by the gallery owner Robert Vose. The *Boston Post* lauds them for "introducing this element of humor" into the art world, but Charles Hovey Pepper, a member of the Boston Five group of Modernist painters, decries the "cheap attempt to discredit the modernist movement."
October 10. George Henschel returns to Boston to conduct the Boston Symphony Orchestra on its fiftieth anniversary. The program is almost identical to the first one played in 1881, except that Weber's *Jubilee Overture* is replaced by the prelude to Wagner's *Die Meistersinger von Nürnberg.*

1932

 The Uphams Corner Municipal Building opens at 500 Columbia Road.

 January 1. Governor's Square is renamed Kenmore Square.

July 1. Denied a place in the Massachusetts delegation to the Democratic convention in Chicago, which supported Al Smith, Mayor Curley casts a vote for Franklin Delano Roosevelt as a delegate from Puerto Rico.
November 8. Joseph Langone, Jr., is elected state senator, becoming the first Italian-American from Boston in the Massachusetts legislature.
March 23. The Boston Municipal Research Bureau is established "to study Boston's fiscal, management, and administrative problems." Bentley Warren is the first chairman. At the organization's sixtieth anniversary in May 1992, its longtime president Sam Tyler describes the "love-hate relationship" between the

Mayor James Michael Curley throws out the first pitch at Fenway Park. (Photograph courtesy of the Boston Public Library, Print Department)

bureau and the city: "They love us when we say nice things, they hate us when we're critical."

A. Lawrence Lowell's *Conflict of Principle* is published.

Rabbi Joseph Soloveitchik arrives in Boston. Known as "the Rav" (Hebrew for "rabbi"), he becomes an international leader in the Orthodox Jewish community for the next fifty years.

Ivan Kreuger commits suicide in his Paris apartment. Later called the "Swedish con man," he had, over the previous ten years, convinced Lee, Higginson and Company to sell $150 million worth of stock in his International Match Corporation. He kills himself when the company sends officials to audit his books. Lee, Higginson is forced to close as a result of the scandal.

Chez Vous roller skating rink opens on Rhoades Street in Dorchester. It is purchased by Bernard and Faye Leventhal two years later and operated by them for many years. John and Dorcas Dunham operate the rink in the 1980s, and it is currently owned and operated by Edward "Bert" Toney.

The Paramount Theatre, designed by Arthur Bowditch in the Art Deco style, opens at 549 Washington Street.

June 21. Jack Sharkey beats Max Schmeling in a fifteen-round decision in Long Island City, New York, to win the world heavyweight boxing championship. A Binghamton, New York, native, Sharkey had moved to Boston after leaving the navy, trained at the Friend Street Gym, and was described by sportswriters as an "adopted Bostonian" (also the "Boston Gob"). He loses the title in a three-round knockout by Primo Carnera on June 29, 1933. After retiring, he operates Sharkey's Ringside Tavern on Causeway Street until 1954.

1933

The Paul Revere Mall (also called the Prado) opens in the North End.

November 7. Democrat Frederick Mansfield (with 70,035 votes) defeats Malcolm Nichols (with 68,312), William Foley (60,776), and others to be elected mayor. A fiscal conservative, Mansfield declares that, despite the Depression, "I am not willing to believe that in meeting the city's obligation to welfare recipients the public money must be wasted, inefficiency must be tolerated, or a system which invites fraud must be permitted."

William Monroe Trotter organizes a demonstration urging African-American businessmen in the Northampton and Dudley Street areas to hire African-American employees. The future Roxbury activist Melnea Cass participates in what is her first demonstration.

December 5. Boston's celebration of the end of Prohibition is said to rival the one at the end of World War I. The first three restaurants granted new liquor licenses in the city are the Copley Plaza, Jacob Wirth's, and Joe and Nemo's. The Dugout Café opens the next day, and reportedly becomes the oldest bar in continuous operation in the same location in Boston.
Menus at the Ritz-Carlton dining room are changed from French to English.
The Ritz-Carlton Roof Garden opens. Eddie Duchin leads the band that performs on opening night. The room is damaged by a hurricane and closes in 1946. It reopens in 1993, with Duchin's son, Peter, leading the band on opening night.

The gangster Charles "King" Solomon, owner of the Cocoanut Grove nightclub, is gunned down in a Boston nightclub. His last words are reportedly "The dirty rats got me." After his death, ownership of the Cocoanut Grove passes to his lawyer, Barnett Welansky, whose bookkeeper is Rosa Gnecchio Ponzi, wife of the convicted swindler Charles Ponzi.

October. James Conant succeeds A. Lawrence Lowell as president of Harvard. Described in a biography as a "Dorchester boy," he creates a more diverse student body, involves the university in national and international issues, and later declares: "Behold the turtle. He makes progress only when he sticks his neck out." He serves until 1953.*
The Boston Center for Adult Education is founded by Dorothy Hewitt as a place where "small groups of men and women would meet together in living room settings to learn, discuss, and create for the sheer pleasure of doing so." The first classes are held in the home of Mr. and Mrs. Walter Baylies at 5 Commonwealth Avenue, a building the institution purchases in 1941.

February. In an article entitled "Boston," *Fortune* magazine reports: "there can be no doubt but that the Bostonian has suffered a decay and disintegration of tragic proportions . . . the Bostonian of today has withdrawn from productive enterprise. He has lost the active management of his industries." The article continues: "The great family trusts stand between the Bostonians and the activities of contemporary life like the transparent but all too solid glass which separates the angel fish of an aquarium from the grubby little boys outside." The author Russell Adams later explains, "As the first city to make large amounts of money, Boston became also the first city to grow preoccupied with conserving it."

The Old Mr. Boston distillery opens at 1010 Massachusetts Avenue, founded by two Boston natives, Irwin "Red" Benjamin and Hyman Berkowitz. The first edition of the company's *Old Mr. Boston Official Bartender's and Party Guide* is published in 1935. ("Old" drops out of the title in 1980.) The company moves to Owensboro, Kentucky, in 1981.

January 18. The Old Howard Theatre is closed down for thirty days after complaints by the Watch and Ward Society of "voluptuous dancing and profane language." It reopens with a production entitled *Scrambled Legs.* "I was continually badgered by the eager, lip-pursing members of the New England Watch and Ward Society," Mayor Curley later writes, "who combined the fervor of bird-feeders and disciples of the Anti-Vivisection Society." He also declares: "the Old Howard is known in every port of the world. It is one of Boston's great institutions."

February 21. Tom Yawkey buys the Red Sox from J. A. "Bob" Quinn and immediately begins to renovate Fenway Park, removing "Duffy's Cliff" and adding a 37-foot high wall in left field. The wall is painted green in 1947 and becomes known as "the Green Monster." Seats are added above the wall in 2003. "It was built in 1912 and rebuilt in 1934," John Updike writes in 1960, "and offers, as do most Boston artifacts, a compromise between Man's Euclidean determinations and Nature's beguiling irregularities."

1934

June 30. The Sumner Tunnel opens to East Boston. It is named for War of 1812 Gen. William H. Sumner.

November 6. Democrat James Michael Curley defeats Republican Gaspar Griswold Bacon to win his only term as governor. Before taking his oath of office at the State House in January 1935, Curley throws a punch at his predecessor, Joseph Ely. Although most biographers describe his gubernatorial tenure as less than successful, the American Federation of Labor president William Green declares, "More progressive, constructive, liberal laws were enacted under Curley in two years than under all previous administrations in any ten-year period."

February 9. The temperature drops to eighteen degrees below zero—the coldest ever recorded in Boston.

Jeremiah Burke High School for Girls, designed by George Ernest Robinson, opens at 60 Washington Street in Dorchester. Named for a former Boston school superintendent, the school later becomes coeducational.

Two Boston City Hospital doctors, George Minot and William Murphy, and George Whipple of Peter Bent Brigham Hospital receive the 1934 Nobel Prize in Physiology and Medicine for developing a successful treatment for pernicious anemia.

Boston Edison ends its practice of providing free replacement lightbulbs to those who bring burned-out bulbs to the company's offices.
James Guilford opens Dunbar Barbers in lower Roxbury. He changes the name to Jimmy Guilford's Men's Hair Salon in 1945 and remains in business until 1973.

Elliot Norton begins reviewing plays for the *Boston Post*. One of the most influential theater critics in the country, Norton soon moves to the *Record-American* (later the *Herald American*). Known for assisting in "play doctoring" (making suggestions to improve plays making their pre-Broadway runs in Boston), Norton is awarded a Tony for his contributions to theater in 1970. He retires, and the first annual Elliot Norton Awards for excellence in local theater are presented, in 1982.
The Tremont, Majestic, and three other New England theaters are bombed. F. E. Leiberman, who leased and operated the theaters, blames theater owners afraid of competition.

1935

October. The Boston Housing Authority is created.

The Christian Science Center's Mapparium opens. Designed by Chester Lindsay Churchill, the stained-glass globe is thirty feet in diameter with a glass bridge running through it that allows visitors to experience a view from "inside" the earth.

Lucius Beebe's *Boston and the Boston Legend* and Samuel Eliot Morison's *The Founding of Harvard College* are published.

The United Way is established. It is originally called the Community Federation of Boston.
August. Father Charles Coughlin visits Boston. A reception for the "radio priest" from Michigan is held by the Boston City Council, and he is invited by Governor Curley to address the Massachusetts legislature, where he warns against Nazism and Communism.

The first Howard Johnson's restaurant in Boston opens at 800 Morrissey Boulevard in Dorchester. The building is destroyed by fire in 1981, and the site is now occupied by a Ramada Inn.
(ca.) Jordan Marsh begins its annual "Enchanted Village" Christmas display. Discontinued in the 1970s, it is resumed in 1989. The display later moves to a temporary structure on City Hall Plaza in 1998, then to the Hynes Convention Center in 2003.
Edward Filene's *Morals in Business* is published.

The Washington Street theater district on a snowy night, 1935. (Courtesy of the Bostonian Society, Arthur Hansen Collection)

George Santayana's *The Last Puritan* is published. Of one of the characters he writes, "never, except to funerals, did Mr. Nathaniel Alden walk *down* Beacon Hill."

There are fifty-five theaters operating in Boston during this year.

September 30. Porgy and Bess, starring Todd Duncan, Anne Wiggins Brown, and John Bubbles, premieres at the Colonial Theatre.

October 7. The Franklin Park Theatre opens at 616 Blue Hill Avenue with a Yiddish performance of *When Hearts Speak*.

November 4. Romeo and Juliet, starring Katherine Cornell and Maurice Evans in his American debut, opens at the Shubert Theatre.

April 19. John Kelley ("the Elder") wins his first Boston Marathon. He wins again in 1945.

May 25. The Braves lose 11–7 to the Pirates in Pittsburgh, despite three home runs by Babe Ruth. Released in February by the Yankees, Ruth signed with the Braves in hopes of later being named the team manager, but announces his retirement at Braves Field a week later.

July 10. Suffolk Downs Raceway opens in East Boston, drawing thirty-five thousand fans. Designed by Mark Linenthal, it is built for thoroughbred horse racing. The first annual Massachusetts Handicap (Mass Cap) is run on October 16. Harness races are held there from 1959 to 1970.

1936

The Charles River Embankment (later the Storrow Memorial Embankment, and today the Esplanade) opens. Filling began in 1931. Although a commission had recommended that a highway be constructed along the riverside park, the proposal was dropped when Helen Osborne Storrow, the widow of James J. Storrow and a $1 million contributor to the project, objected.

Ross Playground in Hyde Park is added to the city's park system.

President Roosevelt's reelection campaign stop in Boston includes a speech to a crowd of 175,000 on Boston Common and a visit to the G & G Deli in Dorchester.

November 3. Republican Henry Cabot Lodge, Jr., defeats Democrat James Michael Curley by 136,000 votes to win election to the U.S. Senate.

Joseph F. Dineen's *Ward Eight* is published.

The Institute of Contemporary Art is established. It is originally called the Boston Museum of Modern Art and is a branch of the Museum of Modern Art in New York. The organization becomes independent and changes its name to the Institute of Modern Art in 1939, then adopts its current name in 1948. James Sachs Plaut becomes the first director in 1939. He is succeeded by Thomas Messer (1957), Sue Thurman (1962), Andrew Hyde (1968), Sydney Rockefeller (1974), Gabriella Jeppson (1975), Stephen Prokopoff (1978), David Ross (1982), Milena Kalinovska (1991), and Jill Medvedow (1998 to the present). Located initially in the Back Bay, the institute moves to various sites in the Back Bay, the Fenway, Allston, and Quincy Market. It has been located at 955 Boylston Street since 1973. A new museum is planned for Fan Pier on the South Boston waterfront and scheduled to open in 2006.

The Boston Symphony Orchestra performs its first Berkshire Summer Music Festival concerts at the Holmwood estate. The orchestra moves to Tanglewood, the former Tappan family estate outside Lenox, in 1937. The six-thousand-seat open-air auditorium (later known as "The Shed") opens there in 1938. Serge Koussevitzky founds the Berkshire Music Center (now the Tanglewood Music Center) as a summer school for training young musicians in 1940. Leonard Bernstein is a member of the first class of students. Seiji Ozawa Hall, designed by William Rawn, opens on July 7, 1994.

February 6. Hamlet, starring John Gielgud in his Boston debut, opens at the Shubert Theatre.

1937

The Community Boat Club (today's Community Boating) is established. Founded by Joseph Lee, Jr., as a summer program for children from the West End, it is the oldest public sailing program in the country.

November 2. On election day, the *Boston Post* runs two front-page "endorsements" of James Michael Curley's opponent, Democrat Maurice Tobin: one by the newspaper, the other a six-year-old quote by Cardinal O'Connell, which makes it appear as if the cardinal is also endorsing Tobin. The *Post* distributes thirty thousand free newspapers to people coming out of Mass on All Soul's Day morning. Tobin (with 105,212 votes) defeats Curley (with 80,376), Nichols (55,247), Foley (28,184), and others to be elected mayor. He is a former state legislator and member of the Boston School Committee.

Mildred Gleason Harris becomes the first woman to serve on the Boston City Council, winning a special election to fill the vacant seat of her late brother, Richard.

The Maimonides School is founded by Rabbi Joseph Soloveitchik and his wife, Tonya. Named for a twelfth-century Jewish philosopher, the school begins with one class of six students. Initially located on Columbia Road in Dorchester, the school later moves to its first school building nearby in 1941, and then to Brookline in 1962.

John P. Marquand's Pulitzer Prize–winning novel, *The Late George Apley*, is published. In it the title character declares to his son: "I wonder if you know exactly what marriage means. It is, my boy, a damnably serious thing, particularly around Boston."
(*ca.*) The Hi-Hat Club opens at 572 Columbus Avenue in the South End. The first nightclub to feature bop, its performers would include Count Basie, Erroll Garner, Dizzy Gillespie, Woody Herman, and Illinois Jacquet. Charlie Parker records a live album there, *New Bird: Hi-Hat Broadcasts, 1953*, on December 14, 1952.

January 6. The Ice Follies makes its first appearance at Boston Garden.

1938

Old Harbor Village opens in South Boston. The first federally funded public housing development in the country, it is later renamed the Mary Ellen McCormack Development.

The Boston Planning Board recommends that the city, the state, and metropolitan communities join together to construct a central artery.

May 10. The state legislature repeals the law that prohibits the mayor of Boston from succeeding himself in office.
November 8. Democrat James Michael Curley is defeated in the gubernatorial election by Republican Leverett Saltonstall. During the campaign, a *Boston Transcript* columnist described Saltonstall as a Yankee with "a South Boston face."

The Ritz-Carlton Bar opens, with a separate area for ladies. Unescorted women are not allowed in the main bar until 1970.

Augusta Bronner becomes the first woman judge on the Boston Municipal Court and the first full-time female judge in Boston.

September 21. The Great New England Hurricane, the most destructive storm in Boston's history, strikes. Its 130-mile-an-hour winds cause six million dollars in damage and deposit enough sand to connect Deer Island to Winthrop. With Mayor Tobin on a speaking tour in California, the Boston City Council President John Kerrigan serves as acting mayor during the emergency.

The Catholic Youth Organization (CYO) is established in Boston. The organization starts chapters within individual Catholic schools to promote recreation and social activities.

Northeastern University moves to its current site on Huntington Avenue. The first building to open is the white-brick Richards Hall, designed by Shepley, Bulfinch, Richardson, and Abbott. Frank Palmer Speare is succeeded as president by Carl Ell (1940), Asa Knowles (1959), Kenneth Ryder (1975), John Curry (1989), and Richard Freeland (1996 to the present).

Surgeons at Children's Hospital perform the first successful surgery to correct a congenital heart defect.

March 14. The first issue of the *Mid-Town Journal* appears. Published by Frederick Shibley, the offbeat publication describes itself as "a local newspaper for local people." Its last issue appears on June 6, 1966.
October 30. Orson Welles's radio broadcast adaptation of H.G. Wells's *War of the Worlds* alarms Boston residents.

February 18. Nadia Boulanger becomes the first woman to lead the Boston Symphony Orchestra, conducting Fauré's Requiem.
January 25. Thornton Wilder's *Our Town*, starring Frank Craven, premieres at the Wilbur Theatre. According to the *Boston Herald* theater critic Elinor Hughes, the audience includes "a sizable group of Mr. Wilder's fellow Peterborough [New Hampshire] residents."
December 13. Thornton Wilder's *The Merchant of Yonkers*, starring Ruth Gordon, opens at the Colonial Theatre. Back in Boston, rewritten and retitled *The Matchmaker* in 1955, Wilder's work is finally a hit after being rewritten, renamed *Hello Dolly*, and recast with Carol Channing, in 1964.

June 29. Seabiscuit is scratched forty minutes before facing the 1937 Triple Crown winner War Admiral in the Massachusetts Handicap, disappointing a record crowd of sixty-six thousand at Suffolk Downs. The explanation for the withdrawal is given as a tendon injury, but there is speculation that the real reason is a desire to avoid running the horse in wet conditions. The two horses compete later in the year, with Seabiscuit winning the Pimlico Special in Baltimore on November 1.

1939

The new Suffolk County Court House building, designed by Desmond and Lord, opens in Pemberton Square. It is currently being renovated.

Eighteen thousand people, including Governor Saltonstall and Mayor Tobin, attend a birthday ball for President Franklin Roosevelt in Boston Garden.

February 28. Six people are killed and twenty-six injured when a trolley jumps the track on the curve at the intersection of Seaver Street and Blue Hill Avenue in Roxbury.

Father Joseph Manton begins preaching at novenas held at Mission Church. The services would attract attendees from all over Boston and the Boston area.

May 10. Ignacy Paderewski performs at the Boston Opera House. An estimated thirty-four hundred people crowd into the three-thousand-seat hall for one of the last concerts of the seventy-eight-year-old artist's career.

October 6. William Schuman's *American Festival Overture* receives its world premiere by the Boston Symphony Orchestra, Serge Koussevitzky conducting, at Symphony Hall.

October 10. Moss Hart and George Kaufman's *The Man Who Came to Dinner* premieres at the Colonial. The authors substantially rewrite the play while staying at the Ritz-Carlton Hotel.

April 16. The Bruins beat the Toronto Maple Leafs 3–1 in game 5 at Boston Garden to win their second Stanley Cup.

April 21. The George Wright Golf Course is dedicated in Hyde Park, with Mayor Tobin hitting a two-hundred-yard drive from the first tee. The eighteen-hole course is designed by Donald Ross. Built as a WPA project, it is named for the former baseball player and manager who later opened a sporting goods store and championed the sport of golf in Boston.

1940

Boston's population is 770,816, the ninth-largest of any city in the United States. Of that number, 25,350 are described as "Negro and Other Races," including 23,679 who are African American. A total of 184,080 are foreign born: 34,983 from Ireland, 28,014 from Russia, and 31,555 from Italy. An estimated 87,000 are Jewish.

The Charlestown, Lenox Street (lower Roxbury), Mission Main, and Old Colony (South Boston) public housing developments open.

Spring. Herbert Philbrick visits the Boston office of the Federal Bureau of Investigation (FBI) at 7 Water Street. Soon after, he agrees to become an informant for the agency and spends the next nine years reporting on Communist infiltration of various Boston area organizations. His testimony in New York on April 6, 1949, leads to the conviction of eleven people for conspiracy to overthrow the government.

Malcolm Little (later Malcolm X) arrives in Boston from Detroit. *The Autobiography of Malcolm X*, written with Alex Haley and published in the 1965, contains this passage: "Soon I ranged out of Roxbury and began to explore Boston proper. Historic buildings everywhere I turned, and plaques and markers and statues for famous events and men. One statue in Boston Common astonished me: a Negro named Crispus Attucks, who had been the first man to fall in the Boston Massacre. I had never known anything like it."

The neon Cities Service sign is erected in Kenmore Square. The company name is changed to CITGO in 1965. Darkened during the energy crisis in 1979, it is again illuminated beginning on August 10, 1983.

November 10. A *Boston Sunday Globe* headline reads, "Kennedy Says Democracy All Done in Britain, Maybe Here." Based on an interview by the reporter Louis Lyons with the ambassador to England, Joseph P. Kennedy, the story quotes Kennedy's declaration that "there's no sense in our getting in [the war]." Reactions to his comments prompts Kennedy to resign his post soon after.

Mabel Munson Swan's *The Athenaeum Gallery, 1827–1873: The Boston Athenaeum as an Early Patron of Art* is published.
January. Cab Calloway and Duke Ellington appear at the Roseland Ballroom.
The Savoy nightclub opens at 441 Columbus Avenue. It moves to 410 Massachusetts Avenue in 1943.
The Latin Quarter nightclub opens on Winchester Street in Bay Village. Originally called the Towne Club, it is owned and operated by Lou Walters, who later sells it to Mickey Redmond. The club closes in 1955.
February 27. Lillian Hellman's *Little Foxes*, starring Tallulah Bankhead, opens at the Colonial Theatre.

January 1. Boston College loses 6–3 to Clemson University in the Cotton Bowl in Dallas.
November 16. Boston College beats Georgetown 19–18 at Fenway Park, as Charlie O'Rourke takes an intentional safety after running twenty-three seconds off the clock on the last play of the game. The sportswriter Grantland Rice later calls it "the greatest college football game every played."
December 16. Joe Louis beats Al McCoy with a sixth round technical knockout to win the only world heavyweight boxing championship fight ever held at Boston Garden.

1941

Oscar Handlin's *Boston's Immigrants* is published. "Once I thought to write a history of the immigrant in America," Handlin later remarks. "Then I discovered that the immigrants *were* American history."

February 16. The Huntington Avenue subway opens; it is the second-largest WPA project to be completed. Stops include Mechanics, Symphony, and Opera Place.

The Victory Gardens are created in the Fenway.

Robert McCloskey's *Make Way for Ducklings* is published. An Ohio native who studied at Boston's Vesper Art School, McCloskey wins the Caldecott Medal for best children's picture book in 1942. The Newton artist Nancy Schön's bronze sculpture, *Mrs. Mallard and Her Eight Ducklings* (Jack, Kack, Lack, Mack, Nack, Ouack, Pack, and Quack), is installed in the Public Garden in 1987.
William Stanley Braithwaite's *The House under Arcturus: An Autobiography* is published.
December 9. Two days after the Japanese attack on Pearl Harbor, and a day

after the United States declares war on Japan, an air raid siren sounds in Boston at 2:00 P.M., causing considerable panic. It turns out that the alarm is only being tested. The United States declares war on Germany and Italy on December 11.

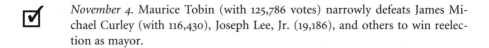 *November 4.* Maurice Tobin (with 125,786 votes) narrowly defeats James Michael Curley (with 116,430), Joseph Lee, Jr. (19,186), and others to win reelection as mayor.

The Ritz-Carlton welcomes the African-American actor and comedian Eddie "Rochester" Anderson as a guest. Dining room staff are directed to serve guests regardless of their race.

The Hildy Ellis controversy begins. When an unmarried Irish Catholic nurse from Boston discovers that the baby she put up for adoption was placed with a Jewish couple in Brookline, she demands the baby's return so she can place the child with a Catholic family. Court action and extensive newspaper coverage follow, and the Ellis family flees with the baby to Florida. They are arrested, but the governor of Florida refuses to extradite them to Massachusetts.

May 18. Adm. Richard Byrd and the members of his Antarctic expedition return to Boston Harbor aboard the barkentine *Bear*. The ship ties up at the same berth at the South Boston Army Base from which it had left Boston for the South Pole in November 1939.

January 1. Boston College beats the University of Tennessee 19–13 in the Sugar Bowl in New Orleans. The Eagles finish 11–0 and claim a share of the national collegiate football championship (along with Stanford and Minnesota). Three days later, the team is met by a crowd of one hundred thousand fans at South Station.
April 12. The Bruins beat the Detroit Red Wings 3–1 in game 4 to sweep the series and win the team's second Stanley Cup in the last three years.
September 28. Ted Williams collects six hits in eight at bats in a doubleheader at Philadelphia to finish the year at .406, becoming the last major league player to bat over .400 for the season. Williams had refused manager Joe Cronin's offer to sit out the games in order to protect his .3995 average—which would have been rounded off to .400.

1942

The New England Mutual Life Insurance Company building, designed by Cram and Ferguson, opens at 501 Boylston Street. The poet David McCord later describes the severe style of the building as an "Urn Burial/For a concern actuarial." The company is acquired by Metropolitan Life Insurance Company in 1996, and the building is sold in 2002.
The Orchard Park (Roxbury), Heath Street (Jamaica Plain), and Maverick (East Boston) public housing developments open.

Ted Williams is shown here batting in the Red Sox 1947 home opener at Fenway Park. (Courtesy of the Boston Herald)

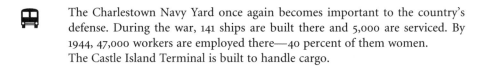

The Charlestown Navy Yard once again becomes important to the country's defense. During the war, 141 ships are built there and 5,000 are serviced. By 1944, 47,000 workers are employed there—40 percent of them women. The Castle Island Terminal is built to handle cargo.

Esther Forbes's *Paul Revere and the World He Lived In* and Samuel Eliot Morison's Pulitzer Prize–winning *Admiral of the Ocean Sea: A Life of Christopher Columbus* are published.

November 3. James Michael Curley is elected to Congress for the first of two consecutive terms.

Wally's Paradise opens at 428 Massachusetts Avenue in the South End. Owned and operated by Joseph Walcott, the club provides an opportunity for local jazz musicians and students to perform. Renamed Wally's Cafe, it moves to 427 Massachusetts Avenue in 1979, and is today owned and operated by Walcott's grandson Joseph.

November 15. Six Boston firefighters are killed and more than forty are injured fighting a fire at the Luongo Restaurant in East Boston. The blaze destroys the one-hundred-year-old Lyceum Hall building in Maverick Square. Although it is one of the most tragic fires in Boston history, it is almost forgotten when an even worse tragedy occurs two weeks later.
November 28. Four hundred ninety-two people are killed and 270 injured in the Cocoanut Grove fire at 17 Piedmont Street in Park Square. It is the greatest tragedy in terms of loss of lives in Boston history, and the worst nightclub fire in U.S. history. Initial reports suggest the fire started when a sixteen-year-old busboy lit a match so he could screw in a lightbulb, which a customer had

The Boston Advertiser *headline following the Cocoanut Grove fire, 1942. (Courtesy of the Bostonian Society)*

loosened to darken a booth. A subsequent investigation casts doubt on that theory, however. Despite a legal capacity of 460, an estimated 1,000 patrons were in the club at the time. The club's owner, Barnett Welansky, and his brother, James, the manager, are convicted of manslaughter and imprisoned. The disaster leads to improved fire and building codes (including the requirement that doors in public buildings open outward). It also leads to improved treatment for burn victims (through the use of penicillin) and for smoke inhalation.

The outbreak of World War II prompts the Museum of Fine Arts to secretly transfer many of its most valuable holdings to a secure, climate-controlled facility in Williamstown, Massachusetts.

The New England Conservatory Opera Workshop is founded by Boris Goldovsky.

December 3. The Boston Symphony Orchestra becomes the last major American professional orchestra to unionize. Its members are allowed to join the American Federation of Musicians, but only after a boycott of the orchestra is threatened by other unionized music institutions and record companies.

February 10. The Bruins beat the Montreal Canadiens 8–1. The "Kraut line" (Woody Dumart, Milt Schmidt and Bobby Bauer—all from Kitchener, Ontario) scores eleven points in their last game before leaving for service with the Royal Canadian Air Force in World War II.

November 28. Undefeated Boston College (a twenty-one-point favorite) loses to Holy Cross 55–12 at Fenway Park, in one of the biggest upsets in college football history. The loss prevents Boston College from playing in the Sugar Bowl, and deters many of the team's fans from attending a planned victory celebration that night at the Cocoanut Grove nightclub.

1943

The repeal by the U.S. Congress this year of the Chinese Exclusion Act of 1882 and passage in 1946 of the War Brides Act would lead to increased Chinese immigration to Boston.

William Foote Whyte's *Street Corner Society* is published.

A public school teacher, Grace Lonergan, challenges the Boston School Committee policy requiring that "a female teacher will resign upon marriage." A teacher at the Charles Taylor Elementary School for nearly twenty years, Lonergan had recently married a soldier who was then shipped overseas. Because of the shortage of teachers created by the war, Lonergan is subsequently allowed to continue teaching—but as a substitute, at a lower salary, and with no benefits. The ban on married teachers is finally overturned in September 1956.

The West Roxbury Veterans Administration Hospital opens.

The *Pilot* criticizes the comedian Bob Hope, who is entertaining troops fighting in World War II, for his mildly risqué humor, declaring that he is encouraging soldiers to "laugh at the wrong things."

January 28. The Duke Ellington Orchestra performs Ellington's *Black, Brown and Beige: A Tone Parallel to the History of the American Negro* at Symphony Hall.
May 15. Rodgers and Hammerstein's *Away We Go!* opens at the Colonial Theatre. The *Herald* theater critic Elinor Hughes comments, "the title could be improved." It is—to *Oklahoma!*—by the time it reaches Broadway.

April 8. The Bruins lose to Detroit 2–0 at the Boston Garden in the fourth and final game of the Stanley Cup championship.

1944

The Boston Society of Architects sponsors a competition, soliciting ideas to improve the city. The first-prize entry calls for creation of a Boston Metropolitan Authority, composed of representatives from all of the communities within twenty-five miles of Boston, governed by a legislative council elected by proportional representation, and run by a city manager. The third-prize entry calls for transforming the North and West Ends into "first-class residential sections."
December. Speaking at Faneuil Hall, the architect William Roger Greeley satirically bemoans the fact that Boston did not suffer "the advantage of widespread destruction by aerial bombardment," as London did, and so must "destroy our own diseased tissues and by heroic will-power rebuild our community as a worthy competitor of the newer type of city."

November 7. Boston's mayor, Maurice Tobin, is elected governor. He resigns as mayor on January 4 to assume the higher office, and the City Council president John E. Kerrigan serves as acting mayor until the next election.

The first Boston Cotillion is held, at which debutantes are presented to society. Organized by Margaret Howell, the event is held annually until 1996, then revived in 2002.

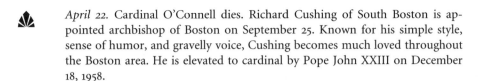

April 22. Cardinal O'Connell dies. Richard Cushing of South Boston is appointed archbishop of Boston on September 25. Known for his simple style, sense of humor, and gravelly voice, Cushing becomes much loved throughout the Boston area. He is elevated to cardinal by Pope John XXIII on December 18, 1958.

The human ovum is successfully fertilized in a test tube at the Free Hospital for Women.

Jean Stafford's *Boston Adventure* is published.
December 1. Béla Bartók's *Concerto for Orchestra* is given its world premiere by the Boston Symphony Orchestra, conducted by Serge Koussevitzky, who commissioned the piece.
October 17. Mary Coyle Chase's *The Pooka*, starring Frank Fay, opens at the Copley Theatre. The play's name is changed to *Harvey* during its Boston run, and it later becomes a hit on Broadway.
November 7. J. P. Marquand and George S. Kaufman's *The Late George Apley*, starring Leo G. Carroll, premiers at the Plymouth Theatre. "For the professional observer was not only watching George Apley and his family across the footlights," the theater critic Elinor Hughes later writes in her review, "but was sitting beside them in the orchestra. It was concentrated Boston, wherever you looked or however you listened."

March 8–9. The Tech Tourney high school basketball tournament moves to Boston Garden from its original site at Tufts University in Medford.
Labor Day. The first annual North American Chinese Invitational Volleyball Tournament is held in Chinatown. The event brings together teams from all over the United States and Canada.

1945

April 29. The "Battle of the Bricks" begins on Beacon Hill. A group of residents, described by the *Boston Post as* "Beacon Hill matrons, maintaining their poise and dignity," stages a demonstration on West Cedar Street to protest the replacement of their brick sidewalks with concrete. Their protest proves successful. Mayor Curley later orders the bricks reinstalled, and the demonstration is credited with sparking the preservation movement on Beacon Hill.

May 8. V-E Day marks the end of World War II in Europe.
August 14. V-J Day marks the end of World War II in the Pacific. A little after 7:00 P.M., news reports are received in Boston of the Japanese surrender. An estimated 750,000 people pour into Boston's streets in celebration.

November 6. James Michael Curley (with 111,824 votes) defeats John Kerrigan (with 60,413), William Arthur Reilly (46,135), and others to win his fourth and final term as mayor. He leaves Congress in midterm to assume the office.

After demonstrations are held calling for the hiring of African Americans in jobs other than elevator operators, Cynthia Belgrave becomes the first African-

American clerk at Gilchrist's downtown department store. Hired to wrap Christmas gifts, she is kept on after the holidays in the glassware department, and the store hires eight more African-American women as clerks.

January 4. In a famous—and possibly true—Boston story, firefighters who are called to the Somerset Club are directed by Joseph, a club employee, to go around to the service entrance in back. After dinner is over, Joseph announces: "There will be no dessert this evening, gentlemen. The kitchen is on fire."

Researchers at the Vincent Memorial Hospital of Massachusetts General perfect the use of the Pap Smear to detect cervical cancer.

Robert Lowell's Pulitzer Prize–winning *Lord Weary's Castle* is published.
Berklee College of Music opens at 284 Newbury Street. Originally called the Schillinger House of Music, the school adopts its current name in 1954 and shifts its emphasis to jazz. Larry Berk is the school's first president, and he is succeeded by his son, Lee (1979), then Roger Brown (2004). The school moves to the former Hotel Bostonian at 1140 Boylston Street, expands to the former Sherry Biltmore Hotel at 150 Massachusetts Avenue, and then to the adjacent former Fenway Theatre in 1972.
October 5. Aaron Copland's *Appalachian Spring* is performed by the Boston Symphony Orchestra, Serge Koussevitzky conducting, one day after its world premiere by the New York Philharmonic Orchestra.
April 3. Annie Get Your Gun, starring Ethel Merman, opens at the Shubert Theatre.
April 14. Rodgers and Hammerstein's *Carousel*, starring John Raitt, opens at the Colonial Theatre.

April 16. The Red Sox grant brief tryouts to three African-American baseball players—Jackie Robinson, Sam Jethroe, and Marvin Williams—but only after they are prodded by the African-American sportswriter Wendell Smith and by city councilor Isadore Muchnick and *Boston Daily Record* sportswriter Jack Egan. None of the players is signed to a contract.

1946

Walter H. Kilham's *Boston after Bulfinch: An Account of Its Architecture, 1800–1900* is published.

June 22. The Quabbin Reservoir begins operation, with the first water flowing through the Winsor Dam Spillway sixty-five miles east to Boston. At the time, it is the largest reservoir in the world devoted exclusively to the supply of water. Construction began in 1927.

January 18. Mayor Curley is convicted of ten counts of using the mails to defraud. The conviction is the results of his participation in a company on whose board he served while out of office, which swindled small contractors. His appeal of the conviction is not decided until 1947.*
November 5. John F. Kennedy, a Democrat, defeats the Republican Lester

Bowen to win election to the U.S. House of Representatives. During his campaign, Kennedy admitted that his long absence from Boston had made him "a stranger in the city of his birth."

Gov. Maurice Tobin is defeated in his bid for reelection by Robert Bradford.

Emily Greene Balch receives the Nobel Peace Prize. Born in Jamaica Plain, she is the first Bostonian to receive the award. A founder of the Denison House, the Boston Women's Trade Union League, and the Women's International League for Peace and Freedom, she is honored for her life's work fighting for peace and social justice.

Fontaine's Restaurant opens on Route 1 in West Roxbury. The neon sign of the flapping chicken is added in 1950. The restaurant is sold in 2004.

February. Malcolm Little (later Malcolm X) is convicted of possession of stolen goods in Middlesex Court. Sentenced to eight to ten years in prison, he is released from Charlestown State Prison in August 1952.

The Lowell Institute Broadcasting Council is established. A cooperative that includes six Boston colleges, it is formed to promote educational radio, and begins by broadcasting the Lowell Lectures on commercial stations.

December 9. Jean Cocteau's *The Eagle Rampant*, starring Tallulah Bankhead, opens at the Plymouth Theatre. A young Marlon Brando is a member of the cast—but only briefly. He is fired after the first performance for overacting in a death scene.

April 9. The Bruins lose to Montreal 6–3 in the fifth and final game of the Stanley Cup championship.

May 11. The Braves lose to the New York Giants 5–1 at Braves Field in the first major league night baseball game played in Boston. The Red Sox beat the Chicago White Sox 5–3 in the first night baseball game played at Fenway Park on June 13, 1947.

October 15. The Red Sox lose to the Cardinals 4–3 in game 7 of the World Series in St. Louis, as Enos Slaughter scores from first base on a double by Harry Walker in the eighth inning. Johnny Pesky is later criticized for holding the ball too long before making the relay throw to the plate. Others blame the substitute center fielder Leon Culberson, inserted for the injured Dom DiMaggio, for not getting the ball to Pesky quickly enough.

November 5. The Boston Celtics lose to Chicago 57–55 in their first home game, played at Boston Arena. The start of the game is delayed when the Celtics' Chuck Connors breaks one of the backboards during warm-ups. The game is the first to be played on the parquet floor, made up of 247 panels of maple, held together by 988 bolts, and constructed by the East Boston Lumber Company. The Celtics beat the Toronto Huskies 53–49 in their first game in Boston Garden on November 16.

1947

The Boston Housing Authority announces the New York Streets project in the South End. Boston's first urban renewal project, it involves demolition of a residential neighborhood to make way for industrial development. The project is completed in April 1964.

The "Old" John Hancock Building, designed by Cram and Ferguson, opens at 200 Berkeley Street. The weather antenna atop the twenty-six-story building is lit in 1950. The lighting code is: "Steady blue, clear view/flashing blue, clouds are due;/steady red, rain ahead/flashing red, snow instead." In summer the flashing red means the Red Sox game at Fenway Park has been canceled because of the weather. The current headquarters building opens in 1976.*
The Boston Trailer Park opens on the site of the former Caledonian Club off V.F.W. Parkway in West Roxbury. It is today the only remaining mobile home park in Boston.

August 29. The Metropolitan Transit Authority (MTA) is created by the Massachusetts legislature. The new entity absorbs the Boston Elevated Railway Company and is charged with providing transit service to Boston and thirteen other cities and towns in the Boston area.

Cleveland Amory's *The Proper Bostonians* is published. It contains marvelous stories of self-satisfied Bostonians, including "the Beacon Hill lady, who, chided for rarely leaving the city, asked simply, 'Why should I travel when I'm already here?'"
Charles Angoff's *When I Was a Boy in Boston* is published.

June 26. After his appeals fail, Mayor Curley is sentenced to serve six to eighteen months in a federal correction facility in Danbury, Connecticut. Because the City Council president, John Kelly, is under indictment for bribery (he is later acquitted), the Massachusetts legislature passes special legislation in order to appoint the City Clerk, John Hynes, acting mayor.
November 26. Curley's sentence is commuted by President Truman, after the entire Massachusetts congressional delegation (except for John F. Kennedy) signed a petition requesting his release. Curley returns to Boston the next day (Thanksgiving) and is greeted by five thousand well-wishers at South Station. Back at City Hall a day later, he boasts: "I have accomplished more in one day than has been done in the five months of my absence." The remark reportedly infuriates Hynes and prompts him to run against Curley in the next mayoral election.

Dr. Sidney Farber of Children's Hospital introduces chemotherapy to successfully treat cancer in children.

September 5. John Deferrari bequeaths over one million dollars to the Boston Public Library. A North End native and fruit merchant, he claims to have become wealthy "without benefit of a banker, a secretary, a bookkeeper, an automobile, or even a telephone." He later donates an additional five hundred thousand dollars to the library.
November 3. Tennessee Williams's *A Streetcar Named Desire*, starring Marlon Brando and Jessica Tandy, premieres at the Wilbur Theatre. The *Herald* theater critic Elinor Hughes credits Brando with "a mature and forceful performance

of the angry, boisterous, resentful Steve [*sic*]." Williams rewrites part of the play while staying at the Ritz-Carlton.

1948

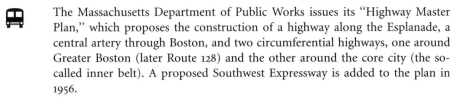

The Massachusetts Department of Public Works issues its "Highway Master Plan," which proposes the construction of a highway along the Esplanade, a central artery through Boston, and two circumferential highways, one around Greater Boston (later Route 128) and the other around the core city (the so-called inner belt). A proposed Southwest Expressway is added to the plan in 1956.

The Boston Public Garden is closed to the public to enable Shirley Temple to ride the Swan Boats. An estimated twenty-five thousand people line the iron fence around the park to watch.

David McCord's *About Boston* is published.

October 27. President Harry Truman speaks at a campaign rally in front of the G & G Deli in Dorchester.

Buzzy's Fabulous Roast Beef opens at 327 Cambridge Street in the West End. The restaurant closes because of bankruptcy in 1996, reopens later in the year, and closes for good on March 17, 2002.

Winter. Total snowfall in Boston is a record 89.2 inches, the most since official statistics began to be kept in 1890.

Boston University moves to its campus along the Charles River and Commonwealth Avenue. All its colleges, except the medical and dental schools, are located there by 1966. Daniel Marsh is succeeded as president by Harold Case (1951), Arland Christ-Janer (1967), John Silber (1971), Jon Westling (1996), and acting president Aram Chobanian (2003 to the present).

May 22. The Jimmy Fund is launched. Speaking from his hospital room, surrounded by members of the Boston Braves, Einar Gustafson, a twelve-year-old cancer patient from Maine (called "Jimmy" to protect his identity), makes a fund-raising appeal for the Children's Cancer Research Foundation (later the Dana-Farber Cancer Institute at Children's Hospital) on the national radio program *Truth or Consequences*. In addition to the Braves' sponsorship, the fund is sponsored by the Variety Club of New England (now the Variety Children's Charity of New England). The Red Sox replace the Braves as sponsors in 1953.

June 9. At 6:15 P.M., WBZ TV broadcasts the first commercial television programming in Boston. After several hours of test patterns, Arch MacDonald reads fifteen minutes of news. A filmed message of congratulations from Catholic, Protestant, and Jewish clergy is then shown, followed by a broadcast of the *Kraft Television Theatre*. According to estimates, more than one hundred thousand viewers watch the broadcast.

May Sarton's *Faithful Are the Wounds* and Dorothy West's *The Living Is Easy* are published.

April 9. Samuel Barber's *Knoxville: Summer of 1915*, inspired by the writing of James Agee, is given its world premiere by the Boston Symphony Orchestra, Serge Koussevitzky conducting, at Symphony Hall.

June 15. The Braves beat the Chicago Cubs 6–3 at Braves Field, in the first televised baseball game in Boston history. Jim Britt is the Braves' announcer.

October 4. The Red Sox lose to Cleveland 8–3 at Fenway Park in the first one-game playoff for the American League pennant. The Red Sox manager, Joe McCarthy, is later criticized for starting journeyman pitcher Denny Galehouse in the game. The Red Sox loss prevents a "streetcar series" with the Braves, who won the National League pennant behind their two great starting pitchers Warren Spahn and Johnny Sain ("Spahn and Sain and pray for rain"). The Braves lose game 6 to Cleveland 4–3 and the World Series at Braves Field on October 11.

1949

Congress passes Title 1 of the Federal Housing Act of 1949. The legislation contains a commitment to a "decent home and a suitable living environment for every American family," calls for slum clearance, makes five hundred million dollars available to local public authorities (LPAs), and spurs Boston's urban renewal efforts.

The West Broadway (also called the D Street) public housing development opens in South Boston.

Joseph F. Dineen's *The Purple Shamrock: The Honorable James M. Curley of Boston* is published.

November 8. Democrat John Hynes (with 137,930 votes) defeats James Michael Curley (with 126,000) to win election as mayor. Hynes is endorsed by most of the Boston newspapers. The *Boston Globe* later said the election "marks the end of one era and the beginning of another." It also marks the last time to date that an incumbent Boston mayor is defeated for reelection. Inaugurated in Symphony Hall on January 2, 1950, Hynes reestablishes a long-absent working relationship between city government and the business community and lays the groundwork for the redevelopment of Boston.

Lawrence Banks loses to David Sullivan by six votes (4,377–4,371) in the Boston City Council election. After an appeal based on voting irregularities, Banks becomes the first African American to serve as an at-large Boston city councilor when he is seated on August 6, 1951.

Voters approve a change in the city charter to a Plan A government, effective in 1952. The change increases the power of the mayor, replaces the twenty-two-member city council elected by wards with a nine-member at-large body, and retains nonpartisan preliminary elections.

February. Freedom House is established. Originally called the Upper Roxbury Project, it is founded at a meeting in the home of Otto and Muriel Snowden. The organization's goals are to reduce barriers for African-American residents to education, employment, and housing. It moves to 14 Crawford Street in Roxbury, the site of the former Hebrew College, in 1952.

March 31. In a speech at the MIT Mid-Century Convocation at Boston Garden, Winston Churchill defends the possible use of nuclear weapons to deter Communism.

January 3. George Georgenes opens the Victoria Diner at 1024 Massachusetts Avenue in Roxbury. His sons Charlie and Nick take over the restaurant in 1956. Jay Hajj buys the diner in 2004.

Archbishop Cushing censures Father Leonard Feeney for preaching that there is no salvation outside the Catholic Church. Feeney is excommunicated in 1953. The excommunication is lifted in 1972, however.

The Boston School Committee is again reorganized. Under the charter change, it is to consist of five members, elected at large, for nonstaggered, two-year terms.

Dr. Charles Bonner becomes the first African-American staff physician at Boston City Hospital.

John Enders, Thomas Weller, and Frederick Robbins of Children's Hospital discover the method for culturing the poliomyelitis virus. The discovery leads to the development of the polio vaccine, and the three men receive the Nobel Prize in Medicine in 1954.

April 8. Leonard Bernstein's Symphony no. 2 (*The Age of Anxiety*) is given its world premiere by the Boston Symphony Orchestra, Serge Koussevitzky conducting and Bernstein playing the piano, at Symphony Hall.

September. Jacqueline Steiner and Bess Lomax Hawes record their song "MTA." It is written for the Progressive Party's mayoral candidate Walter O'Brien, Jr. (who opposed the recent five-cent fare imposed on trolley rides and the state takeover and bailout of the Boston Elevated Railway Company). The song is released by the Kingston Trio in June 1960.

Charles Munch succeeds Serge Koussevitzky as music director of the Boston Symphony Orchestra. He is succeeded by Erich Leinsdorf (1962) and William Steinberg (1969 until 1973*).

March 15. Rodgers and Hammerstein's *South Pacific*, starring Mary Martin and Ezio Pinza, opens at the Colonial Theatre. In her review, the *Herald* theater critic Elinor Hughes writes: "You can think up your own adjectives and then double them, and still you'll be short of the facts."

March 19. Boston College beats Dartmouth 4–3 at the Broadmoore Ice Palace in Colorado Springs to win its first NCAA hockey championship. The Eagles are coached by John "Snooks" Kelly, who is in the midst of his thirty-six-year coaching career at the school.

October 1–2. The Red Sox lose their last two games to New York, 5–4 and 5–3,

Police investigate the scene of the Brink's robbery. (Courtesy of the Boston Herald/Boston Public Library)

in Yankee Stadium and lose the pennant to the Yankees on the final day of the season.

1950

 Boston's population is 801,444, the tenth largest of any city in the United States. Of that number, 758,700 are white; 40,057 are African American (nearly double the number of ten years before); 2,687 are classified as "other." A total of 144,092 are foreign born; 27,737 are from Ireland, 21,686 from Russia, and 25,315 from Italy. An estimated 83,000 are Jewish; this marks the first decrease in the city's Jewish population.

 February 27. The Mystic River Bridge opens, connecting Charlestown to Chelsea. It is renamed the Tobin Bridge in 1967.
The Greyhound Bus Station opens in Park Square. It moves to a temporary station near South Station in 1980, then to the Intermodal Transportation Center there on October 28, 1995.

 June 25. The United States enters the Korean War, which lasts until July 27, 1953.
May 20. A giant Boston baked bean supper is held on Boston Common as part of the city's midcentury jubilee. An estimated twenty-five thousand people (including ten thousand American Legionnaires holding their convention in Boston) consume seventeen thousand pounds of beans.

January. Gabriel Piemonte is elected the first Italian-American president of the Boston City Council.

January 17. The Brink's robbery is carried out at 600 Commercial Street in the North End. It is the largest robbery in U.S. history to this date. Thieves wearing Halloween masks rob the company's countinghouse of $2,775,395.12 in cash, checks, securities, and money orders. The group of eleven men is led by Anthony Pino, and includes Joseph "Specs" O'Keefe. On January 6, 1956—eleven days before the state's statute of limitations was to have run out—O'Keefe, in prison on another charge, confesses to the crime and names his cohorts. The eight surviving thieves are tried, convicted, and sentenced to life imprisonment in August 1956. O'Keefe is provided a new identity, moves to California, and reportedly works as a chauffeur for Cary Grant. Only sixty thousand dollars of the stolen money is ever recovered.

August. Community Auditions first airs on television. A talent show for local performers, it is hosted first by Gene Jones, then Dave Maynard, and remains on the air for thirty-seven years.
September. Starring the Editors first airs on television. A weekly current affairs show, it is hosted by the *Christian Science Monitor* editor Erwin D. Canham, includes a panel made up of the editors of the *Boston Globe, Herald, Post,* and *Record,* and remains on the air until 1975.

A. J. Deutsch's science fiction story "A Subway Named Mobius" is published. Frances Parkinson Keyes's *Joy Street* is published.
September. The Storyville nightclub, operated by George Wein, opens in the Copley Square Hotel at 47 Huntington Avenue. Performers would include Count Basie, Sidney Bechet, Duke Ellington, Billie Holiday, Charlie Parker, and George Shearing. The club relocates to various sites during the summer, moves to the Buckminster Hotel in 1951, returns to the Copley Square Hotel in 1953, and closes in 1959.
The Elma Lewis School of Fine Arts opens on Waumbeck Street in Roxbury. It becomes part of the newly formed National Center of Afro-American Artists in 1968, moves to Elm Hill Avenue, and closes because of a fire and related financial problems in 1985.

April 18. The Braves beat the Giants 11–4 at the Polo Grounds in New York, as Sam Jethroe becomes the team's first African-American player. He is later named the 1950 National League Rookie of the Year.
April 25. The Celtics draft Chuck Cooper, of Duquesne, making him the first African-American player in NBA history. Two days later, the owner Walter Brown hires thirty-two-year-old Red Auerbach as the team's new coach, and in October the team acquires the former Holy Cross star Bob Cousy.

1951 to 1975

1951

Three public housing developments open: the Archdale (Roslindale), Cathedral (South End), and Fidelis Way (later renamed the Commonwealth), Brighton.

June 16. Storrow Drive opens. Construction began in 1950.
August 4. The Long Island Bridge is dedicated.
August 24. The first segment of Route 128 opens between Route 9 in Wellesley and Route 1 in Lynnfield. Construction began in 1936. The highway is extended to Gloucester in 1953 and to Braintree in 1958.
November 10. Tokens are reintroduced on Boston's public transportation system. First used briefly in 1918, the new tokens cost fifteen cents.

September 7. Putzi, a nine-hundred-pound hippopotamus, arrives in Boston. Acquired for the Franklin Park Zoo after a campaign led by the state representative Julius Ansel, the animal is soon after shipped to the Brooklyn zoo (because the city cannot afford his price tag, over three thousand dollars). It is renamed Dodger to bring the local baseball team good luck. (Note: The Giants win the pennant.)

March 8. The Freedom Trail is proposed. William Schofield suggests the creation of "a 'Puritan Path' or 'Liberty Loop' or 'Freedom's Way' or whatever you want to call it," in his column in the *Boston Evening Traveler.* Mayor Hynes and business leaders immediately embrace the idea. Supported by the Advertising Club of Boston, the Chamber of Commerce, and the local businessman and philanthropist Dick Berenson, the Freedom Trail Foundation is established in June. Sites on the eventual five-and-a-half-mile trail include Boston Common, the State House, Park Street Church, the Granary Burying Ground, King's Chapel and the adjacent burying ground, the site of the original Boston Latin School and the Ben Franklin statue on the grounds of Old City Hall, the Old Corner Book Store, Old South Meeting House, Franklin's birthplace, the Old State House, the site of the Boston Massacre, Faneuil Hall, Paul Revere's House, the Old North Church, Copp's Hill Burying Ground, the USS *Constitution,* and Bunker Hill.

November 6. John Hynes (with 154,206 votes) again defeats James Michael Curley (with 76,354), this time by a more than two to one margin, to win reelection as mayor. He is inaugurated on January 4, 1952.

Sullivan's Restaurant opens on Castle Island in South Boston.

Dr. Mildred Jefferson becomes the first African-American woman graduate of Harvard Medical School.

October 6. WGBH first airs on the radio, with a live broadcast of the Boston Symphony Orchestra from Symphony Hall. The station is located initially in Cambridge, and opens its current studio in Allston in 1964.

"Symphony Sid" Torin begins work as a disc jockey at WBMS. He is credited with pioneering jazz on Boston radio, much of it broadcast live from local clubs.

March 6. Rodgers and Hammerstein's *The King and I*, starring Gertrude Lawrence, opens its pre-Broadway run at the Shubert Theatre. The song "Getting to Know You," which had been discarded from *South Pacific*, is added at this time.

September 8. The first episode of the network television detective series *Boston Blackie* airs. The last episode airs on October 13, 1952.

1952

Three public housing developments open: the Franklin Hill (Dorchester), Mission Hill Extension (later renamed the Alice Taylor), and Orient Heights (East Boston).

Chester Square in the South End is destroyed by the widening of Massachusetts Avenue.

The streetcars in East Boston are replaced by buses.

Herbert Philbrick's *I Led Three Lives* is published.

November 3. Republican presidential candidate Dwight D. Eisenhower decries "godless Communism" in a speech at a campaign rally at Boston Garden.

November 4. Democrat John F. Kennedy defeats Republican Henry Cabot Lodge, Jr., to win election to the U.S. Senate. Thirty-six years before, Kennedy's grandfather, the former Boston mayor John "Honey Fitz" Fitzgerald, had been defeated by Lodge's grandfather for the same office. After JFK's victory, his mother, Rose Fitzgerald Kennedy, reminisces about how her father, as a young newsboy, was given shelter by a cook one winter evening in the Lodge house at 31 Beacon Street. "In his wildest dreams that winter's night," she asks, "could he ever have imagined how far both he and his family would come?"

Thomas P. "Tip" O'Neill succeeds Kennedy as a U.S. representative. He is elected Speaker of the House of Representatives in 1977 and retires in 1987.

The Boston Veterans Administration Hospital opens in Jamaica Plain.

Dr. Paul Zoli introduces the pacemaker at Beth Israel (now Beth Israel Deaconess) Hospital.

Ida M. Cannon's *On the Social Frontier of Medicine* is published.

November 8. The Big Brother Show, hosted by Bob Emery, airs on Boston television. Originally a radio show that first aired in Medford in 1921, the television show continues to air in various formats until 1968.

The art critic Bernard Berenson, eighty-seven, who left Boston to live in Italy years before, writes in his diary: "I still consider Boston my home."

June. The first annual Boston Arts Festival is held in the Public Garden. Original poems are commissioned for the occasion from e. e. cummings, Archibald MacLeish, Marianne Moore, Carl Sandburg, and others. The event continues until 1964.

The flutist Doriot Anthony Dwyer of the Boston Symphony Orchestra becomes the first woman to chair a section of a major symphony orchestra.

The Sack Theatre chain is established in Boston. Founded by Benjamin Sack, the chain is sold in 1968 and Sack is forced out as an executive in 1974.

June 17. Red Sox center fielder Jimmy Piersall is sent down to the minor leagues after a series of emotional outbursts in a game against the Washington Senators. Hospitalized in August after suffering a nervous breakdown, Piersall eventually returns to play eight more years with the Red Sox and a total of seventeen years in the major leagues.

September 21. The Braves lose to the Brooklyn Dodgers 8–2 before 8,822 fans in what proves to be the team's last game at Braves Field. The team finishes in seventh place and draws only 281,278 fans for the season. Lou Perini, the team's owner, abruptly announces the team is moving to Milwaukee for the upcoming season on March 13, 1953.

September 23. Rocky Marciano of Brockton knocks out Joe Louis in the thirteenth round in Philadelphia to win the world heavyweight boxing title. Marciano successfully defends the title six times, the last, a ninth-round knockout of Archie Moore on September 21, 1955. He retires with a record of forty-nine wins (forty-three by knockouts) and zero losses.

December 26. Boston University beats Northeastern 4–1, and Harvard beats Boston College 3–2 in overtime in the first Beanpot hockey tournament (originally called the New England Invitational) before 5,105 fans at Boston Arena. Harvard beats Boston University 7–4 the next night before 3,382 to win the first championship. The tournament moves to Boston Garden in January 1954 and switches to February in 1955.

1953

The Whittier Street public housing development opens in lower Roxbury.

February 16. Red Sox outfielder and Air Force pilot Ted Williams lands his plane safely after being hit by enemy fire in Korea.

Fall. Nathan Pusey succeeds James Conant as president of Harvard. Soon after moving from Wisconsin, Mrs. Pusey reportedly remarks at a Back Bay reception that everyone in Boston had been very welcoming—only to be told, "It's obvious, Mrs. Pusey, that you have not met any of the right people." Pusey is succeeded by Derek Bok (1971), Neil Rudenstine (1991), and Lawrence Summers (2001 to the present).

Radio station WILD first airs. Purchased by Sheridan Broadcasting, it becomes the only urban, contemporary music radio station in the United States owned and operated by an African-American-owned company in 1972.

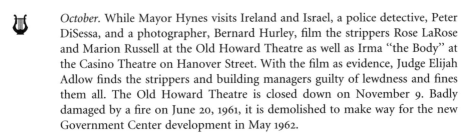

October. While Mayor Hynes visits Ireland and Israel, a police detective, Peter DiSessa, and a photographer, Bernard Hurley, film the strippers Rose LaRose and Marion Russell at the Old Howard Theatre as well as Irma "the Body" at the Casino Theatre on Hanover Street. With the film as evidence, Judge Elijah Adlow finds the strippers and building managers guilty of lewdness and fines them all. The Old Howard Theatre is closed down on November 9. Badly damaged by a fire on June 20, 1961, it is demolished to make way for the new Government Center development in May 1962.

January 10. Ralph DeLeo of Boston Tech sets a schoolboy record by scoring eleven goals against Roxbury Memorial High School in a game at Boston Arena.
April 16. The Bruins lose to Montreal 1–0 at Montreal in the fifth and final game of the Stanley Cup championship.
October 25. The Celtics' radio announcer Johnny Most makes his debut, broadcasting an exhibition game against the New York Knicks in New London, Connecticut.

1954

October 26. Mayor Hynes delivers a speech entitled "Boston, Whither Goest Thou?" in which he lays out his plan for a "New Boston," at the first Boston College Citizens Seminar in Fulton Hall on the BC campus. The program was prompted by a suggestion from Arthur J. Kelly, vice president and treasurer of the R. H. White Company, to the BC Business School Dean W. Seavey Joyce. Mayor Hynes later declares that the seminars "pried open windows long and tightly closed," and his successor, Mayor John Collins, later says they "helped mightily in knitting together a series which sometimes seemed to find division the natural order."

Three public housing developments open: the Bromley Park (Jamaica Plain) and Columbia Point and Franklin Field (Dorchester). The Columbia Point high-rise buildings are later demolished and replaced with a mixed-income development, renamed Harbor Point, in 1988.

The Arthur Fiedler Footbridge, designed by Shepley, Bulfinch, Richardson, and Abbott, opens over Storrow Drive.

East Boston Memorial Stadium is added to the city's park system.

June 9. Joseph Welch, a Boston attorney, denounces U.S. Senator Joseph McCarthy in a hearing in Washington, D.C. After McCarthy attempts to tarnish the reputation of Fred Fisher (a junior member of Welch's law firm, who is not even involved in the proceedings), Welch declares: "Let us not assassinate this lad further, Senator. You've done enough. Have you no sense of decency, sir? At long last, have you left no sense of decency?"

June 16. A reputed mob hit man, Elmer "Trigger" Burke, fires thirty shots in an unsuccessful attempt to kill the Brink's robber James "Specs" O'Keefe at the Victory Road housing development in Dorchester. Arrested the next day, Burke escapes from Charles Street Jail on August 28. Arrested again a year later in South Carolina, he is tried, convicted of a murder in New York, and executed at Sing Sing Prison in January 1958.

August 31. Hurricane Carol strikes Boston, toppling the steeples on the Old North Church and the First Church of Roxbury.
September 11. Hurricane Edna strikes Boston, causing extensive damage.

Muhammad's Mosque no. 11 opens on Intervale Street in Roxbury. Founded by Malcolm X and others, it is the first Nation of Islam temple in Boston.
The 35-foot statue of the Madonna Queen is dedicated on Orient Heights in East Boston.

May 17. In *Brown v. Board of Education of Topeka, Kansas,* the U.S. Supreme Court prohibits segregation in public schools. In its decision the court cites the *Roberts v. City of Boston* case of 1848.
English High School moves to the former Commerce High School building on Avenue Louis Pasteur in the Fenway. The school moves into a new ten-story building on the same site in September 1973, the first new high school built in the city since 1934. English merges with Jamaica Plain High and moves to its current location at 144 McBride Street in 1989.

December 23. Dr. Joseph Murray performs the first successful organ transplant in history at Peter Bent Brigham Hospital—a kidney transplanted from one identical twin to another. He is awarded the Nobel Prize for Medicine in 1990.
The Lemuel Shattuck Hospital opens in Franklin Park.

October 27. Members of Local 11 of the United Packinghouse Workers of America Union are locked out of the Colonial Provision Company. After a strike and a boycott by consumers that lasts more than a year, a settlement is reached in January 1956. The union's name is changed to Local 616 to appease Colonial's president, however, because he had vowed never to sign an agreement with Local 11.

The Boston Camerata is established. Reportedly the oldest early music ensemble in continuous existence in the United States, it is initially affiliated with the Museum of Fine Arts but becomes independent in 1974.

Sunday, June 6. The Red Sox beat Cleveland 7–4 at Fenway Park, as second-year first baseman Harry Agganis hits a two-run homer to win the game. Immediately after the game, Agganis rushes to Boston University's commencement exercises, held at the site of the former Braves Field, where he receives his bachelor's degree. A Lynn native, one of the finest schoolboy athletes in Massachusetts history, and an All American football player at Boston University, Agganis dies a year later from a cerebral blood clot.

1955

The Park Square bus station opens. Originally used by the Boston and Worcester Street Railway, it becomes a Trailways station in 1957 and closes on May 18, 1980. The bus station moves to a temporary location near South Station, and then to the Intermodal Transportation Center there on October 28, 1995.

November 8. John Hynes (with 124,301 votes) beats the Massachusetts Senate president John E. Powers of South Boston (with 111,775) to win reelection as mayor. Inaugurated in Symphony Hall on January 2, 1956, Hynes then drives to the Jamaica Plain home of John Collins to swear him in as a member of the Boston City Council. Collins was elected, despite having been struck down by polio ten days before the September preliminary election.

Jimmy's Harborside Restaurant opens in South Boston. Founded by Jimmy Doulos (an Americanization of his Greek name, Demetrios Efstratios Christodoulos) on the site of his former Liberty Café (established in 1924), it becomes the first restaurant in the nation to offer profit sharing to its employees. The restaurant continues today.

January. The "Siege of Cherry Hill" takes place at Charlestown State Prison. After failing in an escape attempt, Theodore "Teddy" Green, a bank robber, and three others hold five guards hostage, and demand that a car be provided to them so they can leave the prison. The authorities refuse, and Green is subsequently persuaded to give up by his seventeen-year-old daughter. Transferred to Alcatraz for the remainder of his sentence, Green is paroled in 1967 and later becomes a car salesman for Coveny Ford in West Roxbury.

Martin Luther King, Jr., receives his Ph.D. degree from Boston University's School of Theology.
November 23. St. Anthony's Shrine is dedicated on Arch Street.

April 25. Boston schoolchildren are vaccinated with the new polio vaccine developed by Dr. Jonas Salk.

May 2. WGBH TV first airs. The first programs are *Come and See*, a sing-along show for children hosted by Tony Saletan, and a news program with Louis Lyons. A twelve-part series entitled "The Challenge to Greater Boston" airs later in the year.
July 11. Don Kent begins his weather forecasts for WBZ TV. Kent had begun on WBZ Radio a few years before. He continues on television until 1983 and on radio until 1985.

April 12. Richard Adler and Jerry Ross's *Damn Yankees*, starring Gwen Verdon, Stephen Douglas, and Ray Walston, Jr., opens at the Shubert Theatre.
September 13. Arthur Miller's *A View from the Bridge*, starring Van Heflin, Eileen Heckart, and J. Carrol Naish, opens at the Colonial Theatre.
November 15. The Matchmaker, starring Ruth Gordon, opens at the Colonial Theatre.

Construction of the John F. Fitzgerald Expressway/Central Artery, ca. 1955. (Courtesy of the Bostonian Society, Central Artery Collection)

Richard Sinnott is appointed chief of the Licensing Division of the city of Boston. The aptly named unofficial "city censor" retires on November 18, 1975. No one succeeds him, and the position is eliminated in 1982.

 April 1. Tony DeMarco of the North End beats Johnny Saxton with a fourteenth round technical knockout at the Boston Garden to win the world welterweight title. He loses the title to Carmen Basilio in Syracuse, New York, on June 10, then loses a rematch with Basilio at Boston Garden on November 30 in what many call two of the greatest fights in boxing history.

1956

 June 29. President Dwight D. Eisenhower signs legislation in Washington creating the National System of Interstate and Defense Highways.
The Central Artery opens from the Mystic Bridge to Fort Hill. Wags later joke that the reason for its name is that it is always clogged. Demolition work had begun in 1951, and an estimated 20,000 residents, more than 1,000 structures, 573 businesses, and 7,160 jobs were moved from the path of the new highway.

 Edwin O'Connor's *The Last Hurrah* is published. The book is set in an unnamed city, though clearly modeled after Boston, and its fictional hero, Frank Skeffington, is obviously based on James Michael Curley. Although Curley initially threatens to sue O'Connor over the book, he subsequently comes to enjoy it. In a chance meeting outside the Parker House, he tells the author jokingly that his favorite passage was "the part where I die."

Arnie "Woo Woo" Ginsburg debuts on WBOS Radio. He is a sound engineer filling in for the regular disc jockey, and his eccentric style and sense of humor make him immediately popular with listeners. He moves to WMEX Radio and begins his *Night Train* program there in 1958.

April 28. The local television show *Boomtown*, featuring Rex Trailer, first airs.

Walter Muir Whitehill's *The Boston Public Library* is published.

February 3. Aaron Copland's revised *Symphonic Ode* is given its world premiere by the Boston Symphony Orchestra, Charles Munch conducting, at Symphony Hall.

An antitrust ruling ends the Shubert family's control of all seven legitimate theaters in Boston. The Copley, Majestic, and Plymouth theaters become movie houses, the Opera House is sold to Northeastern University, and the Colonial and Wilbur are sold to new owners.

October. Eugene O'Neill's *A Long Day's Journey into Night*, starring Frederick March and Jason Robards, Jr., premieres at the Wilbur Theatre.

October 30. Candide opens at the Colonial Theatre. The book is by Lillian Hellman, the lyrics by Richard Wilbur, the music by Leonard Bernstein.

April 29. The Celtics acquire the second pick in the NBA draft (which they later use to select Bill Russell) from St. Louis in exchange for player Ed Macauley and a draft pick (which the Hawks later use to select Cliff Hagan). Led by Russell, the Celtics go on to win eleven championships in the next thirteen years, a dynasty unmatched in professional sports history.

1957

September. The Boston Redevelopment Authority (BRA) is created. Kane Simonian is the first director. The BRA replaces the Boston Housing Authority as the city's local planning authority and assumes control of the West End and New York Streets Projects.

May. The Massachusetts Turnpike opens between West Stockbridge and Weston. Construction began in 1955. The Turnpike Extension, between Weston and Boston, opens on February 18, 1965. The connection to the Ted Williams Tunnel and Logan Airport opens on January 17, 2003.

George F. Weston, Jr.'s *Boston Ways: High, By, and Folk* is published.

James Michael Curley's autobiography, *I'd Do It Again*, is published.

WGBH TV begins airing a twenty-part series on Boston entitled *City in Crisis*, hosted by Rev. Seavey Joyce.

Jerry Williams debuts as a talk show host on radio station WMEX. He moves to WBZ in 1968, is fired in 1976 and leaves Boston, then returns to WRKO in the mid-1980s. He is fired in 1998, and returns for one show, a few months before his death, on March 1, 2003.

November 29. The Charles Playhouse opens with a production of Sartre's *No Exit*, performed by a company of Boston University students. Located initially

Demolition of the West End. (Courtesy of the Bostonian Society, Robert B. Severy Collection)

at 54 Charles Street, above a fish market, it moves to 74 Warrenton Street in 1958.

April 16. The Bruins lose to Montreal 5–1 at Montreal in the fifth and final game of the Stanley Cup championship.

April 13. The Celtics beat the St. Louis Hawks 125–123 in double overtime in game 7 at Boston Garden to win their first NBA championship. The Celtics lose to St. Louis in 1958 (when Bill Russell misses two games because of injury), but go on to win the championship against the Minneapolis Lakers in 1959, the St. Louis Hawks in 1960 and 1961, and the Los Angeles Lakers in 1962 and 1963.

1958

April. The West End urban renewal plan begins. The Boston Redevelopment Authority (BRA) seizes forty-six acres by eminent domain. Demolition starts in May and is completed in March 1960; 4,050 families are displaced and an estimated 2,800 homes are torn down. A group headed by Jerome Rappaport, a former secretary to Mayor Hynes, is chosen to develop the area. Charles River Park, designed by Victor Gruen, opens in January 1962. The project receives much criticism. Walter Muir Whitehill later writes: "The experience of the West End created a widespread conviction that if urban renewal were necessary in Boston, some less drastic form must be devised." Supporters defend it, however, for attracting much-needed private investment to Boston. The BRA's executive director, Kane Simonian, later tells the *Boston Globe*: "There are people in real estate who believe that if the West End hadn't been cleared, there would have been no Government Center, no development of Faneuil Hall or the waterfront."

The Massachusetts Port Authority (Massport) is established. Created by the state legislature the year before, it is responsible for running Logan Airport as well as the Port of Boston.

Oliver Smoot (MIT '62) is used by his fraternity mates to measure the length of the Harvard Bridge ("364.4 Smoots plus one ear"). When the bridge is rebuilt in 1990, the Smoot marks are repainted on the sidewalk.

November 12. James Michael Curley dies, eight days before his eighty-fourth birthday. His funeral services are later described as the largest in city history: one hundred thousand mourners attend the wake at the State House, and an estimated one million people line the streets for his funeral at the Cathedral of the Holy Cross and burial in Old Calvary Cemetery in Jamaica Plain.

May 3. An estimated six thousand fans riot after the Big Beat Rock 'n' Roll Concert at the Boston Arena, hosted by the New York disc jockey Alan Freed. Performers included Chuck Berry, Buddy Holly and the Crickets, and Jerry Lee Lewis. Mayor Hynes subsequently orders a temporary ban on rock 'n' roll concerts in the city.

June 22. The Boston Symphony Orchestra's "Lagoon Concert" is held at the Public Garden. The closing event of the Boston Arts Festival, it features Richard Burgin conducting eighteen members of the BSO, all riding in Swan Boats, before an audience of twenty-five thousand.

The Greater Boston Youth Symphony Orchestra (GBYSO) is established. Founded by Dr. Robert Choate, the orchestra soon performs at Carnegie Hall and the White House, under the direction of the conductor Marvin Rabin.

The Opera Company of Boston, originally called the Boston Opera Group, is founded by Sarah Caldwell.

Elliot Norton Reviews debuts on WGBH TV. The program continues until 1982.

January 28. John Osborne's *The Entertainer*, starring Laurence Olivier, opens at the Shubert Theatre.

The movie version of *The Last Hurrah* is released and is being screened in Boston at the time of James Michael Curley's death. It stars Spencer Tracy, although Curley had said he would have preferred Claude Rains in the role.

January 18. The Bruins' Willie O'Ree becomes the first African American to play in the National Hockey League.

April 20. The Bruins lose to Montreal 5–3 at Boston Garden in the sixth and final game of the Stanley Cup championship.

Candlepin Bowling first airs on WHDH TV with Jim Britt as host; Don Gillis soon takes over the job. The longest running locally produced sports program in the United States, it continues until 1996.

The East Newton Street Armory, long used for interscholastic indoor track meets, is torn down to make way for construction of the Massachusetts Turnpike Extension.

1959

The Boston Planning Board releases the Government Center Plan. Designed by I. M. Pei and Henry Cobb, it calls for transforming Scollay Square into a site for several new government office buildings. Demolition begins in February 1962, and ground is broken for construction on October 18, 1962. Walter

Muir Whitehill later describes the completed projects as "almost as dramatic in their effect upon the topography of Boston as the filling of the Back Bay." With Boston's tax base 25 percent smaller than it was on the eve of the Great Depression, Moody's Investor Service lowers the city's bond rating from A to Baa, the lowest of any major city in the country.

The Travelers Building opens on High Street and is the first major new office building to be constructed in Boston since the John Hancock Building in 1947. It is demolished on March 6, 1988, to make way for another new office building, 125 High Street.

July 1. The Southeast Expressway is completed from Braintree through the Dewey Square Tunnel to the Central Artery. Construction began in 1954. A study by the Boston Traffic Department later finds that between 1958 and 1964 the number of people walking or using mass transit to get to work declines by 33 percent, and the number using automobiles increases by 35 percent.
July 1. The Metropolitan Transit Authority's Riverside Line begins operation along the former Highland Branch of the Boston and Albany Railroad.
August. The city incinerator begins operation in the South Bay. It shuts down on August 23, 1975.
A dike is constructed from Castle Island to Head Island, enclosing Pleasure Bay in South Boston.

Samuel Eliot Morison's *John Paul Jones* and Walter Muir Whitehill's *A Topographical History of Boston* are published.

October 30. Federal agents raid the Ringside Cafe in East Boston, charging that it is a bookie joint. Four days later, on election day, mayoral candidate John Collins's campaign runs a front-page ad featuring a picture of the building, which displays a large campaign sign for his opponent, John Powers. The ad also includes a picture of the owner with Powers—but with Sen. John F. Kennedy cropped out.
November 3. John Collins (with 114,210 votes) defeats John Powers (with 90,142) in what is later called the biggest upset in Boston political history. In his inaugural address at Symphony Hall on January 4, 1960, Collins declares: "We must restore, rebuild and redevelop." As mayor, he is credited with completing the physical and economic renewal of Boston begun under Mayor John Hynes in the 1950s.

Ruth Batson runs unsuccessfully for the Boston School Committee. A longtime Roxbury community activist, she later describes the sacrifices made by herself and others: "It has not been easy to put yourself out there, you know; it's not easy for yourself, it's not easy for your mate; and it's not easy for your children."

April 25. The Cuban leader Fidel Castro speaks to an audience of nearly nine thousand at Harvard University's Dillon Fieldhouse at Soldiers Field. He stays overnight at the Statler-Hilton Hotel (today's Park Plaza), guarded by what is described as the largest security force ever organized for a visitor to Boston.

Chiang Yee's *Silent Traveler in Boston* is published. In it he writes of being told "to be sure to go to see the American room [at the Museum of Fine Arts], for there I would see something which I never could see in any other museum in the world. I would find a group of people under a certain portrait and their family name would be that of the person in the portrait. All Bostonians were like that. They went to the museum to see their ancestors' portrait and never wanted to see any other picture."

The Boston Coordinating Committee is formed; it is known as "the Vault" because its first meetings are held in the boardroom near the vault of the Boston Safe Deposit Company. The original fourteen members include Ralph Lowell, of the Boston Safe Deposit and Trust Company, and Gerald Blakely, Jr., of Cabot, Cabot, and Forbes, as well as the chief executives of other major Boston companies. The committee is credited with working closely first with Mayor Hynes and then with Mayor Collins on issues regarding city finances and development. It becomes less active in the 1990s, especially as more Boston companies are bought up by out-of-town corporations, and disbands in 1997.

November 25. Elizabeth Hardwick's essay "Boston: A Lost Ideal" appears in *Harper's.* In it she declares: "Boston—wrinkled, spindly-legged, depleted of nearly all her spiritual and cutaneous oils, provincial, self-esteeming—has gone on spending and spending her inflated bills of pure reputation, decade after decade. Now, one supposes it is over at last."

Robert Lowell's *Life Studies* is published.
August 21. A jazz festival produced by George Wein is held at Fenway Park. Performers include Ray Charles, the Dukes of Dixieland, and Pee Wee Russell. The New England Conservatory of Music, under the direction of Gunther Schuller, initiates a Jazz Studies program.

July 21. The Red Sox lose to the White Sox 2–1 in Chicago, in Elijah "Pumpsie" Green's first game with the team since he was brought up from the minor leagues. He is the first African-American player for the Red Sox, which is the last major league team to add African-American players to its roster.
November 22. The newly formed Boston Patriots of the American Football League make running back Ron Burton of Northwestern University the team's first draft choice. After a distinguished career on the field, Burton would distinguish himself even more off the field for his work on behalf of Boston area young people.

1960

Boston's population is 697,197, the thirteenth largest of any city in the United States—a decrease of more than 100,000 in ten years. Of the total population, 628,704 are white, 63,165 are African American; 5,328 are classified as "other." A total of 109,964 are foreign born.

March. Ed Logue arrives in Boston to work as a development consultant to the city after Mayor Collins meets his three demands: a $30,000 salary ($10,000

President John F. Kennedy greets well-wishers on Beacon Hill, 1962. (Courtesy of the Bostonian Society, Walter P. McNaney Collection, Boston Herald *photograph)*

more than the mayor's); a house on Beacon Hill (on West Cedar Street); and a membership in a private club (the Tavern Club). After hearing the last demand, Collins reportedly told Logue: "Are you crazy? I've lived here all my life and I've never even been *invited* to those places." Logue is soon named director of the Boston Redevelopment Authority.

September 22. Collins announces a $90 million development program for Boston, which includes proposals for the redevelopment not only of downtown Boston but of most of the city's neighborhoods.

 November 7. John F. Kennedy, the Democratic presidential candidate, delivers an electrifying campaign speech to a crowd estimated at twenty thousand people at an election-eve rally in Boston Garden. The author and Boston native Theodore White later describes Kennedy being "surrounded on the dais by a covey of the puffy, pink-faced, predatory-lipped politicians." An estimated hundred thousand people lined the streets prior to the event, which turns out to be the last major political rally held at Boston Garden.

November 8. Kennedy defeats Richard Nixon to be elected president. Inaugurated on January 20, 1961, he becomes the first Catholic to hold the office, and he is sworn in using a Bible that had belonged to his grandfather, the former Boston Mayor John Fitzgerald.

October 4. A flock of starlings causes Eastern Airlines Flight 375 to crash into Winthrop Bay during its takeoff from Logan Airport. Sixty-two of the seventy-two people aboard are killed.

Proton beam therapy is first used to treat brain tumors at Massachusetts General Hospital.

 February 8. Dave Maynard of WBZ Radio and other disc jockeys testify before a congressional committee in Washington, D.C., investigating the "payola" scandal, in which record companies are found to have paid to have their records played.

 January 22. A Brookline firefighter, Paul Pender, beats Sugar Ray Robinson in a fifteen-round split decision for the middleweight title at Boston Garden, prompting charges of a "hometown decision." Pender defeats Robinson, again in fifteen rounds at Boston Garden, on June 10. After later losing his middleweight title to the Englishman Terry Downes, Pender regains a share of the title with a fifteen-round decision over Downes in what is reportedly one of the greatest fights in Boston Garden history on April 7, 1962. He retires soon after.

September 9. The Boston Patriots lose to the Denver Broncos 13–10 before 21,597 fans at Boston University's Nickerson Field in the first game in the newly formed American Football League. The Patriots later move their home games to Fenway Park (1963), and then Boston College's Alumni Stadium (1969). The team is renamed the New England Patriots and begins playing in the newly built Schaefer Stadium in Foxborough (1971), then in the new adjacent Gillette Stadium (2002).

September 28. In the last at bat of his career, Ted Williams hits an eighth-inning home run (his 521st) off Baltimore Orioles pitcher Jack Fisher before 10,454 at Fenway Park. John Updike later describes the scene that followed in "Hub Fans Bid Kid Adieu": "The papers said that the other players, and even the umpires on the field, begged him to come out and acknowledge us in some way, but he never had and did not now. Gods do not answer letters."

1961

 The Boston Banks Urban Renewal Group (BBURG) is created. A consortium of twenty-two savings banks, cooperatives, and savings and loan institutions that creates a pool of mortgage money for minority home buyers, it is formed after Massachusetts state representative Royal Bolling of Roxbury files legislation (ultimately unsuccessful) to require banks to loan 40 percent of their mortgage money to borrowers in the communities in which they are located. The lending program does not begin to operate until 1968.*

 The Lenox Street trolley line is discontinued.

November. The Boston Common Underground Garage opens. Plagued by construction delays and charges of corruption, it is declared structurally unsafe and closed for repairs in March 1993, then reopens on July 3, 1995.

November 11. The Callahan Tunnel opens to East Boston. Construction began in 1959. The tunnel is named for William Callahan, Jr., who was killed in battle in World War II and was the son of the Massachusetts Turnpike Authority chairman.

The Pine Street Inn is established. An outgrowth of the Rufus Dawes Hotel, it is a refuge for the indigent, alcoholic, and homeless. Located initially at 8 Pine Street in the 1940s, it moves this year to Harrison Avenue, then to the former Boston Fire Department headquarters on Albany Street in 1978.

The Crittenton Hastings House is established, a merger of the Florence Hastings House and the Crittenton Home and Hospital. In 1962 it opens the first alternative high school within the Boston public schools for young, pregnant women. After the U.S. Supreme Court's *Roe v. Wade* decision in 1973, it opens the first independent abortion clinic in Boston.

November 30. Biography of a Bookie Joint airs on network television. Blacked out in Boston because of a pending criminal investigation, the CBS exposé shows Boston police frequenting the bookie joint in question, Swartz Key Shop, at 364 Massachusetts Avenue.

November 31. Bernie McLaughlin is shot and killed outside the Richards Liquor Store in City Square, Charlestown. The murder reportedly initiates a gangland war that leads to more than forty killings in the next four years, including the murder of McLaughlin's brother, Edward "Punchy" McLaughlin, at a bus stop in West Roxbury on October 20, 1965.

November. Louise Day Hicks of South Boston is elected to the Boston School Committee for the first time. She is elected chairperson in 1963.

George Frazier's column "Another Man's Poison" first appears in the *Boston Herald*. After moving to the *Record American*, Frazier relocates to New York in 1963. He returns to Boston and writes a column for the *Boston Globe* from 1969 until 1971.

The Edge of Sadness by Edwin O'Connor and *Mastering the Art of French Cooking*, by Julia Child, Simone Beck, and Louisette Bertholle, are published.

January 15. The film *Exodus*, based on the founding of the state of Israel, premieres at the Saxon Theatre. The screening prompts an appearance of the American Nazi party leader George Lincoln Rockwell in front of the theater and an estimated two thousand people who demonstrate against him.

March 15. Herb Gardner's *A Thousand Clowns*, starring Jason Robards, Jr., and Sandy Dennis, opens at the Wilbur Theatre.

The Sportsmen's Tennis Club opens at 930 Blue Hill Avenue in Dorchester. Founded by Jimmy Smith to introduce inner-city young people to tennis, it continues in operation today.

January 28. John Thomas of Boston University sets a world's indoor high jump record, clearing 7 feet, 3⅛ inches, in a meet at Boston Garden.

1962

Herbert Gans's *The Urban Villagers*, a sociological study of the West End, and Sam Bass Warner, Jr.'s *Streetcar Suburbs: The Process of Growth in Boston, 1870–1900* are published.

May 3. Mayor Collins unveils a model of the winning design for the new City Hall at press conference at the Museum of Fine Arts. (He reportedly had not seen it previously.) Some applaud the winning design (from among 256 entries) by Kallmann, McKinnell, and Knowles. Some criticize it, including Edward Durrell Stone, who a few days later declares that it looks "like the crate that Faneuil Hall came in."

Samuel Eliot Morison's memoir *One Boy's Boston, 1887–1901* is published.

August 27. In a debate at South Boston High School during the campaign for the Democratic nomination for the U.S. Senate, Edward McCormack, Jr., tells his opponent: "If his name was Edward Moore, with his qualifications— with your qualifications, Teddy—your

Albert DeSalvo in police custody. (Photograph by Dick Thomson, courtesy of the Boston Herald)

candidacy would be a joke." Kennedy's campaign slogan is: "He can do more for Massachusetts." Kennedy defeats McCormack in the primary election on September 18 and Republican George Cabot Lodge in the final election on November 6. He becomes one of the most effective senators in U.S. history and the longest-serving in state history.

Action for Boston Community Development (ABCD) is established. The organization provides education and employment opportunities for residents of Boston and continues today.

June 14. The first of the "Boston Strangler" murders occurs at 77 Gainsborough Street in the Fenway. The last of the thirteen murders (of which eight were in Boston) takes place at 44A Charles Street on January 4, 1964. Albert DeSalvo later confesses to the murders, although some later doubt he was the real killer. Convicted on unrelated charges on January 18, 1967, he receives a life sentence, and is killed in his bed at Walpole State Prison on November 26, 1973.

Rev. John Burgess is installed as suffragan bishop of Boston in Trinity Church. The first African-American Episcopal bishop of a primarily white congregation, he is elected bishop of the Massachusetts diocese in 1969.

May 23. Dr. Ronald Malt performs the first successful reattachment of a completely severed human arm at Massachusetts General Hospital. The patient, a twelve-year-old Little Leaguer, Everett Knowles of Somerville, was injured attempting to hitch a ride on a freight car.

March 30. The *Boston Globe* runs a story describing Ted Kennedy's expulsion from Harvard for cheating. Although the story by the reporter Robert Healy appears on the front page, the newspaper reportedly obliges the Kennedy family by placing it "below the fold."

September. The first issue of today's *Boston* magazine appears. An outgrowth of the *Chamber of Commerce Journal*, which began in October 1909, it becomes a privately owned publication from this time forward.

September 14. Two thousand rhythm and blues fans riot when a concert by the Etta James Band at Boston Arena is canceled.

July 26. After a game against the Yankees in New York (and, reportedly, more than a few beers), Red Sox players Pumpsie Green and Gene Conley leave the team bus, go to the airport, and attempt to board a flight to Israel. Green rejoins the team the next day, Conley a few days later.

1963

November 5. John Collins (with 108,624 votes) defeats the city councilor Gabriel Piemonte (with 73,067), winning nineteen of twenty-two wards to be reelected mayor. Inaugurated in Symphony Hall on January 6, 1964, Collins criticizes Gov. Endicott Peabody in his address for "grossly inadequate" state support "not only to Boston, but to all cities and towns in the Commonwealth."

November 22. President John F. Kennedy is assassinated in Dallas, Texas. In Boston, church bells ring, flags are flown at half-mast, and black borders appear on newspapers.

Malcolm X delivers a speech entitled "God's Solution to the Race Problem" at the Ford Hall Forum, attracting the largest audience to an event in the series in more than thirty years.

September 22. A march on Roxbury is held. An estimated ten thousand people—black and white—protest the poor conditions in that community's schools.

Anthony Athanas opens Anthony's Pier 4 restaurant in South Boston. Known for its seafood and the site of numerous political and civic fund-raising events, the restaurant remains in operation today.

Sal Lombardo opens Lombardo's Restaurant at 220 Border Street in East Boston. Originally a function room over a supermarket, the restaurant becomes the scene of family, neighborhood, and civic functions until its closing on July 15, 2000.

June 11. At a Boston School Committee meeting, Ruth Batson and other members of the Boston branch of the NAACP testify that the Boston public schools are engaging in de facto segregation. A week later, an estimated two to five thousand African-American students take part in a school "Stay Out," boycotting the Boston public schools and instead attending "freedom schools." Over nine thousand students take part in the second annual Stay Out demonstration February 26, 1964.

$ The Magellan Fund is created by Fidelity Investments' Edward Johnson.

●C *February 11. The French Chef,* hosted by Julia Child, first airs on WGBH TV.

♫ *September 9. Nike Driving a Two-Horsed Chariot,* a fourth-century Egyptian gold earring, is stolen from the Museum of Fine Arts, shortly after being featured in a television program. Police subsequently arrest the thief, who reveals that the earring is buried in a Campbell soup can somewhere in the Fens. Florence Wolsky, a Boston University archeology student, digs for the ring, and discovers it on April 16, 1964.
Warren S. Tryon's *Parnassus Corner: A Life of James T. Fields* is published.
The Theatre Company of Boston is formed. It operates in various theaters during the next twenty years.

⛵ *November 9.* The Northeastern University football team beats Tufts 34–0 at Parsons Field to complete the first unbeaten and untied season in school history. Northeastern subsequently loses to East Carolina 27–6 in the Eastern Bowl in Allentown, Pennsylvania, on December 14 in the first post-season bowl appearance in Northeastern football history.

1964

♯ The term "Combat Zone" is first used by a military police officer to describe the area along lower Washington Street. The *Boston Daily Record* then uses the phrase as the title of a series it runs about the area, written by Jean Cole, Al Salie, and Frank Thompson.

🚌 *August 3.* The Massachusetts Bay Transportation Authority (MBTA) begins operation. Created in June by the Massachusetts legislature, it replaces the Metropolitan Transit Authority (MTA) and serves seventy-eight (later seventy-nine) communities in the Boston area. The MBTA takes over the commuter rail lines of the New York, New Haven, and Hartford Railroad on July 28, 1965, and that of the Eastern Massachusetts Street Railway Company in 1968.

★≡ *August 7.* Five days after North Vietnamese patrol boats attack the USS *Maddox,* Congress passes the Gulf of Tonkin resolution authorizing President Johnson to commit U.S. troops to the war between North and South Vietnam. U.S. involvement continues until a peace treaty is signed in Paris on January 27, 1973.
The Museum of Afro-American History is established by Sue Bailey Thurman, among others. It moves to the African Meeting House on Beacon Hill in 1987.

🔥 The University of Massachusetts at Boston is established. Located initially at 100 Arlington Street in Park Square, it moves to a new campus on Columbia Point, where the first classes are held in January 1974.

♫ Robert Lowell's *For the Union Dead* is published.
January 31. Leonard Bernstein's Symphony no. 3 (*Kaddish*) is given its American premiere by the Boston Symphony Orchestra at Symphony Hall.

September 12. The Beatles perform for the first time in Boston—in a thirty-one-minute concert at Boston Garden. The group makes its second—and last—appearance in Boston before twenty-five thousand fans at Suffolk Downs in East Boston on August 18, 1966.

The Jazz Workshop and Paul's Mall open at 733 Boylston Street. Both clubs are operated by Tony Mauriello and Fred Taylor. Performers would include Miles Davis, Elvin Jones, Roland Kirk, and Charlie Mingus. Both clubs close on April 9, 1978.

April 28. King Lear and *The Comedy of Errors* are performed in repertory by the Royal Shakespeare Company, with Paul Scofield, Alec McCowen, and Diana Rigg, and Peter Brook directing, at the Shubert Theatre.

January 5. The Patriots lose to the Chargers 51–10 in San Diego in the American Football League championship game.

April 26. The Celtics defeat the San Francisco Warriors 105–99 in game 5 at Boston Garden to win their sixth consecutive NBA championship—a record in professional sports. During the season, the Celtics featured the first all-African-American starting five in NBA history.

1965

The Combined Jewish Philanthropies issues *A Community Survey for Long Range Planning: A Study of the Jewish Population of Greater Boston.* Noting that an estimated forty thousand residents of Boston are Jewish, less than half the number of fifteen years before, the report declares: "In a single generation, we have witnessed tremendous changes in the population. . . . We have seen the Jewish population break out from the 'ghetto' and central city into the suburbs, and a rise from little or moderate education to high education."

April 19. The Prudential Center, designed by Charles Luckman, is dedicated at a ceremony attended by an estimated thirty-five thousand people. The 52-story, 750-foot-high building is at the time the tallest building in the world outside Manhattan. "Boston was suffering from a major league inferiority complex," the future Boston Redevelopment Authority director Stephen Coyle later declares, "and the Pru began the turnaround." Thirty more downtown office buildings and stores open by 1978. The Prudential Center shopping arcade is expanded and a pedestrian walkway to Copley Place is added in 1995.

August 25. The Massachusetts Bay Transportation Authority introduces the "T" logo and color-coded subway lines: Green for the Emerald Necklace; Blue for the ocean; Red for Harvard University; and Orange because Washington Street was formerly called Orange Street.

The prototype of the Black Heritage Trail is established by J. Marcus Mitchell, curator of the Museum of Afro-American History. The trail is formally presented in a brochure in 1968; sites eventually include the African Meeting House, the Smith Court Residences, the Abiel Smith School, the George Middleton House, the *Robert Gould Shaw and the 54th Regiment Memorial,* the

Phillips School, the John J. Smith House, the Charles Street Meeting House, the Lewis and Harriet Hayden House, and the John Coburn House.

Helen Howe's *The Gentle Americans: Biography of a Breed* and Samuel Eliot Morison's *The Oxford History of the American People* are published.

March 12. An estimated two hundred demonstrators stage a sit-in on the eleventh floor of the federal building in Boston to protest the murder three days before of Rev. James Reeb of Dorchester in Selma, Alabama, where he had been attempting to enroll African-American voters. Police evict the demonstrators two days later, arresting thirty-five.

April 23. Martin Luther King, Jr., leads a march of five thousand people from Roxbury to Boston Common. In his speech King declares: "I would be dishonest to say Boston is Birmingham or that Massachusetts is a Mississippi. But it would be irresponsible for me to deny the crippling poverty and the injustices that exist in some sections of this community." King then meets with Mayor Collins, presenting him with a "bill of particulars" related to housing, welfare, community affairs, and poverty.

April 26. A group called Mothers for Adequate Welfare stages a sit-in at the state welfare office on Hawkins Street, protesting the department's failure to distribute surplus food.

February 24. The War Memorial Auditorium opens. The hall, which has over five thousand seats, is later renamed the Hynes Convention Center after the former mayor. It is expanded and renovated in 1989.

The Boston Police Patrolmen's Association is established. The union receives American Federation of Labor charter number 16,807—the same number originally awarded to the Boston police union that voted to strike in 1919.

November 9. At 5:21 P.M., the Great Northeast Blackout strikes Boston. Thirty-six million people over eight hundred square miles lose electricity, which begins to be restored at 9:08 P.M.

Spring. Jonathan Kozol, a teacher at the Christopher Gibson School, is fired after he teaches Langston Hughes's poem "Ballad of the Landlord." The Boston School Committee member Thomas Eisenstadt later cites "Mr. Kozol's continual deviation from the fourth grade course of study."

August 18. Gov. John Volpe signs the Massachusetts Racial Imbalance Act. Filed by the state representative Royal Bolling, of Roxbury, the law calls for the state to withhold aid to school districts where "the percent of non-white students in any public school is in excess of fifty percent of the total number of students in such school," and so applies only to Boston, Cambridge, and Springfield.

August. Operation Exodus is established. Founded by Ellen Jackson and others, the program takes advantage of the Boston public schools' open enrollment policy by providing transportation to enable African-American students to attend more integrated schools. More than four hundred students participate in the first year, and more than nine hundred in the second.

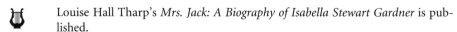

September. Tom Winship succeeds his father, Laurence, as editor of the *Boston Globe*. He would be credited with making it a nationally important newspaper.

September 25. The first issue of *The Bay State Banner* appears. Bryant Rollins is the first editor.

Louise Hall Tharp's *Mrs. Jack: A Biography of Isabella Stewart Gardner* is published.

Arona McHugh's *The Seacoast of Bohemia* is published. The novel contains this passage describing Boston: "For no matter how they might want to ignore it, there was an excellence about this city, an air of reason, a feeling for beauty, a memory of something very good, and perhaps a reminiscence of the vast aspiration of man which could never entirely vanish."

The Standells' single "Dirty Water" is released. Written by a Texan and recorded by the Los Angeles band, the song reaches no. 11 on the national pop music charts and becomes Boston's unofficial rock 'n' roll anthem.

January 25. The Boston Ballet makes its official debut, performing George Balanchine's *Apollo* and *Scotch Symphony* and Anton Dolin's *Pas de Quatre* at John Hancock Hall. The company's first annual performance of *The Nutcracker* takes place on December 19. The company's founder, E. Virginia Williams, is the first artistic director. She is succeeded by Violette Verdy (1980), Bruce Marks (1985), Anna-Marie Holmes (1997), and Mikko Nissinen (2001 to the present). The company's primary venue later changes to the Back Bay Theatre, the Orpheum, the Opera House, the National Theatre, and finally the Wang Center for the Performing Arts.

February 2. Neil Simon's *The Odd Couple*, starring Walter Matthau and Art Carney, opens at the Colonial Theatre. Simon rewrites part of the play while staying at the Ritz-Carlton Hotel.

The first annual Boston Film Festival is held. The festival continues today.

April 15. The Celtics beat the Philadelphia 76ers 110–109 in game 7 at Boston Garden to win the Eastern Conference championship, as John Havlicek steals the ball with five seconds left to preserve the victory. The Celtics go on to beat the Lakers 129–96 in game 5 at Boston Garden to win their eighth NBA championship on April 25.

October. The first annual Head of the Charles Regatta is held. The regatta subsequently becomes the largest rowing meet in the world.

1966

Demolition begins for construction of the proposed Southwest Expressway (I-95) and Inner Belt. More than five hundred buildings are torn down by the time construction ceases in 1973. On October 15 a "Beat the Belt" rally takes place in front of the State House, organized by those opposed to construction of the highways.

The South End Historical Society is established.

September 13. Mayor Collins is defeated by the former governor Endicott Peabody in the Democratic primary for the U.S. Senate seat being vacated by the retiring Leverett Saltonstall. Edward W. Brooke defeats Peabody in the final election on November 8 to become the first African-American elected to the U.S. Senate since Reconstruction.

August 10. The Fort Hill Commune is established in Roxbury. Formed by friends and followers of the musician Mel Lyman, it includes members of the Jim Kweskin Jug Band. The group subsequently purchases a number of houses around Fort Hill Park. Despite Lyman's death in 1978, it continues today.

September. The Metropolitan Council for Educational Opportunity program (METCO) is established. The program provides minority children with the opportunity to attend suburban schools. A total of 220 students in Boston and seven suburban school districts take part in the first year. Over three thousand students in Boston and Springfield and thirty-five school districts participate by 2002.

March 2. The first issue of *Boston After Dark (BAD)*, a weekly entertainment newspaper, appears. After writers at the "underground" Cambridge *Phoenix* go on strike, *BAD* buys that paper and becomes the *Boston Phoenix* in August 1972. Meanwhile, the striking writers form *The Real Paper*. Its first issue appears on August 2, its last on July 12, 1981.
The first annual Channel 2 Auction begins. A fund-raiser, it is hosted by the station president, David Ives, who continues to host the auction for many years.
Robert Manning succeeds Edward Weeks, Jr., as editor of the *Atlantic Monthly*. He is succeeded by William Whitworth (1981 to 1999*).
WGBH Radio's *Morning Pro Musica* debuts. Ron Della Chiesa becomes host in 1969. Robert J. Lurtsema succeeds him in 1971.

An exhibit of Andy Warhol's works is held at the Institute of Contemporary Art. The art rock band The Velvet Underground plays at the opening.
The Massachusetts legislature passes a law giving the state attorney general, rather than the Watch and Ward Society, the authority to prohibit certain books from being sold and exempts booksellers from liability.

Martin Green's *The Problem of Boston* is published. In it he declares: "[Boston] tried hard to be what modern criticism says a culture should be. Its literature should surely bear *some* mark of that virtue, and in *some* way satisfy, rather than so radically dissatisfy, that taste. That is the puzzle. That is the problem of Boston."

The Cheri becomes Boston's first multiplex cinema.

April 19. Roberta Gibb becomes the first woman to complete the Boston Marathon. She runs unofficially since women are still prohibited from participating. A year later, Kathrine Switzer (who had obtained a number by applying as "K. Switzer") nearly has her number torn off early in the race by the Boston Athletic Association official Jock Semple, but she ultimately finishes the race in four hours and twenty minutes.

April 28. The Celtics beat the Los Angeles Lakers 95–93 in game 7 at Boston Garden to win their ninth NBA championship, all of them under coach Red Auerbach, who retires after the game. On April 18, the Celtics had named Bill Russell their next coach, making him the first African-American head coach in a major American professional sport.

October 19. The Bruins beat the Detroit Red Wings 6–2 at Boston Garden, in Bobby Orr's first game with the team. Orr would become one of the greatest hockey players in the history of the National Hockey League, and one of the most popular athletes in Boston history, before knee injuries force him to retire in 1978.

Gil Santos is named radio broadcaster for the New England Patriots. He continues until 1979; he then resumes in 1990 and continues today.

1967

August 4. Ed Logue submits his final report as director of the Boston Redevelopment Authority. In it he envisions Boston in 1975: "Downtown has become a marvelous combination of Olde Boston, still very much here, and a new Boston—apartment towers on the Waterfront with a pedestrian way from Beacon Hill past the new City Hall, Faneuil Hall, Quincy Market, where the old bookstalls joined with food stores and shops of all kinds have replaced the produce market, down to a Waterfront Park where the harbor and the sea open before you. Much of Washington Street is a mall and people love it. Locke-Ober's is still there, but there are new stores and restaurants. . . . Boston's residential neighborhoods are renewed. Their schools and other public services have reached the quality level of the better suburbs and the exodus of families has halted. Neighborhoods are secure about their future, because for one thing, they had a lot to say about it. . . . Boston is still Boston, but newer, fresher, more dynamic—a better place than ever to live and work." The historian Lawrence Kennedy later writes: "[Robert] Moses may have accomplished more [in New York City] in absolute terms over many decades, but Logue transformed proportionally more of a smaller city in less than seven years."

Bainbridge Bunting's *Houses of Boston's Back Bay: An Architectural History, 1840–1917* is published.

January 31. Katherine "Kitty" Craven, a City Councilor, throws an ashtray at fellow councilor William Foley during a meeting in Boston City Council chambers. The second woman elected to the body, Craven also calls Foley a "bald-headed bastard" for making what she later describes as "insulting" remarks.

November 7. Kevin White (with 102,706 votes) beats Louise Day Hicks (with 90,154) to win election as mayor. The Massachusetts secretary of state, White had admitted he was seeking the mayor's office "to raise money for a gubernatorial bid." A few days before the election, the *Boston Globe* had broken its seventy-one-year policy of not endorsing candidates and declared its support for White. Hicks was the first woman to win a preliminary election for mayor in September. Her campaign slogan was "You know where I stand"—a reference to her strong opposition to school busing as a remedy for ending school segregation in Boston.

November 7. Thomas Atkins becomes the second African American to be elected citywide to the Boston City Council.

April 6. William Baird is arrested for violating Massachusetts law by distributing a contraceptive device (spermicidal foam) to an unmarried nineteen-year-old female student during an appearance at Boston University's Hayden Hall. He is later convicted and the verdict is upheld by the Massachusetts Supreme Judicial Court, and Baird spends thirty-six days in the Charles Street Jail. But in *Eisenstadt v. Baird* the U.S. Supreme Court overrules the decision and strikes down Massachusetts' so-called Crimes against Chastity law on March 22, 1972.

June 2. The Grove Hall riots break out. The violence starts when police arrest members of Mothers for Adequate Welfare, a group that had been conducting a two-day sit-in at the Roxbury welfare office on Blue Hill Avenue to protest the state Welfare Department's policies. Four days of looting and property damage follow along a fifteen-block stretch of Blue Hill Avenue in Roxbury. Sixty-eight people are reported injured and more than fifty are arrested.

June 6. When representatives from the Mothers for Adequate Welfare group do not appear for a scheduled meeting with Mayor Collins at City Hall, he calls an impromptu press conference and announces that he will not be a candidate for reelection.

Project Place is established. Founded by Peter Callaway and other seminarians to provide services to the growing number of hippies, street people, and runaways coming to Boston, it opens a counseling service and drop-in center at 37 Rutland Street and a halfway house on Dwight Street in the South End.

October 6. U.S. Army private Raymond Kroll, eighteen, is arrested and removed from Boston University's Marsh Chapel after he attempts to claim sanctuary there as part of his refusal to participate in the Vietnam War.

Jonathan Kozol's *Death at an Early Age* is published.

The first open-heart surgery is performed at Children's Hospital.

The Boston Gas Company constructs the first of two large liquid natural gas tanks on Commercial Point in Dorchester. The second is constructed in 1969.

Summer. The first issue of *Avatar* appears. Published by the Fort Hill Commune, the underground newspaper soon evolves into a quasi-religious tract featuring Mel Lyman's spiritual teachings. The paper ceases publication in 1969.

January 20. The Boston Tea Party opens at 53 Berkeley Street in the South End, with Willie "Loco" Alexander's band The Lost. Boston's first "psychedelic nightclub," it is operated by Ray Riepen and David Hahn in a former synagogue that had most recently been converted to an underground film theater. After the nightclub ceases operation, the building is converted into condominiums with a convenience store on the ground floor.

The annual Playhouse-in-the-Park summer concert series begins, produced by Elma Lewis. Performers would include Duke Ellington, Odetta, Michael Olatunji, Max Roach, Billy Taylor, and the Boston Pops. The series continues until 1978.

May 6. The James Bond Riot breaks out. An estimated four thousand college students riot outside the 4:00 A.M. showing of *Casino Royale* at the Savoy Theatre. As a promotional stunt for the spy-spoof movie, free admission had been promised to everyone wearing a trench coat. When the theater reaches capacity, those who do not get in riot.

February 18. Boston College beats Providence College 83–82 at Chestnut Hill, in one of greatest collegiate basketball games in Boston history. BC is led by Terry Driscoll of Winthrop, Providence by Jimmy Walker of Roxbury. A few months later, Walker becomes the first player from Boston to be the number one pick in the NBA draft.

May 15. The Bruins acquire Phil Esposito, Ken Hodge, and Fred Stanfield from the Chicago Black Hawks for Gilles Marotte, Doug Mohns, and Jack Norris in one of the most beneficial trades for the Bruins in team history.

August 18. The Red Sox beat the Angels 3–2 at Fenway Park, in a game in which the Red Sox outfielder Tony Conigliaro is "beaned" by the Angels pitcher Jack Hamilton. After missing the rest of the season and all of the next one, Tony C. returns to hit a home run on opening day on April 8, 1969, to help the Red Sox beat the Orioles in Baltimore 5–4 in twelve innings. Traded to the Angels on October 11, 1970, he retires because of failing eyesight in 1971.

October 1. The Red Sox beat the Minnesota Twins 5–3 at Fenway Park to win the American League pennant. Dubbed the "Impossible Dream Team" because it had finished half a game out of last place the year before, the Red Sox are led by Carl Yastrzemski, who batted .417 with 9 home runs, 26 runs batted in, and 22 runs in September. After the victory, thousands of people flood the streets across the city to celebrate. The Red Sox lose to the St. Louis Cardinals 7–2 in game 7 of the World Series at Fenway Park on October 12.

1968

April 26–28. The "Tent City" demonstration is organized in a parking lot at 130 Dartmouth Street, in the South End, by the Community Assembly for a United South End (CAUSE) to protest the displacement of residents by urban renewal. Demonstrators pitch tents and occupy the site for a number of days. A community development corporation is subsequently established that builds

the Tent City housing development, designed by Goody, Clancy and Associates, which opens on April 30, 1988.

May 13. Mayor White announces the enactment of the Boston Banks Urban Renewal Group (BBURG) program, a fifty-million-dollar mortgage program for minorities. A decision is later made to restrict it to the predominantly Jewish sections of Roxbury, Dorchester, and Mattapan. Within two years, forty thousand of the existing residents leave, and a study later finds that half of all the homes purchased are lost through foreclosure by 1974. Authors Hillel Levine and Lawrence Harmon, in their 1992 book, *The Death of an American Jewish Community: A Tragedy of Good Intentions*, write: "The Boston Banks Urban Renewal Group program was to housing what court-ordered desegregation was to education: while creating the impression of fairness, in reality it created more problems than it solved."

Inquilinos Boricuas en Accion (IBA) is established. Founded by Puerto Rican residents of the South End to fight displacement and build affordable housing, the group eventually constructs the Villa Victoria housing development, designed by John Sharratt Associates, at 100 West Dedham Street in 1982.

September 28. The "Mothers of Maverick Street," twenty-five East Boston women led by Anna DeFronzo, stage a sit-in on Maverick Street to keep dump trucks bound for Logan Airport from using local streets. After a week of demonstrations, the Massachusetts Port Authority agrees to reroute the truck traffic and subsequently builds a special truck route on airport property.

The Deer Island primary sewage treatment plant opens. A new one is completed in 1995.

Russell H. Greenan's *It Happened in Boston?* and Thomas H. O'Connor's *Lords of the Loom* are published.

January 1. Kevin White assumes the office of mayor in the first inaugural to be held at Faneuil Hall in fifty years. Although he had envisioned the post as a stepping-stone to higher office, White serves as mayor for sixteen years, the longest tenure of any mayor in Boston's history to date. He is credited with helping to make Boston a "livable" and "world-class" city.

March 19. Mayor White announces the creation of "Little City Halls" to "bring government closer to the people." The first one opens in July; eventually, eighteen are opened throughout the city. All are closed because of budget cuts by July 1, 1981.

April 4–6. Following the assassination of Dr. Martin Luther King, Jr., in Memphis, Tennessee, three days of rioting take place in the Grove Hall area of Roxbury.

April 5. In an effort to calm tensions, Mayor White urges that a James Brown concert at Boston Garden be held as scheduled. He persuades WGBH TV, with the support of "the Vault" (the Boston Coordinating Committee), to televise the concert in an attempt to keep people home.

April 6. Nearly five thousand people attend a rally organized by the Black United Front at White Stadium in Franklin Park, at which a list of demands is presented that includes "the transfer of the ownership of . . . [white-owned] businesses to the black community, . . . every school in the black community shall have all-black staff, . . . [and] control of all public, private, and municipal agencies that affect the lives of the people in this community."

June 14. Four members of the so-called "Boston Five" (the pediatrician Dr. Benjamin Spock, Rev. William Sloane Coffin, Michael Ferber, Mitchell Goodman, but not Marcus Raskin) are convicted in Federal District Court in Boston of counseling young men to refuse military service. The four are sentenced to two years in prison on July 10, but the convictions are overturned by the Federal Court of Appeals on July 11, 1969.

Boston High School opens at 332 Newbury Street. A work-study high school program, it later moves to the former Abraham Lincoln School, designed by A. W. Longfellow, at 152 Arlington Street. The school closes in 2002.
September 24. After a student is denied entrance to English High School for violating the dress code by wearing a dashiki, five hundred African-American students walk out of the school in protest.

September 14. The creation of the "Boston Arm" is announced. The artificial, battery-operated, computer-controlled limb, which responds to the wearer's thoughts, was developed by a number of Boston medical and scientific institutions working together.

June. The Unity Bank opens. Described as "the first full service Black bank in Boston," it is later subsumed by the Boston Bank of Commerce. Incorporated on June 30, 1982, the Bank of Commerce is described as "the only fully-insured Black owned and operated bank in Boston and New England."

March 17. Newspaper Row comes to an end when United Press International moves from Washington Street to Ashburton Place. At one time, the *Globe*, *Herald*, *Traveler*, *Advertiser*, *Post*, *Journal*, *Transcript*, AP, UPI, and the International News Service all were located there.
June 25. The *Boston Herald* begins running a series on what it calls Boston's Hippie Invasion, declaring that "flower children by the thousands head here to join those already on the scene."
The *Boston Globe* introduces "Draft Counselor" as a Sunday feature.
WGBH TV begins airing *Say Brother*, a current affairs show on subjects of interest to Boston's African-American community.

January 28. In an article entitled "The Bosstown Sound," *Newseek* features four local bands—the Beacon Street Union, Orpheus, Phluph, and Ultimate Spinach—and describes the music as "anti-drug, anti-hippie."
Summerthing is established. An annual summerlong festival of the arts throughout Boston's neighborhoods, the city-sponsored program ends in the early 1980s because of budget constraints.
August 31. Judy Garland makes her last Boston appearance in concert on Boston Common before one hundred thousand people.
The movies *The Boston Strangler* and *The Thomas Crown Affair* are released.

April 19. The Celtics beat the Philadelphia 76ers 100–96 in game 7 in Philadelphia to win the Eastern Conference title, after trailing in the series three games to one. The Celtics beat the Lakers 124–109 in game 6 in Los Angeles to win the NBA championship on May 2. They beat the Lakers again, 108–106 in game 7 in Los Angeles, to win their eleventh championship in thirteen years on May 5, 1969.

May 4. Dancer's Image, owned by the Boston businessman Peter Fuller, wins the Kentucky Derby. The filly's win is reversed three days later, however, when traces of an illegal painkilling drug are found in the horse's system. After an appeal, the Kentucky Racing Commission rules on December 23 that the horse won the race, but not the purse.

November 23. "Harvard beats Yale 29–29" (according to the next day's *Harvard Crimson*) at Harvard Stadium, when Harvard scores sixteen points in the last minute, tying the game on a two-point conversion pass from substitute quarterback Frank Champi to Pete Varney on the final play.

1969

Langley Keyes's *The Rehabilitation Planning Game*, a book about urban renewal in Boston, is published.

Boston passes a rent control law. Initially regulating rents in buildings of six or more units, the law is expanded to include buildings of four or more units, beginning January 1, 1973. A statewide referendum ending rent control goes into effect January 1, 1995.

February. The new City Hall opens at Government Center. To celebrate, a weeklong series of events is held. At one, Senator Edward Kennedy warns, "If the City of Boston becomes . . . a city lived in only by the very rich and the very poor . . . then our problems will overcome us."

January 25. A "People before Highways" demonstration is held at Boston Common to protest the proposed construction of the Inner Belt and Southwest Expressway.

June 21. The Massachusetts Bay Transit Authority "temporarily" suspends trolley service on the Green Line "A" line through Brighton to Watertown Square because of a shortage of trolley cars. The service is never restored, and the tracks are finally torn up in 1996.

June 27. Rabbi Gerald Zelermyer is attacked in his home in Mattapan by two young men who come to his door, hand him a note demanding that he "lead the Jewish racists out of Mattapan," and throw acid in his face.

October 15. More than one hundred thousand people protest U.S. involvement in the Vietnam War on Boston Common. It is one of many demonstrations held on this day as part of a Vietnam moratorium movement across the country. Speakers include U.S. senators George McGovern of South Dakota and Edward Kennedy of Massachusetts.

December 18. Mel King and other members of the New Urban League demonstrate at a United Way luncheon at the Statler-Hilton, protesting the "crumbs" given to Boston's African-American community.

October. Dorchester district court judge Jerome Troy is ordered to cease filling property he owns along Tenean Beach in Dorchester after photos of him op-

Anti–Vietnam War demonstration, Boston Common. (Photograph courtesy of the Boston Public Library, Print Department)

erating a bulldozer during court hours appear in the newspaper. He is removed from the bench and disbarred in 1973.

June. The New England Aquarium, designed by Cambridge Seven Associates, opens on Central Wharf.
Thalassa Cruso's *Making Things Grow: A Practical Guide for the Indoor Gardener* is published.

The William Monroe Trotter School opens at 135 Humboldt Avenue in Roxbury. An elementary school, it is one of the first citywide "magnet" schools created to encourage integration.

The Advocates first airs on WGBH TV. Featuring debates on current affairs, the show is hosted by Michael Dukakis.

June 17. Hamlet, starring Nicol Williamson, opens at the Colonial Theatre. Disappointed with his performance, Williamson walks off the stage. He reappears twenty minutes later, and is persuaded by the audience to continue.

1970

Boston's population is 641,071, the sixteenth largest of any city in the United States. Of that number, 524,709 are white; 104,707 are African American; and 11,655 are classified as "other." In addition, 83,988 are foreign born.

February 11. Gov. Frank Sargent declares a temporary moratorium on all high-way construction in Greater Boston, except for completion of I-93. "Nearly everyone was sure highways were the only answer to transportation problems for years to come," Sargent declares. "But we were wrong." The moratorium is made permanent, ending plans for the proposed Southwest Expressway and Inner Belt, on November 30, 1972.

Columbia Point Playground is added to the city's park system.

Stephen Fox's *The Guardian of Boston: William Monroe Trotter* and Hiller Zo-bel's *The Boston Massacre* are published.

November 3. Democratic Mayor Kevin White loses to the incumbent Republi-can, Frank Sargent, in the governor's race.
Louise Day Hicks is elected the U.S. Representative from the Ninth Congres-sional District, replacing the retiring John McCormack.
Msgr. Mimie Pitaro, pastor of Holy Redeemer Church in East Boston, becomes the first Roman Catholic priest to be elected to the Massachusetts legislature.

January 29. A student protest against a speech by Dr. S. I. Hayakawa at North-eastern University turns violent when Boston police attempt to disperse the demonstrators.
April 15. An estimated fifty thousand take part in an anti–Vietnam War demon-stration on Boston Common.
May. After four students protesting the U.S. invasion of Cambodia are shot and killed at Kent State University and two at Jackson State University, college students in Boston join their counterparts throughout the country in a student strike to protest the war in Vietnam.
May 10. Violence erupts again at Northeastern University when Boston police are called to break up a block party on Hemenway Street.
The first annual Walk for Hunger is held, sponsored by Project Bread.

The Ritz-Carlton allows unescorted women into its bar and café for the first time.
The first annual August Moon Festival is held in Chinatown.

September 23. A Boston police officer, Walter Schroeder, is shot and killed while responding to a robbery of the State Street Bank and Trust Company in Brighton. The three male members of the group of self-styled revolutionaries who robbed the bank are soon arrested, tried, convicted, and sentenced to prison. The two women become fugitives. Susan Saxe surrenders in 1975 and is released from prison in May 1982; Katherine Power surrenders in 1993, and is released from prison in 1999. Boston police officer William Schroeder, Walter's brother, is later shot and killed by gunmen who robbed a pawn shop on Wash-ington Street in Roxbury on November 30, 1973.

April 22. The nation's first annual Earth Day is held; it is marked in Boston by a demonstration on Boston Common.

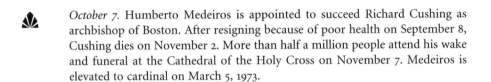

October 7. Humberto Medeiros is appointed to succeed Richard Cushing as archbishop of Boston. After resigning because of poor health on September 8, Cushing dies on November 2. More than half a million people attend his wake and funeral at the Cathedral of the Holy Cross on November 7. Medeiros is elevated to cardinal on March 5, 1973.

Copley High School opens at 150 Newbury Street. Founded as Dorchester Annex High School in 1966, the school is renamed Snowden International High School in 1988.

The Boston Women's Health Book Collective's *Our Bodies, Ourselves* is published.

Evening at Pops first airs on WGBH TV.

Walter Muir Whitehill's *The Museum of Fine Arts: A Centennial History* and David McCord's "Poem for the Occasion" are published to celebrate the museum's one hundredth anniversary.
March 6. Galt McDermot's *Hair* opens at the Wilbur Theatre. The musical is immediately shut down by the city censor (officially, chief of the Licensing Division), Richard Sinnott—not because of the nude scene, but because of one in which the American flag is desecrated. The show reopens four weeks later and runs for forty weeks.
The first annual production of *Black Nativity* by the Elma Lewis School of Fine Arts is performed at the school in Roxbury. A reinterpretation of Langston Hughes's play, the production later moves to Northeastern University, then to the Opera House, and continues today.

May 10. The Bruins beat the St. Louis Blues 4–3 in overtime in game 7 at the Boston Garden to sweep the series and win their first Stanley Cup in twenty-nine years, as Bobby Orr scores the winning goal. The team is also led by Phil Esposito ("Jesus Saves . . . and Esposito Scores on the Rebound" is a popular bumper sticker at the time).

1971

The Shelburne Community Center opens at 2730 Washington Street in Roxbury.
The First National Bank building opens at 100 Federal Street. Designed by Cambridge, Aldrich, Nulty (and sometimes called "the pregnant building" because of the bulge in its middle), it later becomes the Bank of Boston, then the FleetBank Building.
The Boston Housing Authority's controversial Infill I scattered-site housing development opens. Infill II opens in 1972. The program founders when the developer goes bankrupt, leaving unfinished foundations and shells in many neighborhoods.
Harbor Towers, designed by Henry Cobb of I. M. Pei and Partners, opens on India Wharf.

The Friends of the Public Garden and Boston Common is established to oppose the proposed Park Plaza development. Its goal is to protect and preserve those historic parks.

November 2. Kevin White (with 113,137 votes) again defeats Louise Day Hicks (with 70,331) to win reelection as mayor.
Lawrence DiCara, twenty-two, becomes the youngest person elected to citywide office in Boston history when he is elected to the City Council. Albert "Dapper" O'Neil is also first elected to the council.

The first annual Gay Pride Day is held.

The Ritz-Carlton ends its prohibition of women wearing pantsuits in the hotel bar.

Masterpiece Theatre first airs on WGBH TV. Alistair Cooke is the first host. He is succeeded by Russell Baker in 1993.

Corita Kent's mural is painted on one of the two Boston Gas Company tanks on Commercial Point in Dorchester. Reportedly the largest copyrighted work of art in the world, the painting is replicated—after the larger tank is demolished—on the smaller tank in 1994. Although many people claim to see the likeness of the late Vietnamese leader Ho Chi Minh in the rainbow stripes, the artist denies the resemblance was intentional.
George V. Higgins's *The Friends of Eddie Coyle* is published.
November 10. Elvis Presley makes his only Boston appearance, at a sold-out Boston Garden.
December. The J. Geils band releases its eponymously titled first album.

March 20. Boston University beats Minnesota 4–2 in Syracuse to win its first NCAA hockey championship.

1972

July 13. At the Democratic National Convention in Miami, the presidential nominee George McGovern nearly chooses Boston Mayor Kevin White as his running mate, but he selects U.S. Senator Thomas Eagleton of Missouri instead.
November 7. J. Joseph Moakley, running as an Independent, defeats the incumbent Louise Day Hicks to win election as the U.S. representative from the Ninth Congressional District.
Doris Bunte of Boston becomes the first African-American woman elected to the Massachusetts state legislature.

July 15. A fight at the Puerto Rican Festival at Blackstone Park in the South End turns into a three-day riot. Twenty-seven are injured and thirty-five arrested as cars are stoned and stores are looted and burned.

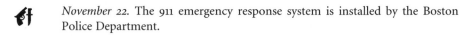

November 22. The 911 emergency response system is installed by the Boston Police Department.

June 17. A fire at the Hotel Vendome on Commonwealth Avenue kills nine Boston firefighters when the floors of the building collapse without warning. Ted Clausen and Peter White's memorial to the firefighters is later installed nearby on the Commonwealth Avenue Mall.

March 15. The *Morgan v. Hennigan* case is filed in the federal district court in Boston. Named for Tallulah Morgan, a twenty-four-year-old mother of three and one of fifteen plaintiffs, and the Boston School Committee chairman James Hennigan, the class action suit charges the Boston School Committee with deliberately creating a dual school system—one for white students and one for African Americans—in violation of the Fourteenth Amendment. The case is decided in 1974.*
Boston Latin School and English High School become coeducational.

Nine to Five is established. Founded by Karen Nussbaum and others, the organization's goal is to promote better pay, treatment, and working conditions for women clerical workers in Boston.

The first issue of the *Sampan*, a Chinese-language weekly, appears.
Zoom, a national program for children, first airs on WGBH TV.

Brian Cudahy's *Change at Park Street Under: The Story of Boston's Subways* and Mark Mirsky's *Blue Hill Avenue* are published.
July 18–19. The start of a concert by the Rolling Stones at Boston Garden is delayed by the arrest in Warwick, Rhode Island, of Keith Richards and Mick Jagger. Mayor White takes the stage and asks the sellout crowd to be patient. The band eventually arrives, and the show begins after midnight.

March 18. Boston University beats Cornell 4–0 at Boston Garden to win its second straight NCAA hockey championship.
April 17. Female runners are allowed to participate in the Boston Marathon for the first time. Nina Kuscsik becomes the first women's winner, finishing in 3:10:26. Finland's Olari Suomalainen wins the men's race in 2:15:39.
May 11. The Bruins beat the New York Rangers 3–0 at Madison Square Garden in game 6 to win their fifth Stanley Cup, their second in three years, and the last to date.
June. The Boston Shootout is established. An annual basketball tournament for high school players from around the country, it is organized initially as a showcase for the so-called Boston Six (Bobby Carrington, Billy Collins, King Gaskins, Ron Lee, Wilfred Morrison, and Carlton Smith), one of the most talented group of players in the city's history.

1973

January 20. A storm shatters sixteen panes of glass and damages forty-nine others in the new John Hancock Building, still under construction, sending a shower of broken glass onto the street. Fortunately, no one is hurt. Eventually, one-third of the 10,344 panes of reflective glass shatter and are replaced, temporarily, with sheets of plywood. The glass is eventually redesigned and new windows are installed.

Tai Tung Village opens in Chinatown. The culmination of a struggle for community control and against urban renewal, the four buildings contain over two hundred units of affordable housing.

I-93 is completed into Boston.

The Massachusetts Bay Transit Authority launches "Dime Time," a reduced-fare program on weekdays between 10:00 A.M. and 1:00 P.M. The program is later discontinued. A prepaid pass program is introduced a year later.

A replica of the Boston Tea Party ship is first moored in the Fort Point Channel.

November 6. Louise Day Hicks is first elected to the Boston City Council. She becomes the first woman president of the council in 1976.

January 22. In *Roe v. Wade*, the U.S. Supreme Court strikes down nearly all state laws against abortion.

August 29. Three members of the Fort Hill Commune attempt to rob the New England Merchants Bank in Brigham Circle. One of the men is shot and killed by police. The other two, Sheldon Barnhard and the actor Mark Frechette, are captured, tried, convicted, and imprisoned. Frechette is later killed in what is described as an accident in the prison weight room.

July 31. A Delta jet crashes while landing in the heavy fog at Logan Airport, killing all eighty-nine persons on board. It is the worst aviation disaster in Boston history.

September 9. A gravel truck slams into a girder of the Tobin Bridge. The driver is killed, two hundred feet of the structure collapses, and the bridge is closed for several months for repairs.

Roxbury Community College is established. Located initially in Grove Hall, it moves to Dudley Street in January 1975, to the former Boston State College campus on Huntington Avenue in 1982, and to its current location, a campus designed by Stull and Lee at 1234 Columbus Avenue, in January 1988.

Bunker Hill Community College opens in Charlestown.

Boston magazine introduces its first annual "Bests" and "Worsts" of Boston issue.

Robert B. Parker's first Spenser mystery, *The Godwulf Manuscript*, is published.

January 8. Bruce Springsteen performs at Paul's Mall in his first Boston appearance. A year later, after Springsteen returns to the Boston area, the *Real Paper* rock critic Jon Landau writes a review on March 22, 1974, in which he declares, "I saw rock and roll future and its name is Bruce Springsteen."

July 27–28. The KOOL/Newport Jazz Festival/New England, produced by

George Wein, is held at Fenway Park. Performers include Ray Charles, Roland Kirk, Charles Mingus, the New Preservation Hall Jazz Band, and Stevie Wonder.

Aerosmith's first album, featuring the hit song "Dream On," is released.

Seiji Ozawa succeeds William Steinberg as music director of the Boston Symphony Orchestra. He serves for twenty-nine years, the longest tenure in BSO history, and is succeeded by James Levine, the first American-born music director in the orchestra's history, in October 2004.

January 30. The New England Patriots choose John Hannah of the University of Alabama with the fourth pick in the National Football League draft. He would become one of the greatest offensive linemen in the history of professional football.

1974

The "Combat Zone" is established as an official "Adult Entertainment District." Fearful of these businesses' spreading to other parts of the city, Boston amends its zoning code to permit them along lower Washington Street and prohibit them elsewhere in the city.

A report by the Boston Observatory, an institute at the University of Massachusetts/Boston, concludes that residential property in some of the city's neighborhoods (e.g., Dorchester and Roxbury) is being assessed at three times the rate of property in others (e.g., the Back Bay, Charlestown, and East Boston).

In *Town of Sudbury v. Commissioner of Corporations and Taxation*, the Massachusetts Supreme Judicial Court rules that all cities and towns in the state must reassess property at 100 percent of their full market value. The ruling has a serious effect on property taxes and the city budget in Boston.

The Mishawum Park public housing development is completed in Charlestown.

July 4. The annual Boston Pops concert on the Esplanade features Tchaikovsky's *1812 Overture* for the first time, complete with church bells, cannons, and—thanks to the businessman David Mugar—fireworks. The event begins to attract hundreds of thousands of spectators and a large television audience.

October 1. A law creating the Boston National Historic Park is signed by President Gerald Ford.

April 28. Boston City Councilors Louise Day Hicks and Albert "Dapper" O'Neil post large letters in the windows of their City Hall offices spelling out ROAR (Restore Our Alienated Rights), the acronym for an antibusing group. After a judge refuses to order the removal of the letters, the windows are broken a number of times by vandals.

November 5. William Owens of Mattapan becomes the first African American elected to the Massachusetts State Senate. Elaine Noble becomes the first openly gay member of the Massachusetts legislature when she is elected state representative from the Back Bay.

The Haymarket People's Fund is established. Founded by George Pillsbury, its purpose is to enable wealthy heirs to contribute to socially progressive causes.

April 14. Rosie's Place opens in the former Rozen's Market on Columbus Avenue in the South End. Founded by Kip Tiernan originally as a drop-in center, it becomes a women's shelter when it moves to Haley House on Dartmouth Street a year later. It moves to 1662 Washington Street in 1978, then to its current location, the former St. Phillip's Church at 886 Harrison Avenue, in 1986.

Douglass Shand-Tucci's *Church Building in Boston, 1720–1970* is published.

June 21. Federal district court judge W. Arthur Garrity rules for the plaintiffs in *Morgan v. Hennigan.* In his decision, the judge declares that the Boston

Students being bused to South Boston. (Photograph by Kevin Cole, courtesy of the Boston Herald)

School Committee "knowingly carried out a systematic program of segregation" and "intentionally brought about and maintained a dual school system" by creating "Byzantine" feeder systems, "manipulating district lines and establishing different grade structures for schools in different neighborhoods." A few days later, Judge Garrity orders "Phase I" of his remedy, which calls for busing four thousand of the school system's approximately ninety-four thousand students to promote integration in the Boston public schools.

September 9. An estimated eight thousand people protest Judge Garrity's busing order at a rally at Government Center. When Senator Edward Kennedy attempts to speak, he is shouted down, pelted with tomatoes and rocks, and chased into the building bearing his late brother's name, the John F. Kennedy Federal Office Building.

July 25. In *Millikan v. Bradley,* the U.S. Supreme Court rules that suburban school districts cannot be forced to be part of the remedy to end segregation in an urban school district.

September 12. On the first day of school, only 124 of 1,300 students report to class in South Boston, and 235 of 900 students report to school at Roxbury High School.

October 4. An evening motorcade demonstration is held in front of Judge Garrity's home in suburban Wellesley. Later that night and the next, patrons of the Rabbit Inn in South Boston clash with members of the Boston Police Department's Tactical Patrol Force (TPF).

October 7. Mayor White requests that federal marshals be assigned to Boston. That afternoon, the Haitian immigrant Andre Yvon Jean-Louis is attacked in South Boston after he stops to pick up his wife at work in a laundry there.

October 8–9. African-American youths stone cars driven by white drivers in Jamaica Plain, Roxbury, and the South End. Protest demonstrations and violent incidents continue sporadically for the next two years.

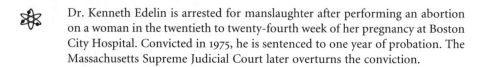

Dr. Kenneth Edelin is arrested for manslaughter after performing an abortion on a woman in the twentieth to twenty-fourth week of her pregnancy at Boston City Hospital. Convicted in 1975, he is sentenced to one year of probation. The Massachusetts Supreme Judicial Court later overturns the conviction.

Nova, a national show focusing on science topics, first airs on WGBH TV.

August. The Rat begins offering live music in Kenmore Square. Opened as the Frog in 1962, then the Rathskeller in 1964, the bar-restaurant is purchased by the former manager Jim Herald, who transforms it into first a rock and then a punk rock nightspot. An album, *Live at the Rat,* is recorded September 27–29, 1978.
November 30. The U.S. representative and House Ways and Means Committee chairman Wilbur Mills, a Democrat from Arkansas, appears on the stage of the Pilgrim Theater in pursuit of the stripper Fanne Fox. Mills later admits to an alcohol abuse problem.

May 12. The Celtics beat the Bucks 102–87 in game 7 at Milwaukee to win their twelfth NBA championship. After flying back to Boston and celebrating the victory, the Celtics star Dave Cowens sleeps overnight on a bench in the Public Garden.
May 19. The Bruins lose to the Philadelphia Flyers 1–0 in Philadelphia in the sixth and final game of the Stanley Cup championship.

1975

To enforce the federal Clean Air Act, the Environmental Protection Agency imposes a cap on the number of privately owned downtown rental parking spaces in Boston at 35,503. The parking cap continues today.

Armando Perez and eight other public housing tenants file a class-action suit charging the Boston Housing Authority with violations of the state sanitary code. The Housing Court judge Paul Garrity finds for the plaintiffs on March 28. The BHA is subsequently placed in receivership from February 1980 to October 1984.*

The Franklin Park Coalition is established to protect and preserve the park. Richard Heath is the first director.

Howard Mumford Jones and Bessie Zaban Jones's *The Many Voices of Boston: A Historical Anthology, 1630–1975* is published.
June 20. The *Where's Boston?* exhibit opens at the Prudential Center.
December. The Boston Landmarks Commission is established to identify, protect, and preserve historic properties in the city.

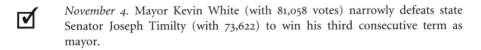

November 4. Mayor Kevin White (with 81,058 votes) narrowly defeats state Senator Joseph Timilty (with 73,622) to win his third consecutive term as mayor.

Massachusetts Fair Share is established. Michael Ansara is the first director. Described by the *Boston Herald* as developing a "lower middle-class following for fights against everything from utility rate hikes to hazardous waste," the statewide organization eventually attracts more than one hundred and fifty thousand members. Individual chapters are started in various Boston neighborhoods.

July 27. Six African-American Bible salesmen from South Carolina are attacked by whites at Carson Beach in South Boston. On August 10, 800 police officers attempt to keep order when an estimated 800 African Americans stage a "picnic" on Carson Beach and are confronted by a crowd of 1,500 whites. Forty people are injured and ten are arrested over the course of the Sunday afternoon.

December 20–22. A storm drops 18.2 inches of snow in Boston, a record for December.

May 10. The U.S. Supreme Court upholds Judge W. Arthur Garrity's ruling in the *Morgan v. Hennigan* case. That same day, Garrity rejects the so-called McCormack Plan, submitted by one of his own court-appointed "Masters," which calls for promoting integration by redrawing school district lines, rather than by busing. Instead, Garrity later issues Phase II of his own plan, which calls for busing an additional ten thousand students in September.

May 5. The *Boston Globe* is awarded a Pulitzer Prize for Meritorious Public Service for what is described as "its massive and balanced coverage of the Boston school desegregation conflict in a bitterly emotional climate."

The Victory Garden, a national show about gardening, first airs on WGBH TV.

April 21. Bill Rodgers wins his first Boston Marathon in a course record time of two hours and nine minutes. Wearing his trademark white gloves, he wins again in 1978, 1979, and 1980. Bob Hall becomes the first official wheelchair entry this year, finishing in a time of two hours and fifty-eight minutes.

October 21. The Red Sox beat the Reds 7–6 in game 6 of the World Series, on Carlton Fisk's twelfth-inning home run off Pat Darcy in one of the greatest World Series games ever played. The Red Sox lose to the Reds 4–3 in the seventh and final game of the series at Fenway Park the next day. Red Sox manager Darrell Johnson is later criticized for replacing pitcher Jim Willoughby with Jim Burton, who gives up the game-winning hit to the Reds' Joe Morgan in the ninth inning.

1976 to 2004

1976

August 26. The renovated Quincy Marketplace, designed by Ben Thompson and developed by the Rouse Company, reopens on the 150th anniversary of its original dedication. A crowd estimated at a hundred thousand people spontaneously turns out to tour the building, a reaction the *New York Times* later calls "instant acceptance." The South Market building opens in 1977, and the North Market building in 1978.

September 29. The John Hancock Tower officially opens at 200 Clarendon Street. Designed by I. M. Pei and Henry Cobb, the 60-story, 790-foot building is the tallest in Boston. Although initially criticized for dwarfing the smaller, historic buildings in Copley Square, it is eventually hailed by many as a great work of architecture. As the humorist poet Felicia Lamport later writes: "'It's a constant delight to the viewer,'/As someone was recently saying,/'And if the old vistas are fewer,/Well, that is the price I. M. Pei-ing.'"

An American Institute of Architects' poll ranks Boston City Hall—along with Trinity Church—as among the ten best works of architecture in the United States.

May 9. Waterfront (later Christopher Columbus) Park opens.

December 31. First Night is established in Boston. Adopted in cities across the country, the New Year's Eve celebration continues today.

July 4. A crowd estimated at four hundred thousand gathers along the Esplanade for the annual Boston Pops concert. It is later recognized by the Guinness Book of World Records as the largest audience ever for a live music performance.

July 10. An estimated 650,000 people witness the parade of the "Tall Ships" into Boston Harbor. Part of the city's Bicentennial celebration, the parade is led by the USS *Constitution*, which goes under sail and fires it cannons for the first time in a hundred years.

July 11. Queen Elizabeth visits Boston. After touring some of the sites on the Freedom Trail, she speaks from the balcony at the Old State House, where the Declaration of Independence had first been read in Boston two hundred years before.

Thomas H. O'Connor's *Bibles, Brahmins, and Bosses: A Short History of Boston* and Francis Russell's *Adams: An American Dynasty* are published.

April 22. At 9:22 A.M. a bomb explodes on the second floor of the new Suffolk County Court House, injuring twenty-five people. The Samuel Melville–Jonathan Jackson Brigade of the New World Liberation Front later claims responsibility and demands improvements in the treatment of prisoners at Walpole State Prison.

A Bicentennial event in front of Faneuil Hall, July 1976. From left to right: Massachusetts Governor Michael Dukakis, his wife, Kitty, Boston Mayor Kevin White, Queen Elizabeth II, and Prince Philip. (Photograph by Frank Hill, courtesy of the Boston Herald)

November 16. Andrew Puopolo, a twenty-one-year-old Harvard student, is stabbed to death in the Combat Zone on the night of the Harvard-Yale football game. After two trials, two men are acquitted and a third is convicted of manslaughter and sentenced to eighteen to twenty years in prison.

February 1. A fire destroys the Thomas Plant Shoe Factory on Centre Street in Jamaica Plain. One of the largest factory buildings in the city, it had been home to hundreds of local artists.

April 5. The American flag is used as a weapon on City Hall Plaza. After an antibusing demonstration, Joseph Rakes, a high school student from South Boston, uses a flagpole to attack Theodore Landsmark, an African-American attorney on his way to a meeting in City Hall. Rakes later pleads guilty to assault and battery, receives a two-year suspended sentence, and moves out of Boston. Landsmark, originally from New York, recovers from his injuries, becomes a high-ranking city official, and is currently president of the Boston Architectural Center. The *Boston Herald American* photographer Stanley Forman is awarded a Pulitzer Prize for his photo of the incident in 1977.

The band Boston's eponymously titled first album, including the hit song "More Than a Feeling," makes it to no. 3 on the pop music charts. The band is made up of five members, four of them from Boston.
The Boston Film/Video Foundation opens at 1149 Boylston Street. Its goal is to provide support and facilities for independent film and video artists.

June 4. The Celtics beat the Suns 128–126 in three overtimes in game 5 of the NBA finals at Boston Garden, in one of the greatest games in NBA play-off history. The Celtics beat the Suns 87–80 in game 6 in Phoenix to win their thirteenth NBA championship on June 6.

1977

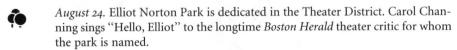

August 24. Elliot Norton Park is dedicated in the Theater District. Carol Channing sings "Hello, Elliot" to the longtime *Boston Herald* theater critic for whom the park is named.

The Boston Historic Neighborhoods organization is established.

Alan Lupo's *Liberty's Chosen Home: The Politics of Violence in Boston* is published.

November 8. John O'Bryant is elected to the Boston School Committee. It is the first time an African American has been elected to the board since 1895.
Madison Park High School, designed by Marcel Breuer and Tician Papachristou, opens at 55 New Dudley Street in Roxbury.

$ Russell B. Adams's *The Boston Money Tree: How the Proper Men of Boston Made, Invested, and Preserved Their Wealth from Colonial Days to the Space Age* is published.

Northeastern University Press is established. One of the areas it would specialize in is Boston history. The press is scheduled to cease operation at the end of 2004.

Robin Cook's *Coma* is published.
Eric in the Evening, a jazz show hosted by Eric Jackson, first airs on WGBH Radio.
Donna Summer's hit single "Love to Love You, Baby" reaches the no. 1 spot on the popular music charts. A graduate of Burke High School, Summer's "MacArthur Park" is no. 1 in 1978, and "Bad Girls" and "Hot Stuff" are nos. 1 and 2 a few years later.
The Next Move Theatre opens at 955 Boylston Street.

May 14. The Bruins lose to the Montreal Canadiens 2–1 in overtime at Boston Garden in the 4th and final game of the Stanley Cup championship series.

1978

The Boston branch of the NAACP sues the federal Department of Housing and Urban Development for allowing the Boston Housing Authority (BHA)

to engage in discrimination. The federal district court judge Walter Skinner subsequently finds in favor of the plaintiffs.

Douglass Shand-Tucci's *Built in Boston: City and Suburb, 1800–1950* is published.

November 7. Massachusetts voters approve a statewide referendum to allow tax classification (setting different tax rates for different kinds of property) by a two to one margin. The measure is particularly important to Boston, where the implementation of tax classification and the large concentration of commercial property combine to keep residential tax rates comparatively low.

Theodore White's *In Search of History: A Personal Adventure* is published. In it he describes the "ethnic ballet; slow yet certain, in every big American city that I have reported, which underlies its politics. The ballet is different in each city." In Boston, he describes how "the old stock Protestants gave way to the Irish, who gave way in turn to Italians or Jews, who gave way in turn to blacks."

The Boston Preservation Alliance is established. An outgrowth of the City Conservation League, which was created in an effort to save the Jordan Marsh block from demolition in 1975, it is an alliance of twenty-five existing preservation organizations. After relocating several times, it moves to its current headquarters in the Old City Hall in 1984.

The city enacts an ordinance that sets aside 10 percent of all city contracts for minority-owned businesses. An executive order increasing the percentage to 15 percent for minority-owned businesses and 5 percent for women-owned businesses is signed in 1987. After recent court rulings strike down such "set aside" programs as unconstitutional, another executive order is signed discontinuing the program in 2003.

April. The Boston Police Department establishes the Community Disorders Unit. A six-man unit, headed by Sgt. (and future police commissioner) Francis "Mickey" Roache, its role is to monitor police response to racial crimes and promote strategies to reduce racial incidents.

February 6–7. The Blizzard of '78 strikes. Snow falls for thirty-three hours, dropping a record 27.1 inches during one twenty-four-hour period—on top of the previous record 21.4 inches that had fallen in twenty-four hours on January 20. Winds reach nearly eighty miles an hour. The storm kills twenty-nine people across Massachusetts and causes an estimated one billion dollars in damage in the state. In Boston, 125 people are arrested for looting on the night of February 7. Roads are closed to all but emergency and public transit vehicles in the city and many surrounding communities for a week, and nonessential businesses are forced to close.

September 5. Downtown Crossing opens. Originally called the Washington Street Mall, the street is a pedestrian mall closed to vehicles to promote retail business.

Blues after Hours first airs on WGBH Radio. The program is hosted by Mai Cramer until her death in 2002 and continues on the air today.

Folk Heritage begins airing on WGBH Radio. The weekly program airs on Sunday evenings until switching to Saturday afternoons in 1981. It is hosted by Dick Pleasants until March 13, 2004, and continues on the air today.

James Carroll's *Mortal Friends* is published.

The Cars' eponymously titled first album is released, which includes the hit song "Just What I Needed."

March 25. Boston University beats Boston College 5–3 in Providence to win the NCAA hockey championship.

May 10. The Bruins lose to the Montreal Canadiens 5–4 in Montreal in game 7 of the Stanley Cup finals.

June. The Boston Celtics draft the junior-eligible player Larry Bird with the sixth pick in the NBA draft. He would go on to become one of the greatest— and probably the most popular—player in the team's history.

August 12. The New England Patriots' wide receiver Darryl Stingley suffers a broken neck and is paralyzed for life as the result of a tackle by the Raiders' linebacker Jack Tatum in an exhibition game in Oakland.

September 7–10. The "second Boston Massacre" takes place. Holding a four-game lead over the Yankees, the Red Sox are swept by New York in a four-game series at Fenway Park by a combined score of 42–9. The teams finish tied for first in the American League, and the Red Sox lose a one-game play-off 5–4, as Bucky Dent hits a three-run home run off the ex-Yankee pitcher Mike Torrez into the net above the Green Monster in Fenway Park on October 2.

1979

Stephan Thernstrom's *The Other Bostonians* is published.

October 20. The John F. Kennedy Library, designed by I. M. Pei, is dedicated on Columbia Point.

March 23. In *Tregor v. Board of Assessors of Boston*, the Massachusetts Supreme Judicial Court rules for the plaintiff and orders the city to refund $143 million to Norman Tregor and other commercial property owners overcharged on their property taxes. The state later assumes the city's debt in return for title to the Hynes Convention Center and the Boston Common Underground Garage as part of the so-called Tregor Bill, passed by the state legislature on June 29, 1982.

November 6. Kevin White (with 78,048 votes) again defeats Joseph Timilty (with 64,269), this time by a bigger margin (54.8 to 45.2 percent) to win reelection to his fourth consecutive term as mayor.

November 7. Senator Edward Kennedy announces his candidacy for president in Faneuil Hall. He is subsequently defeated for the Democratic nomination by incumbent President Jimmy Carter.

Fall. The Boston Resident Jobs Policy Ordinance is signed into law. Proposed by Chuck Turner and others, it sets hiring goals of 50 percent for residents, 25 percent for minorities, and 10 percent for women on all publicly supported construction projects in the city. Struck down by the Massachusetts Supreme Judicial Court in 1982, it is upheld by the U.S. Supreme Court on April 30, 1983. The ordinance is expanded to include major private construction projects in the city on July 12, 1985.

March 30. David Nelson of Roxbury becomes the first African American to be appointed a federal judge in Massachusetts.
The Path of the Law, a series of law-related sites primarily on Beacon Hill and in downtown Boston, is developed as a tour, with an accompanying pamphlet by Edward Bander, the Suffolk University law librarian.
September 28. Darryl Williams, a member of the Jamaica Plain High School football team, is shot while warming up for the second half of a football game at Charlestown High School. Left paralyzed by the attack, Williams goes on to graduate from college and becomes a motivational speaker to youth groups in Boston. A Charlestown teenager subsequently pleads guilty to assault and battery with a dangerous weapon and receives a ten-year prison sentence.

The Boston Urban Gardeners (BUG) is established by a group of neighborhood gardening organizations. Edward Cooper is the first director.

October 1. Pope John Paul II visits Boston. Two million people line the papal motorcade route, and four hundred thousand gather in the rain for a Mass celebrated by the pope on Boston Common.

Radiologists at Massachusetts General Hospital pioneer the use of magnetic resonance imaging (MRI) to diagnose illness and injury.
Artificial skin is invented by Dr. John Burke of Massachusetts General Hospital and Ioannis Yannas of Massachusetts Institute of Technology.

This Old House, a home improvement show, first airs on WGBH TV. The station also begins producing *La Plaza,* a show concerning subjects of interest to Boston's Hispanic community.

July 10. The longtime Boston Pops conductor Arthur Fiedler dies. Harry Ellis Dickson leads the orchestra for the remainder of the season. John Williams is named conductor in 1980; he is succeeded by Keith Lockhart (1995 to the present).

April 16. Joan Benoit, a Bowdoin college senior, wins the Boston Marathon in a women's record time of 2:35:15. She wins the race again in 1983, lowering the women's record time to 2:22:43. Benoit also wins the Olympic women's marathon in Los Angeles in 1984.

1980

Boston's population is 562,994, twentieth among U.S. cities. Of that number, 382,123 are white; 122,203 are African American; 36,068 are Hispanic; 14,910 are

Asian/Pacific Islander; 1,217 are Native American; 6,473 are of other races. A total of 87,056 are foreign born.

Jane Holtz Kay's *Lost Boston* is published.

November 4. Massachusetts voters approve a binding referendum question called Proposition 2½, which places a 2.5 percent cap on both the total amount of revenue cities and towns can raise through property taxes and the percentage those taxes can be increased annually. As a result, the city of Boston must reduce its property tax revenue by $518.7 million in fiscal year 1981 to $374.6 million in fiscal year 1983 and lay off approximately three thousand city workers.

December 6. The Massachusetts Bay Transit Authority shuts down for twenty-six hours for lack of funds. The next day, the Massachusetts legislature passes Chapter 581, the so-called Management Rights Bill, which allows the system to resume operation.

Shipyard Park opens at the Charlestown Navy Yard.

Boston celebrates its 350th anniversary with a summerlong series of events, including a "Parade of Sail" of Tall Ships into Boston Harbor, which is watched by an estimated one million people on May 30.

September 21. An 1,800-pound birthday cake is unveiled and cut into pieces for 15,000 people on Boston Common in the morning. A parade of 20,000 marchers is watched by an estimated 1 to 1.5 million people in the afternoon. The Boston Pops plays for an estimated 120,000 people at City Hall Plaza in the evening.

The Boston Committee is formed to improve race relations. Members include Mayor White; Cardinal Medeiros; Richard Hill, chairman of the First National Bank of Boston; and Davis Taylor, chairman of Affiliated Publications, the parent company of the *Boston Globe.* Frank Jones is executive director.

July 15. Levi Hart, a fourteen-year-old African American attempting to flee in a stolen car, is shot and killed by police near Kenmore Square. His death prompts public outcries against the use of excessive force by the Boston Police Department. Hundreds of people attend Hart's funeral at the Union United Methodist Church on July 21.

October 13. A fire badly damages the Beacon Chambers hotel at 19 Myrtle Street on Beacon Hill, leaving 350 people homeless. The building is rebuilt, converted into affordable housing for the elderly, and reopens on November 22, 1983.

September 8. The Hubert Humphrey Occupational Resource Center, designed by Shepley, Bulfinch, Richardson, and Abbott, opens at 55 New Dudley Street in Roxbury.

Bunker Hill Community College (established in 1973), also designed by Shepley, Bulfinch, Richardson, and Abbott, opens in Charlestown.

July 12. The Brigham and Women's Hospital opens. It is formed by a merger of the Peter Bent Brigham and Robert Breck Brigham hospitals, and the Boston Hospital for Women.

March 15. A *Boston Globe* headline for a story on a speech by President Carter on the nation's economic woes reads, "Mush from the Wimp." The result of a prank by the reporter Kirk Scharfenberg, the headline was to have been corrected before the paper went to press. In later editions, it is changed to "All Must Share the Burden."

July 3–August 31. The artist Judy Chicago's *Dinner Party* is exhibited at the Cyclorama Building.

February 11. Northeastern beats Boston College 5–4 in overtime to win its first Beanpot hockey tournament championship, as Wayne Turner scores the winning goal. For the first twenty-seven years of the tournament, Northeastern had been known as "the team that played at 6:15" (the starting time of the consolation game).

April 21. Rosie Ruiz is crowned the women's winner of the Boston Marathon. She is later disqualified for failing to run the entire race (having taken public transportation part of the way), and Jackie Garreau of Canada is named the official winner on April 29. This is also the first year that Dick Hoyt and his son, Rick, a victim of cerebral palsy, run the race together, a tradition they have continued almost every year since.

June 9. The Celtics trade the first and thirteenth picks in the NBA draft to the Golden State Warriors for Robert Parrish and the third pick, who, the next day, turns out to be Kevin McHale of the University of Minnesota. It is one of the best trades in the team's history.

1981

March 27. Moody's Investors' Service suspends the bond rating of Boston and thirty-six other Massachusetts municipalities, making borrowing impossible.

September. The South Boston Vietnam Memorial is dedicated at M Street Park. Reportedly the first in the United States, it honors twenty-five South Boston residents killed in that war. The inscription on the monument reads, "To All the Men and Women Who Served During the Viet-Nam War, 1961–1975, Welcome Home."

March 27. A planned "birthday party" for Mayor White's wife at the Museum of Fine Arts is canceled after charges are made that it is really a thinly disguised fund-raising event.

November 3. Boston's City Council and School Committee are again reorganized. Voters approve a proposal to make each one a thirteen-member board, with nine members elected by district and four elected at large, all of them serving two-year terms, beginning in 1984.

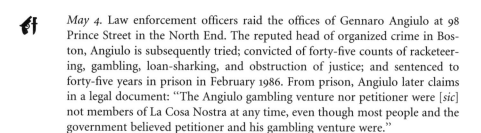

May 4. Law enforcement officers raid the offices of Gennaro Angiulo at 98 Prince Street in the North End. The reputed head of organized crime in Boston, Angiulo is subsequently tried; convicted of forty-five counts of racketeering, gambling, loan-sharking, and obstruction of justice; and sentenced to forty-five years in prison in February 1986. From prison, Angiulo later claims in a legal document: "The Angiulo gambling venture nor petitioner were [*sic*] not members of La Cosa Nostra at any time, even though most people and the government believed petitioner and his gambling venture were."

October 23. Roger Sessions's *Concerto for Orchestra* is given its world premiere by the Boston Symphony Orchestra, Seiji Ozawa conducting, at Symphony Hall.

May 3. The Celtics beat the Philadelphia 76ers 91–90 in game 7 at Boston Garden to win the NBA Eastern Conference championship series, after having trailed three games to one in the series. The Celtics go on to beat the Rockets 102–91 in game 6 in Houston to win their fourteenth NBA championship on May 14.
December 31. Three horses, Great Combination, Dawn's Count, and Needachant finish a triple dead heat in the last race in the final day of the season at Suffolk Downs.

1982

December 17. The City of Quincy files suit against the Metropolitan District Commission (MDC) in Massachusetts Superior Court to halt the discharge of untreated sewage into Boston Harbor. Judge Paul Garrity later finds for the plaintiff, as does a U.S. District Court judge in a similar suit brought by the regional office of the federal Environment Protection Agency on January 31, 1985. A cleanup of the harbor is ordered, which is carried out by a new agency created in 1984.*

Cynthia Zaitzevsky's *Frederick Law Olmsted and the Boston Park System* is published.
The Chinatown Gate is installed. A gift from the Taiwanese government, it is inscribed with several proverbs, including "Everything under the sky is for the people."

January 23. Two passengers are missing and presumed drowned when a World Airways jetliner, while landing at Logan Airport, slides off an icy runway and into Boston Harbor.
June 16. An article in the *New York Times* describes Boston as "the arson capital of the world." Between June 1 and mid-October, nearly two hundred fires of suspicious origin occur throughout the city.

September 22. The Boston Compact is established. The goal of this partnership between the business community and the city's public schools is to improve the schools and the educational and employment opportunities for Boston public school students. The compact is expanded in 1983 to include colleges and universities, and in 1984 to include the building trades. A Boston Compact II agreement is signed in 1989, and Boston Compact III in 1994.

November 20. In another of their "hacks" (practical jokes), MIT students inflate a weather balloon on the 46-yard-line of Harvard Stadium during halftime of the Harvard-Yale football game.

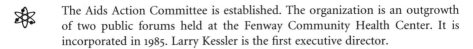

The Aids Action Committee is established. The organization is an outgrowth of two public forums held at the Fenway Community Health Center. It is incorporated in 1985. Larry Kessler is the first executive director.

June 1. Cab drivers go on strike across the city to protest "gypsy" cabs and limousines doing business at Logan Airport.

March 9. The first issue of the *Boston Observer* appears. The self-described "journal of politics, business, media, and the law" is edited and published by Steven Pearlstein. The monthly continues publication until the summer of 1985.

Chronicle first airs on WCVB TV. One of the few, locally produced news and feature programs in the country, it continues today.

July 5. The Concerts on the Common series begins, with a concert by the folksingers Peter, Paul, and Mary. The series of performances by well-known singers and musicians proves to be very popular. As a result of escalating costs and competition from private concert promoters, the series is discontinued in March 1989.

March 5. The Wheelock Family Theatre opens at 180 The Riverway with a production of *Alice's Adventures in Wonderland.*

September 30. The first episode of the network television show *Cheers* airs. A situation comedy set in a fictional Boston neighborhood bar (represented by the exterior of the Hampshire House at 84 Beacon Street), it becomes the no. 1 rated show on television and features guest appearances by local politicians and sports figures. The last episode, one of the most-watched shows in television history, airs on May 20, 1993.

October 26. The first episode of the network television show *St. Elsewhere* airs. It is a dramatic series set at the fictional St. Eligius Hospital (represented by the exterior of the Franklin Square House). The last episode airs on May 25, 1988.

December 12. The Patriots defeat the Miami Dolphins 3–0 in Foxborough. During a blizzard at the newly renamed Sullivan Stadium, a snowplow driver, Mark Henderson, helps the team when he clears a spot on the field for John Smith to kick a game-winning field goal.

1983

December 20. The Boston Zoning Commission adopts the so-called Linkage Ordinance. Sponsored by the city councilor Bruce Bolling, it requires developers of large commercial projects to contribute to the construction of affordable housing. After Superior Court Judge Mel Greenberg rules the ordinance in-

The Hampshire House, 84 Beacon Street, the downstairs pub of which served as a model for the television series Cheers. *(Photograph by Richard Tourangeau)*

valid on April 4, 1986, it is redrafted, passed as state legislation, and signed into law in October 1987. The linkage ordinance is expanded to include contributions to job training programs in 1986.

January 26. Republican President Ronald Reagan visits the Erie Pub in Dorchester. The president's visit is meant to symbolize an effort to reach out to so-called Reagan Democrats. He orders a Ballantine Ale.

May 25. Mayor White announces that he will not run for a fifth consecutive term—after tricking the reporter Peter Lucas and getting the *Boston Herald* to run a front-page story that morning with the headline "White Will Run."

November 15. Ray Flynn (with 128,578 votes) defeats Mel King (with 69,015) to win election as mayor. Turnout for the election was 69.5 percent, the highest in a Boston mayoral election since 1949. King is the first African American to qualify for a final election in Boston history, and Flynn is the first mayor elected from South Boston. Inaugurated before forty-five hundred people at the Wang Center on January 2, 1984, Flynn is later credited with improving race relations and becomes known as the "Mayor of the Neighborhoods."

November 15. The new thirteen-member at-large and district Boston City Council is elected. It includes David Scondras, a district councilor from the Fenway, who becomes the first openly gay member of the council in January 1984.

April 27. The fire alarm operator Karen Harrison becomes the first woman member of the Boston Fire Department. Her father and brother are both firefighters.

Robert Hayden's *Faith, Culture, and Leadership: A History of the Black Church in Boston* is published.

Ray Flynn and Mel King, the 1983 mayoral election finalists. (Photograph by Michael Grecco, courtesy of the Boston Herald)

 November 15. The new thirteen-member Boston School Committee is elected. It includes John O'Bryant, who becomes the first African-American chairman in January 1984.

George Metcalf's *From Little Rock to Boston: The History of School Desegregation* is published. In it he quotes the Harvard sociologist Robert Coles: "The ultimate reality is the reality of class, having and not having, social and economic vulnerability versus social and economic power—that's where the issue is."

 August 7. Michael Barrett's article "The Out-of-Towners" appears in the *Sunday Globe* magazine. In it he argues that Boston gives more than it gets from nonresidents.

The first issue of *Bay Windows*, a newspaper for Boston's gay community, appears.

 The New Edition's hit single "Candy Girl" is released. The band is made up of five teenage boys from Boston. Their first eponymous album is released a year later.

1984

 October 18. Boston regains authority over its public housing after nearly five years of court receivership. Doris Bunte is appointed the Boston Housing Authority administrator. She is the first former public housing tenant to head a public housing agency in a major city, and the first African-American woman to hold the position in Boston.

December 19. The Massachusetts Water Resources Authority (MWRA) is created by the Massachusetts legislature to take over responsibility for providing

water and sewer services for forty-three communities in metropolitan Boston and to manage the cleanup of Boston Harbor. The MWRA's primary treatment plant on Deer Island begins operation in 1995, the secondary plant in 1998, and the outfall pipe in 2000.

George V. Higgins's *Style versus Substance: Boston, Kevin White and the Politics of Illusion* is published. In it he writes: "In Boston, which is large enough to attract and sustain a reasonable number of highly competitive and driven people but still small enough so that each of them can know all of the others' business, envy is robust and vigorous."
Ken Hartnett's *A Saving Grace* is published.
January 10. Newly elected Mayor Ray Flynn demonstrates his hands-on style by riding with snowplow drivers all night during the year's first winter storm. He talks a would-be suicide down from a bridge in East Boston on July 5, leads people to safety from a fire on the fourteenth floor of the Prudential Center on January 2, 1986, and helps police end a siege by a gun-wielding man in Roxbury on July 14, 1987. Flynn also runs annually in the Boston marathon.

January 24. Bernard Law is appointed to succeed the late Humberto Medeiros as archbishop of Boston. Installed on March 23, he is elevated to cardinal on May 25, 1985.

March 22. John Harbison's Symphony no. 1 is given its world premiere by the Boston Symphony Orchestra at Symphony Hall.

May 31. The Celtics beat the Lakers 124–121 in overtime in game 2 of the NBA finals at Boston Garden, as Gerald Henderson steals the ball and scores to tie the score at the end of regulation time. The Celtics go on to beat the Lakers 111–102 in game 7 in Los Angeles to win their fifteenth championship on June 12.
November 23. The Boston College football team beats Miami 47–45 in Miami, as Doug Flutie throws a forty-six-yard "Hail Mary" touchdown pass to Gerard Phelan in the last play of the game. Flutie is named the winner of the Heisman Trophy as the outstanding collegiate football player on December 1. BC beats the University of Houston 45–28 in the Cotton Bowl on January 1, 1985.

1985

August 16. A bomb is found at the offices of the American-Arab Antidiscrimination Committee at 5230 Washington Street in West Roxbury. Two Boston police officers are injured when they detonate the device at the nearby Gardner Street landfill.

September 3. Judge W. Arthur Garrity issues his final orders in the Boston schools desegregation case and returns control of the public schools to the city. On this same day, Laval Wilson becomes the first African-American school superintendent in Boston history.

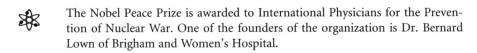

The Nobel Peace Prize is awarded to International Physicians for the Prevention of Nuclear War. One of the founders of the organization is Dr. Bernard Lown of Brigham and Women's Hospital.

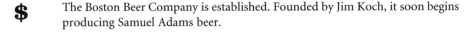

The Boston Beer Company is established. Founded by Jim Koch, it soon begins producing Samuel Adams beer.

March. The first issue of the *West Ender* appears. Edited by James Campano, the newspaper is geared to former residents of the neighborhood who were displaced by urban renewal. It continues publication until 1998.

March. The New Kids on the Block perform for the first time, lip-synching to demo tapes at a concert at the Joseph Lee School in Dorchester. Originally called Nynuk, the band is made up of four teenage boys from Boston. They release their eponymous first album a year later. The group eventually changes its name to NKOTB, releases a final album, *Face the Music,* and disbands in May 1994.
September 20. The first episode of the network television show *Spenser for Hire* airs. The dramatic series, based on Robert B. Parker's mystery novels, continues until May 7, 1988, then airs again for one year in 1993.
November 22. The Sack Theatre chain cancels a scheduled screening of Jean-Luc Godard's film *Hail Mary* in Boston because of protests by local Catholic organizations. The film is shown instead at the Orson Welles Cinema in Cambridge.

June 9. The Celtics lose to the Los Angeles Lakers 111–100 in the seventh and final game of the NBA finals at Boston Garden.

1986

June 28. The Boston Redevelopment Authority (BRA) announces the creation of the South End Neighborhood Housing Initiative. This proposal to construct seven hundred housing units on some seventy parcels of BRA-owned land helps spark the redevelopment of the South End.
The Boston Groundwater Trust is established to monitor low water levels, which have begun to cause serious foundation problems for buildings constructed on filled land, especially in the Beacon Hill Flats area.

The Belle Isle Marsh Reservation opens in East Boston.

J. Anthony Lukas's *Common Ground: A Turbulent Decade in the Lives of Three American Families* and Nat Hentoff's *Boston Boy* are published.

January 6. Bruce Bolling becomes the first African-American president of the Boston City Council.
November 4. Voters in predominantly African-American neighborhoods reject by a three-to-one margin a referendum proposal to secede from Boston and create a new city, to be called Mandela. The question is again defeated convincingly on November 8, 1988.

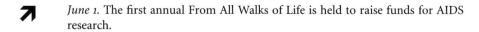

June 1. The first annual From All Walks of Life is held to raise funds for AIDS research.

May 7. More than two hundred people are injured when a commuter train slams into a stalled freight train in Brighton. More than one hundred people are injured in a similar accident at Back Bay Station on November 12.

December 10. Boston University professor Elie Wiesel is awarded the Nobel Peace Prize.

September 21. John Harbison's *The Flight into Egypt* is given its world premiere performance by the Cantata Singers and Ensemble at the New England Conservatory's Jordan Hall. It is awarded a Pulitzer Prize in 1987.

January 26. The Patriots lose 46–10 to the Chicago Bears in Super Bowl XX in New Orleans.
June 8. The Celtics beat the Houston Rockets 114–97 in game 6 at Boston Garden to win their sixteenth championship. Led by "the big three"—Larry Bird, Kevin McHale, and Robert Parrish—the franchise fields what many believe is the best basketball team in history.
October 25. The Red Sox lose to the Mets 6–5 in the tenth inning of game 6 of the World Series in New York. After the Sox lead 5–3 with two outs, their relief pitchers fail to hold the lead and first baseman Bill Buckner allows a ground ball to roll through his legs, and the winning run scores. Red Sox manager John McNamara is later criticized for not making a defensive replacement for Buckner. The Red Sox lose game 7, and the series, to the Mets 8–5 in New York on October 27. McNamara is criticized after this game for taking the starting pitcher, Roger Clemens, out of the game too soon.

1987

James F. O'Gorman's *H. H. Richardson: Architectural Forms for an American Society* is published.
February. One International Place, designed by Philip Johnson and John Burgee, opens. Two International Place opens in 1993.

April 29. Massachusetts governor Michael Dukakis declares his candidacy for president at a rally on Boston Common.
November 3. Mayor Ray Flynn (with 63,714 votes) beats the City Council president Joseph Tierney (with 30,714) to win reelection to a second consecutive term. Flynn wins twenty of twenty-two wards, losing only in his home wards of South Boston, which many attribute to his announcement a few days before that the city would proceed with integrating public housing developments in that neighborhood.
Marilyn Richardson's *Maria W. Stewart: America's First Black Woman Political Writer* is published.

June 12. Andrea Gargiulo, the Boston Licensing Board chair, warns the city's all-male and all-female private social clubs that they must open their membership to both sexes or risk losing their liquor licenses. After a U.S. Supreme Court decision supports Gargiulo's warning in June 1988, she declares: "The powerful men who are members will no longer be able to isolate themselves on a personal level from the cultural diversity of the society they rule."

January 14. In a meeting at Vanessa's sandwich shop in the Prudential Center, three Boston gangsters attempt to extort $500,000 from the reputed top bookie in Boston, eighty-nine-year-old Harry "Doc" Sagansky. He tries to dismiss their threat, explaining that at his age, "I don't even buy green bananas." Gene Dahmen becomes the first woman president of the Boston Bar Association.

May 31. Mother Teresa, an Albanian nun and founder of the Missionaries of Charity in Calcutta, visits Boston. She returns a year later, and again in 1995 to visit the two houses her order established as a result of her previous visits.

February 20. Dr. Rudolph Tanzi of Children's Hospital and researchers at Massachusetts General Hospital identify the gene responsible for Alzheimer's disease.

January 21. The first of Henry Hampton's six-part series, *Eyes on the Prize: America's Civil Rights Years 1954–1965*, airs on WGBH TV. A sequel—*Eyes on the Prize II: America at the Racial Crossroads, 1965–1985*—airs in 1990.

May 2. Chris McCarron, a jockey from Dorchester, rides Alysheba to a victory in the Kentucky Derby. He rides the horse to victory in the Preakness on May 16, but finishes fourth in the Belmont Stakes on June 6. Later in the season, he rides Suffolk Downs–based Waquoit to victory in the MassCap at Suffolk Downs.

1988

November 10. The Boston Redevelopment Authority grants the Dudley Street Neighborhood Initiative the power of eminent domain. Organized in 1985, it is the first nonprofit community development organization in the United States to be granted such authority by a government agency.

May 17. The Boston branch of the NAACP and the Lawyers' Committee for Civil Rights file suit in Federal District Court against the Boston Housing Authority. In the suit, they charge the BHA with steering minorities away from public housing developments in primarily white neighborhoods. The court rules for the plaintiffs and orders the various site-specific waiting lists for those seeking housing to be replaced by a single, citywide list in 1991. Federal officials again allow tenants to choose the development in which they would like to live beginning in 2004.
June 29. The Boston City Council enacts an ordinance that allows the city to regulate the conversion of apartments to condominiums by a vote of nine to four. Mayor Flynn calls the measure "a giant step toward protecting affordable

housing." Edward Shanahan, president of the Boston Rental Housing Association, calls it "devastating" and "a defeat for the free market system."

 June 15. The Boston City Archives is established. Operated by the city clerk, the facility is located in a former school in the Readville section of Hyde Park. Ed Quill is the first city archivist.
Thomas H. O'Connor's *South Boston, My Home Town: The History of an Ethnic Neighborhood* is published.

July 20. Massachusetts governor Michael Dukakis wins his party's nomination for president at the Democratic National Convention in Atlanta. His Republican opponent, Vice President George H. W. Bush, campaigns in Boston and declares Boston Harbor to be "the filthiest harbor in America" on September 1. Bush defeats Dukakis on November 8.

July 6. City Year is established. Founded by the Harvard Law School graduates Michael Brown and Alan Khazei, the service organization for recent high school graduates later expands to other cities across the United States.

August 19. Twelve-year-old Tiffany Moore is shot and killed while sitting on a mailbox at the corner of Humboldt Avenue and Homestead Street in Roxbury. Moore was to have returned to South Carolina the next day, where she and her family had moved to escape the increasing violence in Boston. A twenty-two-year-old man is convicted of firing the shot that killed the young girl, but after doubts are raised over some of the testimony offered in the trial, he is released from prison on November 6, 2003.

September 20. The *Boston Globe* prints the first of two stories containing charges that the South Boston mobster James "Whitey" Bulger is an FBI informant who has for years provided information on the Italian segment of organized crime in Boston. The rumors are later confirmed by the FBI agent Paul Coffey in sworn testimony in court on June 3, 1997. "There's no difference between these guys," the *Boston Globe* later quotes a state trooper as saying, in reference to Italian and Irish gangsters. "Some of 'em got o's before their last name, some of 'em got o's at the end."

May 24. The Bruins are tied with the Edmonton Oilers 3–3 in the second period of game 4 of the Stanley Cup finals when a blackout forces the game to be canceled. When it is replayed two days later in Edmonton, the Bruins lose the game 6–3 and the series 4–0.

1989

August 31. The Boston branch of the Federal Reserve Bank issues a report that finds African-American residents of Boston are twice as likely to be turned down for home mortgages as white residents—even when income differences are taken into account. The Boston Redevelopment Authority releases a study that finds a similar bias in mortgage lending on December 19.

The new Southwest Corridor Park is dedicated.

 Lawrence Carden's *Witness: An Oral History of Black Politics in Boston, 1920–1960* is published.

 Kathleen Hirsch's *Songs from the Alley* is published.

 September 1. Rudolph Pierce becomes the first African-American president of the Boston Bar Association.

September 6–October 16. Four people are killed and 101 are wounded in the worst outbreak of street gang–related violence in Boston.

October 23. Police receive an emergency phone call from a man who says: "I've been shot. My wife's been shot." Soon after, they locate a car containing Charles Stuart and his pregnant wife on St. Alphonsus Street on Mission Hill. Stuart's wife and child die. He barely survives; he claims to have been the victim of an attack by an African-American man. Stuart's story unravels a few months later, however, when his brother confesses to involvement in the incident. Stuart's body is found in the water below the Tobin Bridge on January 4, 1990, an apparent suicide. City and police officials are later criticized for believing Stuart's story and for the manner in which the investigation of the bizarre crime was conducted.

November 20. Lawyers for young minority men file a class action suit against the Boston Police Department for its "Stop and Search" policy.

 February 11. Rev. Barbara Harris becomes the first woman—and first African-American woman—Anglican bishop, when she is consecrated as suffragan bishop of the Episcopal Diocese of Massachusetts.

 May 31. Judge W. Arthur Garrity approves the replacement of the court-designed "geo code" plan, which assigned each student to a school strictly on the basis of race and address, with a so-called controlled choice plan, which employs a lottery and allows some degree of choice, while continuing to use racial guidelines. The new system goes into effect beginning in September 1989.

November 7. In a nonbinding advisory referendum, Boston voters approve by a small margin (37.3 to 36.2 percent) replacing the elected Boston School Committee with an appointed board.

 Scullers Jazz Club opens in the DoubleTree Guest Suites hotel at 400 Soldiers Field Road.

Edward Zwick's movie *Glory* opens; it is based on the experiences of the Massachusetts Fifty-fourth Regiment.

 April 1. Harvard beats Minnesota 4–3 in overtime in St. Paul to win its first NCAA hockey championship.

1990

 Boston's population is 574,283, the twentieth largest of any city in the United States. Of that number, 338,734 are white; 136,887 are African American; 61,955

are Hispanic; 29,640 are Asian/Pacific Islander; 1,531 are Native American; and 5,536 classify themselves as "other." Of the total, 114,597 are foreign born.

Ashburton Park opens behind the State House.

May 30. The Boston's Women's Heritage Trail opens. Initially a single trail honoring the accomplishments of twenty women, it grows to a number of trails in various neighborhoods, honoring more than fifty women. Mary Maynard began advocating for the trails' creation in the late 1970s, Meg Campbell helped implement it, and Patricia Morris is the first director.

June 23. The South African president, Nelson Mandela, speaks before 250,000 people at the Esplanade, and is entertained by a Boston Pops concert featuring Jackson Browne, Dick Gregory, and Paul Simon.

March 3. "The Wall" is erected at the Chez Vous roller skating rink on Rhoades Street in Dorchester by Rev. Bruce Wall and the owners, John and Dorcas Dunham. A plywood memorial, it contains the names of sixty-one Boston teenagers killed since 1984.
December 31. Boston ends the year with a record 152 murders, 17 more than the previous high of 135 in 1973.

December 12. Two hundred eighty people are hurt when an Amtrak Night Owl train from Washington, D.C., jumps the track and crashes into a Massachusetts Bay Transit Authority commuter train at Back Bay Station.

May 31. Judge W. Arthur Garrity ends his jurisdiction over the Boston public schools, and the *Morgan v. Hennigan* case is closed. He later tells the *Boston Globe*, "If I had again the same submissions, the same briefs and arguments, given the same set of circumstances, I am not positive of this, but I do think that the same orders would have issued." In 1970, four years before Garrity issued his busing order, total enrollment in the Boston public schools was 96,696; 64 percent white, 30 percent African American, 4 percent Hispanic, and 2 percent Asian. As of January 2004, the total school enrollment is 60,431; 14 percent white, 46 percent African American, 30 percent Hispanic, and 9 percent Asian.

March 18. On Sunday evening at 10 P.M., the Gardner Museum is robbed of artworks valued according to some estimates at two hundred million dollars, and to many art lovers as "priceless." Two thieves, dressed as police officers, steal thirteen works, including paintings by Vermeer, Rembrandt, Manet, and Degas. The art has never been recovered.
The Museum of Fine Arts closes its front entrance on Huntington Avenue. It is reportedly a "cost-cutting measure," but many believe it is a response to the increase of crime in the area. The entrance is reopened by the director Malcolm Rogers "as a gesture of welcome to the inner city communities of Boston where the museum is located" in 1995.
December. An exhibition entitled *Allan Rohan Crite: A Retrospective* opens at

the National Center of Afro-American Artists in Roxbury. The artist is a life-long resident of the South End.

Shaun O'Connell's *Imagining Boston: A Literary Landscape* is published.

 May 24. The Bruins lose to Edmonton 4–1 in Boston Garden in the sixth and final game of the Stanley Cup championship finals.

1991

 December 24. David Cortiella becomes the first Hispanic American to hold the position of Boston Housing Authority administrator when he succeeds Doris Bunte.

 June 15. Post Office Square Park opens. It is later named for the Boston businessman Norman Leventhal.

Harry Ellis Dickson Park, near Symphony Hall, is dedicated..

 January 16. The United States becomes involved in the Gulf War, which concludes a few months later.

More Than Common Powers of Perception: The Diary of Elizabeth Rogers Mason Cabot, edited by P. A. M. Taylor, and Robert Hayden's *African-Americans in Boston: More Than 350 Years* are published.

 November 5. Mayor Ray Flynn (with 63,582 votes) defeats the Boston Teachers' Union president Edward Doherty (with 21,659)—a three-to-one margin—to win his third consecutive term. Flynn becomes the first mayoral candidate in Boston history to win every precinct in every ward of the city.

 April 20. Eleven-year-old Charles Copney and fifteen-year-old Korey Grant are shot and killed on Highland Avenue in the Fort Hill section of Roxbury. Two local street gangs announce a temporary truce in their hostilities a few days later, and six other gangs agree to a thirty-day truce on May 29.

May 19–26. A Gun Amnesty Week is held in Boston, sponsored by the city councilor Bruce Bolling, in cooperation with city, county, state, and federal law enforcement officials. Guns can be turned in—without penalty—at various neighborhood churches and mosques.

July 26. The reputed South Boston mobster James "Whitey" Bulger claims a one-sixth share of a winning lottery ticket for a $14.3 million Mass Millions jackpot, which entitles him to a payment of $89,000 per year from the state.

 August 20. The "Blinking Madonna" controversy occurs in the North End. A videotape shot by the documentary filmmaker Beth Harrington at the eightieth annual Fisherman's Feast appears to show the eyes of the statue of the Madonna blinking. Thousands flock to the North End in the hope of witnessing a miracle. Others attribute the phenomenon to a malfunction of the camera.

 April 10. The Boston School Committee is reorganized again. The Boston City Council votes to replace the elected thirteen-member committee with a seven-

member board appointed by the mayor. The Massachusetts legislature authorizes the change, which is signed into law on July 5.

$ *January 6.* Federal government regulators declare the Bank of New England insolvent. An attempt at saving the bank fails. It soon closes, and its assets are purchased by the Fleet Financial Group.

1992

Lawrence W. Kennedy's *Planning the City upon a Hill: Boston since 1630* and Hillel Levine and Lawrence Harmon's *The Death of an American Jewish Community: A Tragedy of Good Intentions* are published.

The Last Tenement: Confronting Community and Urban Renewal in Boston's West End is published by the Bostonian Society.

Barbara Moore and Gail Weesner's *Beacon Hill: A Living Portrait* is published.

Jack Beatty's *The Rascal King: The Life and Times of James Michael Curley* is published.

After a young man is attacked attending the funeral of a murder victim, the Ten Point Coalition is founded by seven African-American ministers. Rev. Mickarl Thomas is the first president. The organization takes its name from the ten-point plan it issues calling for increased public safety, economic development, and community building.
The Charlestown After Murder Program (CHAMP) is organized by family members of victims of violence. Its mission is to stop violence and end the so-called Code of Silence that keeps residents from testifying against local criminals.

James M. O'Toole's *Militant and Triumphant: William Henry O'Connell and the Catholic Church in Boston, 1859–1944* is published.

January 6. An appointed Boston School Committee replaces the elected one. Paul Parks is the first chairperson, and George Joe becomes the first Asian American to serve on the committee. Boston voters approve a binding referendum to retain the appointed school committee by a vote of 70 percent to 30 percent in November 1996.

March 17. The Irish rock group U2 performs at Boston Garden on St. Patrick's Day.

June 13. Harvard wins its sixth NCAA men's heavyweight crew national championship since 1983. The school also won in 1985, 1987, 1988, and 1989.

1993

July 12. Mayor Ray Flynn resigns to become the U.S. ambassador to the Vatican. Boston City Council president Thomas Menino is named acting mayor.

November 2. Thomas Menino (with 74,448 votes) defeats James Brett (with 41,052) in a special election to become the first Italian American elected mayor of Boston. Inaugurated on January 18, 1994, Menino is dubbed "the Urban Mechanic" for his focus on delivering basic services.

December 21. Fifteen-year-old Louis Brown is killed by a stray bullet while walking to the Fields Corner MBTA subway station. The teenager was an honor roll student at West Roxbury High School. His father, Joseph Cherry, who later starts an antiviolence program in his son's name, declares: "All kids are beautiful and none of them deserves to die."

Researchers at Massachusetts General Hospital are among those who first identify the genes responsible for Huntington's disease and Lou Gehrig's disease.

April 22. Sunbeam Television Corporation buys WHDH TV (Channel 7) from a group of local businessmen, including David Mugar. Under the new management, the station employs a more fast-paced and graphics-oriented approach to news coverage, which includes more live shots.
October. The *Boston Globe* becomes a wholly owned subsidiary of the *New York Times*.

March 31. The New England Patriots replace the team's longtime logo (a football-playing Patriot designed by the artist Phil Bissell) with a more modern Patriot, quickly dubbed the "Flying Elvis."
July 27. The Celtics' Reggie Lewis collapses and soon after dies after a workout at the team practice facility at Brandeis University, in Waltham.
December 4. The Boston University football team loses 21–14 to the University of Idaho in Moscow, Idaho, in the quarterfinals of the national collegiate football Division 1AA quarterfinals. The team had compiled an 11–0 regular season record and won its first play-off game a week earlier.

1994

Susan Wilson's *Boston Sites and Insights* is published.

March 20. The St. Patrick's Day Parade in South Boston is canceled when a Massachusetts court rules that a gay, lesbian, and bisexual group cannot be kept from marching in the parade. The Massachusetts Supreme Judicial Court affirms the ruling, but in a ruling issued in June 1995, the U.S. Supreme Court rules that the private group that sponsors the parade, the South Boston Allied War Veterans, can exclude groups that it feels do not promote its values.

October 31. Nine-year-old Jermaine Goffigan is shot and killed by a stray bullet while trick-or-treating in the Academy Homes housing development in Roxbury. A sixteen-year-old boy is later wrongly convicted of the crime and is freed after serving five years in prison. Two other men, ages seventeen and fifteen at the time of the shooting, subsequently plead guilty to the crime and receive ten-year sentences in 2004.

March. The total snowfall for the winter is 95.2 inches, breaking the previous record of 89.2 inches set in the winter of 1947–1948. (Official statistics have been kept since 1890.)
June–July. Boston experiences the warmest summer since 1872.

March 10. The minister Louis Farrakhan speaks to fourteen hundred men at the Strand Theatre in Dorchester. After complaints about his excluding women from the event, he returns and speaks to an audience of women at the Mason Cathedral Church of God in Christ in Dorchester in July.

January 29. A new Boston City Hospital opens. The largest single capital construction project in the city's history, it is merged with Boston University Medical Center to become Boston Medical Center on July 1, 1996.

July 13. Cathy Minehan becomes the first woman chief executive of the Federal Reserve Bank of Boston.

June 19. In an editorial, the *Boston Globe* declares: "twenty years ago this newspaper unequivocally endorsed a desegregation plan for Boston schools that included busing students between black and white neighborhoods . . . [but] busing has been a failure in Boston. It achieved neither integration nor better schooling."

James Carroll's *The City Below* is published.
September 9. An estimated sixty-five thousand people attend a free concert by the band Green Day on the Esplanade. Unruly fans and injuries in the "mosh pit" in front of the Hatch Shell force the sudden ending of the concert. A near-riot follows, leading to forty-five arrests. One fan declares that the concert "was great right up until it wasn't."

November 13. The New England Patriots beat the Minnesota Vikings 26–20 in overtime, behind a record-setting performance by Drew Bledsoe (seventy passes attempted, forty-five completed). The next day, the *Boston Globe* sportswriter Dan Shaughnessy declares: "It was one of those rare Foxboro Stadium days when the throws actually outnumbered the throw-ups."

1995

December 15. The Ted Williams Tunnel opens. Construction began in January 1992.

June 20. Piers Park is dedicated on the East Boston waterfront.
October 22. The New England Holocaust Memorial is dedicated in Dock Square. It is designed by Stanley Saitowitz.

Barbara Moore and Gail Weesner's *Back Bay: A Living Portrait* and Thomas O'Connor's *The Boston Irish: A Political History* are published.

January 22. Rose Fitzgerald Kennedy dies at the age of 104 in her home in Hyannisport on Cape Cod. Her husband, Joseph, had died in Hyannisport on

November 18, 1969. Mrs. Kennedy's funeral is held at St. Stephen's Church in the North End, the neighborhood where she was born, on January 24.

The Ritz-Carlton's Bar and Café relax their jacket-and-tie dress code.

January 4. Federal warrants on charges of criminal extortion are sworn out for the alleged organized crime members James "Whitey" Bulger, Stephen "The Rifleman" Flemmi, and Frank "Cadillac" Salemme. Flemmi is arrested in Boston the next day and later convicted of ten murders and sentenced to life in prison. Salemme is arrested in Florida in August, later convicted of extortion and racketeering, and released into the Witness Protection Program in March 2003. Bulger remains a fugitive.

September 25. Paul McLaughlin, an assistant district attorney, is shot and killed at the West Roxbury commuter rail station. A twenty-year-old criminal whom McLaughlin had been prosecuting is later convicted of the murder.

March 19. John Powers's article "How to speak with a Bawstin accent: It's not so bzah when you know how" appears in the *Boston Sunday Globe*. In it the author declares: "Henry Higgins could have taught Eliza Doolittle to tawk Bawstin in a mattah of owahs." The article is expanded to a book, *The Boston Dictionary*, illustrated by Peter Wallace, and published in 1996.

September 27. Seiji Ozawa and the Boston Symphony Orchestra celebrate twenty-five years together with a free performance of Beethoven's Ninth Symphony on Boston Common.

April 1. Boston University beats the University of Maine 6–2 in Providence to win the national collegiate hockey championship.

September 30. The FleetCenter opens adjacent to, and as a replacement for, the Boston Garden.

The Reggie Lewis Track and Athletic Center opens in Roxbury.

1996

June 8. The Dudley Town Common park opens.

November 12. Congress authorizes creation of the Boston Harbor Islands National Park.

Lorie Conway's *Boston: The Way It Was* is published. The book is based on an Emmy Award–winning television series produced by WGBH TV.

January. The Greater Boston Interfaith Organization, a coalition of religious congregations, is established. Lew Finfer is the first director. The goal of the organization, eventually comprising eighty-seven congregations, is to promote solutions to social problems, particularly the lack of affordable housing in the Boston area. Approximately four thousand people attend a kickoff rally at Boston College High School on November 22, 1998.

October 20. Heavy rains cause the Muddy River to flood the Green Line subway tunnels at Kenmore Square.

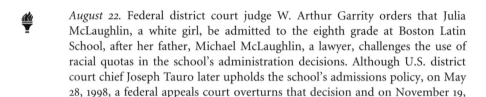

August 22. Federal district court judge W. Arthur Garrity orders that Julia McLaughlin, a white girl, be admitted to the eighth grade at Boston Latin School, after her father, Michael McLaughlin, a lawyer, challenges the use of racial quotas in the school's administration decisions. Although U.S. district court chief Joseph Tauro later upholds the school's admissions policy, on May 28, 1998, a federal appeals court overturns that decision and on November 19, 1998, orders an end to the use of racial quotas at the examination school.

February 1. George Walker's *Lilacs, for Voice and Orchestra* is given its world premiere by the Boston Symphony Orchestra, Seiji Ozawa conducting. Walker is later awarded a Pulitzer Prize for the piece, and is the first African-American classical music composer so honored.

August 1. Calvin Davis of Dorchester, a student at the University of Arkansas, wins a bronze medal in the 400-meter hurdle in the summer Olympics in Atlanta.

1997

September 3. The Lowell Square housing development opens in the West End. Built by the Archdiocese of Boston, it is the first affordable housing built in the area since the neighborhood was torn down as part of an urban renewal project in 1960. Although former West End residents sought preference for all the 183 units, a federal district court judge ruled on January 8 that, because of federal fair housing regulations and a 1993 consent decree, they could receive priority for no more than 55 percent.

January 24. The Frog Pond skating rink opens on Boston Common.

November 4. Thomas Menino (with 48,323 votes) is reelected mayor and becomes the first mayor in Boston history to run without opposition.

December 31. Boston ends the year with 43 homicides, 18 fewer than the previous year and 109 fewer than the record number killed in 1990. The "Boston Miracle" of improved law enforcement and social service delivery and a better relationship between the police and the community are credited for the decline. The number of homicides decreases to 35 in 1998 and 31 in 1999, but it increases during the next five years.

August 12. The City of Boston enacts a Living Wage Ordinance, which requires that all city workers and employees of companies doing business with the city receive a so-called living wage. A revised version of the law is signed into law on September 4, 1998.
The last of the F. W. Woolworth stores are closed in Boston.

Douglass Shand-Tucci's *The Art of Scandal: The Life and Times of Isabella Stewart Gardner* is published.
The movie *Good Will Hunting* is released.
March 4. The first episode of the network television show *The Practice* airs. A

dramatic series set in a fictional Boston law firm, the last episode airs on May 16, 2004.

September 8. The first episode of the network television show *Ally McBeal,* a comedy-drama set in a fictional Boston law firm, is aired. The last episode airs on May 20, 2002.

 January 26. The Patriots lose to the Green Bay Packers 35–21 in the Louisiana Superdome in Super Bowl XXXI.

1998

 September 25. The federal district courthouse opens on Fan Pier in South Boston. Designed by Henry Cobb, it is named for U.S. representative J. Joseph Moakley on April 18, 2001.

 December. The Boston Museum Project is established. A nonprofit entity made up of the Bostonian Society, Boston History Collaborative, Freedom Trail Foundation, and in 2000, the National Park Service, its goal is to create a city history museum.

 Thomas O'Connor's *Boston Catholics: A History of the Church and Its People* is published.

 Boston Arts Academy opens at 174 Ipswich Street in the Fenway. It is the city's first high school for the performing and visual arts.

 June 18. The *Boston Globe* columnist Patricia Smith resigns after it is discovered that she made up characters and quotations in her columns. Another *Globe* columnist, Mike Barnicle, resigns for similar reasons on August 19.

 An exhibit at the Museum of Fine Arts entitled *Monet in the Twentieth Century* attracts more than 565,000 visitors, the largest attendance of any show in the museum's history.

 March 14. Harvard defeats Stanford in the NCAA women's basketball tournament, behind thirty-five points and thirteen rebounds by Allison Feaster. It is the only time a sixteenth seed has defeated a top seed in either the men's or women's college basketball tournaments.

1999

 Gerald Gamm's *Urban Exodus: Why the Jews Left Boston and the Catholics Stayed* is published.

 September 21. The Grove Hall Mall opens on Blue Hill Avenue in Roxbury. Along with Unity Plaza, which opened across the street in 1995, the development replaces commercial properties abandoned or neglected since riots occurred in the area in 1967.

The New Chardon Street Courthouse opens. Designed by Kallmann, McKinnell, and Wood, it is named for the former U.S. senator Edward Brooke on November 16th.

July. Paul Revere Park opens along the Charles River behind North Station.

November 2. Marie St. Fleur becomes the first Haitian-American elected to the Massachusetts legislature when she is elected state representative from Dorchester.

A moose wanders into the Cleveland Circle area. He is eventually caught by wildlife officers, taken to a less populated area, and released.

June 21. On the twenty-fifth anniversary of Judge W. Arthur Garrity's school desegregation ruling, four white parents and an advocacy group sue the Boston School Committee, charging that the use of racial quotas in the so-called Controlled Choice student assignment plan is unconstitutional. The School Committee votes to drop race as the basis for assigning children to schools and allow as many as 50 percent of students to attend their neighborhood schools.

March. Boston magazine devotes an issue to "The Twelve Tribes of Boston." The magazine identifies them as Brahmin, Irish, Black, Jewish, Euro, Italian, Medical, Techno, Culinary, Gay, Intellectual, and Lost (those who inexplicably move to New York). "Because tribalism means that one group often refuses to acknowledge the value of another," the magazine declares, "it can reduce the city to less than the sum of its extraordinary parts."
Michael Kelly succeeds William Whitworth as editor of the *Atlantic Monthly*. Kelly turns the position over to the current editor, Cullen Murphy, in 2002 in order to return to reporting. He is killed while covering the war in Iraq in April 2003.

A Northeastern University freshman, Shawn Fanning, creates "Napster," a program that enables the sharing of music files over the Internet. Asked later why he wrote the software program, Fanning declares: "I was bored. I had some free time." The program becomes immensely popular with high school and college students, but it is criticized by the music industry and many artists. In 2001 various courts order the company that had since been formed to stop the distribution of copyrighted material, effectively shutting down Napster.

2000

Boston's population is 589,141, the twentieth largest of any city in the United States. Of that number, 291,561 are white; 140,305 are African American; 85,089 are Hispanic; 44,280 are Asian/Pacific Islander; 1,517 are Native American; 8,215 classify themselves as other; and 18,174 are multiracial. Of the total, 151,836 are foreign born.

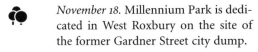

November 18. Millennium Park is dedicated in West Roxbury on the site of the former Gardner Street city dump.

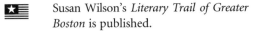

Susan Wilson's *Literary Trail of Greater Boston* is published.

The Boston Foundation publishes *The Wisdom of our Choices: Boston's Indicators of Progress, Change and Stability.* The report provides a scorecard—to be updated yearly—in order to assess how much progress the city is making in areas such as housing, the environment, education, the economy, public health, cultural life, civic health, public safety, technology, and transportation.

November 30. John Corigliano's Symphony no. 2 for String Orchestra is given its world premiere by the Boston Symphony Orchestra. It is awarded a Pulitzer Prize in 2001.

*The Leonard P. Zakim–Bunker Hill Bridge.
(Photograph by Richard Tourangeau)*

June 23. The thirteen-screen Fenway Theatre movie complex opens in the Landmark Center (the former Sears Building) in the Fenway.

October 23. The first episode of the network television show *Boston Public* airs. Set at a fictional Boston High School (represented by the exterior shots of East Boston High School and interior shots of Boston Latin), the show continues until January 2004.

2001

May 1. Pope John Paul II Park opens along the Neponset River.
The City Hall Plaza arcade opens.

Thomas H. O'Connor's *The Hub: Boston Past and Present* is published. It contains the passage "The 'Old Boston'—the Boston as we have known it in history and in literature—no longer exists. Some time ago it ceased to be the Boston of John Winthrop, Josiah Quincy, or James Jackson Storrow. . . . It is equally clear that it is no longer the Boston of John Francis Fitzgerald, James Michael Curley, or John F. Kennedy. . . . All that may be wonderfully romantic and nostalgic, but it is now part of the city's past, not of its future. Instead of Yankees, Irish, and Italians, Boston is increasingly populated by African Americans, Hispanic Americans, and Asian Americans—these are our 'new Bostonians.' "

September 11. Terrorists hijack American Airlines Flight 11 and United Airlines Flight 175 after the two planes leave Logan Airport and crash them into the World Trade Center towers in New York. Two other planes are hijacked in

New York; one is crashed into the Pentagon, the other into a field in Pennsylvania.

December 22. Richard Reid, a British-born Muslim, attempts to detonate a bomb in his shoe on American Airlines Flight 60 from Paris to Miami. He is subdued, and the plane is diverted to Boston.

November 6. Thomas Menino (with 68,011 votes) defeats Peggy Davis-Mullen (with 21,393) to win reelection as mayor.

May. The first issue of the *Boston Haitian Reporter* appears. William Dorcena is publisher.

Dennis Lehane's *Mystic River* is published. A movie version of the novel is released in 2003.

April 7. Boston College beats North Dakota State 3–2 in overtime in Albany, New York, to win the NCAA hockey championship.

2002

July 20. The first section of the Massachusetts Bay Transit Authority's Silver Line opens between Downtown Crossing and Dudley Square in Roxbury. A bus line, its route follows that of the now removed Orange Line elevated subway.

October 4. The Leonard P. Zakim–Bunker Hill Bridge, between downtown Boston and Charlestown, is dedicated. Designed by Christian Menn, it is the world's widest (ten lanes) cable-stayed bridge. The bridge opens to pedestrians on May 12 and October 6, attracting crowds of two hundred thousand and eight hundred thousand, respectively. The bridge opens to northbound traffic, with Zakim's sixteen-year-old daughter, Shari, the first person to drive across it, on March 29, 2003.

October 10–11. Congress votes to authorize the use of force against Iraq. Baghdad is attacked on March 20, 2003.

June 30. Ten-year-old Trina Persad is shot and killed by a stray piece of buckshot from a shotgun used in a shootout between rival gangs. The girl was just leaving Goffigan Park, named for Jermaine Goffigan, an innocent nine-year-old who had also been killed by random gang violence in 1994.

September 8. Eveline Barros-Cepeda, a passenger in a car used in an attempt to run over a police officer, is shot and killed by Boston police. She is the eighth civilian to be killed by Boston police in the last twenty-two months.

December 25. The first major Christmas snowstorm in twenty-eight years strikes Boston.

December 13. Cardinal Bernard Law resigns as archbishop of Boston in the wake of a sexual abuse scandal. The Massachusetts attorney general later confirms there are 789 documented cases of molestation by 250 priests in the

New England Patriot Adam Vinatieri kicks the game-winning field goal against the Oakland Raiders at Foxborough Stadium, January 2002. (Photograph by Michael Seamans, courtesy of the Boston Herald)

Boston archdiocese over a period of more than sixty years. Law is replaced by the temporary apostolic administrator Bishop Richard Lennon.

January 8. President George W. Bush unveils his national education program at Boston Latin School.

January 19. The New England Patriots beat the Oakland Raiders 16–13 in Foxborough in an AFC play-off game, as Adam Vinatieri kicks a forty-five-yard field goal in the snow to tie the game at the end of regulation and a twenty-three-yarder in overtime to win it. The Patriots beat the Steelers 24–17 in Pittsburgh on January 26 to win the AFC championship, then beat the St. Louis Rams 20–17 in New Orleans to win Super Bowl XXXVI, as Vinatieri kicks a forty-eight-yard field goal on the last play of the game on February 3.

Construction on the Big Dig. (Photograph by Mike Adaskaveg, courtesy of the Boston Herald)

2003

March 29. The depressed Central Artery opens to northbound traffic. The highway opens to southbound traffic on December 20. Groundbreaking ceremonies for the so-called Big Dig, the largest public works project in U.S. history, were held on May 13, 1991. Actual construction began September 23 of that year.

March 29. An estimated twenty-five thousand people take part in a march through Back Bay to Boston Common to protest the war in Iraq.

November 4. Felix Arroyo becomes the first Hispanic American elected to the Boston City Council when he wins one of the four at-large seats. Arroyo, who finished fifth in the 2001 election, had been serving on the council since January 6, when he assumed the seat given up by Francis "Mickey" Roache, who became Suffolk County Register of Deeds.

May 5. The city of Boston joins seventy-seven other municipalities in Massachusetts in banning smoking in all workplaces, including bars and restaurants. *November 18.* In *Goodridge v. Department of Public Health,* the Massachusetts Supreme Judicial Court rules 4–3 that state laws excluding same-sex couples from marriage are unconstitutional. In an advisory opinion by a similar margin on February 4, 2004, the court declares that the only way to meet the state constitution's guarantee of equal rights is to grant same-sex couples full marriage rights.

February 5. Adama Hawa Barry, a pregnant, thirty-two-year-old immigrant from Guinea, is hit by a stray bullet fired during an altercation between young men on an Orange Line subway. She survives, but her baby, delivered by emergency cesarean section, dies hours later.

November 20. A report by the U.S. House of Representatives' Committee on Government Reform describes the involvement of agents in the Boston FBI office in crimes committed by their informants as "one of the greatest failures in the history of federal law enforcement."

February 18. A record 27.5 inches of snow falls in a twenty-four-hour period.
September 28. Little Joe, an adolescent gorilla, escapes from the Franklin Park Zoo. He injures two people slightly and is spotted sitting at a bus stop on Seaver Street before he is captured by park officials and police.

July 1. Sean Patrick O'Malley is appointed archbishop of Boston, replacing the temporary apostolic administrator Bishop Richard Lennon. O'Malley is installed as archbishop on July 30.
September 9. The Archdiocese of Boston signs an agreement to pay eighty-five million dollars to 552 people claiming to be victims of sexual abuse by Boston-area Catholic priests.

August 23. Orchard Gardens elementary school opens in Roxbury. Designed by TLDC Architecture and Stull and Lee, Inc., it is one of three new schools (the others are on Columbia Road in Dorchester and on Mildred Avenue in Mattapan) to open this year. These are the first new public schools in Boston since 1978, and the first in these neighborhoods in more fifty years.

June 26. Degas's *The Duchess of Montejasi and Her Daughters* is unveiled at the Museum of Fine Arts. The most expensive painting ever acquired by the museum, it is purchased after the museum sold two paintings by Degas and one by Renoir for a total of $14.5 million the month before.
September 6–7. Bruce Springsteen performs in the first rock concerts held at Fenway Park.
October 25. The former New England Conservatory president Gunther Schuller's *Encounters* is given its world premiere as part of the hundredth anniversary celebration of the opening of Jordan Hall.

March 15. Charlestown High School beats Hoosac Valley 68–51 at the Worcester Centrum to win its fourth straight Massachusetts Division 2 boys' basketball championship.
October 16–17. The Red Sox lose to the Yankees 6–5 in game 7 of the American League championship series in New York, on an eleventh-inning home run by Aaron Boone. Boston had led 5–2 with one out in the eighth inning, and Red Sox manager Grady Little is later criticized for not replacing starting pitcher Pedro Martinez sooner.

2004

June 10. The Boston Convention and Exhibition Center, designed by Rafael Viñoly, is dedicated on Summer Street in South Boston. Construction began in 2000.

June 30. The South Boston Maritime Park opens at D Street and Northern Avenue.

Robert J. Allison's *A Short History of Boston* is published.

July 28. Beacon Hill resident and U.S. Senator John F. Kerry wins his party's nomination for president at the 2004 Democratic National Convention, which is held at the FleetCenter. It is the first national political convention ever held in Boston. President George W. Bush is the Republican party candidate in the election, which is held on November 2. Bush wins.

May 17. Robert Compton and David Wilson, two of the plaintiffs in *Goodridge v. Department of Public Health,* become the first same-sex couple to wed in Boston when they are married at the Arlington Street Church.

February 19. Kathleen O'Toole becomes the first woman police commissioner in the history of the Boston Police Department.

January 10. The temperature reaches minus three degrees, the coldest on this date since 1875.

The Catholic Archdiocese of Boston announces the closing of 65 of its 357 parishes, including 12 in Boston. Five additional parishes in Boston are merged with other parishes.

February 1. The Patriots beat the Carolina Cougars 32–29 in Houston to win Super Bown XXXVIII, as Adam Vinatieri kicks a forty-one-yard field goal on the next-to-last play of the game.
October 20. The Red Sox beat the Yankees 10–3 in game 7 of the championship series at Yankee Stadium to win the American League pennant, becoming the first team in baseball playoff history to win four straight games after losing the first three. The Red Sox go on to beat the St. Louis Cardinals 3–0 in game 4 in St. Louis on October 27 to win their first World Series since 1918.

Select Bibliography

BOOKS AND ARTICLES

Ainley, Leslie G. *Boston Mahatma.* Boston: Bruce Humphries, 1949.

Allison, Robert J. *A Short History of Boston.* Beverly, Mass.: Commonwealth Editions, 2004.

Amory, Cleveland. *The Proper Bostonians.* New York: E. P. Dutton, 1947.

Apollonio, Thornton D. *Boston Public Schools Past and Present: With Some Reflections on Their Characters and Characteristics.* Boston: Wright and Potter, 1923.

Avault, John, Alexander Ganz, and Gregory W. Perkins. "Tax Constraint and Fiscal Policy: After the Property Tax. Raising Revenue for Boston." Boston: Boston Redevelopment Authority, October 1983.

Bacon, Edwin M. *King's Dictionary of Boston.* Cambridge, Mass.: Moses King, 1883.

Barber, Samuel. *Boston Common: A Diary of Notable Events, Incidents, and Neighboring Occurrences.* Boston: Christopher Publishing House, 1914.

Barnhill, Georgia B. "Nathaniel Hurd: Boston Engraver." *Porticus* (journal of the Memorial Art Gallery of the University of Rochester) 20 (2001).

Barrett, Richard C. *Boston's Depots and Terminals: A History of Downtown Boston's Railroad Stations.* Rochester, N.Y.: Railroad Research Publications, 1996.

Bartlett, Cynthia Chalmers. *Beacon Hill.* Dover, N.H.: Arcadia Publishing, 1996.

Beatty, Jack. *The Rascal King: The Life and Times of James Michael Curley (1874–1958).* Reading, Mass.: Addison-Wesley, 1992.

Beebe, Lucius. *Boston and the Boston Legend.* New York: D. Appleton-Century, 1936.

Bellis, Mary. "Stitches—The History of Sewing Machines." Inventors.About.com.

Blake, John B. *Public Health in the Town of Boston.* Cambridge, Mass.: Harvard University Press, 1959.

Bond, Lawrence. *Native Names of New England Towns and Villages.* Topsfield, Mass.: privately published, 1993.

Booth, John Nicholls. *The Story of the Second Church in Boston (The Original Old North), Including the Old North Church Mystery.* Boston: Second Church, 1980.

Bowen, Abel. *Bowen's Picture of Boston, or the Citizen's and Stranger's Guide to the Metropolis of Massachusetts and Its Environs.* Boston: Otis, Broaders and Co., 1838.

Bridenbaugh, Carl. *Cities in Revolt: Urban Life in America 1743–1776.* New York: Alfred A. Knopf, 1955.

Brigham, Clarence S., ed. *History and Bibliography of American Newspapers: 1690–1820. Volume One.* Worcester, Mass.: American Antiquarian Society, 1947.

Brooks, Gladys. *Three Wise Virgins.* New York: E. P. Dutton, 1957.

Brooks, Van Wyck. *The Flowering of New England 1815–1865.* New York: E. P. Dutton, 1936.

———. *New England: Indian Summer 1865–1915.* New York: E. P. Dutton, 1940.

Broyles, Michael. *Music of the Highest Class: Elitism and Populism in Antebellum Boston.* New Haven and London: Yale University Press, 1992.

Budington, William I. *The History of the First Church, Charlestown.* Boston: Charles Tappan, 1845.

Buni, Andrew, and Alan Rogers. *Boston, a City on a Hill: An Illustrated History.* Woodland Hill, Calif.: Windsor Publications, 1984.

Carlock, Marty. *A Guide to Public Art in Greater Boston from Newburyport to Plymouth.* Boston: Harvard Common Press, 1988.

Carruth, Gorton, and Eugene Ehrlich. *Facts & Dates of American Sports from Colonial Days to the Present*. New York: Harper and Row, 1988.

Clark, Judith F., and Robert J. Allison. *Massachusetts from Colony to Commonwealth: An Illustrated History*. Sun Valley, Calif.: American Historical Press, 2002.

Cole, Doris, and Nick Wheeler. *School Treasures: Architecture of Historic Boston Schools*. Weston, Mass.: Font & Center Press, 2002.

Corbett, Bernard M. *The Beanpot: Fifty Years of Thrills, Spills, and Chills*. Boston: Northeastern University Press, 2002.

———. *Boston Sports Trivia*. Boston: Quinlan Press, 1985.

Corbett, Bernard M., and Morgan White, Jr. *Boston Trivia: 1,000 Questions*. Boston: Addison C. Getchell and Son, 1984.

Crawford, Mary Caroline. *Famous Families of Massachusetts*. Boston: Little, Brown, 1930.

———. *Romantic Days in Old Boston*. Boston: Little, Brown, 1910.

Davison, Peter. *The Fading Smile: Poets in Boston, 1955–1960*. New York; Alfred A. Knopf, 1994.

Dentler, Robert A., and Marvin B. Scott. *Schools on Trial: An Inside Account of the Boston Desegregation Case*. Cambridge, Mass.: Abt Books, 1981.

Dezell, Maureen. *Irish America: Coming into Clover: The Evolution of a People and a Culture*. New York: Random House, 2000.

Dictionary of American Biography. New York: Charles Scribner's Sons, 1927.

Drake, Francis S. *The Town of Roxbury. Its Memorable Persons and Places, Its History and Antiquities, with Numerous Illustrations of Its Old Landmarks and Noted Personages*. Roxbury, Mass.: Francis S. Drake, 1878.

Drake, Samuel A. *Old Boston Taverns and Tavern Clubs*. Boston: W. A. Butterfield, 1917.

Drake, Samuel G. *History and Antiquities of Boston*. Boston: L. Stevens, 1856.

Einstein, Charles, ed. *The Fireside Book of Baseball*. New York: Simon and Schuster, 1956.

Emerson, Edward Waldo. *The Early Years of the Saturday Club*. Boston: Houghton Mifflin, 1918.

Ernst, C. W. "Words Coined in Boston." *New England Magazine*, December 1896.

Euchner, Charles C., ed. *Governing Greater Boston: Meeting the Needs of the Region's People*. Cambridge, Mass.: Rappaport Institute for Greater Boston, 2003.

Fahey, Joseph J., ed. *Boston's Forty-Five Mayors: From John Phillips to Kevin H. White*. Boston: City of Boston, 1975.

Fairbrother, Trevor, et al. *The Bostonians: Painters of An Elegant Age, 1870–1930*. Boston: Museum of Fine Arts, 1986.

Foner, Eric, and John A. Garraty, eds. *The Reader's Companion to American History*. New York: Houghton Mifflin, 1991.

Formisano, Ronald P. *Boston against Busing: Race, Class, and Ethnicity in the 1960s and 1970s*. Chapel Hill and London: University of North Carolina Press, 1991.

Fraser, James W., Henry L. Allen, and Sam Barnes, eds. *From Common School to Magnet School*. Boston: Trustees of the Public Library, 1979.

Frederick, Antoinette. *Northeastern University. Coming of Age: The Ryder Years*. Boston, Northeastern University, 1995.

Galvin, John T. *Twelve Mayors of Boston*. Boston: Boston Public Library, 1970.

Gammell, R. H. Ives. "A Reintroduction to the Boston Painters." *Classical America* 3 (1973).

Gans, Herbert J. *The Urban Villagers: Group and Class in the Life of Italian-Americans*. New York: Free Press, 1962.

Goodwin, Doris Kearns. *The Fitzgeralds and the Kennedys*. New York: Simon and Schuster, 1987.

Green, James R., and Hugh Carter Donahue. *Boston's Workers: A Labor History*. Boston: Trustees of the Public Library, 1979.

Gregory, Winifred, ed. *American Newspapers: 1821–1936*. New York: Bibliographical Society of America, 1937.

Haglund, Karl. *Inventing the Charles River*. Cambridge, Mass.: MIT Press, 2002.

Halper, Donna L. "Boston Radio in the Early 1920s." New England Music Scrapbook, http://www.geocities.com/uridfm/r/earlybostonradio.html

Handlin, Oscar. *Boston's Immigrants: A Study in Acculturation.* Cambridge, Mass.: Harvard University Press, 1959.

Hayden, Robert C. *African-Americans in Boston: More than 350 Years.* Boston: Trustees of the Public Library, 1991.

Hazell, Ed. *Berklee: The First Fifty Years.* Boston: Berklee College of Music, 1995.

Herlihey, Elisabeth M., ed. *Fifty Years of Boston: A Memorial Volume Issued in Commemoration of the Tercentenary of 1930.* Boston, 1932.

Higgins, George V. *Style versus Substance: Boston, Kevin White and the Politics of Illusion.* New York: Macmillan, 1984.

Holli, Melvin G., and Jones, Peter d'A., eds. *Biographical Dictionary of American Mayors, 1820–1980: Big City Mayors.* Westport, Conn.: Greenwood Press, 1981.

Howe, M. A. De Wolfe. *The Boston Symphony Orchestra 1881–1931.* Boston: Houghton Mifflin, 1931.

Howland, Llewellyn, ed. *A Book for Boston.* Boston: David Godine, 1980.

Jarvis, F. Washington. *The Roxbury Latin School 1645–1995.* Boston: David Godine, 1995.

Jarzombek, Nancy. *The Nineteenth Century: Rediscovering American Painters of New England and New York.* Boston: Vose Galleries, 1999.

Jennings, James, and Mel King, eds. *From Access to Power: Black Politics in Boston.* Rochester, Vt.: Schenkman Books, 1986.

Johnson, Arthur M., and Barry E. Supple. *Boston Capitalists and Western Railroads: A Study in the Nineteenth Century Railroad Investment Process.* Cambridge, Mass.: Harvard University Press, 1967.

Johnson, H. Earle. *Musical Interludes in Boston: 1795–1830.* New York: Columbia University Press, 1943.

Johnson, Richard A. *A Century of Boston Sports.* Boston: Northeastern University Press, 2000.

Jones, Douglas Lamar, Alan Rogers, James Connolly, Cynthia Farr Brown, and Diane Kadzis. *Discovering the Public Interest: A History of the Boston Bar Association.* Canoga Park, Calif.: CCA Publications, 1993.

Jones, Howard Mumford, and Bessie Zaban Jones, eds. *The Many Voices of Boston: A Historical Anthology, 1630–1975.* Boston: Little, Brown 1975.

Juravich, Tom, William F. Hartford, and James R. Green. *Commonwealth of Toil: Chapters in the History of Massachusetts Workers and Their Unions.* Amherst: University of Massachusetts Press, 1996.

Kaitz, Merrill. *The Great Boston Trivia and Fact Book.* Nashville, Tenn.: Cumberland House, 1999.

Kales, Emily, and David Kales. *All about the Boston Harbor Islands.* Boston: Herman Publishing, 1976.

Kay, Jane Holtz. *Lost Boston.* Boston: Houghton Mifflin, 1980.

Kelley, Walt. *What They Never Told You about Boston (Or What They Did That Were Lies).* Camden, Maine: Down East Books, 1993.

Kennedy, Lawrence M. *Planning the City upon a Hill: Boston since 1630.* Amherst: University of Massachusetts Press, 1992.

Kenney, Herbert A. *Newspaper Row: Journalism in the Pre-Television Era.* Chester, Conn.: Globe Pequot Press, 1987.

Kernfeld, Barry, ed. *The New Grove Dictionary of Jazz,* 2d ed. New York: Grove's Dictionaries, 2001.

King, Mel. *Chain of Change.* Boston: South End Press, 1981.

Kozol, Jonathan. *Death at an Early Age.* Boston: Houghton Mifflin, 1967.

Krieger, Alex, and David Cobb, with Amy Turner. *Mapping Boston.* Cambridge, Mass.: MIT Press, 2002.

Kruh, David. *Always Something Doing: Boston's Infamous Scollay Square.* 1989. Rept., Boston: Northeastern University Press, 1999.

Lane, Roger. *Policing the City: Boston, 1822–1885.* Cambridge, Mass.: Harvard University Press, 1967.

Langtry, Alfred P., ed. *Metropolitan Boston: A Modern History.* New York: Lewis Historical Publishing, 1929.

Levine, Hillel, and Lawrence Harmon. *The Death of an American Jewish Community: A Tragedy of Good Intentions.* New York: Free Press, 1992.

Logan, Roberta. *Long Road to Justice: The African American Experience in the Massachusetts Courts.* Boston: Justice George Lewis Ruffin Society, Northeastern University College of Criminal Justice, 2000.

Lukas, J. Anthony. *Common Ground: A Turbulent Decade in the Lives of Three American Families.* New York: Alfred A. Knopf, 1986.

Lupo, Alan. *Liberty's Chosen Home: The Politics of Violence in Boston.* Boston: Beacon Press, 1971.

Lupo, Alan, Frank Colcord, and Edmund P. Fowler. *Rites of Way: The Politics of Transportation in Boston and the U.S. City.* Boston: Little, Brown, 1971.

Lyons, Louis M. *Newspaper Story: One Hundred Years of* The Boston Globe. Cambridge, Mass.: Harvard University Press, 1971.

Makris, John N., ed. *Boston Murders.* New York: Duell, Sloan and Pearce, 1948.

Marchione, William P. *Allston-Brighton.* Dover, N.H.: Arcadia Publishing, 1996.

———. *The Bull in the Garden.* Boston: Trustees of the Public Library, 1986.

McCord, David. *About Boston: Sight, Sound, Flavor and Inflection.* Boston: Little, Brown, 1948.

McKay, Richard C. *Some Famous Sailing Ships and Their Builder, Donald McKay.* New York and London: G. P. Putnam's Sons, 1928.

McPherson, Bruce, and James Klein. *Measure by Measure: A History of New England Conservatory from 1867.* Boston: Trustees of New England Conservatory of Music, 1995.

Morison, Samuel Eliot. *Builders of the Bay Colony.* 1930. Rept., Boston: Northeastern University Press, 1981.

———. *The Maritime History of Massachusetts 1783–1860.* 1921. Rept., Boston: Northeastern University Press, 1979.

Muir, Diana. *Reflections in Bullough's Pond: Economy and Ecosystem in New England.* Hanover, N.H.: University Press of New England, 2000.

Nordlinger, Edward A. *Decentralizing the City: A Study of Boston's Little City Halls.* Cambridge, Mass.: MIT Press, 1972.

Norton, Bettina A. *The Boston Naval Shipyard, 1800–1974.* Boston: Bostonian Society, 1975.

Norton, Elliot. *Broadway Down East: An Informal Account of the Plays, Players and Playhouses of Boston from Puritan Times to the Present.* Boston: Trustees of the Public Library, 1978.

O'Connor, Thomas H. *Bibles, Brahmins, and Bosses: A Short History of Boston,* 3d ed. Boston: Trustees of the Public Library, 1991.

———. *Boston A To Z.* Cambridge, Mass.: Harvard University Press, 2000.

———. *Boston Catholics: A History of the Church and Its People.* Boston: Northeastern University Press, 1998.

———. *The Boston Irish: A Political History.* Boston: Northeastern University Press, 1995

———. *Building a New Boston: Politics and Urban Renewal, 1950 to 1970.* Boston: Northeastern University Press, 1993.

———. *Civil War Boston: Home Front and Battlefield.* Boston: Northeastern University Press, 1997.

———. *Eminent Bostonians.* Cambridge, Mass.: Harvard University Press, 2002.

———. *The Hub: Boston Past and Present.* Boston: Northeastern University Press, 2001.

———. *South Boston: My Home Town.* 1988. Rept, Boston: Northeastern University Press, 1994.

O'Toole, James M. *Militant and Triumphant: William Henry O'Connell and the Catholic Church in Boston, 1859–1944.* Notre Dame, Ind.: University of Notre Dame Press, 1992.

Philbrick, Herbert. *I Led Three Lives.* New York: McGraw-Hill, 1952.

Pike, James, ed. *History of the Churches in Boston.* Boston: Ecclesia Publishing, 1883.

Price, Michael, and Anthony Mitchell Sammarco. *Boston's Immigrants: 1840–1925.* Charleston, S.C.: Arcadia Publishing, 2000.

Puleo, Stephen. *Dark Tide: The Great Boston Molasses Flood of 1919.* Boston: Beacon Press, 2003.

Quincy, Josiah. *Municipal History of the Town and City of Boston, during Two Centuries, from September 17, 1630, to September 17, 1830.* Boston: C. C. Little and J. Brown, 1852.

Rees, Dafydd, and Luke Crampton, eds. *VH1 Music First Rock Stars Encyclopedia.* London: DK Publishing, 1996.

Richardson, Robert D., Jr. *Emerson: The Mind on Fire.* Berkeley: University of California Press, 1995.

Robinson, Barbara. *Creating Community: The African Experience in Massachusetts.* Boston: Commonwealth Museum at Columbia Point, 1988.

Roessner, Jane. *A Decent Place to Live: From Columbia Point to Harbor Point: A Community History.* Boston: Northeastern University Press, 2000.

Rossiter, William S. *Days and Ways in Old Boston.* Boston: R. H. Stearns, 1915.

Russell, Francis. *The Knave of Boston & Other Ambiguous Massachusetts Characters.* Boston: Quinlan Press, 1987.

Rutman, Darret B. *Winthrop's Boston: Portrait of a Puritan Town.* New York: Norton, 1972.

Ryan, Jerry. *The Forgotten Aquariums of Boston.* Pascoag, R.I.: Finely Aquatic Books, 2002.

Ryczek, William J. *When Johnny Comes Sliding Home: The Post–Civil War Baseball Boom, 1865–1870.* Jefferson, N.C.: McFarland, 1998.

Sammarco, Anthony Mitchell. *Boston: A Century of Progress.* Dover, N.H.: Arcadia Publishing, 1995.

———. *Dorchester.* Dover, N.H.: Arcadia Publishing, 1995.

———. *East Boston.* Dover, N.H.: Arcadia Publishing, 1997.

———. *Hyde Park.* Dover, N.H.: Arcadia Publishing, 1996.

———. *Roslindale.* Dover, N.H.: Arcadia Publishing, 1997.

———. *Roxbury.* Dover, N.H.: Arcadia Publishing, 1997.

———. *West Roxbury.* Dover, N.H.: Arcadia Publishing, 1997.

Sarna, Jonathan D., and Ellen Smith, eds. *The Jews of Boston: Essays on the Occasion of the Centenary (1895–1995) of the Combined Jewish Philanthropies of Greater Boston.* Boston: Northeastern University Press, 1995.

Savage, Edward H. *Boston Events: A Brief Mention and the Date of More than 5,000 Events That Transpired in Boston from 1630 to 1880.* Boston: Tolman and White, 1884.

———. *Police Records and Recollections; or, Boston by Daylight and Gaslight for Two Hundred and Forty Years.* Boston: John P. Dale, 1873.

Seaburg, Carl. *Boston Observed.* Boston: Beacon Press, 1971.

Simon, Clea. *Boston Rock Trivia.* Boston: Quinlan Press, 1995.

Slonimsky, Nicolas. *Music since 1900.* 5th ed. New York: Schirmer Books, 1994.

Smith, Richard Norton. *The Harvard Century: The Making of a University to a Nation.* New York: Simon and Schuster, 1986.

Snow, Caleb H. *A History of Boston, the Metropolis of Massachusetts, from Its Origin to Its Present Period.* Boston: A. Bowen, 1825.

Snow, Edward Rowe. *The Islands of Boston Harbor.* New York: Dodd, Mead, 1984.

Southworth, Susan, and Michael Southworth. *AIA Guide to Boston.* Chester, Conn.: Globe/Pequot Press, 1992.

Sowell, Mike. *The Pitch That Killed: Carl Mays, Ray Chapman and the Pennant Race of 1920.* New York: Macmillan, 1989.

Stott, Peter. *A Guide to the Industrial Archeology of Boston Proper.* Cambridge, Mass.: MIT Press, 1984.

Tager, Jack. *Boston Riots: Three Centuries of Social Violence.* Boston: Northeastern University Press, 2001.

Thwing, Annie. *The Crooked and Narrow Streets of Boston 1630–1822.* Boston: Marshall, 1930.

Trager, James, ed. *The People's Chronology.* New York: Henry Holt, 1994.

Troyen, Carol, Charlotte Emans Moore, and Priscilla Kate Diamond. *American Paintings in the Museum of Fine Arts, Boston: An Illustrated Summary Catalogue.* Boston: Museum of Fine Arts, 1997.

Truettner, William H., and Roger B. Stein, eds. *Picturing Old New England: Image and Memory.* Washington, D.C.: National Museum of American Art, Smithsonian Institution, and New Haven, Conn.: Yale University Press, 1999.

Tuohey, George V. *A History of the Boston Baseball Club.* Boston: M. F. Quinn, 1897.

Van Doren, Mark, ed. *The Portable Emerson.* New York: Viking Press, 1946.

Vensel, Leslie A., ed. *Aesculapian Boston.* Boston: Paul Dudley White Medical History Society, 1980.

Vogel, Morris J. *The Invention of the Modern Hospital.* Chicago: University of Chicago Press, 1980.

Von Schmidt, Eric, and Jim Rooney. *Baby, Let Me Follow You Down: The Illustrated Story of the Cambridge Folk Years.* Amherst: University of Massachusetts Press, 1979.

Vose Galleries. *Mary Bradish Titcomb and Her Contemporaries: The Artists of Fenway Studios 1905–1939.* Boston: Vose Galleries, 1998.

Warner, Sam Bass. *Streetcar Suburbs: The Process of Growth in Boston 1870–1900.* Cambridge, Mass.: Harvard University Press, 1962.

Weston, George F., Jr. *Boston Ways: High, By, and Folk.* Boston: Beacon Press, 1957.

White, Charles William III. "The History of Boston Rock & Roll." *The Beat Magazine,* 1985–1986.

White, Olive B. *Centennial History of the Girls' High School of Boston.* Boston: Paul K. Blanchard, 1952.

Whitehill, Walter Muir. *Boston: A Topographical History.* 2d ed. Cambridge, Mass.: Belknap Press of Harvard University Press, 1968.

———. *Boston in the Age of John Fitzgerald Kennedy.* Norman: University of Oklahoma Press, 1966.

———. *Museum of Fine Arts Boston: A Centennial History.* Cambridge, Mass.: Belknap Press of Harvard University Press, 1970.

Whyte, William Foote. *Street Corner Society: The Social Structure of an Italian Slum.* Chicago: University of Chicago Press, 1943.

Williams, Alexander W. *A Social History of the Greater Boston Clubs.* Barre, Mass.: Barre Publishing Co., 1970.

Wilson, Susan. *Boston Sites and Insights.* Boston: Beacon Press, 1994.

———. *Literary Trail of Greater Boston.* Boston and New York: Houghton, Mifflin, 2000.

Winsor, Justin, ed. *The Memorial History of Boston, including Suffolk County, Massachusetts: 1630–1880.* Boston: James R. Osgood, 1881.

Young, Alfred F. *The Shoemaker and the Tea Party.* Boston: Beacon Press, 1999.

Zaitzevsky, Cynthia. *Frederick Law Olmsted and the Boston Park System.* Cambridge, Mass.: Belknap Press of Harvard University Press, 1982.

GUIDES AND REPORTS

Boston Athletic Association. *2003 Boston Marathon Media Guide.* Boston: Boston Athletic Association with John Hancock, April, 2003.

Boston Directory for the Year Commencing August 1, 1930. Boston: Sampson & Murdock, 1931.

Boston Globe. *Historic Front Pages.* Boston: Boston Globe, 1997.

Boston History Collaborative. *Innovation Odyssey through Boston and Cambridge.* Boston: Boston History Collaborative, 2003.

Boston History Company. *Professional and Industrial History of Suffolk County, Massachusetts, in Three Volumes.* Boston: Boston History Company, 1894.

Boston Landmarks Commission. *Exploring Boston's Neighborhoods: Allston/Brighton.* Boston: Boston Landmarks Commission, 1996.

———. *Exploring Boston's Neighborhoods: Charlestown.* Boston: Boston Landmarks Commission, 1995.

———. *Exploring Boston's Neighborhoods: East Boston.* Boston: Boston Landmarks Commission, 1995.

———. *Exploring Boston's Neighborhoods: Fenway/Kenmore.* Boston: Boston Landmarks Commission, 1996.

———. *Exploring Boston's Neighborhoods: Hyde Park.* Boston: Boston Landmarks Commission, 1996.

———. *Exploring Boston's Neighborhoods: Jamaica Plain.* Boston: Boston Landmarks Commission, 1995.

———. *Exploring Boston's Neighborhoods: Mission Hill.* Boston: Boston Landmarks Commission, 1994.

———. *Exploring Boston's Neighborhoods: North End.* Boston: Boston Landmarks Commission, 1995.

————. *Exploring Boston's Neighborhoods: Roxbury.* Boston: Boston Landmarks Commission, 1994.

————. *Exploring Boston's Neighborhoods: South Boston.* Boston: Boston Landmarks Commission, 1994.

————. *Exploring Boston's Neighborhoods: West Roxbury/Roslindale.* Boston: Boston Landmarks Commission, 1995.

Boston 200 Corporation. *Boston Neighborhood History Series: Black Bostonia.* Boston: Boston 200 Corporation, 1976.

————. *Boston Neighborhood History Series: Brighton.* Boston: Boston 200 Corporation, 1976.

————. *Boston Neighborhood History Series: Charlestown.* Boston: Boston 200 Corporation, 1976.

————. *Boston Neighborhood History Series: Chinatown.* Boston: Boston 200 Corporation, 1976.

————. *Boston Neighborhood History Series: The Fenway.* Boston: Boston 200 Corporation, 1976.

————. *Boston Neighborhood History Series: Mission Hill.* Boston: Boston 200 Corporation, 1976.

————. *Boston Neighborhood History Series: Roslindale.* Boston: Boston 200 Corporation, 1976.

A Brief History of the Somerset Club of Boston—1852–1913—With a List of Past and Present Members. Prepared by a Committee of the Club, 1913.

Chronology of Boston: With the Dates of Discoveries. Boston: Noyes, Snow and Co., 1878.

City of Boston. *Boston Recollections: The Boston History Calendar 2001.* Boston: Office of the City Clerk, Archives and Records Management Division, 2000.

————. *Boston Year Book 1924–1925.* Boston: Statistics Department of the City of Boston, 1925.

————. *Jubilee 350. Boston.* Boston: Mayor's Office, 1980.

Davis Museum and Cultural Center. *Walking Tour of Boston Arts & Crafts Points of Interest.* Wellesley, Mass.: Davis Museum and Cultural Center, Wellesley College, 1997.

Dorchester 350. *Dorchester's 350th Anniversary Calendar & Appointment Book.* Boston: Dorchester 350, 1980.

Ernst, George A. O. *A Chronology of the Boston Public Schools.* Boston: Finance Commission of the City of Boston, 1912.

Friends of the Public Garden and Common. *The Boston Common.* Boston: Friends of the Public Garden and Common.

Heath, Richard. *Calf Pasture: The Elastic Peninsula.* In the collection of the Bostonian Society.

Hitchings, Sinclair, and Catherine H. Farlow. *A New Guide to the Massachusetts State House.* Boston: John Hancock Life Insurance Company, 1964.

Isabella Stewart Gardner Museum. *Guide to the Collection: Isabella Stewart Gardner Museum.* Boston: Isabella Stewart Gardner Museum, 1959.

King, Moses, ed. *King's Hand-Book of Boston.* Cambridge, Mass.: Harvard College, 1878.

————. *King's "How to See Boston": A Practical Guide and an Artistic Souvenir.* Boston, 1883.

————. *King's How to See Boston: A Trustworthy Guide Book.* Boston, 1895.

Krim, Arthur. "Chinatown—South Cove Comprehensive Survey Project Final Survey Report." Boston: Boston Landmarks Commission, 1997.

New England Baptist Hospital. *A Century of Distinction: New England Baptist Hospital.* Boston: New England Baptist Hospital.

Okie, Susan, and Donna Yee, eds. *Boston: The Official Bicentennial Guidebook.* New York: E. P. Dutton, 1975.

O'Neill, Edward B., and Robert E. MacQueen. *A Manual for the General Court for 1991–1992.* Boston: Causeway Print, 1991.

Robinson, Barbara, and Samuel Rubin. *The View at Columbia Point: A Self-Guiding Tour.* Boston: Commonwealth Museum and the John F. Kennedy Library, 1990.

Sharf, Frederic Alan. "Art and Life in Boston, 1837–1850: A Study of the Painter and Sculptor in American Society." Ph.D. diss., Boston College, 1956.

Sketches of Some Historic Churches of Greater Boston. Boston: Beacon Press, 1918.

State Street Trust Company. *Boston's Story in Inscriptions.* Boston: State Street Trust Company, 1908.

Supreme Judicial Court Historical Society Annual Report. Boston: Supreme Judicial Court Historical Society, 1992.

Vose Galleries. "Art and Collecting in America, an Illustrated Timeline." *Vose Art Notes* 6–11, 1996–2003.

NEWSPAPERS

In addition to the sources mentioned above, information used in this book came from thousands of articles, essays, and columns from various newspapers, primarily the *Boston Globe* and *Boston Herald*. Although it would be impossible to list each article, I want to acknowledge the contribution made by each reporter and author to preserving Boston's history. I want to mention specifically Susan Wilson's "History Notebook" column, which formerly appeared in the *Boston Globe*, Thomas F. Mulvoy, Jr.'s "FYI" column, which currently appears in that newspaper, Paul Restuccia's occasional articles on Boston architectural history in the *Boston Herald*, and William Marchione's "Boston Primer" columns in the *Tab* newspapers.

Index

Page numbers in *italics* refer to illustrations and their captions